"As a well-respected, conservative scholar, James Hoffmeier's broad training, depth of knowledge, understanding of Scripture, and love of God emerge in *The Prophets of Israel: Walking the Ancient Paths*. Hoffmeier's thorough overview of Yahweh's servants, the prophets, reflects well on over forty years (which in Bible time represents a lifetime, a generation) of teaching the prophetic literature in university settings. His well-thought-out presentation excels in unpacking the historical circumstances of these men and women of God, bringing to life their stories with archaeological discoveries and cultural connections that are beautifully illustrated. This readable summary of the situations and messages of the prophetic voices of Israel, Judah, and the early church—with insight into how these voices are woven into the larger story of God's messianic mission in the world—will be of immeasurable value to the student, pastor, or lay reader of this important volume."

—Jesse C. Long, Jr.,
Professor of Old Testament and Biblical Archaeology,
Lubbock Christian University

"The prophets of Israel spoke to their contemporaries in their time and place. So, it is essential for us to hear them in their original historical context. James Hoffmeier, a biblical scholar and archaeologist of international reputation, is an excellent guide to help us read the theological message of the prophets in their proper setting. He brings his skill and immense knowledge to bear to orient us to a proper understanding of the prophets. I highly recommend this volume to all who want to read the prophets to truly hear their voice and ultimately the voice of God who speaks through them."

—Tremper Longman III,
Distinguished Scholar and Professor Emeritus of Biblical Studies,
Westmont College

"Does it matter where Jeremiah lived, or when, or Amos, or Zephaniah? The Hebrew Prophets are often difficult to understand; reading them in their contexts can help a lot. James Hoffmeier sheds light on the men and their messages through archaeology and geography. His work will ease the path for Bible readers to explore and recognize the continuing worth of this large part of Scripture."

—Alan Millard,
Emeritus Rankin Professor of Hebrew & Ancient Semitic Languages,
The University of Liverpool

"The prophetic books of the Old Testament can be challenging to understand since they come to us from the unfamiliar world of the ancient Near East. In this inviting book, Professor James Hoffmeier serves as an experienced guide who unfolds the meaning of these marvelous books in their original context as well as unlocking their relevance for today. Readers will enjoy the fruits of Hoffmeier's many years of faithful teaching on the Prophets which have been gathered together in this lavishly illustrated volume."

—Jerry Hwang,
Dean and Professor of Old Testament,
Singapore Bible College

"This is a truly magnificent volume written by a scholar of vast learning. The penetrating, judicious, and captivating analysis of the prophetic books in their historical, archaeological, and religious context alone makes this the perfect textbook for courses on the prophets. Add to that the large number of quality pictures and other illustrative material seeded throughout the book, and this volume is an invitation to reading the Old Testament prophets with eyes wide open in fascination. It is a great accomplishment indeed!"

—Richard E. Averbeck,
Professor of Old Testament and Semitic Languages,
Trinity Evangelical Divinity School

"From the many years that Professor Hoffmeier himself has followed the 'ancient paths' of his archaeological discipline, he turns to direct us along the 'ancient paths' of the prophets. The way is long and treacherous, and Hoffmeier lays down the prophetic map, historically and morally, for all in our generation who stand at the crossroads with the prophets and listen for their commanding geo-spiritual instructions: 'This is the way; walk in it' (Isa. 30:21)."

—C. Hassell Bullock,
Franklin S. Dyrness Professor Emeritus of Biblical Studies,
Wheaton College

"This book serves as a helpful introduction to biblical prophetic writings and is eminently readable and insightful. Hoffmeier invites the readers to tour the world of the biblical prophets while guiding them with historically grounded research and sound theological exposition. This book is comprehensive in its scope, extending its coverage beyond the conventional introductory books on the subject. Hoffmeier weaves together different threads—archaeology, cultural and geo-political perspectives, the role of women prophets, and theological application—to craft a far-reaching and thorough account of the biblical prophets and their message. By integrating such layers and including discussion questions at the end of each chapter, this book is highly recommended as a textbook for undergraduates and seminarians and a guide for pastors and serious readers alike."

—A. S. Melika,
Professor of Archaeology and Anthropology,
California Baptist University

"In this lavishly illustrated text, James Hoffmeier steps outside of his standard role as Egyptologist and archaeologist and offers us the insights of forty years of teaching the Israelite prophets. Unlike many other introductions, Hoffmeier offers us not just the writing prophets, but Moses, Samuel, Elijah, Elisha, and Micaiah as well. His emphasis, of course, is the real people and places that stand behind this corpus. This book is accessible but technical, pedagogically friendly but scientifically up-to-date. There is a slew of new data in here that illuminates the world and the message of the prophets. An excellent resource for student and professor alike."

—Sandra Richter,
Professor of Old Testament,
Robert H. Gundry Chair of Biblical Studies,
Westmont College

THE PROPHETS OF ISRAEL

WALKING THE ANCIENT PATHS

JAMES K. HOFFMEIER

KREGEL ACADEMIC

The Prophets of Israel: Waking the Ancient Paths

Published by Kregel Academic, an imprint of Kregel Publications, 2450 Oak Industrial Dr. NE, Grand Rapids, MI 49505-6020.

ISBN 978-0-8254-4572-9

Printed in the United States of America

21 22 23 24 25 / 5 4 3 2 1

To Mark and Becky Lanier
who do justice,
love mercy,
and walk humbly
with their God

CONTENTS

ABBREVIATIONS OF REFERENCE SOURCES

ABD	*Anchor Bible Dictionary*. 5 vols. Ed. D. N. Freedman. New York: Doubleday, 1992.
ANET	*Ancient Near Eastern Texts Relating to the Old Testament*. Ed. J. B. Pritchard. Princeton, NJ: Princeton University Press, 1969.
Contra Apion	*Josephus: The Life against Apion*. Trans. H. St. J. Thackery. Cambridge, MA: Harvard University Press, 1926.
COS	*Context of Scripture I–IV*. Eds. W. W. Hallo and K. L. Younger. Leiden: Brill, 1997, 2000, 2003, 2016.
ESV	English Standard Version
HALOT	Ludwig Koehler and Walter Baumgartner, *Hebrew and Aramaic Lexicon of the Old Testament*. Leiden: Brill, 2001.
ISBE	*International Standard Bible Encyclopedia*. Ed. G. W. Bromiley. Grand Rapids: Eerdmans, 1979–1988.
OEANE	*The Oxford Encyclopedia of Archaeology in the Near East*. Ed. Eric Meyers. New York: Oxford University Press, 1997.
NEAEHL	*New Encyclopedia of Archaeological Excavations in the Holy Land*. 4 vols. Ed. Ephraim Stern. New York: Simon & Schuster, 1993.
NET	New English Translation
NIDOTTE	*New International Dictionary of Old Testament Theology and Exegesis*. 5 vols. Ed. W. VanGemeren. Grand Rapids: Zondervan, 1997.
NIV	New International Version of the Bible
RSV	Revised Standard Version
Sacred Bridge	Anson F. Rainey and R. Stephen Notely, *The Sacred Bridge: Carta's Atlas of the Biblical World*. Jerusalem: Carta, 2006.

The prophet Jeremiah preached God's word to the people of Judah and Jerusalem for more than four decades beginning in 626 B.C. In one instance he communicated a message with which all his colleagues before him and after could resonate, and to some extent it was the crux of their prophecies:

> This is what the LORD says:
> Stand at the crossroads and look;
> ask for the ancient paths,
> ask where the good way is, and walk in it,
> and you will find rest for your souls. (Jer. 6:16)

Walking (*hālaḵ*) with God is an expression that characterized the life of faithful saints like Enoch (Gen. 5:24) and "blameless" ones like Noah (Gen. 6:9). God instructed Abraham "walk before me and be blameless" (Gen. 17:1). Walking with God is about living one's life in conformity with his word and commandments.

Instead of swerving to alternative routes, Jeremiah urges his audience to "stand at the crossroads (*dᵉrāḵîm*) and look; ask for the ancient paths, ask where the good way (*dereḵ*) is, and walk (*hālaḵ*) in it" (6:16). When there is a choice of roads to take, and there always is, God advises his people to take the ancient path; it is the way toward what is good. Ancient paths were trodden over and over again so that they were well worn, easily recognizable. Ancient routes went somewhere. In fact, they were named by their destination. The path the prophets prescribed is "the good way," that is, to experiencing God's goodness. So effective was the course of many ancient roads in parts of the Middle East and Mediterranean world that modern paved roads and highways often follow the ancient route. You just can't improve on a reliable, proven road for travel.

For Jeremiah the ancient path is marked by God's laws and commandments based in the so-called books of Moses—"you shall walk (*hālak*) in all the way (*derek*) that the LORD your God has commanded you that you may live" (Deut. 5:33). Following God's word and obeying his commandments is how one walks on the ancient path, the good way, and then Jeremiah adds "walk in it and find rest for your souls" (Jer. 6:16c). "Rest" denotes "the ability to live without constant tension and uneasiness."[1]

The picture Jeremiah paints, then, is that of an ancient path that begins with the Sinai covenant and moves toward that which is good. To assist pilgrims who take this path, God discloses, "I appointed watchmen over you" (Jer. 6:17), that is, prophets situated along the route to point them back to God's covenant demands and then to direct them onward. When God called Ezekiel to be a prophet, he told him, "I have made you a watchman for the house of Israel" (Ezek. 3:17 ESV). The prophets are sentries to warn and guide the covenant people along the ancient path. Jeremiah assured his readers of the benefit of walking the ancient path, that "you will find rest for your souls." This outcome is echoed in the New Testament when Jesus urged his listeners to follow his teachings. He condemns places like Bethsaida and Capernaum for rejecting his word even though he taught and performed miracles there. Jesus then invites people: "Come to me, all you who are weary and burdened, and I will give you rest. Take my yoke upon you and learn from me, for I am gentle and humble in heart, and you will find rest for your souls. For my yoke is easy and my burden is light" (Matt. 11:28–30).[2] His teaching was not onerous, a heavy unbearable yoke like the legalistic interpretations of the law that were fashionable in the first century A.D..

The alternative route to the ancient path is perilous: "there is a way (*derek*) that seems right to a man, but its end is the way to death" (Prov. 14:12 ESV). Conversely, the Psalmist affirms, "your word is a lamp to my feet and a light to my path" (Ps. 119:105). This basic understanding of the priority of the Old Testament prophets stands behind the title of this book.

For forty years, it was my pleasure to teach about the Hebrew prophets and their literature in the Hebrew Bible or Old Testament. In my first full-time teaching appointment at Wheaton College (Illinois) in 1980, I was asked to cover a course for a colleague who was on leave. It was on the book of

---

1 William Holladay, *A Commentary on the Book of the Prophet Jeremiah, Chapters 1–25* (Philadelphia: Fortress, 1986), 221.

2 On wearing a yoke as a sign of submission to God and his commandments, see chap. 5.

Jeremiah. Fortunately for me, in my Hebrew classes in graduate school, I had read large portions of that book. So I was not totally unprepared to teach the class, but nevertheless I plunged into serious study of the book so that I could understand it and effectively teach about this intriguing prophet and his wonderful book. Not only did I grow to love the book, but also to appreciate prophetic literature. A couple years later, another colleague, Dr. Hassell Bullock, took a sabbatical leave to work on a major book on prophetic literature, and I again was asked to cover his course in his absence. This opportunity forced me to go deeper into the entire prophetic corpus, and the book that Dr. Bullock produced, *An Introduction to the Old Testament Prophetic Books* (1986)—now in a second edition (2007)—was the main textbook used in my seminary class on prophetic literature at Trinity Evangelical Divinity School for two decades.

This new book is different. While it shares many features with a classic introduction to prophetic literature, such as investigation the type of literature, and the message and theology of a prophetic book, a greater emphasis will be placed on the prophets, their contexts, and the historical circumstances that provided the impetus for their messages. Because of my interest in the prophets as God's servants and not just in their words, chapter 2 is entirely devoted to some of the prophets whose activities are described particularly in 1–2 Samuel, 1–2 Kings, and 1–2 Chronicles. This will allow us to spend time with prophets who are typically overlooked in traditional introductions. Giants like Moses, Samuel, Elijah, and Elisha receive the attention they deserve, but so do lesser-known prophets like Michaiah son of Imlah and Zechariah son of Jehoida. Additionally, some of the woman prophets will be introduced. Miriam (see chap. 1), Deborah, Huldah, and Noadiah are among the women treated in chapter 2. Then in chapter 8, I address the role of prophets and prophecy in the New Testament and early church. This new book, then, offers a more comprehensive perspective on prophets of the Old and New Testaments.

As a practicing field archaeologist, I am convinced that archaeological data offer a powerful tool for setting the stage on which the drama of biblical history is played out. Such data elucidate ambiguous expressions and enables the reader of Scripture to visualize images that would have been familiar to the prophets and their audience but lost to the modern reader. The late Philip King wrote two helpful archaeological commentaries, one on Hosea, Amos, and Micah,[3] and the

3 Philip J. King, *Amos, Hosea, Micah: An Archaeological Commentary* (Philadelphia: Westminster, 1988).

other on Jeremiah.[4] These wonderful books flesh out obscure features found in these prophetic books and clarify aspects of Canaanite religion that figure so prominently in these prophets' denunciations. Archaeological sources go hand in hand with place names (toponyms) and geography.

All the prophets of the Bible lived in real places, most of which can be located in Bible atlases. Knowing where prophets resided and the locations where they delivered their messages provide a rich context for understanding their messages and audiences. An example of geography influencing a prophet's message occurs in the oft-quoted Amos 5:24: "But let justice roll on like a river, righteousness like a never-failing stream!" Most of the streams in Israel only flowed seasonally and not year-round, and thus were unpredictable and unreliable sources of water. God wanted justice to be consistently practiced like a water course that runs year-round.

Furthermore, an appreciation of geography is necessary when following prophets who traveled to deliver their messages. Amos went from Judah to Bethel in Israel. Jonah journeyed hundreds of miles to Assyria, and Jeremiah went south to Egypt. Most of the literary prophets delivered oracles against foreign lands, and books like Jonah, Nahum, and Obadiah are primarily directed at neighboring nations—who are they, and what do they have to do with Israel? Understanding the geopolitics of the day will help clarify our reading of these prophecies.

The main reason for considering archaeological and geographical information goes beyond just setting the stage and fleshing out the context, as vital as that is. Instead it allows a more accurate and complete view of biblical narratives or a prophet's message, which in turn helps one better comprehend the author's message. Ultimately, then the reader is in a better position to make informed theological applications of the text.

The Hebrew prophets spoke for God to ancient Israel and other foreign nations, but their writings, like all of Scripture, "were written down for our instruction" (1 Cor. 10:11 ESV), and thus remain beneficial for God's people for all time. The prophets provided the key information for understanding the identity of Jesus of Nazareth in the NT. The impact of the Hebrew prophets does not stop there, for their writings continue to inspire, challenge, and provoke people of faith from the Jewish and Christian communities to love God with all their hearts and their neighbor as themselves.

---

4 Philip J. King, *Jeremiah: An Archaeological Companion* (Philadelphia: Westminster, 1993).

This book is dedicated to special friends, Mark and Becky Lanier, whose home and library in Houston have been a second home for me. The Lanier Theological Library is a haven for Christian scholarly research, reflection, and fellowship. Like St. Paul, who said of his friend Philemon that "the hearts of the saints have been refreshed" (Philem. 7 ESV), the Laniers through their kindness, generosity, and hospitality are refreshing the saints and helping them to grow in the grace and knowledge of the Lord Jesus Christ.

Scripture quotations throughout are from the NIV, with frequent interaction with ESV and NET. Based on my interactions with students in recent years, these translations seem to be the ones primarily read or consulted when studying English translations of Scripture.

This beautifully illustrated book was made possible through the kindness and generosity of a number of colleagues and friends to who provided the majority of the images. My heartfelt thanks are due to all, but three individuals require special mention. The largest number of illustrations came courtesy of Dr. Todd Bolen (The Master's Seminary) and Bibleplaces.com. The variety and tremendous quality of the images from the biblical world is truly outstanding. Next, particular thanks are owed to Alexander Schick of Sylt, Germany, and Bibelausstellung.de. Not only did Alexander provide images from his bountiful archive; he also obtained important images through his connections in Israel that I was permitted to reproduce here. Furthermore, in combination the creative people at Kregel, he proposed and provided the picture of the view from Mt. Nebo toward the Promised Land. A. D. Riddle, my former Trinity student, provided a number of images from his personal collection and others that were a part of the Bibleplaces.com collection. He is also responsible for creating many of the maps used herein.

I grateful to Kregel for agreeing to take on this monograph. Kregel's vision for the book was a textbook that would be primarily accessible to undergraduate students of the Bible, pastors, and serious-minded laypeople. As a consequence, at the end of each chapter there are discussion questions that could be used with groups of students or Bible study groups. They could also serve as the basis for test questions for instructors and teachers. Through the reading of this book and the Scriptures that it seeks to enliven, it is my hope that readers will grow in their appreciation for the ancient prophets and through them appreciate the wisdom of God anew.

1 INTRODUCTION TO THE HEBREW PROPHETS

THE PROPHETS IN THE BIBLICAL CANON

The prophets of Israel lived and spoke between 2,500 and 3,000 years ago, and yet their voices ring out with some regularity today. Their messages and words survive in the Hebrew Scriptures or Old Testament. We often hear their words but perhaps don't realize their origin. During the Christmas season, for example, the words of the Israelite prophet Isaiah are ubiquitous in the hymns we sing (e.g., "Lo How a Rose," "O Come O Come Immanuel"); and Handel's "Messiah" (also widely played at Eastertime) is replete with the words of Isaiah, the eighth-century B.C. prophet, and other seers. Malachi, the last Israelite prophet of the Old Testament, lived approximately 2,500 years ago, and yet his words "risen with healing in his wings" are sung annually in the classic Christmas carol, "Hark the Herald Angels Sing."

Likewise the message of these prophets is still quoted today when it comes to justice and social issues. When Dr. Martin Luther King Jr. proclaimed in his "I Have a Dream" speech "but let justice roll down like waters," he was quoting the eighth-century prophet Amos (5:24) to make his case for civil rights for all citizens of the United States. As a consequence, of such statements, the expression of speaking with a "prophetic" voice is familiar. One who is prophetic denounces injustice and challenges the status quo and the powerful, while advocating for just causes. Similarly, a person who stands alone on an issue may be likened to Isaiah's "voice of one who cries in the wilderness" (Isa. 40:3). The word "jeremiad," referring to a long bitter complaint or lamentation (or a piece of literature that does the same), derives directly from the name of Jeremiah, the seventh-century prophet known also as the "weeping prophet." According to tradition, he was the author of the book of Lamentations. The expression "seeing the handwriting on the wall," signifying pending doom or bad news, hearkens back to the book of Daniel (5:24–25). Here the vulnerable ruler Belshazzar's imminent demise

Fig. 1.1 – A Torah Scroll
Photo by Alexander Schick/bibelausstellung.de

was etched on the wall where he was holding a massive party while the Persians were about to invade. It is therefore safe to conclude that the Hebrew prophets continue to leave their mark in Western culture, and naturally for Jews and Christians, the prophetic books are a critical part of their shared Scriptures.

Browsing the table of contents of most modern translations of the Bible, the reader will notice that the books of Old Testament are divided into rather logical groupings: the Law, the Historical Books, the Poetic books, and the Prophets (see chart). This arrangement is based on the Greek translation of the Old Testament. Commonly known as the Septuagint, the Greek translation was made in Alexandria, Egypt, beginning in the third century B.C. to service the Greek-speaking Jewish community in Egypt (and elsewhere). It seems that the scribes who rendered the Greek organized the canon more by literary categories or genres. Hence the book of Daniel is placed between Ezekiel and Hosea, whereas in the Hebrew sequence, Daniel is found in the third grouping, namely, the Writings.

The Hebrew Bible offers a simpler organizational scheme, consisting of the same books as found in the Septuagint, but just in three units: the Law (*Torah*), the Prophets (*Neviim*) and the Writings (*Kethuvim*). This tripartite structure is reflected in the Jewish tradition of calling the Hebrew Scriptures as *Tanakh*. The name is an acronym derived by taking the first letter of the three Hebrew words, TNK.

Readers of modern translations may be surprised to see how the Prophets sections vary in the two traditions. In the Hebrew Bible, the *Neviim* begins with the book of Joshua, followed by Judges, Samuel, and Kings, then Isaiah, Jeremiah, Ezekiel, and then what in the Jewish tradition is known as the book of the Twelve, or simply the Twelve (i.e., Hosea to Malachi). It is not clear why this unit of Scripture includes the so-called "historical" books (Joshua through 2 Kings), although it may be that prophets were the authors or compilers of these.[1]

1 Roland Harrison, *Introduction to the Old Testament* (Grand Rapids: Eerdmans, 1969), 664.

English/Greek Canon and the Hebrew Canon	
Greek/English Canon	***Tanakh/Hebrew Canon***
The Law	**The Torah/Law**
Genesis	Genesis
Exodus	Exodus
Leviticus	Leviticus
Numbers	Numbers
Deuteronomy	Deuteronomy
Historical Books	**Neviim/Prophets**
Joshua	*(Former Prophets)*
Judges	Joshua
Ruth	Judges
1–2 Samuel	Ruth
1–2 Kings	1–2 Samuel
1–2 Chronicles	1–2 Kings
Ezra	*(Latter Prophets)*
Nehemiah	Isaiah
Poetic Books	Jeremiah
Job	Ezekiel
Psalms	Hosea
Proverbs	Joel
Ecclesiastes	Amos
Song of Solomon	Obadiah
Prophetic Books	Jonah
Isaiah	Micah
Jeremiah	Nahum
Lamentations	Habakkuk
Ezekiel	Zephaniah
Daniel	Zechariah
Hosea	Haggai

English/Greek Canon and the Hebrew Canon	
Greek/English Canon	***Tanakh/Hebrew Canon***
Joel	Malachi
Amos	
Obadiah	**Kethuvim/Writings**
Jonah	Psalms
Micah	Proverbs
Nahum	Job
Habakkuk	Song of Solomon
Zephaniah	Ruth
Zechariah	Lamentations
Haggai	Ecclesiastes
Malachi	Esther
	Daniel
	Ezra
	Nehemiah
	1–2 Chronicles

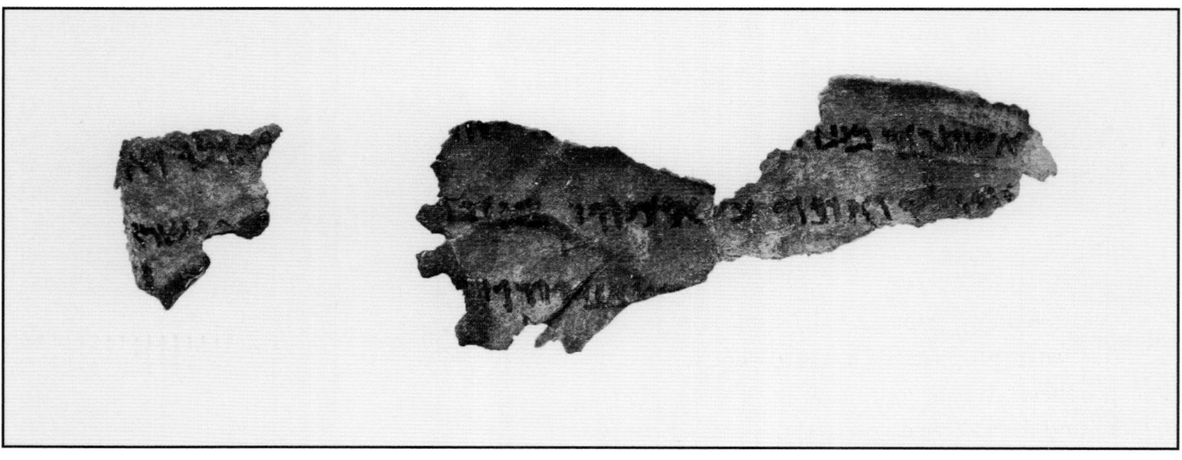

Fig. 1.2 – Dead Sea Scroll Fragment of Amos
Lanier Theological Library – photo by Laurel Wilson

According to the first-century-A.D. Jewish historian Josephus, the prophets of Israel were history writers (*Contra Apion* 1.38–41). This seems to accurately reflect the tradition preserved in 1–2 Chronicles that reports that the author consulted otherwise unknown chronicles written by prophets. The Chronicler actually records the titles of these books and places them as his bibliography at the end of each section on the various rulers. Concerning the reign of David, he lists "The Chronicles of Samuel the seer," "the Chronicles of Nathan the prophet," and "the Chronicles of Gad the seer" (1 Chron. 29:29 ESV), and for Solomon, "the history of Nathan the prophet," "the prophecy of Ahijah the Shilonite," and "the visions of Iddo the seer" (2 Chron. 9:29 ESV), and "the acts of Uzziah from first to last, Isaiah the prophet the son of Amoz wrote" (2 Chron. 26:22 ESV). Since the books of Samuel, Kings, and Chronicles focus on royal history, that is, the reigns of the kings of Judah and Israel, the prophets who sometimes acted as personal chaplains to the rulers were in an ideal position to record the acts of the kings and comment on the their fidelity to God's Law.

The Chronicles of Samuel may well be the book of 1 Samuel. Nothing is known of the Chronicles of Gad and Nathan, nor the writings of Ahijah. The book of Isaiah and segments of 2 Kings may well contain portions from what the Chronicler implies was a detailed, chronological report about king Uzziah written by the great prophet. The association of the prophets with the history writing imbedded in the books of Chronicles may account for the inclusion of the books of Joshua, Judges, Samuel, and Kings in the Prophets section. Moreover, the prophet Samuel is a key figure in the first book that bears his name, and prophets such as Elijah and Elisha are known almost exclusively from the books of Kings. These stories about these remarkable prophets may also have influenced the decision to include these more history-based, narrative books in the *Neviim*.

Fig. 1.3 – Assyrian Scribes writing Nineveh reliefs of Sennacherib. The one on the right is writing on a scroll in Aramaic
British Museum – photo by James K. Hoffmeier

The Book of the Twelve

In the Hebrew canonical tradition, what scholars call "the latter prophets" are made up of the three great prophets—Isaiah, Jeremiah, and Ezekiel, but not Daniel—and the so-called twelve minor prophets. These twelve works of varying size were arranged into a single book or scroll by an unknown compiler/s into what is understood to be "a single coordinated work as well as a composite collection."[2] At first glance, the reader might think that the books are simply arranged chronologically. After all, Hosea dates to the eighth century, as do of other works at the beginning (that is, Amos and Micah), whereas Haggai, Zechariah, and Malachi, the final three works, originate in the post-exilic period (520–450 B.C.). Joel, number two in the sequence, appears to be post-exilic in date, and Obadiah, from just after fall of Jerusalem (586 B.C.), is located between Amos and Jonah. Zephaniah seems to date before Nahum and Habakkuk, but is placed after them. So clearly chronological ordering is not the organizing principle. The compiler of the Twelve, it is argued, was "deliberately connecting the books so that they occur in a particular arrangement in order to communicate the intended theological message."[3] Each book has its own heading or superscription introducing the work, meaning that they need to be studied individually, but macro and canonical[4] perspectives allow the reader to see the bigger picture, and this is partially apprehended by examining the links between the books. A few examples will suffice, and some will be noted when the individual books are treated in subsequent chapters.

Hosea ends with an appeal to the wise to walk in the ways of the Lord (Hos. 14:9), while Joel begins with an appeal for the elders of the community to instruct the youth (Joel 1:2–3). The latter echoes what wisdom literature is all about. Joel 2:1–27 introduces the "Day of the Lord" for Israel as a major theme, which is extended to Israel's neighbors in Amos 1:2–2:3.[5] Then too, the earlier books offer direct warnings of judgment and exile for Samaria and then Jerusalem, while the final three books deal with the restoration of Jerusalem and the temple and then focus attention to the future and eschatological glory of both (Hag. 2:7–9; Zech. 14). This movement suggests a progression from the demise of royal houses of Israel and the devastation of the land to restoration of Israel and Yahweh's establishing his throne on the earth, to which all the nations will flow to worship (Zech. 14:17).

---

2 Christopher Seitz, *Prophecy and Hermeneutics* (Grand Rapids: Baker, 2007), 30

3 Michael Shepherd, *A Commentary on the Book of the Twelve* (Grand Rapids: Kregel Academic, 2018), 21.

4 "Canonical" is concerned with the placement or location of a particular book, believing that its location in the canon is not random. A canonical reading is also interested in a book's relationship to what surrounds it and its function within the Old Testament and how its theological function within the scope of the whole Bible.

5 Seitz, *Prophecy and Hermeneutics,* 120

Since people today tend to be more chronologically oriented in reading texts, and they find it easier to follow movement within such a framework, this book will treat the individual books of the Twelve in their historical setting as best as that can be determined. Thus the books within the Twelve will be treated by the periods where they historically belong, along with the major prophetic books. Thus Micah and Isaiah, both Judaean and eighth-century prophets, appear together, just as Zephaniah and Jeremiah do for the seventh century. At the same time, we need to be sensitive to links between the sequence of books in the Twelve, and it is prudent when reading this small compendium to read it in its canonical order, which is advantageous for literary and theological reasons.

WHAT IS A PROPHET?

Defining what a prophet was in ancient Israel is no easy task as these individuals were engaged in a host of activities, played various roles, used a range of methods of communicating their messages, and functioned in different social and religious settings. According to a Jewish Talmudic tradition, fifty-five men and seven women prophets are mentioned in the Hebrew Scriptures. The classic definition of the Swedish biblical scholar Johannes Lindblom is quite helpful. He suggests that a prophet is an "inspired" person who "claims to share in a particular divine inspiration . . . the prophet does not muse or speculate; his privilege is to receive, to receive thoughts, visions and words as wonderful gifts from heaven. The prophet is, in short, a proclaimer of divine revelations."[6] Prophets who left us collections of their messages, that is, the prophetic books, were most active at times of national crisis or as calamity approached. Hassell Bullock has made the same observation: "the prophets spoke to Israel in times of crisis. In fact, historical and moral crisis, if the list of canonical prophets is any indication, called them forth. Had there been no crisis, there would have been little need for the prophets."[7]

The English word "prophet" actually derives from the Greek word *prophētēs*, who were individuals who made public announcements in the city states Greece. In some instances, the *prophētēs,* a man or woman, spoke ecstatically for a deity, such as the Oracle of Delphi. This background information is important because the word *prophētēs* is used in the Greek translation of the Old Testament (i.e., the Septuagint or LXX) for the Hebrew word *nāḇi'*, the most common word in Hebrew for prophet. While *nāḇi'* (pl. *n^eḇî'îm*) is

6 Johannes Linblom, *Prophecy in Ancient Israel* (Philadelphia: Fortress, 1962), 2.
7 Bullock, *An Introduction to the Old Testament Prophetic Books*, 14.

Fig. 1.4 – Oracle of Delphi, Greece *Photo by Todd Bolen/Bibleplaces.com*

the principal Hebrew word for "prophet," there are several other parallel terms used, foremost among them "man of God." P. Kyle McCarter describes the man of God as "a professional holy man. He was thought of as possessing special skills and powers enabling him to invoke the aide of supernatural forces."[8] This title occurs more than seventy times in the Old Testament and is applied to figures like Moses, Samuel, Elijah, Elisha, Shemiah, and David; it can also be used to refer to anonymous prophets (e.g. 2 Sam. 2:27; 1 Kings 13:1–21).

Another important Hebrew term associated with prophets and prophetic activity is *ḥôzeh*, which is normally translated as "seer," that is, one who sees visions.[9] The common word for vision is *ḥ^azôn.*[10] The opening verse or title of the

8 P. Kyle McCarter, *1 Samuel: A New Translation with Introduction and Commentary*, Anchor Bible Commentary (New York: Doubleday, 1980), 175.

9 *HALOT* 301.

10 *HALOT* 301.

book of Isaiah reads: "The vision (*ḥᵃzôn*) concerning Judah and Jerusalem that Isaiah son of Amoz saw (*ḥāzâ*)." A second word that in English Bibles is translated "seer" is *rō'eh*.[11] This word enjoys only limited use, being applied to only two Hebrew prophets, Samuel (1 Sam. 9: 9, 11, 18, 19) and Hanani (2 Chron. 17:7), a contemporary of King Asa (911–870 B.C.). This word apparently was archaic, and had faded from use in later times, as an explanatory note in 1 Samuel 9:9 makes clear when referring to Samuel as a *rō'eh*: "Formerly in Israel, if a man went to inquire (*dāraš*) of God, he would say, 'Come, let us go to the seer (*rō'eh*), because the prophet (*nāḇi'*) of today used to be called a seer (*rō'eh*).'" This informative note is tucked into the story about Saul, who would later become king. In this story Saul and his servant are searching for lost donkeys, and decide to seek divine direction from Samuel, who is also called "the man of God." "Inquiring" (*dāraš*) is the technical term associated with seeking a word from God. This practice is described as "mantic prophecy," which is defined as "the practice of going to a prophet to gain the Lord's guidance on a specific matter."[12] Indeed, Samuel with divine insight was able to advise them, "As for your donkeys that were lost three days ago, do not set your mind on them, for they have been found" (1 Sam. 9:20 ESV). More on Samuel in the following chapter.

The verb for "prophesy," *nāḇi'*, is related to the Babylonian or Akkadian word *nabû*, meaning one who calls or proclaims, hence a herald or preacher.[13] There is some uncertainty as to whether *nāḇi'* is to be understood in the active voice (as the previous meanings suggest), that is, "one who calls" (i.e., calls out or proclaims), or if it is passive, "one who is called." Indeed, there are numerous examples of prophets who received a call via a dream or vision. Moses himself is encountered by God at the burning bush in Sinai and is summoned to be God's spokesman to Pharaoh and to the Hebrews (Exod. 3). The classic call narrative is that of Samuel while still a youth (*na'ar*) in service to Eli the priest in the dark days when judges ruled in Israel (1 Sam. 3). He hears his name, "Samuel," as he was asleep at night (1 Sam. 3:10). It was the aged priest Eli who realized that the voice young Samuel heard was that of God. When the call came the third time, Samuel responded in those memorable words, "Speak, for your servant hears" (1 Sam. 3:10 ESV).

---

11 *HALOT* 1161–62.

12 Richard Averbeck, "The Test of a Prophet," in *"An Excellent Fortress for His Armies, a Refuge for the People": Egyptological, Archaeological, and Biblical Studies in Honor of James K. Hoffmeier*, eds. R. E. Averbeck and K. L. Younger (University Park: Eisenbrauns/Pennsylvania State University Press, 2020), 2.

13 *HALOT* 661–62.

Isaiah's call came in the form of a vision in which the prophet sees something of that grandeur of Yahweh, the Holy God of Israel (Isa. 6), and then Yahweh himself asks "Whom shall I send, and who will go for us?" to which to prophet responds, "Here am I. Send me!" (Isa. 6:8). Jeremiah was also a "youth" (*na'ar*), probably in his mid-teens,[14] when the word of the LORD came, advising the lad that he was consecrated to God's service and "appointed" as a "prophet to the nations" (Jer. 1:5). Meanwhile, Ezekiel was overwhelmed by sensational heavenly visions, as a priest who was among the exiles taken from Jerusalem to Babylon in 597 B.C. (Ezek. 1–3). He was told, "go to the house of Israel and speak with my words to them" (Ezek. 3:4 ESV).

It is clear, then, that typically prophets received some sort of "call" to be a prophet; it gave him or her authority. Concerning Samuel, it was said, "All Israel from Dan to Beersheba knew that Samuel was established as a prophet of the LORD" (1 Sam. 3:20 ESV). On the other hand, it is evident that one of the chief duties of prophets was to proclaim God's word, the message they divinely received. A portion of Linblom's quotation from above is especially cogent here: "The prophet is, in short, a proclaimer of divine revelations."[15]

From this discussion of the term *nābi'* it is evident that a prophet is both divinely called and calls for the deity. This ambiguity may be intentional so as to include both active and passive meaning of the word, and both possibilities.

While terms *ḥōzeh*, *rō'eh*, and *nāḇi'* offer some insights into how prophets operated, by studying the narratives surrounding various prophets and their activities, further insight will be gained. However, to rightly interpret and correctly comprehend the message of ancient Israel's prophets, one must investigate and understand their historical, political, social, and cultural contexts, as well as the various methods used to convey their message. To grasp the historical and political setting of many prophetic books, we will have to examine the books of Samuel and Kings. Then too, the prophetic books (Isaiah to Malachi) often provide direct contextual information, or clues about the prophets setting, such as where they were from, where they preached, and under which king or kings of Israel and/or Judah they served. On the other hand, some prophetic books like Joel and Obadiah offer very little information about their context.

To flesh out as much contextual information as possible to assist the reader in grasping the message of a prophet, the available information and message

14 It is thought that a *na'ar* was the term for an unmarried lad or adolescent (*HALOT* 707).

15 Linblom, *Prophecy*, 2.

will be investigated through the lens of various types of archaeological and historical data, not to mention a wide range of areas such geographical, environmental, social, and political considerations. The broader context of prophetic literature requires the reader to realize that prophets were not unique to Israel. Rather, prophets were known in the ancient world, especially in Mesopotamia, Syria, Canaan, and Egypt, where they also played an important role in the religious life of their respective societies.

PROPHETS AND PROPHECY OUTSIDE ISRAEL

After the exodus from Egypt and the forty years in the Sinai Wilderness, but before the Israelites entered the Promised Land, they were camped in the land of Moab, east of the Jordan River. Out of fear of these intruders, Balak the king of Moab sent messengers to the prophet (*nāḇi'*) Balaam the son of Beor in order to put a curse on the encroaching Israelites so that Balak could defeat them (Num. 22:5–6). Balaam's home is said to be Pethor on the (Euphrates) River. It is known as Pitru on Assyrian monuments of the ninth century B.C.,[16] and is identified with Tell Aushariye in present-day Syria. It is located at the mouth of the Sajur River where it flows into the Euphrates, around three hundred miles north of Moab. A Danish team of archaeologists has been excavating there since 2000.[17] They have found that the city flourished during the Late Bronze Age (ca. 1550–1200 B.C.), the general period of Moses and the arrival of the Israelites in the Promised Land.

Balaam the prophet must have had quite a reputation for Balak to have gone such a distance to obtain his services. The Moabite emissaries went to distant Pethor armed with "the fee for divination" (Num. 22:7). The idea of paying a prophet for services may sound improper, but this is how many prophets made their living. Proof of this practice is also found within the Bible. When Saul was looking for the missing donkeys, as mentioned previously, his servant suggested consulting with Samuel the prophet. Saul asked, "What can we bring the man?" (1 Sam. 9:7 ESV). The servant responded, "Here I have a quarter of shekel of silver, and I will give it to the man of God to tell us

Fig. 1.5 – Ancient Pethor, Tell Aushariye in Syria, home of Balaam *Courtesy of Tell Aushariye Project*

16 Philip Budd, *Numbers*, World Biblical Commentary (Waco, TX: Word, 1984), 265.
17 "Tell Aushariye: Introduction," https://aushariye.hum.ku.dk/english/introduction.

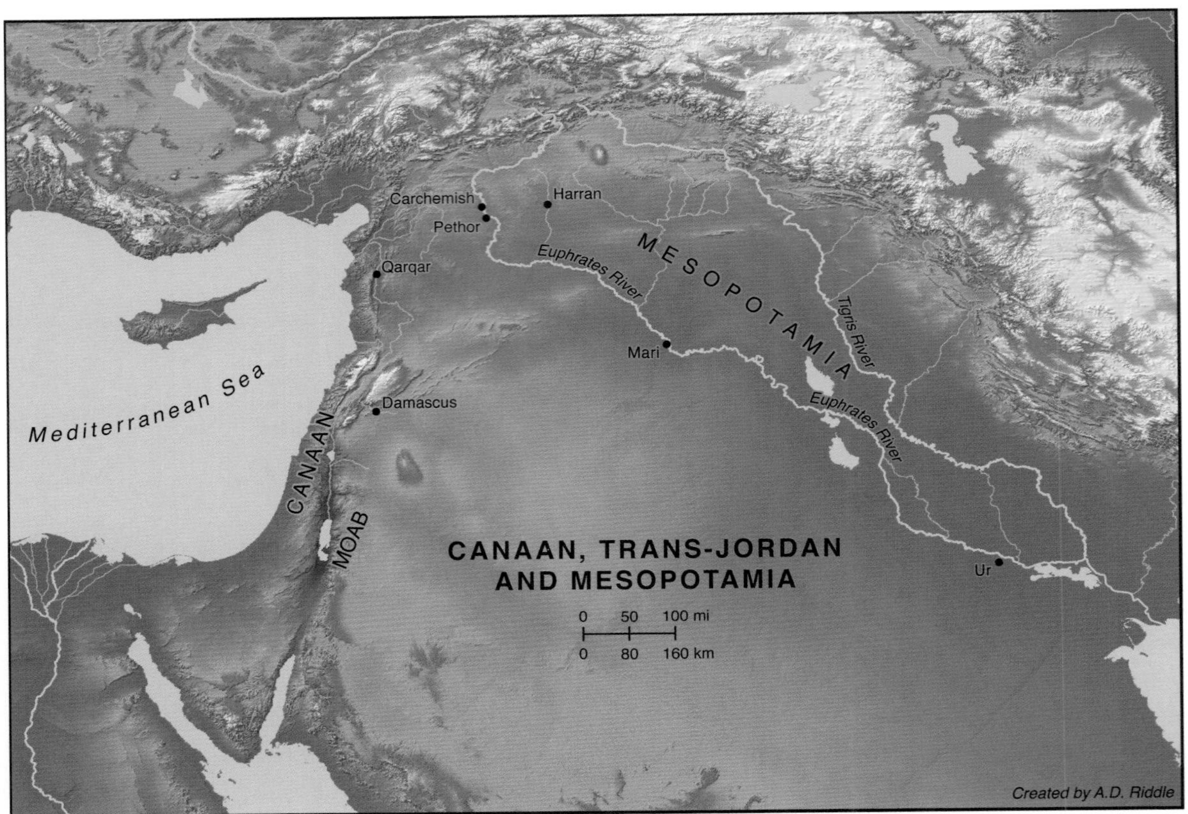

Map 1.1 – Canaan, Trans-Jordan and Mesopotamia at the time of Moses and Balaam. *Map by A. D. Riddle*

our way" (v. 8 ESV).[18] When prophesying at Bethel, Amos was dismissed by the priest Amaziah, who told the prophet to go back to Judah and "earn your bread there" (Amos 7:12), which means "earn your living."[19] This implies that prophets somehow were compensated for their ministry, but how this was practically worked out is not clear.

Divination was the art of ascertaining the disposition of a deity on a matter, and different methods were used throughout the world of the Bible (see below). Balaam received divine messages in dreams or in visions at night, as the narratives disclose: "That night God came to Balaam" (Num. 22:20), and through sacrificing bulls and rams, he anticipates a revelation from the Lord (Num. 23:1–3). One might expect this Syro-Mesopotamian prophet to invoke the name of a local Moabite deity, but instead it is Israel's God

18 This is not a coin, but a small clump of silver that had been weighed. A shekel is about 10 grams/0.02 lbs.
19 F. I. Andersen and D. N. Freedman, *Amos*, Anchor Bible Commentary (New York: Doubleday, 1989), 773.

who appears to him. He declares that "I must speak only what God puts in my mouth" (Num. 22:38), and "Must I not speak what the LORD puts in my mouth?" (Num. 23:12).

Although Balaam is killed in the days of Moses (Num. 31:28), his reputation lived on in this region. In 1967 the Dutch archaeologists, while excavating at the site of Deir 'Alla (five miles or eight kilometers east of the Jordan River), discovered some intriguing pieces of inscribed plaster that had fallen off a wall in a chamber, which had some sort of religious function.[20] Though fragmentary—in fact, consisting of 119 pieces—enough remained to know that it contained words from an ancient book or scroll (*spr*) called "The warning of the Book of Balaam, son of Beor." Dating from about 800 B.C., approximately five hundred years after the events described in the book of Numbers, the inscriptions remember this diviner as a "seer" or "visionary" (*ḥōzeh*), to whom the gods came at night, and who received a vision, hearing the utterance of El, the chief deity of the Syro-Canaanite pantheon or hierarchical group of deities.

The biblical narratives about Balaam and his memory preserved in the Deir 'Alla inscriptions speak of but one prophet in the Mesopotamian tradition. Much more is known about Near Eastern prophets of the second millennium B.C. from the sites of Mari, Alalakh, Emar, as well as from various Assyrian archives of the first millennium B.C.

Mari was a kingdom along the middle Euphrates River, whose king Zimrilim was a contemporary of the Babylonian king, Hammurabi (eighteenth century B.C.). Thousands of cuneiform tablets have survived, some of which describe religious and cultic activity. They reveal that prophets worked closely with temples, seeking clarity and guidance for its kings, especially with regard to military matters. There were a number of different types of specialists involved with seeking divine assistance. The *šā'ilu* was a priest and *šā'iltu* was a priestess who asked for an oracle or inquired of the deity for an answer. There were ecstatic prophets called *mahhû* who proclaimed oracles for various deities. The other frequently occurring term is *āpilum*, which literally means "answerer," but is translated as "prophet" in recent renderings.[21] One Mari oracle is given by a man identified as Abiya, prophet (*āpilûm*) of Adad (i.e. the Syro-Canaanite storm-god, Ba'al's personal name):

---

20 Martti Nissinen, *Prophets in the Ancient Near East* (Atlanta: Society of Biblical Literature, 2003), 207–8.

21 Nissinen *Prophets,* 5–8.

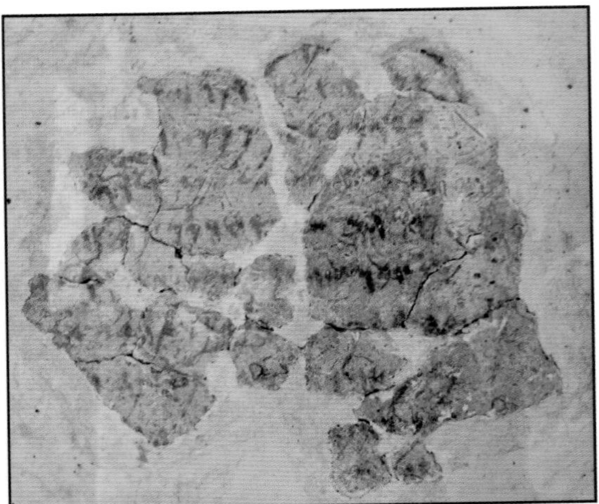

Fig. 1.6 – Balaam Inscription on plaster wall in Amman, Jordan
Photo by James K. Hoffmeier

Fig. 1.7 – Fresco of a priest and bull in a religious procession from Mari in Louvre Museum
Photo by James K. Hoffmeier

> Thus says Adad: 'I have given the whole country to Yahdun-Lim (the king). . . .
> If you go [off] to war, never do so [wi]thout consulting an oracle. [W]hen I become manifest in [my] oracle, go to war. If it does [not] happen, do [not] go out of the city gate.' This is what the prophet said to me. No[w I have sent the hair of the prophet] and a frin[ge of his garment to my lord].[22]

The words for hair and fringe of garments sound like the Akkadian words "wind" and "little breeze," thus associating these items symbolically with the spiritual realm in which there is a close tie between the wind and the spirit.[23] The same is true in the Bible. In Hebrew *rû'aḥ* is the word for wind and spirit (cf. Gen. 1:2; 8:1), just as *pneuma* is in Greek in the NT.

In one instance the prophet Mukanishum, who after making offerings, spoke for the god Dagan and proclaimed that Mari would be victorious over Hammurapi of Babylon: "Babyon . . . I will gather you into a net." The outcome was quite the opposite. Was he a false prophet?

Only in one Mari text is the word *nabû* found, and it occurs in the plural form, referring to a band of prophets who were summoned to give an oracle. The significance of this occurrence is that this word stands behind the Hebrew word for prophet, *nābi'*. This same word is written as *nebi* for "prophet" in Arabic. As noted above, the word *nabû* originates in the Babylonian language and means "one who calls (or calls forth)." This seems to place emphasis on proclaiming or announcing the divine word.

Most of the Near Eastern methods of divination are taboo in the Bible. In Deuteronomy 18 Moses enumerated a list of them just prior to the Israelites entry into

22 Nissinen, *Prophets*, 21–22.
23 Averbeck, "The Test of a Prophet," 5.

Canaan and shortly after the episodes with the shady figure of Balaam. Forbidden is infant sacrifice, divination and sorcery, interpreting omens, witchcraft, casting spells, being or using spirits and mediums, and consulting the dead (necromancy) (vv. 10–12).

Augury involved examining the patterns of flying birds and was practiced in Sumer, as well as Anatolia (ancient Turkey), Syria, and Canaan. Casting lots of various types was also practiced in the Near East. The prophet Ezekiel refers to this Babylonian practice (along with hepatoscopy) by King Nebuchadnezzar: "For the king of Babylon will stop at the fork in the road, at the junction of the two roads, to seek an omen: He will cast lots with arrows, he will consult his idols, he will examine the liver" (Ezek. 21:21). The practice of lot casting plays a prominent role in the Persian Period biblical book of Esther. Haman, the Persian official, "cast the *pûr* (that is, the lot)" (Est 3:7; 9:24) to determine the right day to carry out his program of genocide. "*Pûr*" is actually a Babylonian word (*puru*), and referred to dice-like cubes with writing on each surface.[24] Some have actually survived from the Assyrian period. The statements on them were intended to answer the question posed by the asker. From the term *pûr* comes the name of the Jewish festival Purim first observed in the book of Esther.

Fig. 1.8 – Clay tablet which records the request for an oracle from the sun-god Shamash from the 7th century, in the British Museum
Photo by James K. Hoffmeier

THE BEGINNINGS OF PROPHECY IN ISRAEL

The first use of the word *naḇi'*, or "prophet," in the Old Testament is applied to Abraham in a rather interesting setting. While temporarily dwelling in the territory of Gerar in southern Canaan, Abraham presents his wife Sarah as his sister (Gen. 20). Apparently

> **Divination in the Near East**
>
> Other kinds of divination practices are known from Mesopotamia and the ancient Near East, some of which are listed in Deuteronomy 18. These include extispicy and hepatoscopy. In the former the priest examines the internal organs of a sacrificed goat or sheep. Hepatoscopy entails a specialized version of extispicy that examines the animal's liver. Clay models of livers have been discovered that include writing that explain the oracular meaning of actual livers extracted from the animals by diviner priests.[24]

24 *ABD* 2:637.

25 Ivan Hruša, *Ancient Mesopotamian Religion: A Descriptive Introduction* (Münster: Ugarit-Verlag, 2015), 168–71.

Fig. 1.9 – Babylonian sheep liver model in British Museum
Photo by A. D. Riddle

Fig. 1.10 – A Neo-Assyrian Pur or lot/dice, ca. 8th–7th century
Photo Courtesy of the Yale Peabody Museum of Natural History

in some sort of diplomatic gesture to promote good relations between King Abimelech and Abraham, Sarah is taken into the king's harem.[26] God speaks in a dream to Abimelech, ordering him to return Sarah since she was Abraham's wife, and then God said, "he is a prophet, and he will pray for you and you will live" (Gen. 20:7). Here the role of prophet as intercessor is introduced. Abraham had already been shown to be an intercessor in the earlier story about the destruction of Sodom and Gomorrah. In a theophany or divine appearance, the LORD along with two angels disclosed to Abraham the plan to destroy those wicked cities (Gen. 18:16–21). In response Abraham was "standing before the LORD," an idiom meaning to intercede. He was pleading for the lives of the family of Lot his nephew, and, indeed Lot and his daughters were spared. On the eve of Jerusalem's destruction in 586 B.C., God ordered Jeremiah to stop his intercession for Jerusalem (Jer. 11:14; 14:11) and then added that even "if Moses and Samuel were to stand before me, my heart would not go out to this people" (Jer. 15:1). The point is that Judah's fate was now sealed, and no amount of intercession would dissuade God from the deserved judgment, not even the prayers of the great prophets Moses and Samuel. The mention of Moses, of course, serves as a reminder of arguably the greatest prophetic figure in the Old Testament.

THE FOUNDATION OF ISRAELITE PROPHETISM

The LORD encountered Moses while tending the sheep of his father-in-law Jethro (or Reuel); he spoke through a burning bush. The LORD ordered Moses to return to Egypt and demand of Pharaoh to allow the Hebrews to leave Egypt (Exod. 3:7–22). Moses is

26 James K. Hoffmeier, "The Wives' Tales of Genesis 12, 20 and 26 and the Covenants at Beer-Sheba," *Tyndale Bulletin* 43, no. 1 (1992): 81–100.

understandably reluctant, complaining, "Pardon your servant, Lord, I have never been eloquent, neither in the past nor since you have spoken to your servant. I am slow of speech and tongue" (Exod. 4:10). To which the Lord responds, "Who gave human beings their mouths? Who makes them deaf or mute? Who gives them sight or makes them blind? Is it not I, the LORD? Now go; I will help you speak and will teach you what to say" (4:11–12). Not convinced by the divine encouragement, God offers to have Aaron his older brother to assist him, saying, "I know he can speak well" (4:14). The idea that a prophet speaks to humans for a deity comes through clearly in the dialogue between God and Moses. It is further reinforced once he returns to Egypt: "Then the LORD said to Moses, 'See, I have made you like God to Pharaoh, and your brother Aaron will be your prophet (*nāḇi'*). You are to say everything I command you, and your brother Aaron is to tell Pharaoh to let the Israelites go out of his country'" (Exod. 7:1–2). Just as the prophet is to speak for God or a deity, Aaron was to speak for Moses, and thus be his prophet. Subsequently, however, the reluctant Moses finds his voice and speaks authoritatively to Pharaoh as well as to the Hebrew people.

Fig. 1.11 – Icon of Moses before the burning bush at St. Catherine's Monastery
Photo by Alexander Schick/bibelausstellung.de, courtesy by Father John and Father Justin, St. Catherine's Monastery, Sinai

There is a second episode that not only offers the foundation for Moses's role as prophet but explains why God uses humans as divine spokespersons. After the exodus, the Israelites came to Mt. Sinai, where Exodus 20 reports on the giving of the law audibly with the Hebrew people listening. So overwhelming and terrifying was the encounter, accompanied by the mountain shaking, with fire and smoke billowing skyward, that after the Ten Commandments were proclaimed (Exod. 19:16–19) the people said to Moses, "Speak to us yourself and we will listen. But do not have God speak to us or we will die" (20:19). In other words, the people rejected direct audible communication from God, instead opting to have Moses receive divine messages, which he would in

Fig. 1.12 – St. Catherine's Monastery at the foot of Gebel Musa (Mt. Sinai) which contains the chapel of the burning bush
Photo by Alexander Schick/bibelausstellung.de

turn proclaim the people. Decades later in Deuteronomy, Moses reminds the people that they had asked him to be the voice of God (Deut. 18:15–16). This is the primary task of the prophet, and the people's request captures well the concluding point of Linblom's definition that "the prophet is, in short, a proclaimer of divine revelations."[27]

In addition to Moses and Aaron, their sister Miriam is the first woman identified as a prophet(ess). After the crossing the Re(e)d Sea, which marked the end of the oppression of the Israelites in Egypt, Miriam took an active role in celebrating and leading the worship of God for his intervention and salvation. Exodus 15 recalls:

> Then Miriam the prophetess, Aaron's sister, took a timbrel [tambourine] in her hand, and all the women followed her, with timbrels and dancing. Miriam sang to them:
> "Sing to the Lord, for he is highly exalted.
> Both horse and driver he has hurled into the sea."
> (Exod. 15:20–21)

This is the only reference to Miriam as a prophetess, and it is noteworthy that it has to do with singing and worship, not proclaiming oracles. (This aspect of prophecy will be explored further below when discussing a prophesying incident in the book of 1 Samuel.) Later in the wilderness period, Aaron and Miriam appear to challenge Moses's leadership role, defiantly asking, "Has the Lord spoken only through Moses? . . . Hasn't he also spoken through us?" (Num. 12:2). God's response drives home the point of the unique status of Moses and that there are gradations of intimacy in how God communicates to human prophets. With Moses, God spoke directly, face to face, an indication of intimacy and favor.

27 Linblom, *Prophecy*, 2.

When there is a prophet among you,
I, the Lord, reveal myself to them in visions,
I speak to them in dreams.
But this is not true of my servant Moses;
he is faithful in all my house.
With him I speak face to face,
clearly and not in riddles;
he sees the form of the LORD.
Why then were you not afraid
to speak against my servant Moses? (Num. 12:6–8)

Fig. 1.13 – Clay figures of women playing tambourines
Photo by Christian Walker/bibelausstellung.de, courtesy Israel Museum, Jerusalem by Amalyah Keshet

In the previous chapter, at God's command, Moses appoints seventy men to serve as elders for the Israelites (Num. 11:16). The LORD announces that he will take some of the Spirit from Moses and place it on these elders who were to provide leadership for the people in order to reduce the burden on Moses (Num. 11:17). When this occurs, "they prophesied—but did not do so again" (Num. 11:25). Eldad and Medad, who were among the seventy, for unexplained reasons were not at the Tabernacle when the phenomenon of the group prophesying occurred. They rather prophesied in the camp. Joshua, Moses's lieutenant, took this as an affront and called on Moses to muzzle the two seemingly rogue prophets (Num. 11:27–28). But Moses saw no problem with this incident, and rather says, "Are you jealous for my sake? I wish that all the LORD's people were prophets and that the LORD would put his Spirit on them!" (Num. 11:29). While the prophetic experience is not explained, it was considered to be an activity only possible when God's Spirit is placed on a person that allows them to communicate in divine speech.

In addition to being a divine spokesman, Moses is also portrayed as an intercessor between the people and God. This happens on numerous occasions, including after the people made and worshiped the image of a golden calf (Exod. 32), when the people

Moses the Prototype Prophet

So Moses, the prototype of the prophet in ancient Israel, proclaimed divine oracles, warned and interceded, and performed miracles for the Hebrews in Egypt and in the wilderness. Consequently, Moses is the standard for future prophets, as God makes clear near the end of the leader's life: "I will raise up for them a prophet like you from among their brothers; I will put my words in his mouth, and he will tell them everything I command him" (Deut. 18:18). This promise comes with a warning to any who might arrogate to themselves the authority to speak in God's name without his sanction: "But a prophet who presumes to speak in my name anything I have not commanded him to say, or a prophet who speaks in the name of other gods, must be put to death" (Deut. 18:20). These, of course, are false prophets.

complained over their harsh circumstances in the wilderness (Num. 11:1–15), after Miriam was struck with leprosy (Num. 11:10–15), and famously after the report of the twelve spies described the challenges of conquering the land of Canaan (Num. 14:11–19).

Fig. 1.14 – Pharaoh Senusert I stands face to face before the god Ptah in Cairo Museum.
Photo by James K. Hoffmeier

The exclusive nature of God's relationship with Moses is recalled in the obituary of Israel's great leader: "Since then, no prophet has risen in Israel like Moses, whom the LORD knew face to face, who did all those miraculous signs and wonders the LORD sent him to do in Egypt—to Pharaoh and to all his officials and to his whole land. For no one has ever shown the mighty power or performed the awesome deeds that Moses did in the sight of all Israel" (Deut. 34:10–12).

THE EXODUS FROM EGYPT

The exodus of the Hebrews from Egypt is one of the constant motifs found in prophetic literature. According to the Genesis narratives, Joseph the son of Jacob was sold to slave traders out of jealousy and taken to Egypt (Gen. 37:12–36). Although he began as a lowly household servant, the talented teenager quickly advanced in the service of an Egyptian official named Potiphar. After being falsely charged with attempted rape against Potiphar's wife, Joseph landed in jail (Gen. 39). Thanks to the prophetic gift of dream interpretation, he was afforded the opportunity to interpret the dreams of Pharaoh, which anticipated seven prosperous years, followed by seven years of famine (Genesis 41). Dream interpretation is often done by prophets throughout the Near

Fig. 1.15 – Dream interpretation manual of the type used in Joseph's day
Pap. Chester Beatty BM 10683, Courtesy of the Trustees of the British Museum

Fig. 1.16 – Michelangelo's Moses in San Pietro in Vincoli, Rome
Photo by Martin Zeindl/bibelausstellung.de

East (e.g. Dan. 2), and in Egypt papyri have survived that were used by priest to discern the meaning of dreams.

Promoted to a top position in the government to manage the looming crisis, Joseph met his brothers, who had come to Egypt for grain as the famine had also struck Canaan (Gen. 42). These circumstances resulted in Jacob and his extended family moving to Egypt at Pharaoh's invitation (Gen. 45:17–20). For several generations, Jacob's family thrived with their flocks and herds as invited guests or sojourners in Egypt. These events seemingly took place during the era between 1700 and 1550 B.C., when the Hyksos rulers controlled northern Egypt. These Semitic speaking kings, originally from Syria-Canaan,[28] dominated Egypt until they were defeated and driven out of Egypt between 1550 and 1525 B.C. by the kings of Thebes in southern Egypt.

With the ouster of the foreign kings Pharaoh Ahmose, the new Egyptian rulers adopted a policy to contain the remaining foreign populations of northern Egypt by trying to limit the population growth of people like the Hebrews and forcing them into hard labor for the state (Exod. 1:8–14), and a program to kill newly born Hebrew boys was introduced (Exod. 1:15–22). This period of slavery had been projected in Genesis 15 when God pronounced the covenant with Abraham to give his descendants the land of

28 Manfred Bietak, *Avaris the Capital of the Hyksos* (London: British Museum, 1996).

Canaan, when he said, "Know for certain that for four hundred years your descendants will be strangers [i.e., sojourners or aliens] in a country not their own, and they will be enslaved and mistreated there. But I will punish the nation they serve as slaves, and afterward they will come out with great possessions" (Gen. 15:13–14).

It is in the midst of this oppressive crisis that Moses from the tribe of Levi emerges as a prophet-leader to fulfill God's promise made to Abraham, Isaac, and Jacob to bring them to the land of Canaan (Exod. 3:16–17). The events surrounding Israel's deliverance from the clutches of Pharaoh and the enslavement in Egypt—namely the ten plagues, the escape from Egypt's army and chariotry and safe passage through the Re(e)d Sea—would stand for all time for the Jews as God's greatest saving deed and would be celebrated in annual festivals like Passover and sung in hymns in the book of Psalms (e.g. Ps. 78, 105, 135, 136).

Fig. 1.17 – Cairo Museum stela of Pharaoh Ahmose who drove the Hyksos rulers out of Egypt
Photo by James K. Hoffmeier

The exodus, which is believed by many to have occurred in the thirteenth century B.C.,[29] and the subsequent forty years in Sinai are dominating themes in the prophetic books. These will be examined when reviewing the literary prophets in following sections. The impact of the Exodus on the prophets and the messages they proclaimed was profound, even centuries later. Similarly, the giving of the law or the Sinaitic Covenant left a deep impression on the prophets and their preaching and their writings.

---

29 This dating is followed by the author, while other scholars hold to an earlier date around 1450 B.C., while others advocate a twelfth-century date. See Mark Janzen, ed., *Five Views on the Exodus: Historicity, Chronology, and Theological Implications* (Grand Rapids: Zondervan, 2021).

Fig. 1.18 – Jebel Musa, the traditional site of Mt. Sinai in south central Sinai
Photo by Alexander Schick/bibelausstellung.de

Fig. 1.19 – Parity treaty written in Egyptian hieroglyphs between Ramesses II of Egypt and Hatusilis of Hatti at Karnak Temple dating to 1259 B.C. *Photo by James K. Hoffmeier*

THE SINAI COVENANT AND PROPHETIC LITERATURE

At Mt. Sinai, most likely somewhere in the southern Sinai Peninsula,[30] God and Israel entered into a solemn covenant relationship. Before departing Egypt, the LORD had announced his intentions for the Israelites: "I will take you as my own people" (Exod. 6:7). The verb "take" in Hebrew is used of a man taking a woman in marriage (e.g. Gen. 24:3, 4, 7; Exod. 21:10; Lev. 21:13; Deut. 22:13; Judg. 14:3; 1 Sam. 25:39). So the prophets regarded the Sinai Covenant as the LORD's marriage to Israel (cf. Ezek. 16:1–14 for an allegorical presentation), and therefore the worship of pagan deities was playing the harlot or committing adultery (cf. Hos. 1:2–2:13; Ezek. 16:16–58). God therefore dispatched his sinful wife into exile with a certificate of divorce (Isa. 50:1; Jer. 3:8).

The idea of the marriage between God and Israel is rightly understood as a "covenant," that is, a legally binding relationship. Human marriage since biblical times has been described as entering a covenant. This idea originated in the Hebrew Scriptures. An adulterous wife in Proverbs 2:17 is the one who "who has left the partner of her youth and ignored the covenant she made before God." Similarly, the prophet Malachi decries the infidelity of a man to his wife "because the LORD is the witness between you and the wife of your youth. You have been unfaithful to her, though she is your partner, the wife of your marriage covenant" (2:14). The marriage between a man and a woman was intended to mirror the union between God and his wife, Israel. This theology carries over into the NT where Paul identifies the mystical nature of human marriage as relating to

30 For various Mt. Sinai candidates, see James K. Hoffmeier, *Ancient Israel in Egypt: The Evidence for the Authenticity of the Wilderness Tradition* (New York: Oxford University Press, 2011), 115–48.

the relationship between the church—the new covenant community—and Christ: "For this reason a man will leave his father and mother and be united to his wife, and the two will become one flesh. This is a profound mystery—but I am talking about Christ and the church" (Eph. 5:31–32).

Fig. 1.20 – The Hittite king's copy written in Akkadian and discovered at Hattusas, Turkey. Now in the Oriental Museum, Istanbul
Photo by Mark Fairchild

In recent decades it has been possible to understand better the Sinai Covenant in a new and fresh way thanks the discovery and literary analysis of ancient treaty texts and law codes. The word "covenant" was used throughout the Old Testament to describe what occurred at Mt. Sinai. *Berith* is the Hebrew word in question, and it is used in the Bible in contexts where a treaty is made (e.g. Genesis 21:25–34; 26:26–33; 31:46–50). The same word is found in texts found in Mesopotamia, Syria, and Egypt during the second millennium B.C., indicating that the word *berith* was used in international diplomacy at that time.[31]

Nearly one hundred treaties and law codes have now been discovered and translated.[32] Among the treaties, two types are discernable: the one type was made between kings of equal status (Parity Treaty), and the second form was drafted between a ruler and a subject (Suzerainty Vassal Treaty). In the former, the two parties mutually negotiate the terms of the agreement, whereas in the Suzerainty Vassal type, the subject has no say. The master merely dictates the terms and the vassal, like the Israelites at Mt. Sinai, respond by saying, "All the words which the LORD has spoken we will do" (Exod. 24:3 ESV).

Study of the literary form of the treaties reveals a structure that was consciously followed in both Exodus and Deuteronomy. The actual form varies over the centuries in the ancient Near East.[33] Those from third millennium are different than those of the second and first millennia. Interestingly, those from the second half of the second millennium B.C. are closest in style to the covenant structure Exodus 20 and Deuteronomy. The following is an

---

31 *NIDOTTE* 1:747–55.
32 Kenneth Kitchen and Paul Lawrence, *Treaty, Law and Covenant in the Ancient Near East*, vol. 1 (Mainz: Harrasowitz Verlag, 2012).
33 Kitchen, *Treaty, Law and Covenant*, 2:253–68.

example of the six parts of the treaty structure based on Kenneth Kitchen's exhaustive analysis.[34]

1. **Preamble/Title:** Here the names of the parties involved in the treaty are introduced
2. **Historical Prologue:** Prior relations with the parties are reviewed, and these typically provide the reason(s) why the vassal is obliged to the king. This is especially the case with the vassal who has summoned the great king for help against an enemy.
3. **Stipulations:** The tribute, conditions, and laws which the vassal were expected to meet are listed.
4. **Deposition of Text and Public Reading:** The text of the treaty was to be copied and placed in the temples of both parties, and the text was to be read publicly at designated times.
5. **Witnesses Summoned:** Because it is a legal arrangement, the treaty had to be witnessed. In the case of the ancient treaties, the gods of the parties were listed, or features from nature could serve as witnesses.
6. **Curses and Blessings:** The treaty ends with a list of curses and blessings that would be administered by the deities who had acted as witnesses. The curses and blessings are applied for violating or upholding the stipulations.

Here is how this pattern works in Exodus 20.

1.	**Preamble/Title:**	Exodus 20:1–2a: "Then God spoke all these words: 'I am the LORD your God.'"
2.	**Historical Prologue:**	Exodus 20:2b: "who brought you out of the land of Egypt, out of the house of slavery."
3.	**Stipulations:**	Exodus 20:3–17: "you shall have no other gods before me" . . . 22–26; 21:1–23 and other laws that follow (Exod. 25–31; Lev. 1–25)
4.	**Deposition of Text:**	Exodus 25:16: "Then put in the ark the tablets of the covenant law, which I will give you."
	and **Public Reading:**	Exodus 24:7: "Then he took the Book of the Covenant, and read it to the people. They responded,

34 Kenneth Kitchen, *On the Reliability of the Old Testament* (Grand Rapids: Eerdmans, 2003), 283–94.

	'We will do everything the Lord has said; we will obey.'"
5. **Witnesses:**	Exodus 24:4: "He [Moses] got up early the next morning and built an altar at the foot of the mountain and set up twelve stone pillars representing the twelve tribes of Israel"[35]
6a. **Blessings:**	Leviticus 26:3–5: "If you follow my decrees and are careful to obey my commands, I will send you rain in its season, and the ground will yield its crops and the trees their fruit. Your threshing will continue until grape harvest and the grape harvest will continue until planting, and you will eat all the food you want and live in safety in your land."
6b. **Curses**	Leviticus 26:14–17: "But if you will not listen to me and carry out all these commands, and if you reject my decrees and abhor my laws and fail to carry out all my commands and so violate my covenant, then I will do this to you: I will bring on you sudden terror, wasting diseases and fever that will destroy your sight and sap your strength. You will plant seed in vain, because your enemies will eat it. I will set my face against you so that you will be defeated by your enemies; those who hate you will rule over you, and you will flee even when no one is pursuing you."

The foregoing illustrates that the biblical writer, Moses according to tradition, was familiar with this late-second-millennium-B.C. literary convention, and by using it, the people would have understood the solemn and legal nature of a treaty-covenant that had been established between God and Israel, and their profound responsibility to obey its laws and statutes. It is the covenant laws made at Mt. Sinai that stands at the foundation Hebrew prophets' messages. The task of the prophet is to bring people back to a right relationship with God vis-à-vis the covenant. This is why in Malachi 3:1 God's messenger, or prophet, is called "messenger of the covenant" and explains the refrain "The

35 While twelve stones are not explicitly identified as "witnesses," they clearly serve as witnesses or signs in other covenant or memorial ceremonies or where oaths are made (Gen. 28:18–22; Gen. 31: 44–52; Josh. 4:1–7; Josh. 22:10–29, esp 26–28).

LORD warned Israel and Judah through all his prophets and seers: 'Turn from your evil ways. Observe my commands and decrees, in accordance with the entire Law that I commanded your fathers to obey and that I delivered to you through my servants the prophets'" (2 Kings 17:13).

DEPOSITING THE COVENANT TEXT IN THE ARK OF THE COVENANT

In the fourth section of the covenant formula, a copy of the text would be deposited in the holiest place of the sanctuary. For Israel this entailed placing the tablets of stone in the ark of the covenant (Exod. 25:16), which in turn was situated in the Holy of Holies of the tabernacle and then in later history, in the temple's innermost chamber. Subsequently, the books of Deuteronomy were also deposited in the ark beside the original tablets (Deut. 31:26). The idea is that the covenant or

Fig. 1.21 – Model of the Tabernacle at Timnah, Israel
Photo by Mark Bolen/BiblePlaces.com

Fig. 1.22 – Temple at Tell Tayinat of the 8th–7th Centuries
Photo Courtesy of the Tayinat Archaeological Project

treaty text would be under the watchful eye of the deity who witnessed the sworn oath and would hold accountable the parties making the treaty or covenant.

Recently a startling discovery was made at Tell Tayinat, Syria, by Timothy Harrison of the University of Toronto. While excavating in the holy of holies in a small temple of the eighth and seventh centuries, copies of treaty texts made between the great Assyrian ruler Esarhaddon (680–669 B.C.) with the local king were recovered. This marks the first time an actual treaty text or covenant was found within the sanctum of a temple.

Fig. 1.23 – Discovering the tablets of treaty texts in the sanctuary by Dr. Timothy Harrison
Photo Courtesy of the Tayinat Archaeological Project

PROPHECY: PAST, PRESENT, AND FUTURE

One might be inclined to think that the Hebrew prophets were preoccupied with the distant future, matters regarding the coming of the Messiah or Christ (i.e., the anointed one) and the end times (i.e., the end of the world as we know it!). One analysis reveals the following surprising results: less than 2 percent of OT prophecy is messianic, less than 5 percent specifically describes the New Covenant Age (i.e., the Christina era), and less than 1 percent is concerned with events yet to come.[36] The reality is that Israel's prophets preached messages that were based on the covenant relationship God had established at Mt. Sinai (i.e., Exodus 20–Leviticus 27) and the earlier covenant with Abraham, Isaac, and Jacob. The latter began with a "promise" to Abraham that included three facets: land, posterity, and a blessing or relationship with this deity (Gen. 12:1–3). This promise, in turn, is guaranteed subsequently by the covenant or treaty agreement in which God introduces himself to Abraham as "the LORD, who brought you out of Ur of the Chaldeans to give you this land (Canaan) to take possession of it." The covenant ceremony concludes with the LORD affirming, "to your descendants I give this land." This promise is reiterated to Isaac (Gen. 26:2–5, 24) and Jacob (Gen. 28:10–15; 35:11–15).

The "Abrahamic Covenant" further anticipates the four hundred years of living as sojourners or aliens in an unnamed land (Gen. 15:13). At the height of the Hebrew enslavement in Egypt, the book of Exodus observes, "God heard their groaning and he remembered his covenant with Abraham, with Isaac and with Jacob" (Exod. 2:24), implying that he was about to act to fulfill that old promise regarding the land. Again prior to the exodus itself, the LORD again speaks to Moses saying, "I will take you to be my people, and I will be your God, and you shall know that I am the LORD your God, who has brought you out from under the burdens of the Egyptians. And I will bring you to the land I swore with uplifted hand to give to Abraham, to Isaac and to Jacob. I will give it to you as a possession. I am the LORD" (Exod. 6:7–8 ESV). When God says "I will take," as noted previously, the verb is the same one used for marriage, when a man takes a wife.[37] This term points to a marriage covenant between God and Israel (cf. Mal. 2:14; Prov. 2:17).

The Sinai covenant was established after the exodus from Egypt, and there as we observed in the previous section, the LORD is identified as the God who brought Israel out of Egypt. By virtue of entering into the covenant relationship that was sealed in the oath ceremony affirming allegiance to the LORD, the laws or stipulations were rehearsed. The people of Israel obligated themselves to lives of obedience to this God and the commandments he introduced through the prophet-leader Moses. By virtue of this covenant relationship, Israel became God's people, and using the marital motif, Israel became God's bride (cf. Ezek. 16).

---

36 Gordon Fee and Douglas Stuart, *How to Read the Bible for All Its Worth* (Grand Rapids: Zondervan, 1982), 50.
37 *HALOT* 534.

One of the components of the treaty structure was the covenant curses and blessings. Blessings come as a result of keeping the laws and the curses are experienced as punishment for violations. Once again, the focus is on the land. God will make it fertile by the seasonal rains and thus provide for their needs, and the Lord will also provide security from hostile neighbors: "I will grant peace in the land" (Lev. 26:6), that is, shalom (*šālôm*): peace and well-being.

In Deuteronomy, which is regarded by many interpreters as the renewal of the Sinaitic covenant with the new generation who would actually take possession of the promised land of Canaan (cf. Deut. 31:9–13), heaven and earth are summoned as witnesses to the renewal (Deut. 4:26; 30:19; 31:28), and similar blessings and curses are announced (Deut. 28), with an additional caveat: disobedience to God's laws (especially those dealing with idolatry) will result in the loss of the land and exile in distant foreign countries (Deut. 4:25–27). However, the prospect of return and restoration for Israel is held out *if* there is a genuine repentance and a sincere seeking after God (Deut. 4:29–30), because "the Lord your God is a merciful God; he will not abandon or destroy you or forget the covenant with your forefathers, which he confirmed to them by oath" (Deut. 4:31).

This discussion about the Abrahamic and Sinaitic covenants lays the foundation for the preaching of the prophets of Israel. It is what God has said in the past (especially in the Sinaitic legislation) that is used as the measuring rod that is applied to the present (i.e., the prophet's time), which naturally has implications for the future. This threefold focus on past, present, and future must always be borne in mind when reading the prophets and understanding their message. Therefore, the task of the prophet, as Richard Averbeck has recently observed, "focused primarily on reforming the behavior of the people and the nation as a whole by calling them back to exclusive and heartfelt covenant loyalty and obedience to the Lord and his word already revealed."[38]

38 Averbeck, "The Test of a Prophet," 3.

DISCUSSION QUESTIONS

- What are some of the characteristics and tasks of a prophet?
- What role does the exodus play in the prophets' duties?
- What is the relationship between the Sinai covenant and prophetic activity?
- Discuss how the prophets' messages are connected to the past, present, and future.
- How are Abraham and Moses prophets?
- What do we know about prophetic practices outside of Israel and the Bible?

2

"This Is What the LORD, the God of Israel, Says"

PROPHETS IN THE OLD TESTAMENT WHO LEFT NO WRITINGS

Prophets typically proclaimed God's messages publicly to the covenant people. Fortunately for future generations, some of these prophetic words were recorded. The LORD instructed Moses, "'Write down these words, for in accordance with these words I have made a covenant with you and with Israel.' Moses was there with the LORD forty days and forty nights without eating bread or drinking water. And he wrote on the tablets the words of the covenant—the Ten Commandments" (Exod. 34:27–28). Isaiah orders that his law or instruction (*tôrâ*) be recorded: "Bind up the testimony; seal the teaching among my disciples" (Isa. 8:16 ESV). This statement is taken to not only mean to record the Isaiah's messages, but to treat it as a legal, unalterable document.[1] God tells Jeremiah to have the messages he had received recorded in a scroll (Jer. 36; see detailed discussion in chap. 5), while Habakkuk is told, "Write down the revelation and make it plain on tablets so that a herald may run with it" (Hab. 2:2). Such tablets, apparently, were to be publicly posted for all to see. In the book of Daniel we find the prophet himself recording the visions he received (Dan. 7:1).

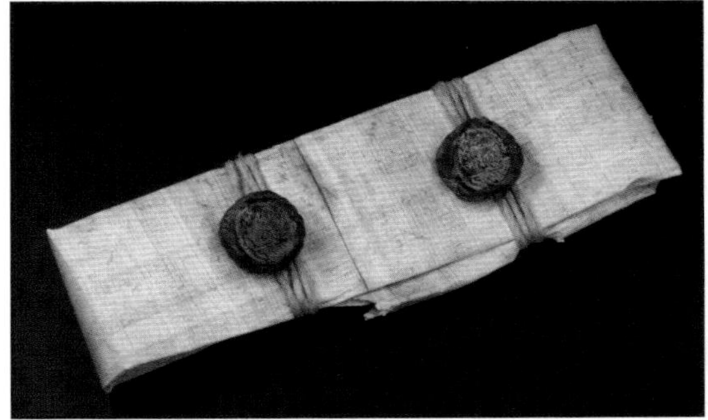

Fig. 2.1 – Double-sealed papyrus document
Photo by Helmut von Grabowiecki/ bibelausstellung.de

The prophets whose messages were actually recorded and preserved in the Bible represent only a small portion of prophets mentioned in the Bible. Some of the better known are Deborah, Samuel, Nathan, Elisha, and Elijah, but there are also lesser-known prophets such as Jehu son of Hanani, Uriah son of Shemiah, and a woman named Huldah.

The death of Moses ushered in a long period of prophetic silence. While Joshua his successor was a brilliant military leader and was faithful to God,

1 J. Alec Motyer, *The Prophecy of Isaiah: An Introductions and Commentary* (Downers Grove, IL: InterVarsity Press, 1993), 95–96.

Fig. 2.2a – Inscribed bronze plaque with a treaty text designed for public display
Photo by A. D. Riddle/Bibleplaces.com

and even proved to be an able religious leader (cf. Josh. 24), he was not called a prophet like Moses. Following the death of Joshua, Israel plunged into the political, social, and spiritual dark age known as the Judges period that spans around two centuries (ca. 1220–1030 B.C.). The Israelites quickly got entangled in syncretistic worship with Canaanite deities (Judg. 2:11–15; 3:7–8). A hillside sanctuary was discovered in recent years and in it a bronze bull, possible representing Baal, was found.

Our knowledge of this period comes through the book of Judges and the opening chapters of 1 Samuel. We do, beginning in this era and beyond, encounter faithful prophets who did not leave us books, nor apparently did future generations preserve their messages in written form.[2] These prophets are sometimes called nonliterary prophets. What we know about these prophets concentrates on their activities more than their words. The following are some the better-known nonliterary prophets, along with some lesser-known individuals whose stories need to be told.

UNNAMED PROPHETS OF THE BOOK OF JUDGES

The book of Judges explains that "the LORD raised up judges, who saved them out of the hands of these raiders" (Judg. 2:16). These judicial-military leaders arose at times of crisis, typically military harassment or invasion by hostile nations "because this nation has violated the covenant that I laid down for their forefathers and has not listened to me" (Judg. 2:20). Prophets played only a limited role in the book of Judges. As we shall see with Deborah, she is the only prophet mentioned by name in this book (see below). Two unnamed prophets, however, make brief appearances. In response to seven years of Midianite and Amalekite raids and the people crying out to God, "he sent them a prophet, who said, 'This is what the LORD, the God of Israel, says: 'I brought you up out of Egypt, out of the land of slavery. I snatched you from the power of Egypt and from the

2 One cannot rule out the possibility that their messages were recorded and simply did not survive.

hand of all your oppressors. I drove them from before you and gave you their land.' I said to you, 'I am the LORD your God; do not worship the gods of the Amorites, in whose land you live.' But you have not listened to me'" (Judg. 6:8–10).

The result was that God called Gideon to be the military leader and judge who liberated the Israelite tribes. Other than Deborah in Judges 4–5, prophetic silence followed until the very end of the Judges period, when another unnamed "man of God" issued a condemnation of the judge-priest Eli (1 Sam. 1:27–36) on account of his corrupt sons.

Because prophetic voices were scarcely heard in the Judges period, during the judgeship of Eli the priest we read, "In those days the word of the LORD was rare; there were not many visions (*ḥāzôn*)" (1 Sam. 3:1). This statement also seems to be a criticism of the priesthood that had the ephod and the Urim and Thummim as tools for ascertaining God's will (cf. Exod. 28:29–30; Lev. 27:21), but God was silent, apparently not speaking through the priesthood either.

DEBORAH: PROPHET AND JUDGE

The lone named prophet of the Judges period is Deborah, who receives the following introduction: "Deborah, a prophetess, the wife of Lappidoth, was leading Israel at that time. She held court under the Palm of Deborah between Ramah and Bethel in the hill country of Ephraim, and the Israelites went up to her to have their disputes decided" (Judg. 4:4–5). This is the same area where Samuel would be active a century or more later in history. Best known for her prophetic role with Barak, a military leader (see further below), her regular duty was sitting under a palm tree as a judge hearing and arbitrating cases, "a legal functionary rendering judicial decisions."[3] Thus she is both a judge and a prophet,

Fig. 2.2b – Code of Hammurabi in the Louvre Museum
Photo by Todd Bolen/Bibleplaces.com

3 K. Lawson Younger, *Judges/Ruth*, The NIV Application Commentary (Grand Rapids: Zondervan, 2002), 140.

Fig. 2.3 – Bronze bull from a cultic center in the hill country of Samaria from the Judges period *Photo by Todd Bolen/Bibleplaces.com*

active in southern territory of Ephraim, about fifty miles south of Hazor, whose armies threatened Israel and led of the major battle with her associate, Barak.[4]

She prophesied in response the rise of the power of Jabin king of Hazor in northern Israel who had "cruelly oppressed the Israelites for twenty years" (Judg. 4:3), inspired Barak the military leader to rally the militias of the tribes of Israel to challenge Jabin. She summoned him from his home in the territory of Naphtali, in which Hazor was located, to communicate God's plan to defeat the armies of Jabin and his general Sisera. At Barak's insistence, she accompanied him to the arena of the battle (Judg. 4:8–9). Barak is not the only leader who wanted to have a prophet involved in matters of war (see Samuel, Elisha, and Micaiah below). The battle took place well south of Hazor in Jezreel Valley, east Megiddo in sight of Mt. Tabor where Barak mustered Israel's troops.

Around 1400 B.C. the Pharaoh Thutmose IV had fought chariot battles with troublesome Canaanites in the same region, which provides us with a glimpse into the types of chariots likely used by Jabin's forces. That pharaoh's own chariot body contained illustrations of a chariot battle against Canaanites.[5] They were lightweight, two-wheeled

Fig. 2.4 – Aerial view of Hazor, capital of King Jabin *Photo by William Schlegel/Bibleplaces.com*

4 A. E. Cundall, *Judges and Ruth: An Introduction and Commentary* (Downers Grove, IL: InterVarsity Press, 1980), 83.

5 Theodore Davis, *The Tomb of Thoutmôsis IV* (London: Archibold Constable, 1904), plates X–XI.

Fig. 2.5 – View of the Jezreel Valley with Mt. Tabor in the background *Photo by Todd Bolen/Bibleplaces.com*

vehicles, and pulled by a pair of horses. The bearded Canaanite charioteers sometimes wore protective helmets, wielded bows, and in some instances a second warrior held a shield to protect the driver. This formidable chariotry was an existential threat to the disorganized, leaderless, and poorly equipped Israelite militias, and clearly was the reason Hazor "cruelly oppressed the Israelites for twenty years" (Judg. 4:3). Thus Deborah's divinely inspired prophetic role encouraged Barak to rally and lead Israel's forces to take on the Canaanite oppressor.

That the Israelite ragtag militia did ultimately defeated the chariot forces of the northern Canaanite king Jabin was worthy of celebration, which was put in the form of a song commonly referred to as "the Song of Deborah" (Judges 5). The song praises the LORD and "recite[s] the victories of the LORD" (5:10) over Israel's foes.

Fig. 2.6 – Drawing of a scene on chariot body of Thutmose IV (1400–1390 B.C.). in Theodore M. Davis, *The Tomb of Thoutmôsis IV* *London: Archibald Constable & Co, 1904), pl. X.*

While little else is known about Deborah's activity as prophet, what Judges 4 and 5 underscores is that the major duty of a prophet in the "historical" books is to advise Israel's leaders in military matters by bringing God's word to them. Secondly, we see the importance of music and worship within prophetism. Like Miriam who is called a prophetess and sang after a great victory (Exod. 15:20–21), Deborah celebrated victory in song (Judg. 5)

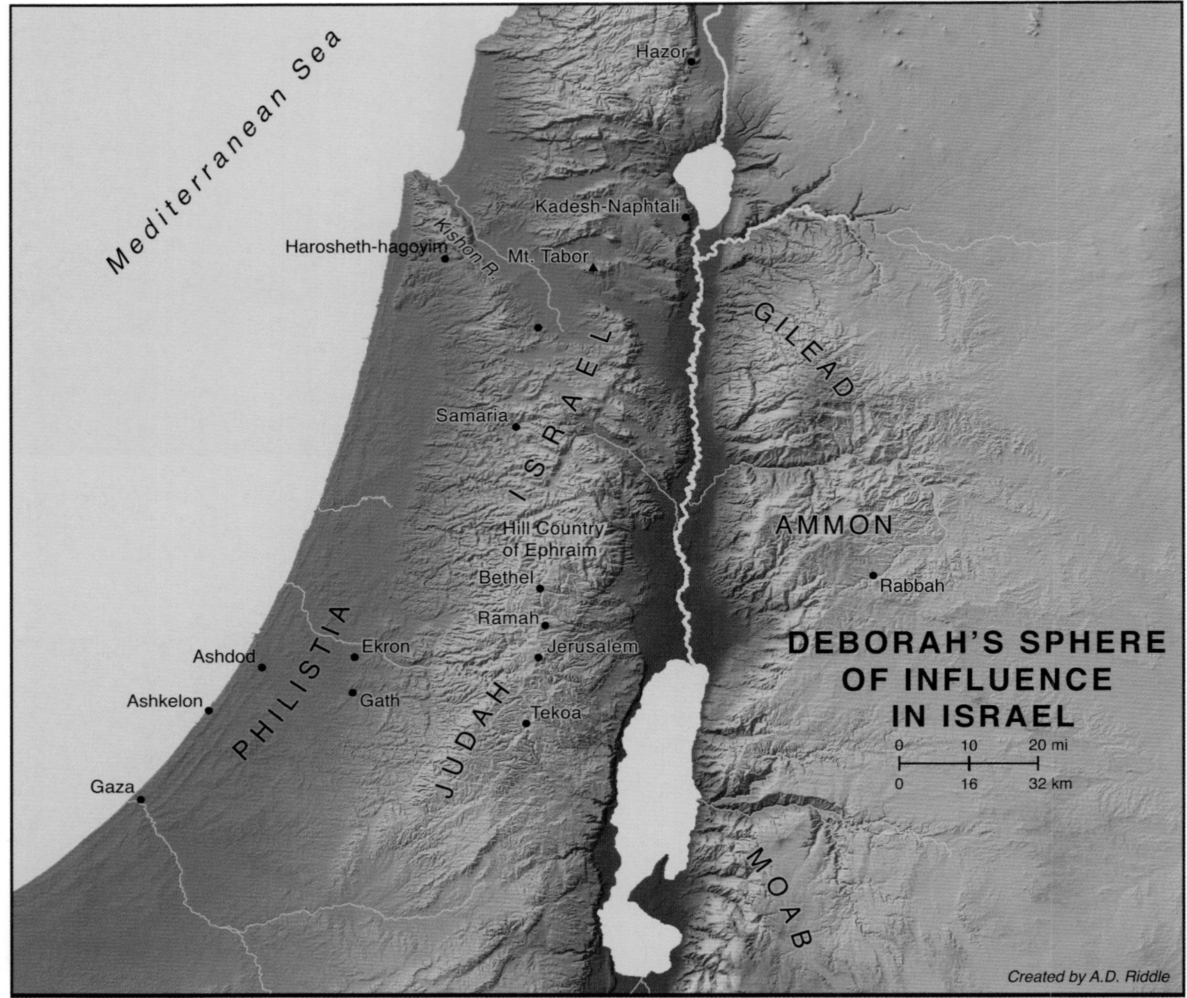

Map 2.1 – Deborah's sphere of influence in Israel *Map by A. D. Riddle*

SAMUEL THE KINGMAKER

Into this period of divine silence that characterized by the Judges period, the birth of Samuel marks a new era in biblical history (ca. 1050–1020 B.C.). From this point onward there is a regular appearance of prophets, especially as the monarchy begins and beyond. Samuel's parents dedicate him to the service of the LORD when Eli was priest and judge (1 Sam. 1:24–27; 2:11, 26). Since the days of Joshua, Shiloh had been Israel's religious capital, and the tabernacle and the ark of the covenant were located there. Without a political capital, Shiloh as the religious center was a de facto capital for the tribes of Israel.

In response to the answered prayers of Hannah dedicated her son to the Lord's service at the central shrine (1 Sam. 1). While still a young lad, Samuel received a nocturnal revelation or call to be a prophet (1 Sam. 3:1). A prophetic call appears to be one factor for recognizing that a prophet is truly sent from God, which is why at the end of the "call" passage, we read that "all Israel from Dan to Beersheba recognized that Samuel was attested as a prophet of the Lord. The Lord continued to appear at Shiloh, and there he revealed himself to Samuel through his word" (1 Sam. 3:20–21).

Fig. 2.7 – View of Shiloh from the west. Possible sacred area in the foreground
Photo by Todd Bolen/Bibleplaces.com

Early in the period of the Judges, the Philistines settled in the southwestern quadrant of ancient Canaan. They had attempted to invade Egypt, but were repulsed by Pharaoh Ramesses III along with the invading "Sea

Fig. 2.8 – Northern Wall of Medinet Habu Temple showing naval invasion of Egypt by Philistines and other Sea Peoples *Photo by Alexander Schick/bibelausstellung.de*

Map 2.2 – Israel and Philistia in the Judges period. *Map by A. D. Riddle*

Peoples" around 1175 B.C. They occupied five earlier Canaanite cities: Gaza, Ashkelon, Ashdod, Ekron, and Gath (Josh. 13:3); and from there the Philistines encroached periodically on Israelite settlements to the east.

A half century later in Samuel's day, the Philistines' power posed a threat to Israel's sovereignty. It was this rising power of Philistia that prompted hostilities and war between these neighboring nations, as reflected during Samson's judgeship (Judg. 13–16), and in the era of Eli's judgeship (1 Sam. 2–6). Samuel likely witnessed the destruction of Shiloh and the loss of the ark of the covenant to Israel's archenemy the Philistines. Although the narratives in 1 Samuel do not specifically mention the destruction of Shiloh where the tabernacle was located, its appearance at Nob (possibly near Jerusalem) a few decades later (see 1 Sam. 21:1; 22:9, 11, 19) implied that the tabernacle had been moved prior to the destruction and the abandonment of Shiloh. Excavations at Shiloh indicate that it was destroyed in the eleventh century, a memory the seventh-century prophet Jeremiah recalls (1 Sam. 7:12; 26:6).To mark this low point in Israelite history, Eli's daughter-in-law gave birth shortly after the ark was captured and named her son Ichabod, meaning "no glory" for "the Glory has departed from Israel" (1 Sam. 4:21–22).

Fig. 2.8 – Philistine prisoners
Photo by Alexander Schick/bibelausstellung.de

It was in the aftermath of this national calamity that Samuel steps forward to give spiritual leadership and rally the nation to strike back against the Philistines. Near his hometown of Ramah within the tribal territory of Benjamin, Samuel mustered the people at Mizpah. In his priestly capacity he offered sacrifices, and Israel's armies defeated the Philistines (1 Sam. 7:7–11). To commemorate the victory, Samuel set up a stone which he named Ebenezer, literally meaning "stone of help," which is explained in the narrative by saying, "the Lord has helped us" (1 Sam. 7:12).

Fig. 2.9 – Excavated area of Shiloh
Photo by Todd Bolen/Bibleplaces.com

Like Deborah before him, Samuel was a prophet and judge. In his capacity as judge, Samuel "went on a circuit from Bethel to Gilgal to Mizpah, judging Israel in all those places. But he always went back to Ramah, where his home was, and there he also judged Israel. And he built an altar there to the Lord" (1 Sam. 7:16–17). Despite being one of Israel's best-known leaders, his circuit was quite small, covering part of the small territory of Benjamin and north to Bethel, which lies just inside southern Ephraim.

Samuel is a unique leader because in addition to being a prophet and judge he was also a priest, and thus stands as something of a transitional figure between the period of the judges and the monarchy. A military leader, however, he was not, which was held against him later in

Fig. 2.10 – Mizpah, Tell el-Nasbeh
Photo by Todd Bolen/Bibleplaces.com

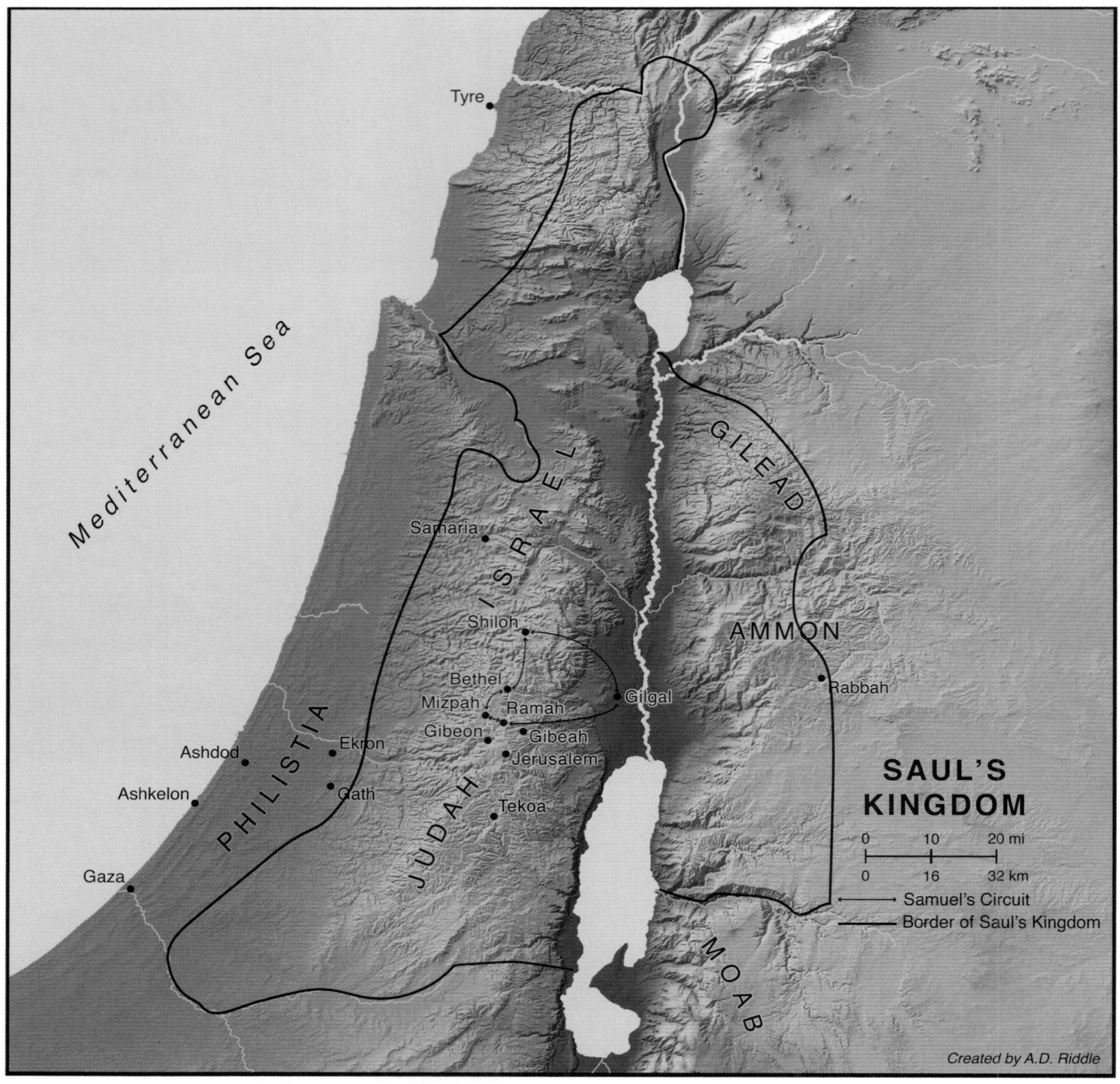

Map 2.3 – Map of Saul's kingdom with Samuel's circuit. *Map by A. D. Riddle*

life as the people were looking for a military hero to lead Israel's armies against the Philistine menace that had started up again. Consequently, the people demanded a king (cf. 1 Sam. 8:4–20). From this point onward, Samuel's role as prophet takes center stage as kingmaker and royal advisor.

In the previous chapter, "the seer" (*hārôeh*) was introduced. Only a few prophets were labelled a *rôeh*, and Samuel was the most important of them (1 Sam. 9:8–10). It was in his capacity of "the seer" that Saul the son of Kish of the tribe of Benjamin and his servant came to Samuel for assistance with the lost donkeys of Kish. He was able to advise them that they had been discovered and were back home. Through divine revelation, God informed Samuel that a man from Benjamin would come to him the next day in search advice about the location for his father's lost donkeys. God announced to Samuel that this man was his designated leader for Israel: "Anoint him ruler over my people Israel," God tells him, for "he will deliver them from the hand of the Philistines. Anoint him leader over my people Israel; he will deliver my people from the hand of the Philistines" (1 Sam. 9:16). The Hebrew word translated "anoint" (*māšaḥ*) is from the Hebrew word from which comes the word "Messiah," an anointed one—that is, one designated or ordained by God for a particular task or mission. Anointing endowed the individual with recognition and authority.

Fig. 2.11 – Iron Age defense wall at Mizpah
Photo by Todd Bolen/Bibleplaces.com

Fig. 2.12 – Ancient stone walls at Ezbet Sartah, Ebenezer
Photo by Todd Bolen/Bibleplaces.com

In the aftermath of his private anointing by Samuel (1 Sam. 10:1), the prophet informed Saul that on his way home from Ramah he would have a transformative prophetic experience:

> After that you will go to Gibeah of God [i.e., Gibeah Elohim], where there is a Philistine outpost. As you approach the town, you will meet a procession of prophets coming down from the high place with lyres, timbrels, pipes and harps being played before them, and they will be prophesying. The Spirit of the Lord will come powerfully upon you, and you will prophesy with them; and you will be changed into a different person. (1 Sam. 10:5–6)

Fig. 2.13 – Gibeah, Saul's home and Israel's first political capital, in 1965
Photo by Paul Lapp/Bible places.com

Indeed these things happened as 1 Samuel 10:10 reports, and Saul was caught up in prophetic ecstasy with the other prophets. The connection between music and prophetic worship was first encountered with Miriam after the crossing of the sea (see chap. 1). From the reference to a high place, it is evident that this band of prophets had been engaged in some sort of cultic activity, which likely included animal sacrifice. While the identity of this group of prophets is not made, it may be that they were disciples of Samuel. Prophetic understudies, normally called "son/s of the prophet," are well known in the ninth century, the period of Elijah and Elisha (2 Kings 2:3, 5, 7; 2 Kings 6:1; 2 Kings 9:1).

It was the prophet Samuel who rallied the tribes together at Mizpah, situated between Bethel and Gibeah, to have a ceremony to recognize publicly Saul as king (1 Sam. 10:17–24). Owing to his priestly connections, Samuel used lots casting, to identify the tribe, clan, family, and individual the LORD intended to be king. The Urim and Thummim were the divinely sanctioned method of "inquiring of the LORD" for the priesthood, and was associated with the ephod worn by the priest (cf. Exod. 28:6–14, 30). Through this process of elimination, Saul was ultimately selected. Samuel then "explained to the people the rihts and duties of kingship. He wrote them down on a scroll and deposited it before the LORD" (1 Sam. 10:25). This ceremony follows the instructions set out by Moses regarding the kingship in Deuteronomy 17:18–20.

Although initially rejected by some Israelites, Saul's rule was subsequently accepted after he had proved himself militarily against the Ammonites who had attack the Israelite city of Jabesh in Gilead, that is, northern Trans-Jordan (1 Sam. 11:1–11). This occasion prompted Samuel to initiate a renewal of kingship at Gilgal, a ceremony over which he presided.

Fig. 2.14 – Gibeah today *Photo by Todd Bolen/Bibleplaces.com*

EXCURSUS ON GILGAL

The reference to Gilgal after Saul and the Israelites returned victoriously from east of the Jordan River evokes memories from centuries earlier when Joshua and the Israelites camped at Gilgal after crossing over the Jordan from victories in the Trans-Jordan (Josh. 4:19). Gilgal had served as a base camp for military missions and a place for religious observances and cultic activity since the day of Joshua (Josh. 4:20; 5:9–10). The name Gilgal means roll away as the episode in Joshua 5:9 (emphasis added) indicates: "Today I have *rolled* away the reproach of Egypt from you. So the place was called Gilgal to this day." Gilgal means "circular" and "wheel" (Isa. 5:28; Ezek. 10:6). In Joshua 4, we are informed that twelve stones were erected at Gilgal, as the name suggests, some scholars think that these sacred stones were set up in a circular pattern.

It may be because of historic and sacral significance of Gilgal to the founding of Israel that Samuel settled on this site for renewing Saul's kingship. Gilgal was also one of the stops on Samuel's circuit as judge (1 Sam. 7:16), and it remained a place of religious sacrifice in connection throughout Saul and Samuel's lifetime.

The identification of Gilgal has eluded archaeologists. The Bible clearly places it at the edge of the border of the city-state of Jericho (Josh. 14:19), whose location is well established. Thus it must have been located within the vicinity of Jericho, west of the Jordan River. While conducting archaeological surveys in central Israel, the late professor Adam Zertal of the University of Haifa recently discovered a most intriguing site in the Jordan Valley called Bedhat esh-Sha'ab, which was investigated thoroughly and excavated in 2002 and 2003. This mysterious foot or sandal-shaped site is 370 meters long and about 90 meters at its widest. It is built against a bleacher-like terraced stone hill on its west side. The surrounding walls are only a stone or two high, indicating that this was not a defensive structure or even a very large animal pen as the walls were too low. Consequently the excavator theorizes that the feature, which has what appears to be a circular stone altar and a higher walled area within outer circuit walls, functioned as a place to gather for religious festivals and services. The pottery from the site spans from the thirteenth and twelfth centuries and down to the tenth centuries, and then fell out of use in the eighth century B.C. The heel area of this large feature is rounded and has two low parallel walls with a cobbled path between them. Zertal wonders if this site is a Gilgal-type site where the Israelite tribes may have assembled, and the circular path outline walls used for some sort a festive circuit. An earlier generation of biblical interpreters had thought that Gilgal was a place of sacred reenactment

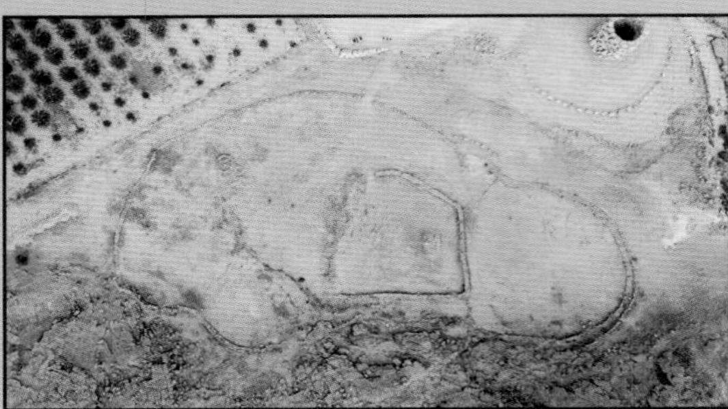

Fig. 2.15 – Bedhat esh-Sha‘ab, a Gilgal site, from the air
Photo by WS/Bibleplaces.com

Fig. 2.16 – Bedhat esh-Sha‘ab walls and possible animal pen on right
Photo by James K. Hoffmeier

of liturgies commemorating the saving acts of God, from bringing the Hebrews from Egypt, through the Sinai wilderness and into the Promised Land.

Bedhat esh-Sha‘ab is located about 65 km (41 miles) north of Jericho, and thus appears to be too far north to be Gilgal of Joshua's day. This site, however, is not the only such foot-shaped one. Zertal's team has identified several others, including one at el-Unuq, situated about 24 km (15 miles) west of Bedhat esh-Sha‘ab, and yet another one was found 17 km farther west at Mt. Ebal; this mountain was known to have been an important early religious center for the newly arrived Israelites in the land of Canaan (cf. Josh. 8:30–33).[6] Then too, between Bedhat esh-Sha‘ab and Jericho, two more foot-shaped sites have been documented in the Jordan Valley. The closest to Jericho is at Yafit, around 38 km (24 miles) to the north. Currently it is unclear whether any of these can be equated with Gilgal of Joshua and Samuel, but these sites may well have been replicas of the original one that were similarly used. It is evident from the various occurrences of Gilgal throughout the Old Testament that this name applied to different sites in different locations. Now that at least five possible Gilgal-type sites have been found, and there may have been more, we can understand why the name occurs at different locations (see Map 2.3).

6 Adam Zertal and Dror Ben-Yosef, “Bedhat esh-Sha‘ab: An Iron Age I Enclosure in the Jordan Valley,” in *Exploring the Longue Durrée: Essays in Honor of Lawrence E. Stager*, ed. J. D. Schloen, 517–29 (Winona Lake, IN: Eisenbrauns, 2009).

Gilgal continued to be associated with the prophetic tradition in the centuries after Samuel. During the eighth century, Gilgal was once again a place of religious observances, although the practices must have involved a blending with pagan practices, for they are roundly condemned by Hosea and Amos. The latter put it this way:

> "Go to Bethel and sin; go to Gilgal and sin yet more." (Amos 4:4)

> "Do not seek Bethel, do not go to Gilgal, do not journey to Beersheba. For Gilgal will surely go into exile, and Bethel will be reduced to nothing." (Amos 5:5)

Fig. 2.17 – A possible altar at Bedhat esh-Sha'ab
Photo by James K. Hoffmeier

During the early years of Saul's reign, Samuel served as prophet, advising the king of God's plans. Saul demonstrated his propensity to be impatient in awaiting Samuel's divine guidance before battles. The first occasion was against the Philistines (1 Sam. 13) and they were getting the upper hand. Saul rallied his troops at Gilgal and awaited Samuel's word on how to proceed, but Samuel's arrival

Fig. 2.18 – Philistine warriors *Photo by Alexander Schick/bibelausstellung.de)*

was delayed, and the troops were beginning to scatter, with some crossing into Trans-Jordan (13:7–8). So the king presided over sacrifices, thus usurping Samuel's priestly role. When Samuel arrived he castigated Saul, "You have done a foolish thing. . . . You have not kept the command the LORD your God gave you" (13:13).

The final blow for Saul occurred in the aftermath of fighting in southern Israel (and into Sinai) against the Amalekites, a desert people who had attacked and harassed the Israelites in the wilderness in Moses's day (Exod. 17:13; Deut. 25:17–19). Once again Saul failed to follow Samuel's instructions from God. Instead of totally destroying the sheep and cattle as an act of dedication (*ḥerem*) to God, he kept some of the best, and then told Samuel he had kept them in order to make sacrifices to the LORD (1 Sam. 15:17–21). In response, Samuel uttered the memorable words:

> Does the LORD delight in burnt offerings and sacrifices
> as much as in obeying the voice of the LORD?
> To obey is better than sacrifice,
> and to heed is better than the fat of rams.
> For rebellion is like the sin of divination,
> and arrogance like the evil of idolatry.
> Because you have rejected the word of the LORD,
> he has rejected you as king. (1 Sam. 15:22–23)

With this stinging indictment, Samuel turns away to leave and Saul grabs the hem of his robe, suggesting that he may have been groveling at his feet. In so doing, he tore Samuel's gown. In response Samuel declared, "The LORD has torn the kingdom of Israel from you today and has given it to one of your neighbors" (1 Sam. 15:28). This tearing of the garment is an early example of a prophet using various dramatic acts to illustrate divine messages. A torn garment is once again used to illustrate the severing of the kingdom and nation at the end of Solomon's reign when the prophet Ahijah rips apart a garment into twelve portions to symbolize the united kingdom splitting (1 Kings 11:29–32; see further below). While Saul's kingship continued until his death in battle with the Philistines (1 Sam. 31), his hold of the kingdom began to unravel, and there would be no Saulide Dynasty. Most significantly, he

Fig. 2.19 – Shasu/Bedouin desert people captured by Pharaoh Seti I (ca. 1294 B.C.) may the same people known as Amalekites in the Bible
Photo by Alexander Schick/bibelausstellung.de

was cut off from access to God's word as Samuel shunned him: "Until the day Samuel died, he did not go to see Saul again" (1 Sam. 15:34).

With Saul disgraced and isolated, the scene shifts to Bethlehem where the LORD sent his prophet to the home of Jesse to anoint one of his sons to be the next king. That son was David, who was destined to be the founder of a royal dynasty that would rule from Jerusalem for over four centuries (1 Sam. 16).

Samuel as a prophet-leader guided the nation between the judges period and the early monarchy, and as noted already was directed by God to anointed the first two kings of Israel, Saul and David. More than a dozen years passed from the time David was designated as God's anointed ruler and when he became king at age thirty (2 Sam. 5:4). By this time Samuel had passed away and it was left to the next generation of prophets, Gad and Nathan, to communicate God's counsel to David.

Later biblical reflection on Samuel holds him up as one of the greats. Psalm 99:6 places Samuel along luminaries like Moses and Aaron: "Moses and Aaron were among his priests, Samuel also was among those who called upon his name; they called to the LORD and he answered them."

When King Josiah promoted the national celebration of Passover in Jerusalem on a grand scale, the Chronicler adds an interesting comment: "No Passover like it had been kept in Israel since the days of Samuel the prophet. None of the Kings of Israel had kept such a Passover as was kept by Josiah, and the priests and the Levites, and all Judah and Israel who were present, and the inhabitants of Jerusalem" (2 Chron. 35:18 ESV). Although the book of 1 Samuel does not report on the prophet's role in this great celebration of Passover, it was remembered centuries later as a credit to Samuel's faithfulness and greatness. Lastly, Jeremiah 15:1 recalls Samuel as a great intercessor and matches him once again with Moses, Israel's greatest prophet-intercessor.

Fig. 2.20 – The cave of Adullam where Gad joined David in exile
Photo by William Schlegel/Bible places.com

GAD AND NATHAN: DAVID'S PROPHETS

Although he had been anointed king, thus having received divine-prophetic legitimacy to rule, David had to wait over a decade till Saul's death, which was followed by a two-year civil war before being accepted as king of all the tribes of Israel. During this period, David found himself on the run, trying to stay one step ahead of Saul. Gad the prophet is closely associated with David and is even called "David's seer" (*ḥōzeh*) (2 Sam. 24:11), but little is known about him. Neither his father's name nor his hometown are recorded. Gad joined David while hiding out at the Cave of Adullam. It was Gad who warned David to leave his cave hideout and to head for the forest of Hereth in Judah to get ahead of Saul (2 Sam. 22:1–5). Gad then comes into the picture again late in David's reign after the king had taken the census that had angered God. This prophet received God's word condemning David's self-serving act and presented him with three different forms of punishment from which the king could choose. Then Gad instructed David to build the altar at the threshing floor of Araunah, where the death angel was about to strike Jerusalem in punishment for the census (2 Sam. 24:18–19). This threshing floor was situated on the north side of Jerusalem and

Fig. 2.21 – Jerusalem from the air: David's Jerusalem is located on the left center side of the image, and the temple area is on the right side, presently covered by the Dome of the Rock complex
Photo by WS/Bible places.com

was subsequently purchased by David who designated it to be the site of the temple of the LORD that was constructed by King Solomon, David's successor.

In keeping with prophets' role in music and worship, Gad, along with Nathan (his successor), played a role in the organization of the Levitical musicians for temple worship in Jerusalem (2 Chron. 29:25). Then too he is mentioned as one of the prophets who recorded the history of David's reign (1 Chron. 9:29).

Nathan was associated with King David, and must have been younger than Gad his contemporary. Like Gad, Nathan's roots are not mentioned, but his activity seems to be centered in Jerusalem, and should be considered a court prophet (i.e., one who served the king and was likely compensated for his service). As is often the case with court prophets, they appear in the biblical

Fig. 2.22 – Aerial view of the City of David
Photo by William Schlegel/Bible places.com

episodes at important or crisis situations. Nathan is first mentioned after David had completed building his palace in Jerusalem. Perhaps feeling guilty over having built a palace for himself, he resolves to build a temple for God, observing, "Here I am, living in a house of cedar, while the ark of God remains in a tent" (2 Sam. 7:2). Nathan is consulted on the matter and his natural impulse is to approve David's idea—surely God deserves a glorious temple! That night, however, the word of the Lord came to Nathan, which he conveyed to the king (7:4–17). God indicated that he did not need a temple and rather preferred the mobility and accessibility to the people afforded by the tabernacle, but agreed that a temple could be built by David's son. The future temple is associated with David's dynasty, which would be an enduring one.

Nathan plays a prominent role in the episode of David's sin of adultery with Bathsheba and the murder of her husband Uriah, one of David's loyal generals. It is Nathan who confronted David regarding the scandal (2 Sam. 12:1). In order to expose the king's attempt to cover up his heinous crimes, Nathan told David a parable about a poor man who had but a single ewe lamb, while a near neighbor had larger herds and cattle. And yet when it came time to serve a meal to an out-of-town guest, the rich man took the poor man's lamb. David was enraged at this man's maltreatment of his poor neighbor: "the man who did this must die!" he exclaimed. Nathan had skillfully drawn David into the story, which caused him to condemn himself. When Nathan announced, "You are the man!" David had to confess, "I have sinned against the Lord" (12:5, 7, 13).

The child of this adulterous union died shortly after birth, as Nathan announced, but David took Bathsheba as his wife. The next child from this union would be the future king. When this birth occurred, Nathan came to David with a message from God indicating that "the Lord loved him," hence the name Jedidiah ("beloved of Yahweh") is given (2 Sam. 12:24–25). Only here is this name mentioned. Through the Bible we know him by his royal name: Solomon!

Nathan was also instrumental in the accession of Solomon. Well advanced in years, David had become senile and was losing grip on his kingdom toward the end of his life. His eldest son Adonijah took advantage of the situation and made his move to succeed his father even before the king died (1 Kings 1). Supporting Adonijah were Joab, David's top general, and Abiathar the priest. Significantly Nathan, though the main prophet of that time period, was not invited to a ceremony designed to coronate David's successor (1:9–10). This development was quite startling since the first two kings of Israel had been divinely acclaimed by prophetic anointing.

Fig. 2.23 – The Gihon Spring
Photo by Todd Bolen/Bibleplaces.com

Upon hearing of this development, Nathan swung into action! He went to Bathsheba to inform her of what was taking place. Bathsheba in turn apprised David of what was occurring. Nathan followed the queen into David's presence by confirming that a royal succession was underway without David's knowledge or approval. Although not recorded previously in 2 Samuel, it seems that David had announced to Bathsheba and Nathan that Solomon was to be his intended successor despite not being the eldest son. It may be that when Solomon was born, the prophetic word Nathan received implied that because he was loved by the LORD he was God's chosen successor. So amid the confusion that must have been rippling through Jerusalem, David proclaims "I will surely carry out today what I swore to you by the LORD, the God of Israel: Solomon your son shall be king after me" (1 Kings 1:30). David directs young Solomon to go with Zadok (another priest), Benaiah (captain of David's elite bodyguards), and Nathan who would anoint him at the Gihon Spring, located just below the City of David. Recent excavations around the Giḥon springs has revealed that is was located within ancient fortified walls and one of the gates of the city. The horn of oil came from "the sacred tent" which may explain why Zadok the priest joins Nathan in anointing Solomon as coregent and soon to be king. The anointing of Solomon was Nathan's last recorded act in the Bible.

DAVID: GOD'S ANOINTED AND THE MESSIAH

The Hebrew word anoint is *māšaḥ*, behind which stands the English word Messiah, an anointed one. When translated into Greek for the Septuagint, the Scriptures of Hellenistic Jews and the early Christian community, the word is *xrēstos* (= Christos) was used. Both "Messiah" and "Christ" mean "anointed one." From the Torah we learn that part of the act of consecrating priests was being anointed with olive oil (Lev. 21:10, 12), so too with some Israelite kings (e.g. Saul, David, Solomon, Jehu, Joash). The prophet Elisha was also anointed to be a prophet by his mentor Elijah (2 Kings 19:16). The practice of anointing was not unique to ancient Israel, but was known in Mesopotamia as early as the early third millennium B.C.

Fig. 2.24 – A relief from ancient Kish in Mesopotamia (ca. 2800 B.C.) showing a man being anointed.
In Henri de Genouillac, Fouilles français d'El-'Akhyer *[Brussels, 1925], pl. 1.1*

David was anointed by Samuel after a divine process in which God communicated with the prophet. Seven sons of Jesse were eliminated until David was identified. Anointing followed, accompanied by "the Spirit of the LORD" coming on him (1 Sam. 16:13). Even though he had been anointed king, David was emphatic that neither he nor his men who were fleeing from Saul would harm the king. Even though they had a chance to kill him, David declined, saying, "The LORD forbid that I should do such a thing to my master, the LORD's anointed, or lay my hand on him; for he is the anointed of the LORD" (1 Sam. 24:5–6). The sentiment expressed here is that LORD's anointed is special, if not sacrosanct.

David became the archetype for the Messianic King, his failures notwithstanding. He was a military hero, from his slaying Goliath the giant as a young man, through his conquests as king when he carved out a small regional kingdom that stretched north to Syria and east through the Trans-Jordan. Particularly significant was his seizure of Jerusalem, with its stronghold Zion, from the Jebusites who had controlled it since before the days of Joshua's conquest (Judges 1:21; 1 Samuel 5:6–10). Jerusalem became Israel's capital and under Solomon, the temple was constructed there, thus binding together temple and state.

Fig. 2.25 – Tell Dan Inscription with the reference to "the House of David"
Photo by James K. Hoffmeier

While David did not build the temple, it was through the agency of Nathan that God announced to David, "Your house and your kingdom will endure forever before me; your throne will be established forever" (2 Sam. 7:16). Known as the "Davidic Covenant," it was reaffirmed with Solomon at the dedication of the temple, provided that the king obey God's laws (1 Kings 9:4–5). As a consequence, the kingship and the temple will be a subject frequently addressed by the prophets.

David's dynasty continued till the fall of Jerusalem and the destruction of the temple in 586 B.C. at the hands of the Babylonians. The "House of David" is an expression used for that dynasty and the kingdom of Judah when the nation was divided in 931 B.C. In 1993 the fragmentary remains of an inscription of a king of Damascus (probably Hazael) was discovered. The text, which dates to approximately 841 B.C., refers to the "House of David."[7] This surely means that throughout the region, the rulers of Jerusalem in the kingdom of Judah were descendants of David.

Because David was the archetype of the ideal, anointed king, when his dynastic line was severed in 586 B.C., the Jewish people began to look toward the reestablishment of the kingship in keeping with the Davidic Covenant. Shortly after King Jehoiachin was deported to Babylon, Jeremiah prophesied: "'The days are coming,' declares the LORD, 'when I will raise up for David a righteous Branch, a King who will reign wisely and do what is just and right in the land'" (Jer. 23:5). From Babylonian exile, the prophet Ezekiel anticipated the return of the Jews to Israel and proclaims, "My servant David will be king over them" (Ezek. 37:24). The coming messianic king is an unresolved matter in the Hebrew Scriptures or Old Testament when its history comes to a close, and around four centuries of prophetic silence followed.

AHIJAH AND SHEMAIAH: THE KINGDOM SPLITS

While David is credited for uniting the tribes of Israel and establishing a kingdom with neighboring nations like Philistia, Moab, and Aram being subject to him (ca. 1010–970 B.C.), it was Solomon who built up the defenses of the nation (1 Kings 9:15–19) and constructed the temple in Jerusalem (1 Kings 6–7; ca. 970–931 B.C.). It appeared that this small but vibrant kingdom was on a good footing. In order to complete the numerous building projects, Solomon had to employ a system of forced labor. Men were drafted to do the heavy lifting, and this resulted in resentment toward the Davidic king. One of Solomon's officials was Jeroboam from the tribe of Ephraim, who was an able

7 Avraham Biran and Joseph Naveh, "An Aramaic Stele Fragment from Tel Dan," *IEJ* 43, nos. 2–3 (1993): 1–18; Avraham Biran and Joseph Naveh, "The Tel Dan Inscription: A New Fragment," *IEJ* 45 (1995): 1–15.

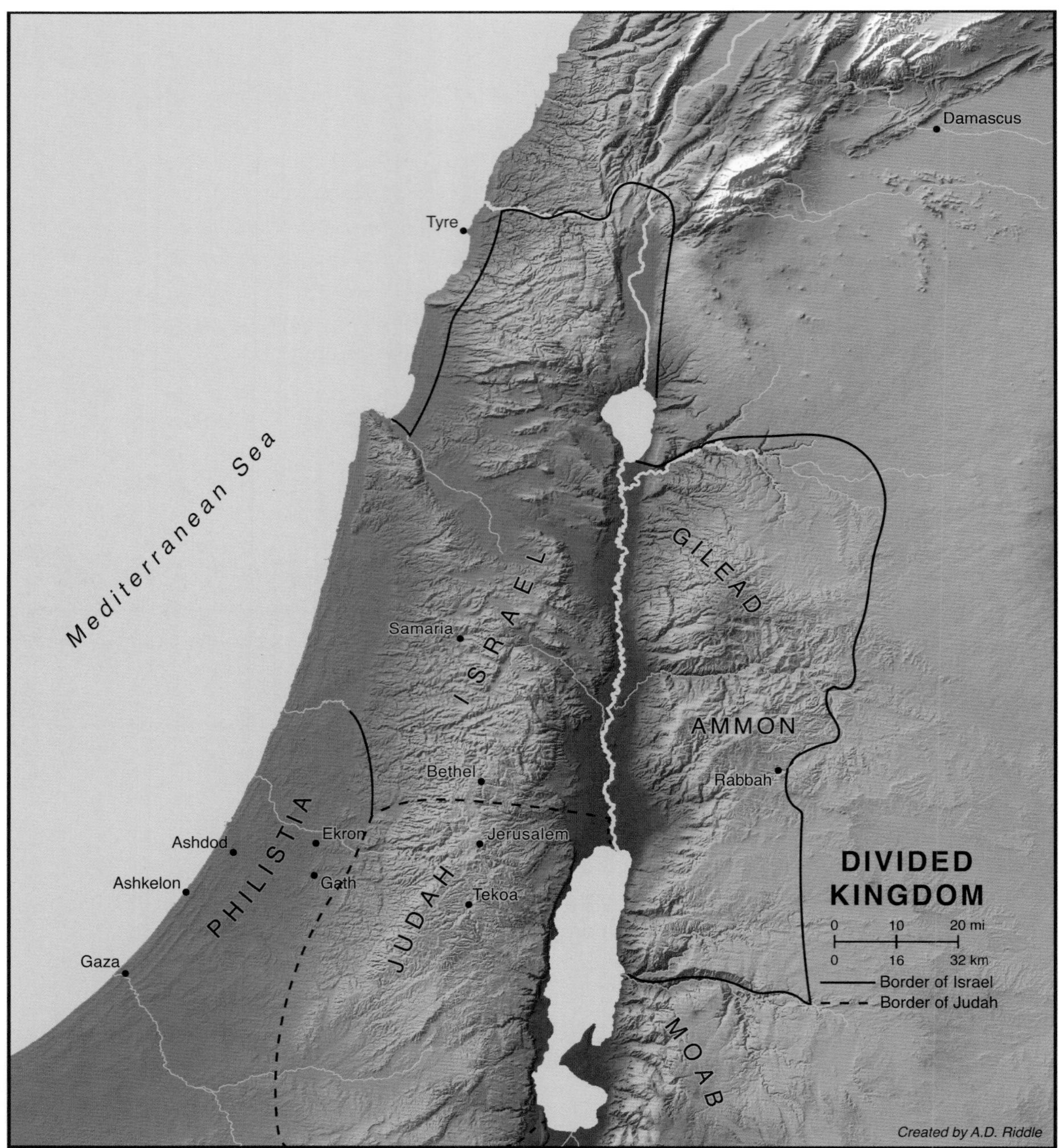

Map 2.4 – The divided kingdom of Israel and Judah *Map by A. D. Riddle*

overseer of the workforce from his tribe along with the draftees from neighboring Manasseh (1 Kings 11:26–28).

On one occasion when Jeroboam was leaving Jerusalem, he was encountered by Ahijah, the prophet from Shiloh. Shiloh had been home to the tabernacle from the days of Joshua until Philistines attacked during the priesthood of Eli (1 Sam. 4). It may be that a band of prophets were stationed at Shiloh as a tribute to the important role it had played in early Israelite history. The prophet took hold of Jeroboam's "new cloak" and tore it into twelve pieces, offering ten of them to the future king (1 Kings 11:29–33). He explained that God was about to tear Israel apart—with Jeroboam, who was from the north, receiving the lion's share. Clearly the new garment represented the relatively new kingdom that would be torn in pieces. As we saw with Samuel and Saul, the torn garment dramatically illustrated what was

Fig. 2.26 – Karnak Temple triumph scene celebrating Shoshenk/Shishak's victory over Israel and Judah
Photo by Todd Bolen/Bibleplaces.com

about to happen with Solomon's kingship and the nation. Ahijah did, however, indicate that a smaller portion would remain with David's successors.

This prophetic pronouncement apparently encouraged Jeroboam to foment rebellion against Solomon who in turn tried to kill the rebel. Jeroboam fled to Egypt for sanctuary and was taken in by Shishak (1 Kings 11:40). This king was in fact Shoshenk I of Egyptian texts, a man of Libyan origin who was the founder of Egypt's twenty-second Dynasty (ca. 945–715 B.C.). Upon Solomon's death, Rehoboam his son succeeded him. Jeroboam returned to negotiate a better arrangement for the northern tribes with the Davidic king. When he would not ease the work burdens that had been imposed by Solomon, the northern tribes seceded and made Jeroboam the first king of the fledgling northern kingdom of Israel. This division of united Israel was understood as a fulfillment of "the word the LORD had spoken to Jeroboam son of Nebat through Ahijah the Shilonite" (1 Kings 12:15). The northern tribes as a nation was called Israel, while the Judah was the name of the southern kingdom.

Ruling in Jerusalem, Rehoboam initially had a military and organizational advantage over Jeroboam and the upstart northern kingdom. He was determined to invade and reclaim his lost territory. As if to reinforce Ahijah's earlier prophecy, "the word of God came to Shemaiah the man of God" indicating that this schism was God's design and that he should give up his aspirations (1 Kings 12:22–24).

Jeroboam and the northern tribes had two serious problems to address: one political (the need for a capital) and the other religious (where would they worship?). Shechem, the city where Jacob had contracted agreements with the locals (Gen. 34) and where Joshua had renewed the Sinaitic Covenant with the twelve tribes before his death (Josh. 24), was initially built up and made the capital, as well as Peniel in the Trans-Jordan. Jeroboam feared that if the people went to Jerusalem for the various religious festivals and ceremonies, their political loyalties would shift back to Rehoboam. So he established two rival worship centers, one in Bethel at the southern end of his kingdom, and Dan in the far north. By locating official sanctuaries at these locations facilitated access to the shrines for Israelites. Bethel was a historically special place. It was there that God renewed the promise to Jacob that was made to Abraham regarding the "promised land" (Gen. 28:13–17), and it was God's appearance to Jacob in his famous dream that stands behind the name Bethel: "When Jacob awoke from his sleep, he thought, 'Surely

Fig. 2.27 – Beitin/Bethel with stone structure of the Byzantine Period
Photo by Todd Bolen/Bibleplaces.com

the LORD is in this place, and I was not aware of it.' He was afraid and said, 'How awesome is this place! This is none other than the house of God [i.e., Bethel]; this is the gate of heaven'" (Gen. 28:16–17).

Ancient Bethel is probably to be identified with the site Beitin, but it was only excavated briefly by W. F. Albright in 1927 and 1934 and by James Kelso for three seasons in the 1950s. The temple area of the Iron Age was not discovered in the course of these excavations. Just recently a team of Japanese archaeologists have begun to survey Beitin with the intent to excavate.[8] Hopefully these excavations at Bethel will reveal what was considered to be "the king's sanctuary and the temple of the kingdom" where Amos denounced Jeroboam II and Israel's religious failures (Amos 7:13). Fortuitously, the counterpart to the Bethel sanctuary was discovered at Tell Dan in the excavations of the late Avraham Biran in the 1980s. The altar area and high place where the "golden calf" once stood have been uncovered. The excavations reveal that this cult center enjoyed repeated use and refurbishment over the centuries until it was destroyed and abandoned in the seventh century.

Fig. 2.28 – Aerial view of Dan sacred precinct with altar area in foreground, behind which is the "high place"
Photo by William Schlegel /Bible places.com

Fig. 2.29 – The high place
Photo by James K. Hoffmeier

In response to Jeroboam's building of these illicit sanctuaries, an unnamed "man of God" from Judah faced off with him at Bethel and denounced them, saying that a son of the House of David named Josiah would destroy the altars (1 Kings 13:1–5). It may be that Shemiah, who is also called "man of God" is this prophet, but there is no way to know for certain. This prophetic word anticipates the reforms of King Josiah (ca. 640–609 B.C.) who sought to obliterate all vestiges of pagan and unauthorized worship centers (2 Kings 23:4–16).

Jeroboam responded angrily, ordering his soldiers to "seize him." As he pointed to the man of God, his arm "shriveled up" and then the altar "split apart"

---

8 Since this work has only just begun, publications have not yet appeared, but one can see a brief report about the work on the project's website: http://www.jcic-heritage.jp/en/project/middle_east_palestine_201312.

(1 Kings 13:4–5). Terrified, Jeroboam cried out for divine intercession and healing. The man of God prayed for healing and restoration followed. Jeroboam's character vis-à-vis the prophetic word was revealed, as the text subsequently records; "Even after this, Jeroboam did not change his evil ways" (1 Kings 13:33) but continued the religious operations at his religious centers.

Engaging in miracles and healings are not typically associated with the Hebrew prophets; none are recorded among the literary prophets. Elijah and Elisha are exceptions (see below). Thus the report of this unnamed "man of God" involved in the healing of king Jeroboam's withered hand is an important detail.

Toward the end of Jeroboam's reign, Ahijah makes one last but significant appearance in the Bible (1 Kings 14). Abijah, Jeroboam's young son, was ill. So Jeroboam sent his wife to Shiloh disguised as a commoner rather than in her regalia to inquire concerning the fate of the boy, Abijah. Though advanced in age and blind, with divine insight, he knew who she was! As she arrived Ahijah greeted her by saying, "Come in, wife of Jeroboam" (14:6). He disclosed that not only would the lad die, but because the king had angered God with his disobedience and idolatry, the nation would in the future be exiled to Mesopotamia (14:15). While the son died upon her arrival home some days later, the nation would hang on for nearly two centuries before being overwhelmed by the Assyrians in 722 B.C.

Fig. 2.30 – Close-up of toponyms on Shishak list, Karnak Temple
Photo by Alexander Schick/bibelausstellung.de

Rehoboam, though the son of Solomon the wise king, was no better than Jeroboam I in that he too introduced foreign deities and practices in Judah (1 Kings 14:22–24). As a consequence of this behavior, the Pharaoh Shishak (i.e., Shoshenk I) invaded the land, and according to Shemaiah this judgment came because "you have abandoned me [God]; therefore I now abandon you to Shishak" (2 Chron. 12:5). In response, "The leaders of Israel and the king humbled themselves" (2 Chron. 12:6), which resulted in a partial reprieve. Shishak would not destroy Jerusalem but simply take away the "treasures of the temple of the LORD and the treasures of the royal palace" (2 Chron. 12:9).

Although the Bible does not mention that Shishak also invaded his erstwhile friend Jeroboam in the north, archaeological evidence indicates that he did. In his victory reliefs carved on the walls at Karnak Temple in Egypt, Shishak celebrated his campaign by showing himself smiting the heads of his enemy before the standing image of the patron deity Amon-Ra. The scene also includes the names of scores of cities and areas the Pharaoh claims to have conquered. And these include Israelite sites such as Penuel and Tirzah (two of Jeroboam's capitals), and Megiddo. In fact at a number of archaeological sites there are signs of the Egyptian demolition. At Megiddo a fragment of an inscribed block was discovered with the name Shoshenk on it. This campaign occurred in Shishak's penultimate year, 925 B.C.

Fig. 2.31 – Top of Shoshenk I/Shishak stela from Megiddo
Photo by Alexander Schick/bibelausstellung.de

TROUBLERS OF THE ISRAELITE KINGS: ELIJAH, ELISHA, AND MICAIAH

Civil strife marred Israel in the early ninth century B.C., with factions divided between an obscure figure named Tibni and Omri the military commander (1 Kings 16:21–23). Around 885 B.C. Omri won out and was founder of a powerful dynasty that included his infamous son Ahab. At this time Samaria was established as the capital. Meanwhile the Assyrian empire was growing in strength as evidenced by Shalmaneser III's military conquests west of the Euphrates River. In 853 B.C. at Qarqar, located southwest of Aleppo in Syria on the Orontes River, the Assyrian armies met a powerful coalition of regional monarchs. Included in the

Fig. 2.32 – The Hill of Samaria, on which the capital city of the northern kingdom was built by king's Omri and Ahab
Photo by Todd Bolen/Bibleplaces.com

opposition was "Ahab the Israelite" who contributed two thousand chariots and ten thousand foot soldiers to this conflict, an event not attested to in the Bible.

Omri and Ahab had close ties with the Phoenicians, who ruled the seas from present-day Lebanon. The dowager queen Jezebel was the daughter of the king of Sidon and was married to Ahab, and mother of the next king, Jehoram. Through her agency, hundreds of pagan prophets were brought to Israel along with other idolatrous practices. These circumstances set the stage for a series of prophets of the Lord to challenge the royal family and its practices. Two of these prophets, Elijah and Elisha, stand out as miracle workers, a characteristic not usually associated with prophets. Micaiah is the third prophet who proved to be a thorn in the flesh of king Ahab.

Elijah the Tishbite

Felix Mendelssohn's great oratorio, "Elijah," is based on the life and ministry of this remarkable prophet. Little, however, is actually known of his personal life. In fact the location of his home Tishbe is unknown, but likely was located in Gilead (1 Kings 17:1), which is east of the Jordan River, opposite the territory of Manasseh. A suggested location for Tishbe is on the Cherith Brook or Wadi.[9] Elijah bursts on the scene to announce to King Ahab that there would be a prolonged drought (1 Kings 17:1–2). During the drought he spent time by the Cherith (1 Kings 17:3–7), until this stream also dried up. He then migrated to Zarephath, a small town near Sidon (the Phoenician capital), to avoid arrest by Ahab (1 Kings 17:8–16). There he met a destitute widow (1 Kings 17:8–24) whom he asked for water and bread, as she was about to run out of flour and oil. He told her that the Lord the God of Israel would not let her flour and oil run out if she fed the prophet. That indeed happened "according to the word of the Lord." Later on the widow's son fell ill and died (1 Kings 17:24), a tragedy she blamed on Elijah. He implored God to restore his life, and the child lived. For a non-Israelite, her confession is significant: "Now I know that you are a man of God and that the word of the Lord from your mouth is the truth" (17:24). These stories about the foreign widow serve as a rebuke to Ahab and

9 Barry Beitzel, *The New Moody Bible Atlas* (Chicago: Moody, 2009), 180–81.

the Israelites who did not heed the word of God as announced by the prophet, and while they were turning to the pagan deities like Baal, Asherah, and Astarte, this Sidonian woman was turning to the God of Israel.

Elijah returned to Israel to challenge Ahab as the drought and famine dragged on (1 Kings 18). He met Ahab's palace manager, Obadiah, who feared the Lord as demonstrated by him hiding a hundred prophets of the Lord and feeding them in order to escape Queen Jezebel, who had been killing off God's prophets (1 Kings 18:13). Obadiah arranged a meeting with Ahab and Elijah. The king called him the "troubler of Israel" as if Elijah were at fault. The prophet retorted, "I have not made trouble for Israel. . . . But you and your father's family have. You have abandoned the Lord's commands and have followed the Baals" (1 Kings 18:18). On this occasion he challenges the prophets of Baal and Asherah, 950 in all, whom Jezebel sponsored, to a showdown to determine whether Yahweh or Baal was the true god.

Fig. 2.33 – Kurkh Stela of Shalmaneser III in the British Museum that mentions the Israelite king, Ahab
Photo by James K. Hoffmeier

Baal means "lord," "master," and "husband" and is used as a title for the storm-god Hadad.[10] He was associated with storm, lightning, and rain, and hence fertility. In summer, according to the Baal Myth, Baal died, which parallels the long rainless period in the west Mediterranean. When the rains came with the clouds from the sea in the Autumn, Baal was thought to have come back to life. The contest between Elijah and the 950 prophets was to answer the ultimate question: Who is the true God, the one who controls nature? The prolonged drought, and the location on Mt. Carmel, set the stage for this dramatic event.

The Carmel range runs in a southeasterly direction from the present-day coastal city of Haifa, where it arises about from around 170 m (550 ft.) at the north end to a height of around 554 m (1800 ft) some 20 km (13 miles) to the southeast. The name Carmel, meaning finest vineyard or orchard, reflects the fertility of this

10 *HALOT* 142.

Fig. 2.34 – Stela depicting the Storm-god Baal of Ras Shamra (Syria)
Photo by Todd Bolen/Bibleplaces.com

area.[11] There Elijah proposed a duel occur in which two bulls would be sacrificed and placed on different altars, one for Baal and the other for the Lord. The bull was the animal most associated with Baal, and such images have been discovered that had been used for religious purposes. Baal's prophets and then Elijah each would take a turn summoning their respective deities to see which one responds "by fire" (i.e., lightning; 1 Kings 18:24). Elijah appeals here to another fitting symbol, as images of Baal frequently show him holding a lightning bolt, poised to hurl it like a spear. For hours Baal priests danced, cried out, and sought Baal to act. Standing by, Elijah mocked their efforts and suggested they shout louder as "he is deep in thought, or busy, or traveling. Maybe he is sleeping and must be awakened" (1 Kings 18:27). The scene was pathetic. The Baal priests went even further; they danced and chanted and "slashed themselves with swords and spears, as was their custom until their blood flowed." from morning till midday (1 Kings 18:28). No response came.

The Baal prophets' bizarre and grisly "custom" of slashing themselves may be alluded to in the prohibition in Leviticus 19:28 and Deuteronomy 14:1, which specifically forbids cutting oneself on behalf of the dead, a known Canaanite practice. In ritual texts in the Baal Myth, Baal dies fighting Mot, death. Just as the agricultural year ends with annual dry period, plants wither and die until autumn rains move off the Mediterranean and resuscitate the land. The protracted drought in the days of Ahab and Jezebel, from a Canaanite/Phoenician perspective, surely meant that Baal had not come back to life. In the Baal Myth, when the fertility god dies, one of the measures used to show great distraught and aid his resurrection was ceremonial body cutting. In texts from ancient Ugarit,

11 *HALOT* 499.

located about 280 km (174 m) north of Sidon on coast of Syria, several of Baal's fellow deities, including El, head of the pantheon and Baal's consort Anat, engage in body cutting: "With a stone he scratches incisions on (his/El's) skin, with a razor he cuts cheeks and chin. He harrows his upper arms, plows (his) back like a (garden in a) valley. He raises his voice and cries aloud."[12]

Fig. 2.35 – Fertility figurines found in Israel, thought by some to be the goddess Asherah
Photo by A. D. Riddle/Bibleplaces.com

The Baal prophets who were slashing themselves were most likely Phoenicians, part of Jezebel's religious entourage that came to Samaria with her. She was the daughter of Ethbaal of King of Sidon (1 Kings 16:31), the maritime power in present-day Lebanon. As this king's name suggests, "with (him) is Baal,"[13] was a devotee of the dying-reviving fertility god of the West Semitic world. The failure to get Baal to bring a life-giving storm was utter defeat for his worshipers, but the ultimate test was, would YHWH God of Israel respond where Baal was silent?

Elijah then took his turn, erecting an altar from twelve stones, and preparing the cuts of the sacrificial bull and the firewood. This twelve-stone altar no doubt was meant to draw a connection to the altar made at Mt. Sinai in connection with God's powerful manifestation when the covenant was made with Israel, and in both cases each stone represented one of the twelve tribes (cf. Exod. 24:4–5; 1 Kings 18:31). Elijah then had water poured over the offering and then he prayed: "Lord, the God of Abraham, Isaac and Israel, let it be known today that you are God in Israel and that I am your servant and have done all these things at your command. Answer me, Lord, answer me, so these people will know that you, Lord, are God, and that you are turning their hearts back again" (1 Kings 18:36–37). Lightning struck, and the offering was consumed (v. 38). The response of the onlookers was one of awe! "The Lord—he is God! The Lord—he is God!" (v. 39). Elijah then oversaw the execution of the pagan prophets. After he prayed again, the storm clouds gathered, and heavy rains began—the drought was over. In this dramatic narrative once again one can see the intercessory role of the prophet as well as bringing the people back to a right relationship with God.

---

12 *COS* 1:268.
13 *HALOT* 101.

Fig. 2.36 – Mt. Carmel looking east toward the Mediterranean Sea
Photo by Todd Bolen/Bibleplaces.com

Ahab, whose presence had not been mentioned in the contest episode but apparently was standing by, was directed to hitch up his chariot and head down to Jezreel about 27 km (16.5 miles) away, lest he be overwhelmed by the coming storm and not be able to negotiate the muddy roads back to his palace (1 Kings 18:44). With pouring rain falling, Elijah is gripped by "the power of the Lord" (v. 46) and runs all the way to Jezreel. There Ahab had built a palace, a site which was excavated in the 1990s and again since 2012. Iron II period (ninth-century) stone fortified walls were uncovered that covered eleven acres.[14] It is believed that this was the winter residence located away from the cooler, higher elevations of Samaria, and that this site with adjacent broad plains was home to some of Ahab's chariotry.

Ahab reported to Jezebel the dramatic events that had occurred at Mt. Carmel. She was furious and lashed out at Elijah, threatening to kill him by the next day. So he fled south, passing Beer-Sheba in southern Judah. He continued

14 David Ussishkin, "Jezreel—Where Jezebel Was Thrown to the Dogs," *Biblical Archaeology Review* 36, no. 4 (2010): 32–42.

going south, with no destination specified. There in the darkest moment of despair, an angel of the LORD appeared to him, providing water and food for the prophet, telling him that a long journey lay before him. "Strengthened by that food, he traveled forty days and forty nights until he reached Horeb, the mountain of God" (1 Kings 19:8). It may be that he had been directed to this mountain, known as Mt. Sinai in other biblical passages, where God had appeared to Moses and the Israelites centuries earlier, but we are not explicitly told so in the text. The reference to the forty days and nights evokes memories of Moses spending forty days and nights on the same mountain (Exod. 24:18; 34:28; see Fig. 1.18).

Fig. 2.37 – Statue of Elijah slaying the prophets of Baal on Mt. Carmel. A 19th-century Carmelite monastery was erected over the area thought to be where Elijah faced off with the false prophets.
Photo by James K. Hoffmeier

Despite experiencing dynamic phenomena, powerful wind, fire, and earthquake—similar to the revelation of God at Mt. Sinai (Exod. 19:16–19)—Elijah encountered God in a "gentle whisper" (1 Kings 19:12). Elijah's complaint to God was understandable: "I have been very zealous for the LORD God Almighty. The Israelites have rejected your covenant, broken down your altars, and put your prophets to death with the sword. I am the only one left, and now they are trying to kill me too" (v. 14). Nevertheless, God ordered him back to Israel with three assignments: first to anoint Hazael king over Aram or Syria, second to anoint Jehu king of Israel (thus signaling the end of the Omride Dynasty), and third to anoint Elisha to succeed him as prophet (vv. 15–17).

For a Hebrew prophet to anoint a foreign king was unprecedented. Elisha became the great prophet's understudy and assistant (1 Kings 19:21), but Elijah's work was not over. Jezebel and Ahab plotted to seize the inherited property that included a vineyard of Naboth at Jezreel so that the king could plant a garden by his palace. When he refused to sell the land, at Jezebel's urging, Ahab had Naboth killed and then confiscated the property (1 Kings 21:1–16). Elijah once again had to condemn the royals, announcing their bloody demise (1 Kings 21:17–24). A large winepress was uncovered at Tell Jezreel recently, which the excavators posited could have been connected to Naboth's vineyard that Ahab coveted and for which he had the owned murdered.[15]

A short while later Ahab, while inspecting his newly acquired land, found himself face-to-face with Elijah, who offered a stinging reproof and announced his doom and that of his entire family: "I am ready to bring disaster on you. I will destroy you and cut off every last male belonging to Ahab in Israel," and concerning Jezebel, the instigator of the brutal death of innocent Naboth, "Dogs will devour Jezebel by the wall of Jezreel" (1 Kings 21:21, 23). Surprisingly Ahab responded, not calling the prophet his "enemy" as he had at the beginning of the encounter (21:20), but by tearing his clothes and donning sackcloth. These are gestures of mourning and contrition.[16]

This behavior was viewed as a genuine humbling of himself before the Lord, leading God to mitigate his sentence. God asked Elijah, "Have you noticed how Ahab has humbled himself before me? Because he has humbled himself, I will not bring this disaster in his day, but I will bring it on his house in the days of his son" (21:29). The change of heart on God's part should not

Fig. 2.38 – The site of Jezreel from the air, where Ahab built his winter palace
Photo by WS/Bible places.com

15 Norma Franklin, et al., "Have We Found Naboth's Vineyard at Jezreel?" *Biblical Archaeology Review* 43, no. 6 (2017): 49–54.

16 D. J. Wiseman, *1–2 Kings*, Tyndale Old Testament Commentaries (Leister/Downers Grove, IL: Inter-Varsity Press, 1993), 184.

be viewed to indicate that God could be manipulated by human acts or prays. As Samuel had stated earlier: "He who is the Glory of Israel does not lie or change his mind; for he is not a man, that he should change his mind" (1 Sam. 15:29). Unlike humans who make decisions arbitrarily and out of sinful and self-centered motives, God alters a judgment based on his mercy and compassion. In many cases, a prophet will utter a warning of pending judgment on God's behalf to produce repentance, a reversal of behavior. In Ahab's case, his repentance was viewed by God as genuine and so the judgment against his dynasty was not actualized in his lifetime, but in stages in the coming years.

Elijah is also remembered for the miracles he performed. As long as he stayed with the widow of Zarephath, her oil and flour did not run out during the challenging days of the drought (1 Kings 17:8–16), and when her son became ill and died, the prophet prayed for the life to return to the lad and God answered his prayer, leading the Phoenician woman to declare, "Now I know that you are a man of God and that the word of the LORD from your mouth is the truth" (1 Kings 17:24).

How Elijah's life ended is unique among the prophets, somewhat mysterious like that of Moses (Num. 34:4–5). It is described as being taken "up to heaven in a whirlwind" (2 Kings 2:1). Knowing the day of his passing, Elijah traveled with Elisha to Jericho and then to the Jordan River nearby where his destiny awaited. There the great prophet was swept into eternity: "As they were walking along and talking together, suddenly a chariot of fire and horses of fire appeared and separated the two of them, and Elijah went up to heaven in a whirlwind. Elisha saw this and cried out, 'My father! My father! The chariots and horsemen of Israel!' And Elisha saw him no more. Then he took hold of his garment and tore it in two" (2 Kings 2:11–12). Perhaps due to this sensational departure rather than a normal death and burial, the prophetic perspective was that Elijah would one day return. Malachi the post-exilic prophet announced that the prophet would appear before the day of the LORD: "See, I will send you the prophet Elijah before that great and dreadful day of the LORD comes" (Mal. 4:5). The New Testament Gospels pick up on the Elijah theme and Jesus directly associates John the Baptist with him (see chap. 8). Elijah was recognized by his attire; he wore "a garment of hair and had a leather belt around his waist" (2 Kings 1:8), and John the Baptist was similarly dressed (Matt. 3:4; Mark 1:6).

Because of the way that Elijah and Elisha's careers overlap and how the latter witnessed the unique departure of his mentor, we shall return below to investigate further these episodes below.

Micaiah

A second prophet who was active during the two-decade reign of Ahab was Micaiah son of Imlah. Though not mentioned in the OT, it would appear that as contemporaries, Micaiah and Elijah were allied in their criticism of Ahab and the royal family's behavior. He only appears in the pages of the OT in one incident, but it is clear that he and King Ahab had a long confrontational history. Indeed, Ahab complained to his Judean counterpart, Jehoshaphat, "There is still one man through whom we can inquire of the Lord, but I hate him because he never prophesies anything good about me, but always bad. He is Micaiah son of Imlah" (1 Kings 22:8). Beyond his name, we only know that he faithfully and fearlessly communicated God's messages to the king, even though they were viewed by Ahab as hostile to him.

Second Kings 22 begins by noting that there had been a three-year truce between Israel and the Aramean kings based in Damascus. This peaceful interlude may be attributed to the fact that these traditional enemies had to cooperate against a more powerful foe: namely, the Assyrians. It seems that the events of Micaiah's prophecy that anticipated the death of Ahab occurred just after the Assyrian westward drive was temporarily thwarted by the coalition of Levantine kings at Qarqar on the Orontes River in Syria (Aram) in 853 B.C. that was mentioned previously (see Fig. 2.33 & Map 1.1).

The story about Micaiah the prophet is important on a number of levels. First we again see the clash between the genuine prophet and the false prophets that Moses had warned about (Deut. 18:17–22). Such confrontations are recorded between Jeremiah and a band of bogus prophets in the sixth century B.C. (Jer. 28). Second, we get a glimpse into the heavenly "divine council" or *sôd*, an enigmatic feature of prophetism that remains poorly understood.

Fig. 2.39 – Possible site of Ramoth Gilead in northern Trans-Jordan
Photo by Todd Bolen/Bibleplaces.com

Micaiah's story is set against the background of a war proposed by Ahab to liberate Israelite Ramoth Gilead, a city in the northern Trans-Jordan taken by the Arameans some years previously. Jehoshaphat king of Judah, described in the Bible as a righteous king, had imprudently made a marriage alliance with Ahab (1 Chron. 18:1). As an ally, Jehoshaphat was obliged to help Ahab in his military activities, but would not join in battle without a clear prophetic word indicating God's approval of the plan. Ahab produced four hundred prophets who encouraged them to go. Jehoshaphat was suspicious of the source of this assurance, and so asked his ally, "Is there no longer a prophet of the LORD here whom we can inquire of?" (1 Kings 22:7). Ahab's agitated response is humorous, indicating he and Micaiah had some history between them and that there was another "troubler" of the king who had, like Elijah, confronted periodically this incorrigible king. Ahab states, "There is one man through whom we can inquire of the LORD, but I hate him because he never prophesies anything good about me, but always bad. He is Micaiah son of Imlah" (v. 8). He was summoned to appear before the two kings who were holding court in the entrance to city gate of Samaria where the prophetic conclave was occurring (v. 10).

Fig. 2.40 – Bull gouging a warrior, representing the pharaoh defeating his enemies. Bull Palette, the Louvre Museum, Paris
Photo by A. D. Riddle/Bibleplaces.com

As he arrived, Micaiah is greeted by hundreds of prophets prophesying ecstatically, chanting "attack Ramoth Gilead and be victorious" (v. 12), while one of their number, Zedekiah son of Kenaanah, had iron (bull) horns in hand an declares, "With these you will gore the Arameans until they are destroyed" (v. 11). This dramatic brandishing of the horns appears to replicate the portrayals of ancient kings as a wild bull gouging their enemies. Prophets using props in dramatic acts is a powerful tool to communicate messages in the prophetic books (examples will be introduced when the books of Hosea, Isaiah, Jeremiah, and Ezekiel are treated in later chapters)

Micaiah was urged by the king's official to concur with the majority report. So when Ahab asked if he should go to war, Micaiah mimicked the prophets, with tongue in cheek: "Attack and be victorious" (v. 15). Realizing that the prophet was being disingenuous, the king poses the question, "How many times must I make you swear to tell me nothing but the truth in the name of the LORD?" So he disclosed the vision he saw that Israel would be without a shepherd (the king). Ahab felt vindicated that Micaiah only prophesied negatively about him—but apparently did not believe him!

Micaiah continued: "Therefore hear the word of the LORD: I saw the LORD sitting on his throne with all the host of heaven standing around him on his right and on his left. And the LORD said, 'Who will entice Ahab into attacking Ramoth Gilead and going to his death there?'" (vv. 19–20).

This vision presents one of the clearest pictures of the workings of divine council (*sôḏ*), in which the LORD sits enthroned and presides over the heavenly court made up of angels and spirits. Micaiah points to his presence in the divine council to show his credentials as a prophet and to authenticate his message. In other words, he professes something like: "I was in the divine counsel. I heard the divine deliberations on how God's purpose would be fulfilled." Similarly the sixth-century prophet Jeremiah appealed to his access to the LORD's council to challenge the false prophets of his day. He questioned his audience about the other prophets: "But which of them has stood in the council of the LORD to see or to hear his word? Who has listened and heard his word?" (Jer. 23:18)

God defends Jeremiah's special status:

> I did not send these prophets,
> yet they have run with their message;
> I did not speak to them,
> yet they have prophesied.
> But if they had stood in my council,
> they would have proclaimed my words to my people
> and would have turned them from their evil ways
> and from their evil deeds. (23:21–22)

The heavenly council can also be seen in action in the narrative part of Job's story (Job 1:6–12; 2:1–7). There we find the sons of God, angels, interacting with God about matters on earth.

Despite his audience in the divine council and having a genuine message from the LORD, Micaiah was shamefully treated and abused for his truthful declaration. First, Zedekiah son of Kenaanah stepped up and "slapped Micaiah in the face" (1 Kings 22:24). Although Zedekiah's identity is not mentioned in the narrative, his actions with the bulls' horns suggest that he was possible the leader of the band of prophets whose message Micaiah had challenged.[17] The slap is meant not just to inflict pain, but to humiliate the speaker.[18] Ahab then incarcerated Micaiah, and ordered that he only be given bread and water till he returned (1 Kings 22:27), but not before the prophet warned, "If you ever return safely, the LORD has not spoken through me" (22:28). This warning notwithstanding, Ahab and Jehoshaphat went to war, with the Israelite king disguising himself as a regular charioteer, just in case the prophet was correct. In the fray, a stray arrow, however, found its mark and Ahab subsequently died from his injury after returning to Samaria (22:35–38). As it turns out, Micaiah proved that access to the divine council rather than large numbers of prophets agreeing on a message was how prophetic authority and authenticity was achieved.

---

17 *ISBE* 5:1186.
18 Mordechai Cogan, *1 Kings*, The Anchor Bible (New York: Doubleday, 2001), 492.

In this remarkable episode, the test of a genuine prophet is on display. Moses had explained that God would raise up prophets after him to proclaim divine truths, but false prophets too would appear:

> I will raise up for them a prophet like you from among their fellow Israelites, and I will put my words in his mouth. He will tell them everything I command him. I myself will call to account anyone who does not listen to my words that the prophet speaks in my name. But a prophet who presumes to speak in my name anything I have not commanded, or a prophet who speaks in the name of other gods, is to be put to death. (Deut. 18:18–20)

Fig. 2.41 – Hittite leader shot in the back while riding to battle in his chariot
Photo by James K. Hoffmeier

The consequence for prophesying falsely in God's name is dangerous for the people, and there would be severe punishment for that prophet. The test to distinguish between a true and false prophet is laid out by Moses: "If what a prophet proclaims in the name of the LORD does not take place or come true, that is a message the LORD has not spoken. That prophet has spoken presumptuously, so do not be alarmed" (Deut. 18:22). The test was a simple one. The false prophet's words or predictions would fail, whereas the true prophet who hears from God, either from the divine council, or in a dream or vision, would come to pass. The narrative with Ahab and Michaiah well illustrates this. Micaiah warned Ahab when he decided to go against the prophet's advice: "Micaiah declared, 'If you ever return safely, the LORD has not spoken through me.' Then he added, 'Mark my words, all you people!'" (1 Kings 22:28). Micaiah's ominous prophecy proved correct. Ahab did not return safely from the battle field, and conversely, Zedekiah and his band of bogus prophets were exposed as frauds. Of this band of false prophets, the LORD might condemn them with words like those used against the pseudo-seers of Jeremiah's day that were quoted above, and add:

> The prophets are prophesying lies in my name. I have not sent them or appointed them or spoken to them. They are prophesying to you false visions, divinations, idolatries and the delusions of their own minds. Therefore this is what the Lord says about the prophets who are prophesying in my name: I did not send them, yet they are saying, "No sword or famine will touch this land." Those same prophets will perish by sword and famine (Jer. 14:14–15)

Jehu, Son of Hanani

King Jehoshaphat escaped injury during the battle at Ramoth Gilead and returned to Jerusalem only to be confronted by Jehu the seer (*ḥôzeh*). He chided the king for allying and helping wicked king Ahab (2 Chron. 19), exclaiming: "Should you help the wicked and love those who hate the LORD? Because of this, the wrath of the Lord is on you. There is, however, some good in you, for you have rid the land of the Asherah poles and have set your heart on seeking God" (2 Chron. 19:2–3). Because he had been such a faithful king in regard to God's law and carrying out religious reforms, including purging the land of pagan elements, Jehoshaphat was not dethroned. During the reign of Jehoshaphat's father, Asa, Jehu also rebuked that king for not trusting God completely in a military crisis (2 Chron. 16:7–10). Asa was enraged at Jehu and had him arrested. While the narratives of 2 Kings tend to focus on the prophets who addressed the wicked kings of Samaria, we also see (especially in 2 Chronicles) that prophets were active in Judah too, fearlessly opposing kings who strayed from God's law and who ignored the prophets' messages. King Asa was regarded as one of the better kings of Judah:

> Asa did what was right in the eyes of the LORD, as his father David had done. He expelled the male shrine prostitutes from the land and got rid of all the idols his ancestors had made. He even deposed his grandmother Maakah from her position as queen mother, because she had made a repulsive image for the worship of Asherah. Asa cut it down and burned it in the Kidron Valley. Although he did not remove the high places, Asa's heart was fully committed to the LORD all his life. He brought into the temple of the LORD the silver and gold and the articles that he and his father had dedicated. (1 Kings 15:11–15)

From a good king like Asa, we might have expected a more contrite response. His reaction to Jehu the seer's reprimand, however, serves as a reminder that even for the godly, being confronted for one's shortcomings and infidelities is unpleasant. The typical human response is to push back. Regardless of opposition, we find the prophets largely do the right, even if unpleasant, thing in speaking God's word to the people in general and Israel's leaders in particular.

Elisha and Elijah's Final Years

Elijah's successor was Elisha the son of Shaphat, whose home was Abel Meholah (1 Kings 19:16), a site located in northern Israel, 10 miles (16 km) south of Beth Shean in the Jordan Valley. It is mentioned as the place where the Midianites fled after being routed by Gideon's three hundred fighters (Judg. 7:22). Rehob is situated four miles south of Beth Shean and six miles north of Abel Meholah. This site was extensively excavated between 1997 and 2012 under the able direction of Amihai Mazar.[19] Some tantalizing discoveries were made there that are seemingly related to Elisha the prophet. The divine directive given to Elijah at Mt. Horeb to anoint Jehu son of Nimshi to be king of Israel (1 Kings 19:16) was left to Elisha to carry out, although he actually

---

19 Amihai Mazar, *It Is the Land of Speech: Discoveries from Tel Reḥov the Early Days of the Israelite Monarchy* (Jerusalem: The Hebrew University, 2016).

Fig. 2.42 – Tell Rehob
Photo by Alexander Schick/bibelausstellung.de

assigned that duty to one of his assistants to act on the prophet's behalf (2 Kings 9:1–3). At that time, Joram the son Ahab was king. He had succeeded Ahaziah, his brother who reigned but two years. He died from injuries that occurred after an accidental a fall (2 Kings 1:1–17). Israel was at war with the Arameans in Gilead (northern Trans-Jordan), and Jehu was the commander of the army (2 Kings 9:5). The unnamed assistant completed the LORD's and Elisha's directive—who was acting on the command given earlier on to Elijah (1 Kings 19:16)—anointing Jehu privately.

Naturally, the other officers wanted to know what had been communicated to Jehu, referring to the prophet as "a madman" but not naming him (2 Kings 9:11). The use of this term likely signals the association of a prophet to ecstatic behavior, not one who is mentally ill or a lunatic.[20] What is clear is that even if a derisive term was intended toward Elisha, when the other senior officers heard what had been communicated and that Jehu had been anointed, they cast their cloaks on the ground for him to stand on, blew the trumpet, and announced "Jehu is king" (2 Kings 9:13). Elisha's word was clearly recognized as God's authoritative communication.

Jehu had a long reign from 841–814 B.C., twenty-eight years (2 Kings 10:36). He zealously carried out Elisha's command, given some years earlier (2 Kings 10:17) to wipe out the dynasty or Ahab and the worship of Baal in the land. Such pagan religions dramatically increased during the reign of Ahab under Jezebel's influence (2 Kings 9:6–10, 14–37; 10:1–27). Although Elisha is not connected by name to Jehu again, recent evidence from the excavations at Tell Rehob suggests an ongoing association.

The Hebrew name *nmš*, Nimshi, has been discovered engraved in two vessels at Rehob, while a third one came to light at nearby Tel 'Amal, 3.7 miles (6 km) northwest of Rehob.[21] This appears to be the family name of Jehu, either his father or grandfather. One of these occurrences was on a large jar found in an apiary. This site was a major producer of honey for this region. Regarding the presence of the Nimshi name, the excavators concluded: "The threefold recurrence of the name in the same region during the same time period leads to the assumption that the Nimshi family was one of influence and prominent

20 Wiseman, *1–2 Kings*, 220.
21 Mazar, *It Is the Land of Speech*, 28e.

status at Tel *Reḥov*, which may have also been the family's seat, being the largest and most significant city in the region during this period. Moreover, we suggest that the Nimshi family may have also been the one to build the apiary and profit from it."[22] They also believe that this is the family name of Jehu.

The connection with Elisha is that an unusual building was uncovered from the ninth century. It was larger than a house, but not designed like a temple. It had larger rooms in which small altars were uncovered, along with vessels that would have been used in religious rites, and large cooking installations. Most remarkably, an ostracon with the letters [']*lš*' ([E]lisha) etched on it was discovered, leading Mazar to label this structure "House of Elisha."[23] It seems quite likely that this building complex was used by the biblical prophet for various cultic rituals, including ceremonial meals. This type of building is presently without parallel in ancient Israel, but it might be recalled that the prophet Samuel presided over sacrifices at a high place and communal meals were shared, with thirty individuals in the case described in 1 Samuel 9 (see vv. 11–18, 22–24). It may be that just as Samuel traveled in a regional circuit visiting religious sites like Bethel and Gilgal (1 Sam. 7:15–16), Elisha may have done the same with one of the stops being Rehob. After all, it was the home of the Nimshi family, whose dynasty ruled the northern kingdom for nearly a century from ca. 841–752. Consequently, Jehu might naturally want to support Elisha's ministry out of thanks for being God's vehicle in becoming king.

Elisha was clearly well-to-do, as the story of his call states that he was plowing with twelve yoke of oxen—that is, twelve pairs of oxen (1 Kings 19:19).[24] This means that Elisha was possibly supervising men in his employment. In dramatic fashion Elijah without speaking approached, took his cloak and wrapped it around Elisha, and then he walked away. Elisha evidently understood this gesture as an invitation to follow the prophet, for he "ran after Elijah. 'Let me kiss my father and mother good-bye,' he said" (1 Kings 19:20). Perhaps as an indication of his devotion to the LORD and his willingness to serve Elijah, he slaughtered the oxen and used the wooden plowing equipment to cook the meat and fed the people. Then he "followed Elijah and

Fig. 2.43 – Ostracon with [E]lisha on it
Photo by Alexander Schick/bibelausstellung.de, courtesy Tel Rehov Expedition by Amihai Mazar

22 Mazar, *It Is the Land of Speech*, 28e.
23 Mazar, *It Is the Land of Speech*, 33–34e.
24 Cogan, *1 Kings*, 455.

became his servant" (19:21). Elisha's action demonstrated that he was making a clear break with his past—a radical career change—not just walking away, but by sacrificing family wealth and standing he was putting his hands on a different kind of plow to follow a prophetic call with no looking back. The parallels with Jesus's call of some of his disciples while they were engaged in their jobs is quite striking (cf. Peter, Andrew, James, and John were at work fishing, and Levi/Matthew was at his tax collecting post; Matt. 4:18–22; 9:9).

Elijah's ministry continued for some time after Elisha joined him. Most memorable is his condemnation of king Ahab for killing Naboth, a landowner at Jezreel, in order to seize his vineyard (1 Kings 21), which was reviewed above. Although Elisha is not named in this episode nor during the reign of Ahab's immediate successor, it could well be that he was present.

Ahab was succeeded by his short-lived son Ahaziah (853–852 B.C.), who early on had injured himself in a fall from the upper room of his palace (2 Kings 1). In order to determine if he would recover, he sent messengers "to inquire of" (i.e., seek an oracle from) Baal-Zebub, the god of Ekron. Ekron was one of the principal Philistine cities. Baal-Zebub means "lord of the flies," possibly associated with healing although this epithet for Baal remains unattested in extrabiblical literature.[25]

An angel instructed Elijah to meet Ahaziah's messengers with the questions, "Is it because there is no God in Israel that you are going off to consult Baal-Zebub . . . ?" (1:3). The messenger returned to the king with the message, "You will certainly die!" (1:4). The messenger seemed unaware of Elijah's identity, and so described him as a man with "a garment of hair and . . . a leather belt around his waist" (1:8). This description made it clear to the king that it was Elijah. It may be that this garb was or would become a way to identify prophets, as we find in the New Testament was the case for John the Baptist (Matt. 3:4). Wearing a particular garment that would identify a prophet accordingly would be similar to various orders of Christian monks adopting the dress code of an earlier mentor.

Elijah's influence extended to Judah, where Jehoshaphat's evil son Jehoram reigned, who "had forsaken the LORD" according to the Chronicler (2 Chron. 21:10). In response to his reintroducing Canaanite pagan practices to Judah that his father had removed, Elijah sent a prophetic message in the form a letter. It began as follows: "This is what the LORD, the God of your father David

25 Mordechai Cogan and Hayim Tadmor, *2 Kings*, The Anchor Bible (New York: Doubleday, 1988), 25.

says" (21:12). He goes on to blast him for not following the example of his godly father, but behaving like Ahab, and then announced that his punishment would be that his kingdom and palace would be attacked and members of his family killed, and then he would soon die a painful death by disease (2 Chron. 21:12–15). These prophecies indeed happened. Jerusalem was attacked by Philistines and Arabs, and subsequently he died of a gruesome intestinal disease at age thirty-two after just an eight-year reign (2 Chron. 21:18–20).

Elijah's life ended in a mysterious way, as noted already. Elijah and Elisha traveled together (at God's directive?) to the Jordan River where the senior prophet was destined to be taken up to heaven (2 Kings 2:1–14). It was something of a farewell tour, in which the prophets first passed by Bethel and Jericho where companies of prophets (i.e., sons of the prophets) lived at these locations. Fifty is the figure given for the group at Jericho (2 Kings 2:7). It will be recalled that during the attacks on God's prophets by Jezebel, Ahab's

Fig. 2.44 – Jordan River near Jericho *Photo by Todd Bolen/Bibleplaces.com*

God-fearing steward Obadiah hid the prophets in groups of fifty (1 Kings 18:12–14). Both bands of prophets must have received some sort of revelation that Elijah was soon to depart this world, for they asked Elisha, "Do you know that the LORD is going to take your master from you today?" (2 Kings 2:3, 5).

The two pressed on to Jordan River, with the "company of prophets" following from a distance. Elijah offers his assistant one last request: "When they had crossed [the Jordan], Elijah said to Elisha, 'Tell me, what can I do for you before I am taken from you'?" "Let me inherit a double portion of your spirit," Elisha replied (2 Kings 2:9. The "double portion" touches on inheritance; in essence he is requesting "twice as much as any other heir, not double the amount Elijah had."[26] After crossing the river a fiery chariot and fiery horses swooped down and whisked Elijah away as Elisha exclaimed, "My father! My father! The chariots and horsemen of Israel!" (2:12).

This is expression curious. How is it that the prophet is likened to chariots and horsemen?

Later in Elisha's ministry, the report is made of the king of Syria coming to Israel with his vast army and chariotry (2 Kings 6:8–19). Each of his movements were anticipated by the Israelite armies, thanks to Elisha's prophetic insight. After several failed attempts to launch a surprise attack on Israel, the Syrian king is frustrated that his every move was anticipated. He naturally thought he had a spy in his circle that was signaling plans to Israel (2 Kings 6:11). One of his officers attributed this "early warning system" to the prophet Elisha, prompting the Syrian monarch to order his capture. At that time, Elisha was residing in Dothan in northern Israel (2 Kings 6:13). The Syrian forces moved on Dothan, surrounding it with their horses and chariots. Elisha's servant understandably panicked: "Oh no, my lord! What shall we do?" (2 Kings 6:15). Elisha knows that behind the visible enemy was the invisible or spiritual armies of God, and so prays: "'Open his eyes, LORD, so that he may see.' Then the LORD opened the servant's eyes, and he looked and saw the hills full of horses and chariots of fire all around Elisha" (2 Kings 6:17). The fiery horses and chariots are a part of God's army and the prophets seemingly play a role in their deployment. In a sense, then, as Samuel Meier explains, "The prophet functions as Israel's chariots and horsemen all merged into one person."[27] This understanding of the prophet is further supported in the episode of Elisha's

26 T. B. Hobbs, *2 Kings*, Word Biblical Commentary (Waco, TX: Word, 1985), 21.
27 Samuel A. Meier, *Themes and Transformations in Old Testament Prophecy* (Downers Grove, IL: IVP Academic, 2009), 151.

death. Before he passes, Jehoash king of Israel came to pay his respects to the ailing prophet, and in an emotional burst, cries: "My father! My father! . . . The chariots and horsemen of Israel!" (2 Kings 13:14). The loss of this powerful prophet who had access to the invisible world left Israel vulnerable to its enemies. Again in Meier's words, "With Elisha dead, Israel's true chariots and horses would no longer be protecting the land."[28] Elisha's involvement in a military campaign against Moab will be discussed below, which will illustrate how the prophet was the real army for Israel.

In stories about the deaths of Elijah and Elisha a powerful prophet was passing from this life. It is as if in the spiritual realm, human eyes cannot see the supernatural forces marshalled to battle evil that the prophet has a role in directing. Certainly some of the episodes in the Elisha narratives will bear this out.

Fig. 2.45 – Tell Dothan with surrounding hills *Photo by A. D. Riddle*

28 Meier, *Themes and Transformations*, 151.

Elisha Alone

After the supernatural appearance of horses and a chariot of fire which snatched Elijah away, all that remained was his cloak that had been used to strike the Jordan's water's (like Moses's rod in the exodus story) so that the two prophets could cross over to the eastern bank. Elisha then struck the waters, and they parted allowing him to return to the west side (2 Kings 2:13). All along, the sons of the prophets viewed these spectacles. Having witnessed them, they proclaimed that "the spirit of Elijah is resting on Elisha." He was now their master.

Elisha's prophetic ministry often mirrors that of his mentor. Like Elijah, he was known for performing miracles, especially caring for his followers. At Jericho, where he was initially staying after Elijah's passing, the spring—the life source of the city—was yielding toxic water (2 Kings 2:19–22). In response, Elisha took a bowl of salt, which was thrown into the water, and declared:

Fig. 2.46 – Elisha's Spring/Ain Sultan located at the edge of the ancient site of Jericho
Photo by Todd Bolen/Bibleplaces.com

"This is what the LORD says: 'I have healed this water'" (v. 19). The author observes that "the water has remained pure to this day" (v. 22).

From Jericho he retraces the footsteps of Elijah, passing by Bethel, then on to Mt. Carmel, the scene of the great triumph over the prophets of Baal, and then went to Samaria the capital (2 Kings 2:24). While passing by Bethel, he is mocked by a group of youths, who jeered, "Get out of here, baldy!" He cursed them in the name of the LORD, and two bears "mauled the forty-two of the boys" (2:24). The translations "little children" (KJV) and "small boys" (ESV) for *nᵉʿārîm* is misleading. A youth or member of a guild are acceptable meanings of this word, and in military contexts a *naʿar* is a soldier,[29] thus pointing to young men who are likely at least twenty years old.[30] Forty-two youths is suggestive of a mob, not a group of children jesting with Elisha.[31]

Some have thought that in mocking Elisha's baldness was belittling him as a prophet, which assumes that the head was shaved or partially shaved as a sign of service to God like Franciscan monks. But there is no evidence for such a practice in the Bible. Rather those who made vows to the LORD were *not* to cut their hair (Num. 16:1–20), and shaving oneself bald as a mourning rite is prohibited (Deut. 14:1). Elisha himself would have been a young man at the time, and hence being bald was unexpected, but apparently in his case he was likely naturally bald.[32] But why the mockery "Get out of here, baldy!" should be taken as so offensive that such harsh punishment resulted is unclear. Elisha's angry curse suggests their words (and actions?) were highly offensive. Bears were not unknown in the area, and those mentioned in the Bible were likely the Syrian brown bear, depictions of which are shown a tomb in Egypt.

Fig. 2.47 – Syria bear in the tomb of Rekhmire, Western Thebes (ca. 1450 B.C.)
Photo by James K. Hoffmeier

The death of Ahab in 853 B.C. resulted in the rebellion of Moab against Israel, its overlord since the days of Omri. The Old Testament reports that Mesha king of Moab, a sheep breeder, paid annual tribute in the form of lambs, rams, and wool (2 Kings 3:4–7), but with Ahab's passing, the tribute stopped. Mehsa

29 *HALOT* 707.
30 According to Numbers 1:2–3, the minimum age of twenty is set for men eligible to be conscripted into Israel's army.
31 Wiseman, *1–2 Kings*, 198.
32 Hobbs, *2 Kings*, 24.

declared his independence on a stela he explained the circumstances from the Moabite perspective.

> I am Mesha, the son of Kemosh[yatti], the king of Moab, the Dibonite. . . .
> Omri was the king of Israel and he oppressed Moab for many days,
> For Kemosh was angry with his land.
> And his son succeeded him and he said—he too—"I will oppress Moab!"
> In my days did he say [so] but I looked down to him and on his house,
> And Israel has gone to ruin, yes, it has gone to ruin forever![33]

In the aftermath of these developments, Ahab's successor Joram or Jehoram decided to reclaim the lost vassal state. Once again, Jehoshaphat king of Judah was called on to form a military coalition. The two kings decided to march south through Judah and around the southern end of the Dead Sea, where they were joined by the king of Edom. After a seven-day march, they were in a desert area and had no water. Joram was alarmed that they found themselves in this desperate situation, while Jehoshaphat as he did with Ahab years before asked, "Is there no prophet of the Lord here, hrough whom we may inquire of the Lord?" (2 Kings 3:11). To which an officer responded that Elisha was among the force, although no mention of his presence had been made at the beginning of the narrative. His inclusion on a military campaign was likely standard practice for Israel's army. It might be recalled that David had priests and prophets with him on his campaigns so he could seek God's will (1 Sam. 22:3–5, 20–23; 1 Sam. 30:10; 2 Sa, 5:17–21).[34] Although this incident would have been early in his career, the Judean king acknowledged, "The word of the Lord is with him" (3:12).

Fig. 2.48 – Stela of Mesha king of Moab that names Omri king of Israel as an oppressor
Photo by James K. Hoffmeier

It is not surprising to find a prophet accompanying a military campaign. As observed in the episode about

33 *COS* 2:137.

34 In 2 Samuel 5: 19 and 23, David "inquired" can be done either with a prophet or the priest who has the oracular ephod.

Ahab and Jehoshaphat launching their campaign to liberate Ramoth Gilead, prophets were consulted to determine God's will in the battle. Indeed, consulting an oracle or a prophet before going to war was the norm among ancient Near Eastern nations.

Elisha ridicules Joram, wondering why he would want to consult him, the prophet of the Lord, rather than inquiring of Ahab and Jezebel's prophets. Because of godly Jehoshaphat's presence, Elisha agrees to cooperate (2 Kings 3:14). He asks for a musician. As he played "the hand of the Lord came on Elisha" and he announced that water would fill the valley in which they were situated, and he indicated that victory would be theirs (2 Kings 3:15–17). The next day, water flowed into the valley, perhaps from a flash flood caused by a localized thunderstorm that periodically occur in that region.

This verse offers a rare glimpse of the mechanics of prophet seeking to obtain an oracle. It would be wrong, however, to believe that the use of a minstrel in this manner was the norm. The term used for the musician is a general one, although it might refer to a harpist (so NIV). In the passage cited above about the band of musician prophets that met king Saul, the harp and lyre were included in the list of instruments used (1 Sam. 10:4–5).

Fig. 2.49 – Harpist playing before a king, from Megiddo 13th century B.C.
Photo by A. D. Riddle

The allied force took city after city in southern Moab. When the king of Moab saw that his defeat was looming, he made a desperate move. Taking seven hundred of his swordsmen, he made a direct assault on the Edomite contingent of the invading army, "but they failed. Then he took his firstborn son, who was to succeed him as king, and offered him as a sacrifice on the city wall" of Kir Hareseth (2 Kings 3:26–27). The result of this incomprehensible and ghastly act was that the coalition force was appalled and suspended their assault.

The practice of sacrificing a child on the wall of a city that is under attack and in great duress is documented on thirteenth-century-B.C. temple scenes in Egypt. In one instance, the Canaanite city of Ashkelon in southern Canaan is under siege by Pharaoh Merneptah (1213–1203 B.C.). As other defenders are shown with hands upraised in a gesture of prayer, a bearded man (a priest?) holds up an incense brazier, while to his right another man is shown dangling an infant over the wall as a knife is at the little one's throat.

In the case of king Mesha, there is some ambiguity as to whose son was sacrificed. The statement is as follows: "he took his firstborn son, who was to succeed him as king, and offered him as a sacrifice on the city wall" (3:27). Traditionally it is thought that it was Mesha's own successor who was sacrificed in hopes of bringing divine intervention.[35] There is an alternative interpretation, namely that Mesha undertook his desperate measure an attack on the king of Edom's forces (3:26), who was an ally of Judah and Israel. "He took his firstborn son" could apply to the king of Edom who was just mentioned.[36] This interpretation means that the Moabites captured Edom's prince and killed him in a visible and dramatic way. This turn of events so repulsed the coalition that they withdrew despite being in a superior position militarily at that moment.

Elisha, like his master Elijah before him, is credited with helping a poor widow of one of the "sons of the prophet" by the miracle of giving her a bountiful supply of oil from her jar so that she could support the family (2 Kings 4:1–7, cf. 1 Kings 17:7–16). He also raised from the dead the son of a family in Shunem who had periodically offered him a guest room (2 Kings 4:8–37). The boy was especially precious to his parents, as he was born in their old age after Elisha had announced "about this time next year about the same time . . . you will hold a son in your arms" (4:15). Some years later the boy was taken ill and died. The Shunammite woman rode her donkey to Mount Carmel where Elisha was staying, possibly the very place scene of Elijah's great triumph over the prophets of Baal. The woman

35 Cogan and Tadmor, *2 Kings*, 47.
36 Rainey, *Sacred Bridge*, 205.

Fig. 2.50 – Scene showing city of Ashkelon under attack by Pharaoh Merneptah (ca. 1208 B.C.), while residents pray for divine intervention; and on far right a child is being sacrificed on city wall
Photo by James K. Hoffmeier

reached the man of God, but he had had no premonition of her coming nor the calamity that had befallen her son, admitting, "The LORD has hidden it from me and has not told me why" (4:27). His admission suggests that the prophet was not all-knowingly clairvoyant, but only as God revealed his word to him was he able to diagnose situations and announce what is about to happen.

After Gehazi, Elisha's assistant, was unable to rally the lad despite following the prophet's instructions, Elisha himself came and after offering prayers, the boy's life returned to him (4:32–37).

One of the more memorable episodes from the Elisha narratives involves the healing of the Aramean general Naaman, who was a leper (2 Kings 5). Elisha's reputation as a miracle worker had reached Damascus in Syria. There, a young girl who had been taken prisoner from Israel became the servant of Naaman's wife. The girl told her mistress of Elisha and how he could heal the general. With the blessings of the king of Aram, and a letter of introduction, Naaman went to the king of Israel. When Elisha heard of the king of Israel's exasperation over the Aramean coming to see him, he sent a message to see him. Rather than personally meet the general and treat him like a celebrity when he arrived at his home, Elisha sent a servant with the simple instructions for Naaman. "Go, wash yourself seven times in the Jordan, and your flesh will be restored" (5:10).

No doubt insulted by the impersonal treatment, and angered by the simple remedy, Naaman complained: "I thought that he would surely come out to me and stand and call on the name of the Lord his God, wave his hand over the spot and cure me of my leprosy" (5:11). After some persuasion from his attendants, the general drove his chariot to the Jordan and followed Elisha's instructions, and he was cured.

Another case where the prophet's influence reached Israel's neighbor is when Elisha went to Damascus, summoned by King Ben-Hadad, the reigning king who was ill (2 Kings 8:7–15). The bedridden monarch sent a generous gift with one of his officers, Hazael, to meet the prophet who had come to Damascus, to determine if he would "recover from this illness" (8:8). Elisha offered a curious response: "'You will certainly recover.' Nevertheless, the Lord has revealed to me that he will in fact die" (8:10). Then the man of God stared at Hazael with a penetrating look, until the general was embarrassed. To Hazael's amazement, Elisha wept. He explained his emotional outburst: "Because I know the harm you will do to the Israelites," he answered. "You will set a fire to their fortified places, kill their young men with the sword, dash their little children to the ground and rip open their pregnant women" (8:12). Incredulous, Hazael asked, "How could your servant, a mere dog, accomplish such a feat?" (8:13). As a nonroyal individual, Hazael did not understand how he could be a conquering king. Elisha assured him, "The Lord has shown me that you will become king of Aram" (8:13). Hazael returned to his master, reporting only the first half of Elisha's message. Then the following day, he suffocated Ben-Hadad and seized the throne!

On an inscribed statue of the Assyrian ruler, Shalmaneser III (858–824 B.C.) calls Hazael a "son of a nobody," a derogatory term applied to an illegitimate usurper.[37] While Elisha came to Damascus at Ben-Hadad's invitation, he

37 K. Lawson Younger, *A Political History of the Arameans* (Atlanta: Society of Biblical Literature, 2016), 598.

may have taken the opportunity of this mission to fulfill the divine order given to Elijah at Mt. Horeb in Sinai (1 Kings 19:15) to anoint Hazael to be king of Damascus. If indeed Elisha anointed Hazael, the text does not disclose this detail. Elisha did subsequently send a member of his prophetic band to anoint Jehu king in accordance with the same directive given to Elijah (2 Kings 9:1–13).

Elisha's concerns for Hazael's aggression against his homeland were not unfounded. Once king, Hazael did engage in battle against Israel (2 Kings 8:28; 9:14; 10:32; 13:22). When Jehoram of Israel and Ahaziah of Judah once again tried to recapture Ramoth Gilead (as Ahab and Jehoshaphat had previously tried), Hazael's troops were up to the task, and wounded the Israelite monarch. He returned to Jezreel to recover from his injuries but was killed by Jehu the military commander and charioteer who had been commissioned at Ramoth Gilead to rid Israel of the successors of the evil rulers Ahab and Jezebel (2 Kings 9:14–28). Ahaziah, Jehoram's cousin, king of Judah was also killed by Jehu at the same time. Thus in 841 B.C. the kings of Judah and Israel, both grandsons of Ahab and Jezebel, died on the same day in keeping with Elisha's word that the whole house of Ahab be cut off, "every last male" (2 Kings 9:9). These events fulfill the word of God against the house of Ahab.

Fig. 2.51 – View of Gath, Tell es-Safi *Photo by A. D. Riddle*

Hazael later invaded Judah, besieging Gath, the former Philistine metropolis that was now under Judah's control (2 Kings 12:17). Evidence of the protracted siege has been discovered in recent excavations at Tell es-Safi, ancient Gath. A large siege trench has been found that encircled the site, apparently excavated by the Aramean armies to discourage Judaeans from fleeing the siege. Hazael, the presumed author of the Tell Dan Stela (see above regarding the reference to the house of David; Fig. 2.25), also takes credit for slaying the Israelite Jehoram and Ahaziah from the house of David (i.e., Judah). In view of the Bible crediting Jehu with their deaths (2 Kings 9:14–28), it may be that the Aramean king is taking credit for their deaths even though they did not occur directly by his hand, but indirectly by the circumstances he had unleashed in Israel.

A prophetic postscript to Hazael's atrocities was offered by Amos, who announced divine judgment on the violent excesses of this king:

> This is what the LORD says:
> "For three sins of Damascus,
> even for four, I will not relent [my wrath].
> Because she threshed Gilead
> with sledges having iron teeth,
> I will send fire upon the house of Hazael
> that will consume the fortresses of Ben-Hadad." (Amos 1:3–4)

Just prior to his death, Elisha engaged in one last prophetic act of a military nature. Joash king of Israel (798–782 B.C.) came to bid the prophet farewell. It was then that he uttered the words "the chariots of Israel" (2 Kings 13:14) discussed above. Perhaps in a gesture to show that victory was God's doing, not the prophet's, Elisha urges him to directly take on Syria:

> "Take a bow and arrows." So he took a bow and arrows. Then he said to the king of Israel, "Draw the bow," and he drew it. And Elisha laid his hands on the king's hands. And he said, "Open the window eastward," and he opened it. Then Elisha said, "Shoot," and he shot. And he said, "The LORD's arrow of victory, the arrow of victory over Syria! For you shall fight the Syrians in Aphek until you have made an end of them." And he said, "Take the arrows," and he took them. And he said to the king of Israel, "Strike the ground with them." And he struck three times and stopped. Then the man of God was angry with him

> and said, "You should have struck five or six times; then you would have struck down Syria until you had made an end of it, but now you will strike down Syria only three times." (2 Kings 13:15–19 ESV)

We learn following Elisha's final prophetic act that Israel was able to regain Israelite territory that Hazael was conquered in three campaigns: "When Hazael king of Syria died, Ben-hadad his son became king in his place. Then Jehoash the son of Jehoahaz took again from Ben-hadad the son of Hazael the cities that he had taken in war from Jehoahaz his father. Three times Joash defeated him and recovered the cities of Israel" (2 Kings 13:25 ESV).

The ultimate episode regarding Elisha deals with the miraculous power happened posthumously. Second Kings 13:20 gives an extremely short notice of his passing: "So Elisha died, and they buried him." No elaborate narrative like that of his mentor Elijah. No sensational rapture. But the text continues: "Now bands of Moabites used to invade the land in the spring of the year. And as a man was being buried, behold, a marauding band was seen and the man was thrown into the grave of Elisha, and as soon as the man touched the bones of Elisha, he revived and stood on his feet" (2 Kings 13:20–21). Amazingly, this miracle-working prophet's divine powers continued after his death.

Three Woman Prophets

The feminine form of the word prophet (*nāḇi'*) occurs a number of times in the OT. *Nāḇi'â* or "prophetess" was applied first to Miriam (Exod. 15:20; see discussion in chap. 1) and Deborah (Judg. 4:4; see discussion in chap. 2), but also to several other women. Isaiah's anonymous wife is referred to as "the prophetess" (Isa. 8:3) when the prophet had sexual relations with her and she bore a son, Maher-shalal-hashbaz (for a discussion of this child's symbolic names, see chap. 4). Some may think that the title prophetess is an honorific extension to Isaiah's wife, but like the practice in Germany, a wife can take on the title of her husband, for instance, Frau Professor (Mrs. Professor) or Frau Doctor (Mrs. Doctor). This seems not to be the case as the practice is not otherwise attested in the OT. So either Isaiah's wife was recognized as a prophetess like Miriam, Deborah, or Huldah (see next paragraph), or more narrowly, she proclaimed God's word by giving birth to the son whose name contained God's message to his.[38] Beyond this lone reference, nothing more can be said about this prophetess and her divine service.

---

38 John Watts, *Isaiah 1–33* (Waco, TX: Word, 1985), 113.

Huldah is another prophetess who makes a brief appearance at a most crucial moment in biblical history. When young Josiah became king of Judah, the nation had been ravaged by decades of apostacy and idolatry under king Manasseh (697–642 B.C.) and his son Amon (642–640 B.C.), Josiah's father. The land was ripe for reform, and through the preaching of prophets like Zephaniah and Jeremiah, followed by the faithful response of Josiah, transformation began (2 Chron. 34:1–7). In his eighteenth year, when temple renovations were underway, Hilkiah the high priest made a dramatic discovery, namely the "Book of the Law of the LORD given through Moses" (2 Chron. 34:14–21; 2 Kings 22:8–12). How this scroll, thought to be the book of Deuteronomy, was out of circulation or hidden is not explained. After the scroll was read to Josiah, he was struck with grief (2 Kings 22:11), and apparently feared that the covenant curses listed at the end of Deuteronomy (28:15–68) might be unleashed due to the infidelity to God and his covenant demands. Here is what happened next:

> When the king heard the words of the Book of the Law, he tore his robes. He gave these orders to Hilkiah the priest, Ahikam son of Shaphan, Acbor son of Micaiah, Shaphan the secretary and Asaiah the king's attendant: "Go and inquire of the LORD for me and for the people and for all Judah about what is written in this book that has been found. Great is the LORD's anger that burns against us because our fathers have not obeyed the words of this book; they have not acted in accordance with all that is written there concerning us." (2 Kings 22:11–13)

The response to the king's order "inquire of the Lord" was that a delegation led by the high priest himself was sent in search for a prophet. One might think that the king and his inner circle might seek counsel from Jeremiah, but that was not the case. Rather, "Hilkiah the priest, Ahikam, Akbor, Shaphan and Asaiah went to speak to the prophet Huldah, who was the wife of Shallum son of Tikvah, the son of Harhas, keeper of the wardrobe. She lived in Jerusalem, in the New Quarter" (2 Kings 22:14). It seems that due to the king's urgency, Huldah was called upon because she lived near the royal quarters—perhaps just to the north of the palace complex,[39] and that her husband, Shallum, keeper of the wardrobe, was a man of some prominence. It is unclear whether Shallum's duties were connected to the royal wardrobe or that of the temple where he would have cared for

39 Hobbs, *2 Kings*, 327.

the priestly vestments.[40] Either way, Shallum and Huldah had connections and physical proximity to the palace or the temple, and her reputation was such that she was sought at this moment of crisis for the godly king. Jeremiah on the other hand, lived in the village of Anathoth (Jer. 1:1), a priestly city about 4 km (2.5 miles) from Jerusalem, within the territory of Benjamin.[41] Apparently he was not as accessible at the moment of Josiah's crisis, and the closest reliable prophet who could communicate God's word was Huldah.

She responded to the king's query by three times proclaiming, "This is what the LORD says" (2 Kings 22:15, 16, 18). Huldah's message (2 Kings 22:15–20; 2 Chron. 34: 23–28) basically agrees with the unpopular warnings of Jeremiah that judgment and destruction of Jerusalem and the temple was forthcoming (see chap. 7). However, due to the king's penitent heart and remorse over the nation's sins, Huldah indicates that the disaster would not strike until after his life (2 Kings 22:18–19; 2 Chron. 34:26–27). Her message seems to fail at one point. She indicated that Josiah would go to his death in peace, that is, live out his life (2 Kings 22:20; 2 Chron. 34:28). As it turns out, Josiah died violently from wounds received in battle at Megiddo against the Egyptian army led by Pharaoh Neco (2 Kings 23:29–30; 2 Chron. 45:22–24). Some interpreters see this conflict between Huldah's message and the king's death as an obvious contradiction. However, her words can be understood differently. Here is what she said: "Therefore I will gather you to your fathers, and you will be buried in peace. Your eyes will not see all the disaster I am going to bring on this place'" (2 Kings 22:20). First of all, the expression "I will gather you to your fathers" does not imply a peaceful death. Of Ahab a similar expression is found: "Ahab rested with his fathers" (1 Kings 22:40), but he died in battle like the later ruler, Josiah. Huldah's message, therefore, could be saying that Josiah would die and not see the calamity that would strike;[42] Jerusalem would survive beyond the king's lifetime. Indeed, Josiah died in 609 B.C. and Judah and Jerusalem survived for two dozen more years, falling in 586 B.C.

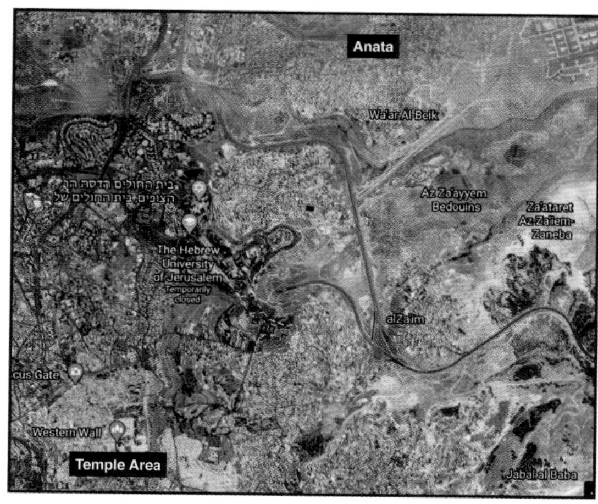

Fig. 2.52 – Google Earth image of present-day Jerusalem and surrounding areas. Note the Temple Mount and the location of Anata/Anathoth.

---

40 *ABD* 3:321.
41 *ABD* 1:227.
42 C. F. Keil and F. Delitzsch, *1–2 Kings, 1–2 Chronicles, Ezra, Nehemiah, Esther*, Commentary on the Old Testament, vol. 3 (Edinburgh: T&T Clark, 1890), 481.

Like the two other prophetesses treated in this section, Noadiah (Neh. 6:14) appears but once, but in a negative way. During Nehemiah's efforts to refortify Jerusalem after the exile (444–443 B.C.), he met considerable opposition from regional governors (Neh. 4–6). Sanballat was the Samaritan leader, Tobiah was from Amon and Geshem was called "the Arab." This cabal solicited help from a band of prophets to oppose Nehemiah's endeavors, and Noadiah was among them. Her name incorporates name of Yahweh the God of Israel, suggesting that she is Judean, her name meaning something like "Yahweh has met by appointment," or "Yahweh has gathered together."[43] Understandably, Nehemiah was frustrated by this opposition, and calls on God to deal with these enemies: "Remember Tobiah and Sanballat, my God, because of what they have done; remember also the prophet Noadiah and how she and the rest of the prophets have been trying to intimidate me" (Neh. 6:14). The fact that Noadiah is the only prophet mentioned by name in this verse indicates that she played a leading role. Here the role of Balaam the prophet might be recalled, when he was hired by Balak king of Moab to prophecy against Moses and the Israelites to thwart their efforts to take their Promised Land.

Zechariah Son of Jehoida

Other nonliterary prophets could be included in this chapter, but the best-known ones have been introduced, along with a few others whose stories give important insights into the nature of prophetic ministry or bear on the prophet-king relationship. Zechariah son of Jehoida should be mentioned because Jesus referred to him by name. Jehoida was the faithful priest who preserved the Davidic line when the evil queen Athaliah (daughter of Ahab and Jezebel!) sought to purge all royal competition so that she could rule. Jehoash or Joash was just a baby who would have been killed, but princess Jehosheba, Jehoida's wife, whisked him away, saving him from a sure death. Seven years later he would be anointed king by Jehoida (2 Kings 11; 2 Chron. 22:10–12; 23:1–21). The priest served as young king Joash's top advisor, which helped keep him faithful to the Law. However, upon the venerable priest's death, other advisors stepped forward who turned the king and the nation away from the LORD: "After the death of Jehoiada, the officials of Judah came and paid homage to the king, and he listened to them. They abandoned the temple of the LORD, the God of their fathers, and worshiped Asherah poles and idols. Because of their guilt, God's anger came upon Judah

---

43 *ABD* 4:1122.

and Jerusalem" (2 Chron. 24:17–18). Following the centuries-old pattern, God raised up prophets to address the infidelity: "Although the LORD sent prophets to the people to bring them back to him, and though they testified against them, they would not listen" (2 Chron. 24:19). One of those prophets was "Zechariah son of Jehoiada." We are informed that "He stood before the people and said, 'This is what God says: "Why do you disobey the LORD's commands? You will not prosper. Because you have forsaken the LORD, he has forsaken you"'" (2 Chron. 24:20). Angered by Zechariah's denunciation, Joash apparently had him falsely charged with a capital crime, resulting in the prophet being stoned to death within the temple court next to the altar (2 Chron. 24:21–22).

This outrageous and vile act by the king is cited by Jesus in the Gospels. Just days before his own death in Jerusalem, Jesus, in a prophetic-like discourse, leveled charges against the religious leaders of his day for their insensitivity to God's word as represented by the law and God's prophets (Matt. 23; Luke 11:37–54). Not only were they insensitive and irresponsive to God's word, but frequently throughout history they had killed those who were righteous along with God's prophets (Matt. 23:29–35; Luke 11:47:51). Jesus charges the present generation with the responsibility of all the righteous martyrs throughout Scripture: "Therefore this generation will be held responsible for the blood of all the prophets that has been shed since the beginning of the world, from the blood of Abel to the blood of Zechariah, who was killed between the altar and the sanctuary. Yes, I tell you, this generation will be held responsible for it all" (Luke 11:50–51).

The addition of the location of Zechariah's murder "between the altar and the sanctuary" assures us that Zechariah son of Jehoida was the victim in question.[44] While other prophets were killed by kings who rejected their confrontations (e.g., Jehoiakim killed Uriah son of Shemaiah [Jer. 26:20–23]), Zechariah is the last prophet killed in the OT. In the Hebrew canonical order, 2 Chronicles was the last book in the sequence in the Hebrew Bible. Genesis, of course, was first. Consequently, Jesus is holding the recalcitrant Jerusalem

---

44 In Matthew 23:35, Zechariah's father is said to be Barachiah. Zecharaiah son of Barachiah is none other than the name of the prophet responsible for the penultimate book of the Book of Twelve or the Minor Prophets (cf. Zech. 1:1, 1:7, which adds the name of his grandfather, Iddo). Luke's citation does not include Zechariah's patronym. Thus Matthew's inclusion of "son of Barachiah" is thus perplexing, and may be attributed to a copyists error at some point in the transmission. For a detailed discussion of this textual problem, see D. A. Carson, *Matthew: Expositor's Bible Commentary* (Grand Rapids: Zondervan, 1984), 485–86 n35.

temple leaders accountable for the death of all the martyrs throughout OT history, from the beginning to the end.

As the son of a priest, Zechariah was also a priest, and his presence in the temple aligns with his status. He is not explicitly called a prophet, however. He might have been a temple or cultic prophet, that is, a temple official or priest whose principal duties were prophetic, namely seeking oracles or other prophetic activities as we saw with Samuel (2 Sam. 10:10:4–13). In Zechariah's case, the text literally states "the spirit of God came on Zechariah" (2 Chron. 24:20). This usage suggests that prompted by a spiritual gift or endowment by the Spirit of God, Zechariah spoke (cf. Luke 24:49; Gal. 3:27).

Concluding Thoughts on Nonliterary Prophets

The prophets treated in this chapter are some of those whose lives and activities are recorded in the "historical books," but they have not left books containing their prophetic messages. The books of Samuel, Kings, and Chronicles deal largely with kingship in Israel, through the time of the divided kingdom. Consequently, the prophets encountered in these books, by and large, interact with the kings. As noted in the first chapter, kings across the Near East appealed to various types of divination, including prophets, in order to ascertain divine purposes and plans. The Israelite kings were no different. In as much as the rulers of Samaria and Jerusalem regularly departed from the covenantal stipulations and its laws (especially with regard to worship and inquiring of foreign deities), the prophets were particularly confrontational. Their long history of communication, their messages warning the leaders to turn back to God's ways, were typically ignored or at best provoked short-lived penance.

As we move into the final fifty years of the northern kingdom, we meet a new type of prophet: those whose messages, or parts thereof, were recorded and preserved. Because they were deemed to be "God's word," these books have become part of the Jewish and Christian Scriptures. While our knowledge of the nonliterary prophets centers on their activities, the prophetic books within the Bible concentrate largely on the messages and less on their actions. To these we now turn.

DISCUSSION QUESTIONS

- What are some of the fundamental differences between the nonliterary prophets and literary prophets?
- Discuss the various roles displayed by Deborah.
- What makes Samuel such a unique prophet figure?
- Discuss the ups and downs of Elijah's prophetic ministry.
- What are some of the unusual aspects of Elisha's prophetic career?
- What is the divine council and its significance?
- Review the women who prophesied in the OT and discuss their contribution to biblical events.

3

"Assyria, the Rod of My Anger"

The Eighth-Century Prophets of Israel

The "prophetic books" of the Hebrew Scriptures cluster around three crisis periods of history. The first crisis was the expanding Assyrian Empire whose forces periodically invaded Israel and then in 722 B.C. destroyed the northern kingdom and its capital Samaria. This event was accompanied by the mass deportation of its population to exile in Mesopotamia. Indeed, Assyria proved to be "the rod of my anger" to punish Israel, as Isaiah 10:5 explains.

Although located south of Aram (Syria) and Israel, the epicenter of Assyrian military action in West Asia throughout most of the eighth century, Judah was not exempt from Assyria's imperialistic designs and felt its blow in 701 B.C. The present chapter will deal with the eighth century, the period of classical prophets Hosea, Amos, Jonah, Micah, and Isaiah. The two latter books will be treated in chapter 4, as their focus is directed at the southern kingdom of Judah. The messages of these earlier prophets were directed toward particular individuals and localized situations (with implications for the nation); the literary prophets, however, focus on Israel and Judah as nations. In addition, these prophets, especially the "major prophets" (i.e., Isaiah, Jeremiah, and Ezekiel) expand their repertoire to include oracles against foreign nations to their warnings to Israel and Judah.

The three earliest prophets in the prophetic corpus have much to say to the northern kingdom. The ninth century was characterized by periodic hostilities between the Arameans of Damascus, with intrusions into the region by the Assyrians from the region of the upper Tigris River in present-day northern Iraq. Throughout most of this period, Nineveh was the capital of the empire and is mentioned in a number of different prophetic books (e.g., Jonah, Zephaniah, Nahum). Thirty-seven times the national name Ashur or Assyria occurs in the book of Isaiah, and nine times in Hosea. These are all indicators that the major power of the day that impacted Israel and Judah was the Nineveh-based Assyrian Empire.

The ninth century B.C. was a period of Assyrian expansion that witnessed the armies of Ashurnasirpal II (884–859 B.C.) extending east to the Phoenicians

Fig. 3.1 – Ashurnasirpal II on stela from Nimrud *Photo by A. D. Riddle/Bibleplaces.com*

coast, exacting tribute from Tyre, Sidon, Byblos, and other cities and kinglets. He was succeeded by Shalmaneser III (858–824 B.C.), who sought to control permanently the northern Levant (present-day Lebanon and Syria), but was challenged by a coalition of regional rulers that confronted the Assyrians at Qarqar on the Orontes River. Ahab of Israel was one of the participants in that battle (see chap. 2 for further discussion). After an initial setback, Shalmaneser subsequently crossed the Euphrates numerous times, claiming years later to have crossed the Euphrates twenty-one times by his twenty-first regnal year.[1] Clearly he extended his hegemony over most of this region as his inscriptions report.[2] King Jehu of Israel (841–814 B.C.) was the first to feel the results of this encroachment of

1 *COS* 2:269.
2 *COS* 2:264–70.

Israel, paying tribute to Shalmaneser III, thereby forestalling an invasion of Israelite territory. In the famous "Black Obelisk" Jehu, or his ambassador, is depicted prostrating himself before Shamaneser III to present Israel's tribute, consisting of "silver, gold, a golden bowl, golden goblet, golden buckets, tin, a staff of the king's hand, (and javelins [?])."[3]

With the passing of king Adad-nirari III (810–783 B.C.) of Assyria, its international prowess dissipates for several decades, resulting in an unprecedented period of prosperity and even expansion for Israel. This unexpected turn of events led the Israelites to think that all was well and that they were enjoying God's blessings. Amos and Hosea in particular take us behind the impressive façade of this era to see the religious, moral, and social decay that was festering and would ultimately lead to the collapse of the edifice. These failures were symptomatic of the spiritual climate related to violating God's law, the Sinaitic covenant stipulations.

Just over fifty years later, Samaria the glorious capital and many Israelite cities lay as smoldering ruins. Second Kings 17 offers the following theological explanation for what had just occurred:

> All this took place because the Israelites had sinned against the LORD their God, who had brought them up out of Egypt from under the power of Pharaoh king of Egypt. They worshiped other gods and followed the practices of the nations the LORD had driven out before them, as well as the practices that the kings of Israel had introduced. The Israelites secretly did things against the LORD their God that were not right. From watchtower to fortified city they built themselves high places in all their towns. They set up sacred stones and Asherah poles on every high hill and under every spreading tree. At every high place they burned incense, as the nations whom the LORD had driven out before them had done. They did wicked things that aroused the LORD's anger. They worshiped idols, though the LORD had said, "You shall not do this." The LORD warned Israel and Judah through all his prophets and seers: "Turn from your evil ways. Observe my commands and decrees, in accordance with the entire Law that I commanded your ancestors to obey and that I delivered to you through my servants the prophets." (2 Kings 17:7–13)

Fig. 3.2 – The Black Obelisk of Shalmaneser III in the British Museum
Photo by James K. Hoffmeier

3 *COS* 2:270.

Fig. 3.3 – Jehu or his ambassador bowing before Shalmaneser III on Black Obelisk
Photo by James K. Hoffmeier

Fig. 3.4 – Excavated remains of the Israelite citadel at Samaria destroyed in 722 B.C.
Photo by A. D. Riddle/Bibleplaces.com

Among God's unnamed servants, prophets, and seers were Amos and Hosea, along with the other eighth-century prophets discussed in this and the following chapters.

THE LION ROARS! THE BOOK OF AMOS

"The LORD roars from Zion
and thunders from Jerusalem" (Amos 1:2)

Amos of Tekoa

Little is known about most of the literary prophets, but in the case of Amos aspects of the personal life are disclosed within the book that bears his name. Although his father's name is not recorded, which would be the normal way of giving one's family name, his home Tekoa is mentioned. Tekoa is located 16 km (10 miles) south of Jerusalem in the highlands of Judah at 825 m (2,700 ft.) above sea level. During the reign of Rehoboam (930–913 B.C.), Tekoa became one of his defense cities (2 Chron. 11:6). It likely remained a military outpost till 586 B.C. to judge from Jeremiah's warning cry to Jerusalem at the approach of the Babylonian armies: "Sound the trumpet in Tekoa!" (Jer. 6:1). Trumpets were used to sound alarms and rally troops in ancient Israel (Num. 10:1–9) and in Egypt.

Amos is introduced as "one of the shepherds" (*nōqdîm*), but the word used is not the common word for "shepherd," which is *rō'eh*. In fact the same word (*nōqdîm*) is used to describe king Mesha of Moab as a "sheep breeder" (2 Kings 3:4 ESV).[4] Later in the book, Amos describes himself as a *bôqēr*, a "shepherd" (NIV) or "herdsman" (ESV) in Amos 7:14, a term that extends to cattle as well as sheep and goats.[5] The combination of these terms suggests that Amos may have been in a

4 Stuart, *Hosea-Jonah*, 29.
5 *HALOT* 116.

managerial position. So he seems to have been a man of higher status. Consequently he has been called "a man of some reputation and substance."[6]

Furthermore, Amos informs Amaziah the priest of Bethel that he "took care of sycamore-fig trees" (7:14). This is understood to refer to seasonal work required to help sycamore figs develop properly and not spoil before their harvest which occurred more than once a year. Tools necessary for such work have survived from ancient Egypt.[7] While still developing, a small notch had to be cut into each fig to enhance the ripening process. Amos appears to have supplemented his income with such work. This type of sycamore should not be confused with the tree with the same name in North America, namely *planata occidentalis*, nor should the fruit or fig of the Levantine tree be confused with the common fig tree, *ficus carica*.

Fig. 3.5 – Ivory carving from Nimrud of lion attacking a Nubian, in British Museum
Photo by Todd Bolen/Bibleplaces.com

Even though Amos was a man of some standing, he was clearly a man from the country, not the city. His familiarity with that world, especially shepherding, is evident regularly in

Fig. 3.6 – Soldiers and trumpeter from funerary temple of Hatshepsut
E. Naville, The Temple of Deir el-Bahri VI *(London: EES, 1908) plate CLV*

6 G. von Rad, *Old Testament Theology*, vol. 2 (New York: Harper & Row, 1965), 131.
7 Philip J. King, *Amos, Hosea, Micah: An Archaeological Commentary* (Philadelphia: Westminster, 1988), 116.

Fig. 3.7 – Sycamore fig tree with figs
Photo by Todd Bolen/Bibleplaces.com

the language he uses in his messages. Some examples here will suffice. In his opening message, Amos describes the LORD roaring like a lion from Zion, with the consequence that "the pastures of the shepherds dry up, and the top of Carmel withers" (Amos 1:2). As a herdsman himself, he was sensitive to the hardships that pastoralists faced when the land withers in drought. Additionally, he likens God communicating his word to a roaring lion. Lions were a menace to sheep. David the young shepherd could claim before facing the Philistine champion Goliath that "when a lion or a bear came and carried off a sheep from the flock, I went after it and struck it and rescued the sheep from its mouth" (1 Sam. 17:34–35). Amos speaks of future survivors from Israel and Damascus in similar terms: "As a shepherd rescues from the lion's mouth only two leg bones or a piece of an ear, so will the Israelites living in Samaria be rescued. with only the head of a bed and a piece of fabric from a couch" (Amos 3:12).

So Amos plainly has rural connections, a simple man from the hill country of Judah. He claimed to have been "neither a prophet nor the son of a prophet" (Amos 7:14), rather just a herdsman, "But the LORD took me from tending the flock, and said to me, 'Go, prophesy to my people Israel'" (7:15). The point seems to be that up until his commission to prophesy to Israel, he had not been a prophet, and certainly not a "son of a prophet." A son of a prophet is not a biological expression, but a way to classify a prophet as the student of a master prophet. In other words, Amos is saying that he lacked the proper résumé of a prophet. As Shalom Paul translates this line, "I was not a prophet nor was I a member of a prophetic guild."[8] Amos considers his authority to be based on his calling and his response to God's word. It compelled him to announce divine messages no matter how unpopular. He may even have been thinking of his calling when he said: "the lion has roared—who will not fear? The Sovereign LORD has spoken—who can but prophesy?" (3:8).[9]

Fig. 3.8 – Sheep in the Negev of Israel
Photo by Todd Bolen/Bibleplaces.com

8 Shalom Paul, *A Commentary on the Book of Amos* (Minneapolis: Fortress, 1991), 238.
9 Andersen and Freedman, *Amos*, 400.

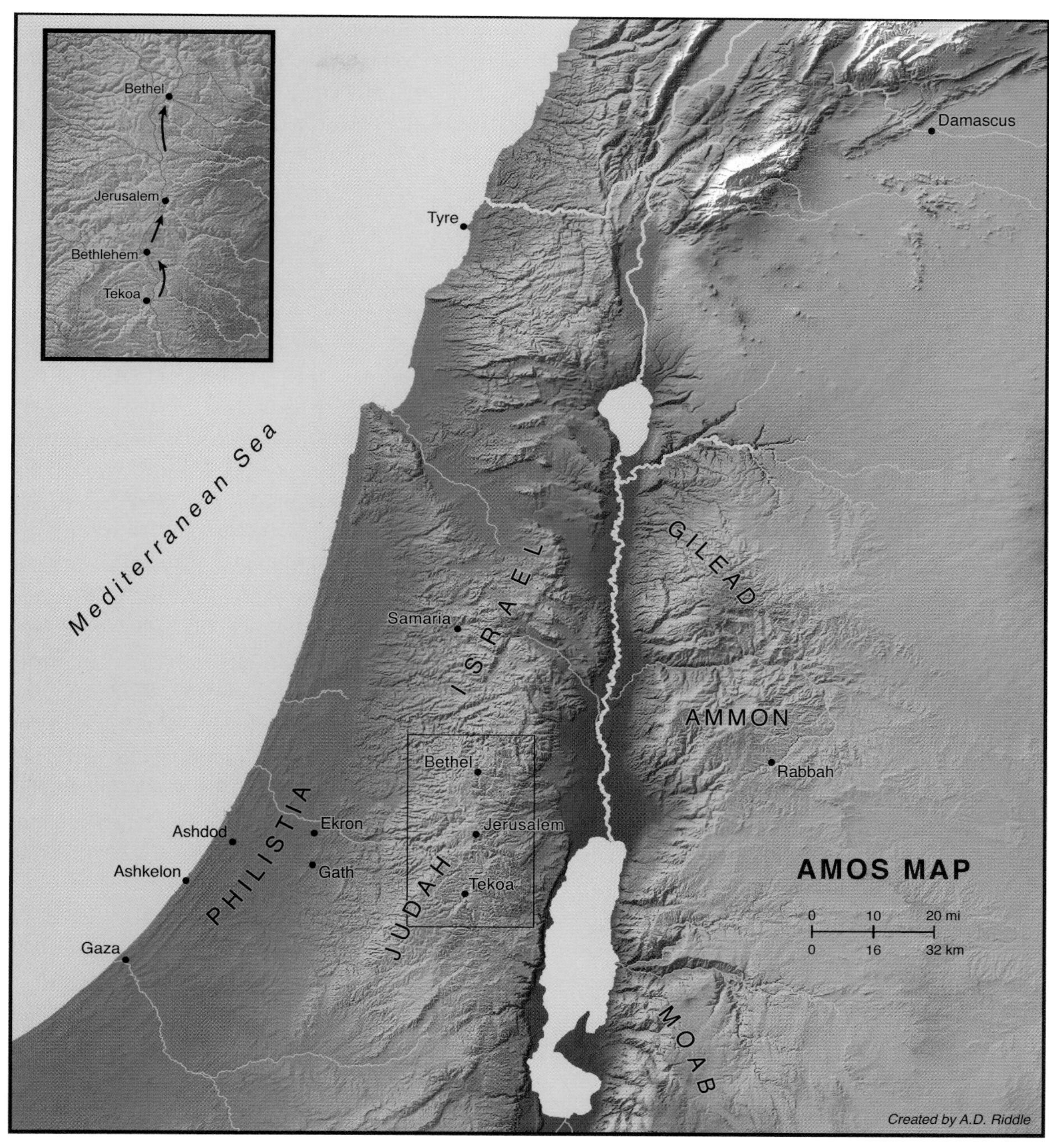

Map 3.1 – Amos's World and His Audience *Map by A. D. Riddle*

The reason to classify him with the northern prophets is because he took his message to Bethel, the religious capital located in southern Israel. We learn in chapter 7 that he was preaching at Bethel, but it is unclear how much of the message of the earlier chapters was presented there, or if he made more than one trip to the north (more on this below).

The Times of Amos

The time frame of Amos is clear. His visions came "two years before the earthquake, when Uzziah was king of Judah and Jeroboam son of Jehoash was king of Israel" (Amos 1:1). These kings both enjoyed long reigns (fifty-two and forty years, respectively) including their coregencies with their predecessors.[10] The period where the two reigned independently was between 765–755 B.C. Reference to the earthquake is significant in two ways. First it is a chronological marker. Among some of Israel's neighbors at different points in history natural phenomena or important events were ways to identify or recall a particular year. In fact, the prophet Zechariah recalls this particular earthquake more than four hundred years later. He announces that when the LORD himself comes to Jerusalem to defend it against its enemies, he will stand on the Mount of Olives causing the mountain to be split, sending people running "as you fled from the earthquake in the days of Uzziah king of Judah" (Zech. 14:5). Obviously, this earthquake in the days of Uzziah and Amos was a terrifying and memorable one that was considered an indication of God's displeasure with Judah and Israel (see below). Archaeological evidence has come to light demonstrating that this earthquake was indeed powerful. Archaeologists have found toppled walls and large cracks have been identified that are believed to have resulted from this eighth-century seismic event.[11] Ongoing excavations at Tell es-Safi (biblical Gath) have recently uncovered toppled walls that are associated with this same earthquake.[12]

On the political and economic front, the Bible portrays the kingdoms of Judah and Israel as prospering in the mid-eighth century. Uzziah, 1 Chronicles 26 reports, enjoyed military success against the Philistines to Judah's southwest, as well as in the lands of Ammon and Edom in Transjordan. Taking the latter regions allowed the king to control the economically vital Red Sea coastal port

---

10 Edwin Thiele, *A Chronology of the Hebrew Kings* (Grand Rapids: Zondervan, 1977), 75.

11 King, *Amos*, 22.

12 The excavations are directed by Professor Aren Meir of Bar Ilan University. For a brief report, see https://mfa.gov.il/MFA/IsraelExperience/Pages/BarIlan_archaeologists_Philistine_temple_Biblical_Gath_28-Jul-2010.aspx.

Fig. 3.9 – The altar at Dan
Photo by James K. Hoffmeier

of Eloth/Elath (26:2), and the maritime trade with Arabia and Africa, from which luxury commodities such as gold, ivory, spices, incense, and exotic woods came. Judah had not enjoyed such access since Solomon's day (1 Kings 9:26–28, 10:14–22). All of this success is attributed to Uzziah's multiplying the military and building up defenses.

In the north Jeroboam II also enjoyed a period of expansion. "He restored the border of Israel from Lebo-Hamath as far as the Sea of the Arabah (Dead Sea)" (2 Kings 14:25 ESV). This territory, including the northern part of the Transjordan, Syria, and Lebanon (Phoenicia), represents territories Israel had controlled in the days of David and Solomon, but lost when the kingdom was divided in 931 B.C.

The Prophecy of Amos

The structure of the book is relatively simple, thematically arranged, and not necessarily along chronological lines. This approach to organizing prophetic books is typical in the biblical tradition. Because of the nonchronological nature of the book and the limited historical references within, it is difficult to determine how the various messages fit together.

It is not until chapter 7, in the midst of a series of visions, that we learn that Amos was actually prophesying at Bethel. Some commentators believe that the span of Amos's ministry was relatively short, and may have begun two years before the earthquake and ended shortly thereafter (an earthquake is vividly described in Amos 9:1–5). The opening verse of the book does refer to him seeing visions (*ḥāzâ*) concerning Israel, not Judah. While the prophet's preaching was directed at the northern kingdom, it may be that the book was produced for a Judean audience. Judah is mentioned in a few instances (Amos 2:4–5, 6:1, 9:11).

Oracles against the Nations, Judah, and Israel (Amos 1:2–2:16)

As the book begins the LORD roars like a lion: "The LORD roars from Zion and thunders from Jerusalem" (Amos 1:2). If this was the opening salvo in a series of messages delivered at Bethel, it drove home two important points. First God was angry and, through his prophet, was thundering out his displeasure against Israel. Second, the LORD was based in Zion and Jerusalem, and not Bethel as believed by the northern Israelites. Clearly this is an indictment against the northern religious sanctuary, despite its significant history. Bethel means "house of God," and its naming hearkens back to the patriarch Jacob, who had a vision of God when he slept at the site formerly known as Luz. In response to the theophany, Jacob declared, "How awesome is this place! This is none other than the house of God; and this is the gate of heaven" (Gen. 28:17). No doubt this is the historical precedent that led king Jeroboam I to select Bethel as one of his religious capitals. As Amos delivered his messages at Bethel, he is confronted by one Amaziah, "the priest of Bethel" (Amos 7:10). The fact that he is "the" priest suggests he occupied a leadership position,[13] if not high priest.[14] Amaziah rebukes Amos, charges him with treason for saying that the king would die and that Israel would go into exile (7:10–12). He excoriates the prophet, telling him to go home and make his living prophesying there, and explains that Bethel was "this king's sanctuary, and the temple of the kingdom" (7:13). The sanctuary at Bethel likely shared the same blueprint as the one discovered at Dan in the 1980s, though it may have been a larger version. Here Jeroboam I had built the temple for the northern part of his kingdom (see chap. 2, Figs. 2.28 & 2.29).

For Amos, then, Bethel represented a center of apostate worship, a rival to Jerusalem where the house of the LORD was located. For this backwoods prophet to travel the 40 km (25 miles) from Tekoa north to Bethel, approximately a two-day hike, was not an overwhelming task, but it meant leaving his comfort zone in Judah and crossing the border to unfriendly Israel. There he communicated bravely a message to a religiously hostile audience. That he obediently did as God commanded is a testimony to his courage and conviction that as a prophet, he had to deliver the divinely given message regardless of the personal consequences, as he explains: "The lion has roared—who will not fear? The Sovereign LORD has spoken—who can but prophesy?" (Amos 3:8).

Opening a prophetic book with foreign-nation oracles is unprecedented in the prophetic corpus. Usually they are tucked away later in a book (e.g. Isa. 13–23; 46–47; Jer. 46–51; Ezek. 25–32). It may be that the frontal placement of these oracles is strategic, and actually reflect Amos's approach to the anticipated hostile audience at Bethel. In other words, it is placed first for rhetorical reasons as the speech of a messenger that employs the formula "thus says the LORD" or "this is what the LORD says."[15] The prophet throughout this opening section uses the same numeric pattern for all eight oracles: "For three sins of X, even for four, I will not turn back [my wrath]" (Amos 1:3, 6, 9, 11, 13; 2:1, 4, 6). The

13 Hans Walter Wolff, *Joel and Amos* (Philadelphia: Fortress, 1977), 310.
14 Paul, *Amos*, 239.
15 Paul, *Amos*, 13–14.

3 + 4 sequence is not to be understood literally, as in most cases only one or two offenses are enumerated, although in the case of Israel six transgressions are cited. Consequently, the numeric pattern formula is a literary device meant to highlight the multiplicity of offenses.[16]

This numerical pattern may originate and be modified from wisdom literature. It occurs a number of times in the book of Proverbs: "There are three things that are never satisfied, four that never say, 'Enough!'" (Prov. 30:15), followed by a list. (See further Proverbs 30:18, 21, 24 and 29; and Proverbs 6:16, which uses the sequence six and seven.) Unlike Amos's appropriation of the numeric formula, in Proverbs the four or seven matters are actually listed.

Amos's rhetorical approach indicates that he was holding back his condemnation of Israel for its sins until God's pending judgment against Israel's neighbors were voiced. Over the centuries there had been many conflicts and wars fought between Israel and adjacent states. Some of the offences of these nations are enumerated, but whether they are contemporary or earlier transgressions is not certain, but by beginning there, the Israelites may have thought they were not the focus of Amos's mission to Bethel.

The geographical sequence of the oracles is not insignificant. Damascus, the first mentioned (1:3–5), was a perennial foe that had in earlier days seized control of Gilead in northern Trans-Jordan during Ahab's day, and more recently under the usurper king Hazael had taken control of northeastern Israel (see chapter 2). So word that God was bringing fire on the house of Hazael was welcome news!

The Philistines are next mentioned (Amos 1:6–8), followed by the Phoenicians, represented by their principal city, Tyre. Both were maritime nations and used their position for exploit other nations through their trade practices, and both nations are similarly charged. God explains Tyre's transgression: "Because she sold whole communities of captives to Edom, disregarding a treaty of brotherhood" (1:9) is the charge against this maritime power. With whom Tyre had violated the treaty is not stated. This reference could hearken back to the days of David and Solomon when brotherhood treaties (i.e., between equals) were established (2 Sam. 5:11–12; 1 Kings 5:1–12). The inhuman sale of people into slavery seems to be in view and the Phoenicians would have acted as the middlemen.[17] By treating Israelites in this manner, the Tyrians perhaps were violating the old sense of brotherhood that the Phoenicians had had toward Israel and Judah. While the Philistine city-states were engaging in a similar exiling of

16 Douglas Stuart, *Hosea–Jonah*, Word Biblical Commentary (Waco: Word, 1987), 310.
17 Anderson and Freedman, *Amos*, 261.

people (Israelites or Judeans?) to Edom, no reference is made to the "covenant of brotherhood" as apparently none had existed (Amos 1:6–8).

The next group of nations has familial ties to Israel. The Edomites (i.e., Edom = Esau, who was Jacob's brother) had shown hostility to the Israelites going back to Moses's day when they did not deny transit through their territory when coming out of Egypt (Num. 20:14–21), and regularly since then. Ammon and Moab (i.e., descendants of Lot the nephew of Abraham: Gen. 19:36–38) are named next. They are indicted for inhumane behavior to their neighbor Israel (Amos 1:13–14; 2:1–3). Ammon is condemned with slaughtering pregnant Israelite women in Gilead (1:13).

Surely Amos's audience was delighted to hear that their troublesome neighbors were in line for divine wrath. Their mood must become euphoric when the Judean Amos had harsh words for his own nation (Amos 2:4–5). Of what was Judah guilty? "They have rejected the law of the LORD and have not kept his decrees, because they have been led astray by false gods" (2:4). Hence Jerusalem would be attacked!

By now Amos must have captured the hearts of his audience, only to shift to their own condemnation. "For the sins of Israel . . . I will not relent [in my wrath]" (Amos 2:6). His indictment of Israel is the focus of following section:

> This is what the LORD says:
> "For three sins of Israel,
> even for four, I will not relent.
> They sell the innocent for silver,
> and the needy for a pair of sandals.
> They trample on the heads of the poor
> as on the dust of the ground
> and deny justice to the oppressed.
> Father and son use the same girl
> and so profane my holy name.
> They lie down beside every altar
> on garments taken in pledge.
> In the house of their god
> they drink wine taken as fines." (Amos 2:6–8)

Doubtless, grave social injustice is in view by the charge of selling the needy for a pair of sandals, even though the statement is somewhat obscure. Debt slavery in Israel was a way of dealing with financial obligations but was mitigated by a statute of limitations on the length of indenture, and a family member could always redeem a relative, thus canceling that persons debt and setting them free (Exod. 21:1–6; Lev. 25:23–55). In this case, Amos addresses the problem of unscrupulous debtholders changing the terms of a contract resulting in the "righteous," that is "innocent," individual being enslaved.[18]

A pair of sandals, the selling price for the poor (Amos 2:6), may hyperbolically point to the incredibly low price offered for a slave, or possibly the sandal refers to a practice associated with land transactions,[19] as reflected in the story of Boaz and Naomi: "Now in earlier times in Israel, for the redemption and transfer of property to become final, one party took off his sandal and gave it to the other. This was the method of legalizing transactions in Israel" (Ruth 4:7).

Israel's sin also includes the men having sexual relations likely with temple prostitutes, and explicitly, a man and his son having sex with the same young woman (*na'arâ*) (4:7), and to make matters worse, laying down "on garments taken in pledge" beside pagan altars. A garment could be taken as collateral on a loan or debt, but according to Exodus 22:6, the cloak should be returned at sunset as it was used to keep oneself warm. Evidently the guilty party referred to here was holding on to the garment, showing no compassion, and then engaging in pagan fertility acts while lying on illegally held garments. The altar would have been associated with either Canaanite deities or syncretized high places where the God of Israel and worship of pagan deities were commingled. God's people, like believers throughout history, were able to rationalize this blending of devotion to Yahweh and foreign gods and goddesses. Glen Taylor frames it this way: "Rationalization that leads to religious compromise is not new. In effect, then, the Israelites found a way to reconcile the worship of Baal, Asherah and other deities with the Yahweh worship."[20] God, however, demands undivided loyalty: "You shall have no other gods before me" (ESV) or "but me" (TLV). As a consequence of their infidelity to the Lord, he laments that, in essence, Israel was becoming like the local population, the Amorites are named (2:9), and God emphatically declares, "Yet I destroyed the Amorites,"[21] recalling the days of the conquest of the Promised Land.

---

18 Allen Guenther, *Hosea, Amos*, Believers Church Bible Commentary (Scottdale, PA: Herald, 1998), 259.
19 Stuart, *Hosea–Jonah*, 316.
20 J. Glen Taylor, "Hosea," in *Zondervan Illustrated Bible Backgrounds Commentary*, ed. J. H. Walton (Grand Rapids: Zondervan, 2009), 10.
21 My translation. Stuart's (*Hosea–Jonah*, 306) translation underscores the emphasis: "I am the one who destroyed . . . "

A final comment on the foreign-nation oracles: though they are brief in Amos, they illustrate something profound. God's word is not limited to the Israelites, his covenant people, but extends to Gentile nations. As Amos learned, "Surely the Sovereign LORD does nothing without revealing his plan to his servants the prophets" (Amos 3:7). By referring to the divine "plan," the prophet is claiming to have been in the "divine council" (see the section on Micaiah in chap. 2), where God's plans for other nations were being revealed.

Warnings for Israel (3:1–6:14)

Israel's obligations to obey God are based on his saving them from Egypt, and there is that constant reminder of their liberation from that enslavement. "I brought you up out of Egypt, and I led you forty years in the wilderness" (Amos 2:10). He goes even further: "Hear this word the LORD has spoken against you, O people of Israel, against the whole family I brought up out of Egypt: 'You only have I known of all the families of the earth; therefore I will punish you for all your iniquities'" (Amos 3:1–2 ESV). Israel here is reminded of the unique relationship she has with the LORD because of the exodus and the subsequent marital covenant. Literally "chosen" means "know" (*yāda'*), a term used in Hebrew especially in the prophets, to signify an intimate, marital relationship between God and Israel.[22] It is because of this special relationship, Israel was not to worship other gods.

Fig. 3.10 – The altar of Beer-sheba
Photo by Alexander Schick/bibelausstellung.de, courtesy Israel Museum, Jerusalem by Amalyah Keshet

Israel's penchant for pagan worship and blending these practices with their worship of God are mentioned in Amos's messages. "Go to Bethel and sin; go to Gilgal and sin yet more" (Amos 4:4). "Seek me and live; do not seek Bethel, do not go to Gilgal, do not journey to Beersheba" (5:4–5). Gilgal, it will be recalled, was an important religious worship center from the days of Joshua, Saul, Samuel and in later times (see discussion in Chapter 2). Beersheba is located in southern Judah—quite a distance to travel for a religious pilgrimage! At Beersheba the remains of a large horned altar (1.6 x 1.6 m = 5' 3" x 5' 3") were discovered reused in a public building. The fact that the altar was dismantled has

22 *NIDOTTE* 2:411–13.

been attributed to the reforms of Hezekiah (715–686 B.C.), which likely closed down this illicit Judean sanctuary.

Another consideration presents itself regarding Bethel, Beersheba, and Gilgal. All three locations had in earlier history as places where God had revealed himself or where historically and theologically significant events had occurred. Abraham "built an altar to the LORD" at Bethel shortly after his arrival in the Promised Land (Gen. 12:8), and there God encountered Jacob, repeating the promise made to Abraham regarding the land (Gen. 28:10–22). Because of these encounters with God, king Jeroboam I of Israel settled on Bethel for the Northern Kingdom's sanctuary (1 Kings 12:26–33; Amos 7:12–13). Beersheba had been where Abraham, Isaac, and Jacob lived at various times. Genesis (21:25–34) credits the name "Beersheba" to the covenant Abraham made with Abimelech of Gerar, which involved swearing an oath (*šāḇaʿ*) and sacrificing seven (*šeḇaʿ*) lambs.[23] There too Abraham "called there on the name of the LORD, the Everlasting God" (Gen. 21:33 ESV). The significance of Gilgal lies in its role in the days of Joshua. Gilgal was the base of operation after crossing the Jordan River, where those not circumcised in the wilderness underwent the covenant ceremonial procedure and where Israel celebrated its first Passover in Canaan (Josh. 5:2–12). (See excursus on Gilgal in chap. 2.)

Fig. 3.11 – Sacred pillars from Canaanite sanctuary at Hazor *Photo by Alexander Schick/bibelausstellung.de*

23 There is a clear wordplay in Hebrews between the words "seven" and "swear" (*HALOT* 1396), hence the name Beersheba could be the well of "swearing an oath" or "seven." Notice that both words are connected to the naming in Genesis 21:30.

All three of these sites, then, had wonderful theological precedents with the founders of Israel and worshiping God. So what was wrong with pilgrimages to these significant holy sites? Amos is not specific on that. It could be that making offerings and worshiping at sites other than Jerusalem once the temple is built was prohibited (Deut. 12:13–13), and this explanation could be Amos's concern.[24] Alternatively, it could be that Israelites were trusting these earlier holy sites over obedience to God's law, hence the reference to "transgress" and "multiply transgression" (Amos 4:4 ESV). *Pešaʿ* is an extremely strong sin-related word used earlier in Amos 1 and 2 that today would be equated with war crimes and crimes against humanity.[25] In other words, they were practicing religious piety while engaged in moral and criminal behavior. A third option is that the people were engaged in syncretistic religious practices out of the reach

Fig. 3.12 – Arad sanctuary from the general period of Hosea and Amos *Photo by Todd Bolen/Bibleplaces.com*

24 Stuart, *Hosea–Jonah*, 337–38.
25 Paul, *Book of Amos*, 138–39.

of accountability to the priests and Levites in Jerusalem. As is often the case, rather than one obvious problem sin in mind, the prophet could be allowing for a range of violations of the Sinai covenant stipulations.

Even though Judah had Solomon's temple within its territory, it was also guilty of intermingling religious beliefs and practices. A small sanctuary was found in excavations at Arad, situated about 30 km (18 miles) east of Beersheba. This small sanctuary located within a fortified outpost, has an altar made of unshaped fieldstones in the outer court. The use of fieldstone does comport with the prescriptions of the law against hewed stone (cf. Exod. 20:25). A broad, narrow chamber separated the court from the small holy of holies at the entrance of which a pair of small incense altars stood inside the doorway. One or more standing stones, or pillars, stood in the most holy place. Such "pillars"

Fig. 3.13 – Holy of Holies of Arad sanctuary
Photo by Alexander Schick/bibelausstellung.de, courtesy Israel Museum, Jerusalem by Amalyah Keshet

are associated of Canaanite religious practice that God had ordered destroyed when Israel entered the land (cf. Deut. 7:5). The Arad and Beersheba sanctuaries represent the forbidden worship centers that Amos railed against (cf. Amos 5:5 for reference to Beersheba). In a sense, Judah is more guilty than Israel because it had the official Jerusalem temple and priesthood, while engaging in the same religious practices as her northern counterpart.

A further symptom of Israel's religious failings was its oppression of the poor, a point introduced previously. Some of the elite women of Israel are called "cows of Bashan on Mount Samaria, you women who oppress the poor and crush the needy and say to your husbands, 'Bring us some drinks!'" (Amos 4:1). Oppression of the poor might include corrupting the judicial system where the poor were denied fair treatment due to bribery and excessive (or unauthorized) taxes (5:10–12). Alternatively, the word "oppress" (*'āšaq*) also includes underpaying or withholding wages from a worker, which is prohibited in the Law (cf. Lev. 25:13). Thus the woman may have been drinking expensive wine purchased with funds that had been swindled from the disadvantaged. The women are also depicted as being depicted as disrespectful to their husbands.[26] This is reflected by using the imperative form "bring" when ordering their drinks.

God opposed the religiosity of the people who went to great lengths and expense for their offerings. He, however, rejected false piety that was devoid of obedience to all aspects of the Law. Amos speaks often of justice (*miškppāṭ*: Amos 5:7; 5:15; 5:24; 6:12) and righteousness (*ṣedāqâ*), used in parallelism with justice, indicating that the two words are semantically related (Amos 5:7; 5:24; 6:12). The basis for justice and righteousness is the Sinai covenant and its stipulations (see chap. 1).

Fig. 3.14 – Ivory inlay from Samaria
Photo by A. D. Riddle/Bibleplaces.com

Even if some were worshiping the LORD in these various sanctuaries—Amos mentions Bethel, Gilgal, and Beersheba (Amos 5:5)—Amos demands that they "Seek the LORD and live" (5:6). "I hate, I despise your religious festivals; your assemblies are a stench to me," God says. "Away with the noise of your songs! I will not listen to the music of your harps. But let justice roll on like a river, righteousness like a never-failing stream!" (5:21, 23–24). For the prophet, "justice" included both social, religious, and moral faithfulness to the Law. Neither the Law nor

26 Shepherd, *Book of the Twelve*, 169.

the prophets bifurcate social and spiritual matters. This interconnection is well illustrated in Amos 2:6–7, discussed above, where God at the same time rails against oppressing the poor, pagan worship, and the related sexual actions. It is misguided to think as some do, that the primary focus of the Hebrew prophets was social justice. Hassell Bullock rightly challenges this popular misperception, maintaining, "The prophets were not social reformers. They were theological reformers, for their basic motivation was generated with their commitment to the fundamental laws of God."[27] Failures in social and religious matters are both symptoms of sinful violations of the covenant stipulations.

The great economic boom in Jeroboam II's reign in Israel and Uzziah's Judah, in combination with the widespread religious observances, made the people feel that God must be pleased with them, and they felt very secure. In

Fig. 3.15 – Assyrian King Ashurbanipal and his queen lounging while drinking wine from bowls
Photo by Todd Bolen/Bibleplaces.com

27 Bullock, *Old Testament Prophetic Books*, 29.

response, Amos warned, "Woe to you who are complacent in Zion, and to you who feel secure on Mount Samaria. . . . You lie on beds inlaid with ivory and lounge on your couches" (6:1, 4). When Samaria was purchased by King Omri (885–874 B.C.) for his capital, it was called the "hill" or "mountain" (*hāhār*) of Samaria (1 Kings 16:24); it stands 430 m (1,377 feet) above sea level. Nahman Avigad described the advantages of this location: "its topographic and strategic advantages were probably why the site was chosen for the capital of the kingdom of Israel."[28] Omri then fortified it, and Ahab (874–753 B.C.) added additional

Fig. 3.16 – Scene from tomb of Rekhmire, Thebe, showing ivory tusks being brought to Egypt as tribute from Nubia in the 15th century B.C.
Photo by James K. Hoffmeier

28 Avigad, *NEAEHL* 4:1300.

defenses in the form of a casemate wall.[29] The manmade walls, when coupled with the landscape, made it a strategic and defendable location. No doubt these considerations explain the sense of well-being and security the people of Samaria felt (see Figs. 2.32 & 3.4).

The opulence of the lifestyle of the upper classes in Samaria is further described by the prophet: "You dine on choice lambs and fattened calves," and "You drink wine by the bowlful and use the finest lotions" (Amos 6:4, 6). Amid the excavations at Samaria, and other royal cities like Nimrud in Assyria, scores of exquisitely carved ivory inlays were discovered. Such ivories were set into wooden furniture. Such costly furnishings demonstrate the economic prosperity of the times. The portrayal of the elites of Samaria lounging on ivory couches and drinking wine from bowls is precisely the way the Assyrian emperor Ashurbanipal presented himself on a relief from his palace.

Fig. 3.17 – Stone plumb bob in Fitzwilliam Museum, Cambridge
Photo by James K. Hoffmeier

Since ivory was shipped from Africa via the Red Sea, it was highly valued. Solomon sent ships to Africa for exotic products, including ivory (1 Kings 10:22), which he used to deck his throne (1 Kings 10:18). Ahab too built a palace "adorned with ivory" (1 Kings 22:39). This could refer to ivory inlaid furniture, or perhaps wood paneled walls with ivory insets.[30]

The prophet is not denouncing wealth and prosperity per se, only when wealth is gained by oppressing and defrauding others (Amos 2:8; 6:4). He also attacked their self-assurance, and perhaps even relying on God's past acts of deliverance and their special relationship with Yahweh as a guarantee of future success, rather than ongoing fidelity to the Sinaitic covenant. On this point, God reminds Israel of that special status in Amos 3:1–2 (ESV): "Hear this word that the Lord has spoken against you, O people of Israel, against the whole family that I brought up out of the land of Egypt: 'You only have I known of all the families of the earth; therefore I will punish you for all your iniquities.'"

---

29 Rupert Chapman, "Samaria: Capital of Israel," *Biblical Archaeology Review* 43, no. 5 (2017): 24–30.

30 Cogan, *1 Kings*, 495.

Fig. 3.18 – Weighing scales used in final judgment. Plumb line in hand of the god Anubis. Papyrus Hunefer, British Museum
Photo by James K. Hoffmeier

Fig. 3.19 – Gezer agricultural calendar in Istanbul Archaeological Museum
Photo by Mark Fairchild

The use of the word "know(n)" (*yāḏa'*) refers to intimately and sexually having a relationship with another (see further treatment of "know" in Hosea), and thus implies a marital relationship between God and Israel that resulted at Mt. Sinai after the exodus from Egypt (see further treatments of Ezekiel 16 in chap. 6). Israel as God's wife is expected to be faithful.

Book of Visions (Amos 7:1–9:10)

A series of five visions drive home the fact that God's judgment would be sudden and decisive.[31] In the first two visions, God shows Amos swarms of devouring locust followed by destructive fire. In response to these the prophet intercedes, and God relents (7:1–6). People today are well aware of the destructive power of fires to demolish forests and urban areas. Locust swarms can wipe out the fields and orchards alike, and they remain a menace in parts of the Middle East and Africa. (For further discussion on locust hordes, see chapter 7 and the discussion of Joel.) It may be recalled that the eighth plague of the exodus was a locust swarm that wrecked the land of Egypt. Pharaoh's advisors ask their master, "Do you not yet understand that Egypt is ruined?" (Exod. 10:7).

The third vision portrays the Lord himself standing beside a wall (in Bethel?) and holding a plumb line, an instrument used by masons and architects to ensure that a wall is being built straight (Amos 7:7–17). Actual plumb bobs have been discovered in Egypt, and plumb lines were frequently attached to scales to aid in making accurate readings of items being weighed.

It is not clear why at this point the sequence of visions is interrupted by confrontation between Amaziah

31 The observations here are largely drawn from the author's article. See James K. Hoffmeier, "Once Again the 'Plumb Line' Vision of Amos: An Interpretive Clue from Egypt?" in *Boundaries of the Ancient Near Eastern World: A Tribute to Cyrus H. Gordon*, eds. Meir Lubetski, et al. (Sheffield: Sheffield Academic Press, 1998), 304–19.

the priest of Bethel and Amos (see above). Were the visions being publicly announced by Amos to his audience? If so, this may explain why Amaziah rebuffs the prophet, and the reason Amos stops interceding for Israel. Then the next vision announces her "end." This comes in the form of a "basket of summer fruit" (*qāyiṣ* = Amos 8:1 ESV). Fruits in Israel were harvested in summer, marking the end of the agricultural cycle.[32] The word *qāyiṣ* plays on the word *qēṣ*, meaning "the end."[33] Hence he announces, "The end has come upon my people Israel" (8:2 ESV). When the fruit, figs, grapes, and olives were picked, the long, dry summer sets in for several months. The so-called Gezer Calendar, a limestone tablet discovered at the site of Gezer with an inscription on it that dates to the tenth century B.C., records the seasons of the agricultural cycle, concluding with the gathering of summer fruit (*qṣ*), which marks the end of the agricultural year. Months without rain turn the lush landscape into a dry tinder box.

The fifth and final vision has the LORD standing by "the altar," the one at Bethel (Amos 9:1–10). God shakes the structure, bringing its blocks crashing down (9:1). "The Lord GOD of hosts, he who touches the earth and it melts, and all who dwell in it mourn, and all of it rises like the Nile, and sinks again, like the Nile of Egypt" (9:5 ESV). The rising of the water reflects the annual Nile flood in Egypt during the months of August, September, and October. This vision graphically portrays the land convulsing during the earthquake mentioned in the opening verse of the book (Amos 1:1), a sure indication of trouble for the land that presages the eventual doom of Israel. In about thirty years Amos's warnings were fully realized when Israelite kingdom was destroyed in 722 B.C.

Fig. 3.20 – Reconstructed canopy over throne pedestal inside city gate at Dan
Israel Ministry of Tourism, provided by Alexander Schick/bibelausstellung.de

The Restoration of Israel (9:11–15)

While much of Amos's message was devoted to doom and destruction, the book ends on a positive note, in which God announces, "I will restore David's tent" (Amos 9:11 NIV) or "booth" (ESV). The meaning of the "booth of David" is disputed. One suggestion is that this booth refers to the type that a king would sit under to administer justice publicly. While excavating the Iron Age gate of Tell Dan, the remains of a platform

32 Wolff, *Joel and Amos*, 218–19.
33 *HALOT* 1098.

was uncovered with four carved stones with a hole bored into the top into which poles were inserted to support a shade canopy for the ruler to sit under.[34] The idea of this future day is that David's kingship would be restored, and rather than Israel being divided, one king would rule over the nation.

This picture of restoration proved to be significant when early Jewish Christians struggled with the question of the salvation of the Gentiles, those outside of the covenant relationship with God.

Paul and his companions brought this issue to the apostles in Jerusalem in Acts 15. After deliberating on the matter, and acknowledging that both Paul and Peter had witnessed the conversion of Gentiles, James made what turned out to be an authoritative word that has guided the church ever since: "When they finished, James spoke up: 'Brothers,' he said, 'listen to me. Simon has described to us how God first intervened to choose a people for his name from the Gentiles. The words of the prophets are in agreement with this, as it is written: "After this I will return and rebuild David's fallen tent. Its ruins I will rebuild, and I will restore it, that the rest of mankind may seek the Lord, even all the Gentiles who bear my name, says the Lord," who does these things—things known from long ago'" (Acts 15:13–18). For James and the early Jewish Christian community, then, the ultimate fulfillment of the restoration of the Davidic kingship was realized in the person of Jesus Christ, who opened the door for non-Jews to be "a people" for God.

FAITHFUL HUSBAND, FAITHLESS WIFE, PATIENT FATHER, PRODIGAL SON: THE BOOK OF HOSEA

> The LORD said to me, "Go, show your love to your wife again, though she is loved by another and is an adulteress. Love her as the LORD loves the Israelites, though they turn to other gods and love the sacred raisin cakes." (Hos. 3:1)

Little can be said about Hosea son of Beeri, such as the location of his home and if he came from the professional guilds of prophets, was a priest or if he, like Amos, was involved in agricultural work. Hosea does display familiarity with agrarian life, as evidenced by some of the illustrations he uses (cf. Hos. 6:11; 8:7; 9:10; 10:1, 11–13). His personal life, however, is unveiled for us in painful detail.

---

34 *NAEAHL* 1:329–30.

The Times of Hosea

The title verse of the book indicates that the word of the Lord came to the prophets during the reigns of Uzziah, Jotham, Ahaz, and Hezekiah, kings of Judah; and during the reign of Jeroboam son of Jehoash, king of Israel. The mention of Uzziah and Jeroboam as kings of Judah and Israel respectively shows that Hosea was a contemporary of Amos, and the four kings of Judah are the same four mentioned in connection with the Judean prophet, Isaiah (see Isa. 1:1). Isaiah's prophetic call came in the year that king Uzziah died (cf. Isa. 6:1 = 740 B.C.),[35] and it is likely that Hosea's prophetic work began in the final years of Uzziah's long reign, otherwise his service would have endured around ninety years. Even if his period of activity were reduced from the final decade of Uzziah and through the first ten years of Hezekiah, a period of forty-five years is covered.[36] Clearly Hosea had a long period of prophetic service.

Since he is generally regarded as a prophet to the northern kingdom, it is odd that he lists Judean kings whose reigns cover the period of the fall of Samaria and beyond (i.e., Ahaz and Hezekiah). If Hosea originally lived in Israel, it may be that as he saw the kingdom beginning to unravel after Jeroboam II's death he may have moved to Judah. Judah is in fact mentioned in the book more than a dozen times, but he never tells us if he lived there.

The political and economic circumstances described above for the period of Amos are identical with what was the case in Hosea's day.

Fig. 3.21 – Canaanite god, possibly El, the head of the pantheon; in the Oriental Institute Museum, Chicago
Photo by James K. Hoffmeier

The Message of Hosea

The book uses two powerful themes to illustrate that Israel had been unfaithful to God. The first motif is that of Israel as an adulterous wife, while the second one portrays the relationship between God and Israel as a loving father and his prodigal son. Because of such infidelity, punishment in the form of foreign exile was sure to come: "My God will reject

35 Thiele, *Hebrew Kings*, 75.
36 Bullock, *Old Testament Prophetic Books*, 101–3.

them because they have not obeyed him; they shall be wanderers among the nations" (Hos. 9:17).

The organizational scheme of the book is complex, but can be reduced to two major units, within which there are various thematic units.

Hosea's Faithless Wife

Isaiah, Hosea's contemporary in Judah, points out, "Here am I, and the children the LORD has given me. We are signs and symbols in Israel from the LORD Almighty, who dwells on Mount Zion" (Isa. 8:18). Isaiah's point is that his life, his marriage, and his children are vehicles used by God to communicate the message in powerful ways. The same was true for Hosea, which is the focus of the first three chapters.

Fig. 3.22 – Canaanite goddess, possibly Qodshu or Astarte, in the Israel Museum
Photo by James K. Hoffmeier

Hosea's story begins with God's directive: "Go, marry a promiscuous woman and have children with her, for like an adulterous wife this land is guilty of unfaithfulness to the LORD" (Hos. 1:2). The narrative continues by reporting on the marriage to Gomer, daughter of Diblaim. While both names were not common, and otherwise not attested in the OT, they lack any notable symbolic meanings.[37] The word *gmr* means "bring to completion" or "accomplish" and may be a shortened form like the name Gemariah (Jer. 29:3; 36:10–11, 25), "Yahweh has accomplished."[38] The new couple proceeds to have three children.

Interpreters have long wrestled with God's instruction "Go, marry a promiscuous woman" (Hos. 1:2). Some take "promiscuous" (*z^enûnîm*) to mean that the woman was a professional prostitute or one who was a ritual prostitute from a pagan cult who participated in religious fertility rites, while others think she was a loose woman who had tendencies indicative of a woman who would prove faithless in time.[39] Regardless of which interpretation one follows, it is clear that she represents Israel who had entered into a marriage covenant with

37 Stuart, *Hosea–Jonah*, 27.
38 *HALOT* 198
39 Guenther, *Hosea, Amos*, 40–41.

Fig. 3.23 – Sowing and plowing in the tomb of Paheri at El-Kab, Egypt
Photo by A. D. Riddle/Bibleplaces.com

God in Sinai, and Israel's faithlessness to God.[40] It is certainly true that Hosea's marriage to a woman of questionable character is paralleled by the LORD entering into the covenant relationship with Israel, even though the sovereign Lord knew beforehand that she would soon after swearing an oath of loyalty to God would worship the golden calf in a matter of days (cf. Exod. 19–24; 32).

The names of the three children are meant to signify Israel's standing before God. Jezreel, the firstborn son (Hosea 1:4), means "God scatters or sows." Here the image of a farmer scattering seed across his field is understood. God explains: "I will soon punish the house of Jehu for the massacre at Jezreel, and I will put an end to the kingdom of Israel. . . . I will break Israel's bow" (Hos. 1:4–5). Earlier on Elisha had commissioned Jehu to terminate the house of Ahab, which he did, but his purge was excessive and brutal beyond expectations (see chap. 2), and much of the slaughter occurred in and around Jezreel, Ahab's winter residence.

A daughter was then born named Lo-Ruhamah (Hos. 1:6), which means "no mercy" (ESV), indicating that God's gracious treatment toward Israel was about to shift, but God states, "I will have mercy on the house of Judah" (Hos. 1:7 ESV). God's extension of mercy on Judah may be due to Hezekiah's reforms that were occurring during the end of the eighth century B.C. A second son is produced from this union named "Lo-Ammi," meaning "not my people," to which the

40 J. Andrew Dearman, *The Book of Hosea* (Grand Rapids: Eerdmans, 2010), 89–91.

Fig. 3.24 – Jezreel Valley near Megiddo
Photo by James K. Hoffmeier

additional note is added, "and I am not your God" (Hos. 1:8). This name would have special significance for the audience, because "my people" hearkens back to the exodus and indicates that God had a unique relationship with Israel. In Exodus 6, God relates the following: "I will take you as my own people, and I will be your God" (v. 7). The verb "take" here, as in Hosea 1:2, is used of marriage.[41] The name Lo-Ammi signified the severing of the marriage covenant relationship with Israel due to her infidelity.

After the third child's birth, Gomer abandons her prophet husband and takes up with other lovers (Hos. 2:2–13). Israel's idolatry is equated with adultery, a breaking of the first and second commandments to not have other gods nor to make images for purposes of worship (cf. Exod. 20:3–5).

41 *HALOT* 534.

The understandably wounded husband (Hosea, representing God) resolves to file for divorce in a court setting. This is clear from the twofold use of the word "rebuke" (Heb. *rîḇ*) is used in Hosea 2:2 (and also in 4:1, 4; 12:3). This is a term with legal force, meaning to bring a suit or make charges.[42] It is widely used in prophetic literature (see below on Micah). In this case, the father calls upon the children to act as hostile witnesses against their adulterous mother (2:2). The husband is torn. On the one hand he wants to punish the infidelity, but on the other hand he wishes to restore the marriage. This tension is revealed by Hosea 2:13–14: "'I will punish her for the days she burned incense to the Baals; she decked herself with rings and jewelry, and went after her lovers, but me she forgot,' declares the LORD. 'Therefore I am now going to allure her; I will lead her into the wilderness and speak tenderly to her.'"

The allusion to the desert wilderness is a reminiscence of the period after the exodus when the LORD entered into the covenant with Israel in the Sinai desert; these themes are all interwoven in Hosea.[43] It is as if God were saying that the wayward wife will experience punishment for her deeds (inevitably all wrong behavior has natural consequences!), but then God would take her back to the desert and woo her, and there say to her: "I will betroth you to me forever; I will betroth you in righteousness and justice, in love and compassion" (2:19), with the result that "you will acknowledge the LORD" (2:20). Put another way, God will remarry Israel, beginning with the betrothal (making the legal arrangements for marriage), followed by intimate union of the relationship that is characterized by "acknowledging" or "knowing" the Lord. "Knowing the LORD" is a repeated expression in Hosea and throughout the prophets to signify an intimate relationship, as one expects in a marriage. Often "knowing" God is the missing dimension of Israel's relationship, which the prophets repeatedly point out. This restoration is understood as occurring after the exile with the return of the Jews from captivity in Mesopotamia to rebuild Jerusalem and the LORD's temple.

The scene then shifts, in chapter 3, to God instructing Hosea to "Go, show your love to your wife again, though she is loved by another and is an adulteress" (3:1). In accordance with ancient Israelite practice, even though he had already

---

42 Dearman, *Hosea*, 108–9.

43 Jerry Hwang, "'I Am Yahweh Your God from the Land of Egypt': Hosea's Use of the Exodus Tradition," in *"Did I Not Bring Israel Out of Egypt?": Biblical, Archaeological, and Egyptological Perspectives on the Exodus Narratives*, Bulletin for Biblical Research Supplement 13, eds. J. Hoffmeier, A. Millard, and G. Rendsburg (Winona Lake, IN: Eisenbrauns, 2016), 245.

Fig. 3.25 – Pieces of silver, not coins, would be weighed out to total 15 shekels
Photo by Alexander Schick/bibelausstellung.de, courtesy Israel Museum, Jerusalem by Amalyah Keshet)

paid a bridal price for her when they first married, and now after she had diminished herself by her infidelities, God tells him to do it all over again! Silver and other commodities would be given to the father of the bride, who in turn was to give it to his daughter when the marriage is finalized as her inheritance—social security, if you will (cf. Gen. 29:18–20; 31:14–16). The price Hosea paid was 15 shekels of silver (150 gm/5.4 oz.), and about 330 liters (350 quarts) of barley. Thirty shekels was the price of a slave in the days of the exodus (Exod. 21:32), but was likely higher in the eighth century. It may be that this combination of silver and grain was equal to the thirty shekels.[44]

What makes this rapprochement so unthinkable is that Deuteronomy 24:1–4 specifically outlaws the reclaiming for marriage an unfaithful, divorced spouse who had remarried. God asks his prophet to do something truly disturbing, but it was meant to illustrate that this is what God was willing to do for his faithless wife Israel, who had committed adultery with pagan deities. Eric Tully has suggested that "sometimes an author uses a vivid story or motif so powerful that it captures the imagination and subsequently dominates one's view of the entire literary work."[45] He suggests this is the case for Hosea's restoring his marriage with Israel and that it sets the framework for the rest of the book by emphasizing the themes of "rebellion, judgment and reconciliation in YHWH's relationship with Israel."[46]

44 Dearman, *Hosea*, 135.
45 Eric Tully, "Hosea 1–3 as the Key to Literary Structure and Message of the Book," in *"An Excellent Fortress for His Armies, a Refuge for the People": Egyptological, Archaeological, and Biblical Studies in Honor of James K. Hoffmeier*, eds. R. E. Averbeck and K. L. Younger (University Park: Eisenbrauns/Pennsylvania State University Press, 2020), 369.
46 Tully, "Hosea 1–3," 369.

THE BOW AS A SYMBOL

When God warns, "I will break Israel's bow" in Hosea 1:5, a highly symbolic statement was being made about the northern kingdom's demise. This expression is also used to refer to various foreign powers. In a foreign nation oracle of Jeremiah, God warns, "See, I will break the bow of Elam, the mainstay of their might" or "chief source" (Jer. 49:35 NET). The same fate would befall Babylon: "A destroyer will come against Babylon; her warriors will be captured and their bows will be broken" (Jer. 51:56). In an even earlier poetic prayer, the prophet Samuel's mother affirms that God will triumph over his enemies: "the bows of the warriors are broken" (1 Sam. 2:4).

Bows were viewed by all ancient cultures as the most lethal weapon, as Jeremiah acknowledged when he said that the bow was "the mainstay of their might." Bows and arrows were used in warfare in the Mediterranean world more than ten thousand years ago. The earliest bows were made of a single piece of wood, sometimes recurved to increase its power and range. If made of a single piece of wood, it is known as a self-bow. The second type of bow is the composite bow, made of

Fig. 3.26 – Ramesses II firing arrows from his chariot in battle
Photo by James K. Hoffmeier

Fig. 3.27a – Assyrian archers stringing a bow
Photo by James K. Hoffmeier

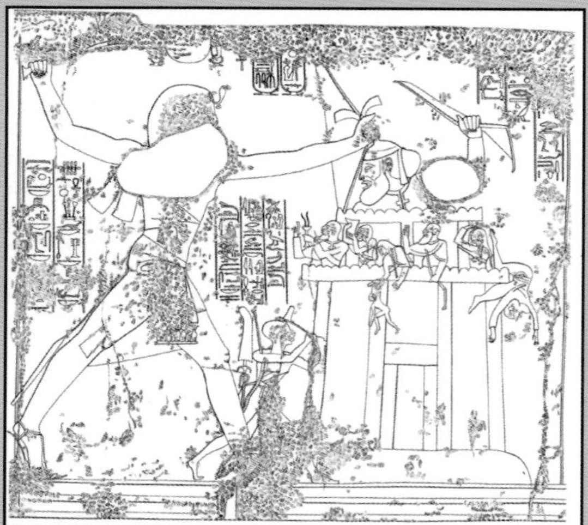

Fig. 3.27b – Rameses II dispatches a Canaanite ruler who holds a broken bow in his hand as a gesture of surrender
Herbert Ricke, George Hughes & Edward Wente, The Beit el-Wali Temple of Ramesses II *[Chicago: University of Chicago Press, 1967], Plate 12*

laminated woods with animal sinew, and a more powerful weapon. Based on pictorial evidence, it is believed that the composite bow (known for its triangular shape when relaxed) is found in Mesopotamia in the twenty-fourth century B.C. This more advanced weapon apparently did not make its way to Egypt until the early second millennium B.C. When King Tutankhamun's undisturbed tomb was discovered, it included fourteen self-bows and twenty-nine composite bows of different sizes.[47] The Assyrians during the period of divided monarchy also used composite bows. It may be that archers in Israel and Judah's armies likewise deployed composite bows, but we lack surviving bows or representations to know for sure.

In most ancient Mediterranean cultures, the bow was the most important long-distance weapon and consequently became a symbol closely associated with warriors of a particular ethnic group or nation and men in general. Consequently, to break a bow was symbolically breaking its owner, a tribe or nation.

Vanquished enemies in some instances in Near Eastern military scenes were sometimes shown breaking their weapons as a

47 W. McLeod, *Composite Bows from the Tomb of Tut'ankhamūn* (Oxford: Oxford University Press, 1970); W. McLeod, *Self Bows and Other Archery Tackle from the Tomb of Tut'ankhamūn* (Oxford: Oxford University Press, 1982).

gesture of complete surrender and defeat. In a battle scene from 2400 B.C. Egypt, a defender of a city is portrayed breaking his bow as an attacker hacks him with an axe. Within a walled city of the same tomb scene, another warrior voluntarily breaks his bow. In one instance when Pharaoh Ramesses II (1279–1213 B.C.) attacked a fortified city, the ruler is presented holding up a broken bow. In this case waving the broken bow seems to be comparable to waving a white flag! Because of the association between warring enemies and bows, Egyptian illustrations show the two together carved on footstools. Examples of this motif were found in the king Tutankhamun's tomb.

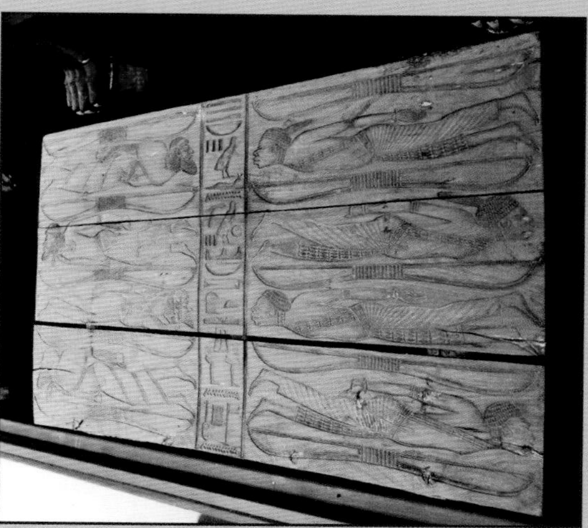

Fig. 3.28 – Footstool of Tutankhamun with foreign enemies and bows together
Photo by A. D. Riddle/Bibleplaces.com

When Israel's prophets spoke of breaking the enemy's bow, it signaled their defeat, and when the bow is banished, peace was the consequence. In Hosea, God says, "Bow and sword and battle I will abolish from the land, so that all may lie down in safety" (2:18). The Psalmist echoes this sentiment: "He makes wars cease to the ends of the earth. He breaks the bow and shatters the spear; he burns the shields with fire" (Ps. 46:9).

Indictments against Israel, God's Prodigal Son

The largest unit of the book is made up of many smaller messages with various themes and motifs (chap. 4–14). One dominant theme, however, is the portrayal of Israel as the Lord's son. Thirty-six times Israel is identified with Ephraim. Ephraim was one of the sons of the patriarch Joseph, the other one being Manasseh (Gen. 41:50–52). Rather than Joseph having a territory named after him like the other sons of Jacob, Ephraim and Manasseh's names were used for the central hill country of Israel, along with Manasseh's adjacent land in the Transjordan (Josh. 16–17). The elevation of Joseph's sons follows their grandfather Jacob's expressed wish that "Ephraim and Manasseh shall be mine, as Reuben and Simeon are" (Gen. 48:5 ESV). It may be that Ephraim is

Fig. 3.29 – The Hill Country of Ephraim with agricultural terraces
Photo by A. D. Riddle/Bibleplaces.com

singled out to represent Israel as a whole because within it was the nation's first religious capital, Shiloh. Bethel was also in Ephraim, which was "the temple of the kingdom" as the priest Amaziah reminded Amos (Amos 7:13).

Just as the first section of the book portrayed the northern kingdom as an adulterous wife being put on trial, the legal perspective is in view in the second section. "Hear the word of the Lord, you Israelites, because the Lord has a charge to bring against you" (Hos. 4:1). The word "charge" (*rîḇ*) demonstrates that a legal case was being filed based on Israel's failure to uphold the terms of the Sinaitic covenant.[48] "Israelites" in this instance, as elsewhere in the Old Testament, literally means "sons of Israel" (sometimes rendered "children of Israel"). The reason for representing Israel as a son is likely linked to ancient

48 Dearman, *Hosea*, 146.

treaty language.[49] Vassal kings were frequently called "son" by their overlords, while the great king is called father.[50]

The exodus narratives also have God speaking of the Hebrews as his son. He directed Moses to say to Pharaoh, "This is what the LORD says: Israel is my firstborn son, and I told you, "Let my son go, so he may worship me" (Exod. 4:22–23).

God's charge against the people in Hosea 4 is expanded as follows:

> There is no faithfulness, no love (*ḥesed*),
> no acknowledgment of God in the land.
> There is only cursing, lying and murder,
> stealing and adultery;
> they break all bounds,
> and bloodshed follows bloodshed. (4:1b–2)

Though sometimes translated "love" and "mercy," the word *ḥesed* in the prophets is normally used to mean "covenant" or "marital loyalty"; faithfulness to God is reflected in obedience to the commandments of Sinai, Israel's marital vows.[51] The sins reviewed here are clearly pointing to the latter six of the Ten Commandments. Loyalty or faithfulness to the covenant laws is how one shows love for God. Here one might recall words of Jesus in the Gospel of John to illustrate the essence of *ḥesed*: "If you love me you will obey my commandments" (John 14:15 NET).

Hosea's language in which God speaks of Israel as his son is especially touching as he recalls how he loved his young son, taught him to walk, and led him out of Egypt:

> When Israel was a child, I loved him,
> and out of Egypt I called my son.
> But the more they were called,
> the more they went awayfrom me.
> They sacrificed to the Baals
> and burned incense to images.

49 *NIDOTT* 1:676–677

50 Some of the fourteenth-century-B.C. Amarna Letters, were written by vassals who use this language in communicating with Pharaoh; see William Moran, *The Amarna Letters* (Baltimore: Johns Hopkins University, 1992), 141, 147, 152 & 170

51 *NIDOTTE* 2:211–13

It was I who taught Ephraim to walk,
taking them by the arms;
but they did not realize
it was I who healed them. (Hos. 11:1–3)

As with the opening chapters of the book of Hosea, Israel's involvement in pagan practices, namely the worship of Baal, is mentioned. Some scholars believe that Israel was not rejecting their God Yahweh entirely but was engaged in religious syncretism, that is, merging the pagan and Yahwistic elements. One possible piece of archaeological evidence that reflects on the fascination with or even the overt worship of Baal in the northern kingdom is found on ostraca (potsherds with writing on them) discovered in Samaria. Recent analysis of these small texts discovered in 1910 have shown that some personal names incorporated Baal and Yahweh in them—for instance, 'Abi-baal (My father is Baal), Baal-zakar (Baal has remembered), Baal-Zemar (Baal is Protection or Strength), 'Abi-yaw (My father is Ya[h]weh'), 'Ur<i>-yaw (Ya[h]weh is my Light), and Yada'-yaw (Ya[h]weh Knows).[52]

These inscribed fragments date to the eighth century based on the writing style, showing that they fall into the period of Hosea's ministry. The use of the Lord's name and that of Baal in personal names at Samaria at this time well reflects the divided loyalties the Israelites had between the Lord and the Canaanite deity Baal (=Hadad).

In chapter 6, the prophet urges his audience to turn back to Yahweh:

"Come, let us return to the Lord. He has torn us to pieces
but he will heal us; he has injured us
but he will bind up our wounds.
After two days he will revive us;
on the third day he will restore us,
that we may live in his presence.
Let us acknowledge the Lord;
let us press on to acknowledge him.
As surely as the sun rises, he will appear;
he will come to us like the winter rains,
like the spring rains that water the earth."
"What can I do with you, Ephraim?

---

52 Jeffrey Tigay, *You Shall Have No Other Gods: Israelite Religion in the Light of Hebrew Inscriptions* (Atlanta: Scholars Press, 1986), 47–68.

What can I do with you, Judah?
Your love is like the morning mist,
like the early dew that disappears."
(Hos. 6:1–4).

Fig. 3.30 – Canaanite incense altar from Megiddo in Israel Museum
Photo by Alexander Schick/bibelausstellung.de, courtesy Israel Museum by Amalyah Keshet)

The formula verses 1–2 directed at wayward Israel, that "after two days he will revive us; on the third day he will restore us," should not be taken literally but to indicate that soon, at a set time, the Lord "would again visit his people in mercy" thereby restoring their wounds.[53] The restoration of life and on the third day here in Hosea undoubtedly influenced New Testament writers when they thought about the resurrection of Jesus. After all, it was Jesus himself who taught them "that everything written about me in the Law of Moses and the Prophets and the Psalms must be fulfilled. Then he opened their minds to understand the Scriptures, and said to them, 'Thus it is written that the Christ should suffer and on the third day rise from the dead'" (Luke 24:44–46 ESV).

The call to "acknowledge the LORD," that is, "know" by having an intimate relationship with God and be restored is in view here, and the invitation is extended to Judah also (Hos. 4:4), illustrating that while Hosea seems (at least initially) a northern prophet speaking primarily to Israel, he also prophesies to the southern kingdom. The encouragement to "know the LORD" (2 x in v. 3) underscores the problem for both kingdoms. God is not looking for a token expression of fealty to Yahweh as their God. God's desire for his covenant people to have a heartfelt love that is characterized by obedience to the Torah, the same point is made by Jesus when initiating the New Covenant: "If you love me you will obey my commandments" (John 14:15 NET). The people of Israel excelled in pious displays of religiosity, but that is not what God wanted. This becomes clear in 6:6, arguably the theological center of Hosea's message: "For I desire steadfast love and not sacrifice, the knowledge of God rather than burnt offerings" (Hos. 6:6 ESV). Here there is

53 Stuart, *Hosea–Jonah*, 108.

the reverberation of the stinging words of Samuel to King Saul (see chap. 2). Sacrifices and rituals are no replacement for "steadfast love."

Hosea issues a condemnation of the priests, likewise bringing charges (*rîḇ*). Their fault is that they have failed to faithfully teach God's laws to the people, so God will reject the priests for leading people away from knowing God's laws:

> My people are destroyed from lack of knowledge.
> Because you have rejected knowledge,
> I also reject you as my priests;
> because you have ignored the law of your God. (Hos. 4:6)

So what will God do with his prodigal son who fails to obey his laws, both social and religious? The king and the high places will be swept away (Hos. 10:7). And the nation will face foreign invasion. Hosea declares, "the roar of battle will rise against your people, so that all your fortresses will be devastated—as Shalman devastated Beth Arbel on the day of battle" (10:14). Reference to Shalman seemingly points to the Assyrian conquering king Shalmaneser III, whose military activity in the region confronted Israelite king Ahab a century before. This hints that the coming enemy would be Assyria.

Fig. 3.31 – Statue of Shalmaneser III in the Oriental Museum, Istanbul
Photo by James K. Hoffmeier

God is portrayed as a father who struggles emotionally with having to punish his son:

> How can I give you up, Ephraim?
>   How can I hand you over, Israel?
> How can I treat you like Admah?
>   How can I make you like Zeboyim?
> My heart is changed within me;
>   all my compassion is aroused. (Hos. 11:8)

Mentioning Admah and Zeboiim means that God does not want to destroy Israel by invoking the covenant curses of Deuteronomy, which warns: "The whole land will be a burning waste of salt and sulfur—nothing planted, nothing sprouting, no vegetation growing on it. It will be like the destruction of Sodom and Gomorrah, Admah and Zeboyim, which the Lord overthrew in fierce anger" (Deut. 29:23). Admah and Zeboyim are two of the four cities destroyed in God's wrath in Abraham's day along with the infamous Sodom and Gomorrah (cf. Gen. 14:2, 8). So he resolves not to obliterate Israel, but to punish by exile (Hos. 11:10–11a). But then the LORD announces, "I will return them to their homes" (Hos. 11:11b ESV). The book ends with a final invitation for the people to return to God (Hos. 14:1).

THE ASSYRIANS

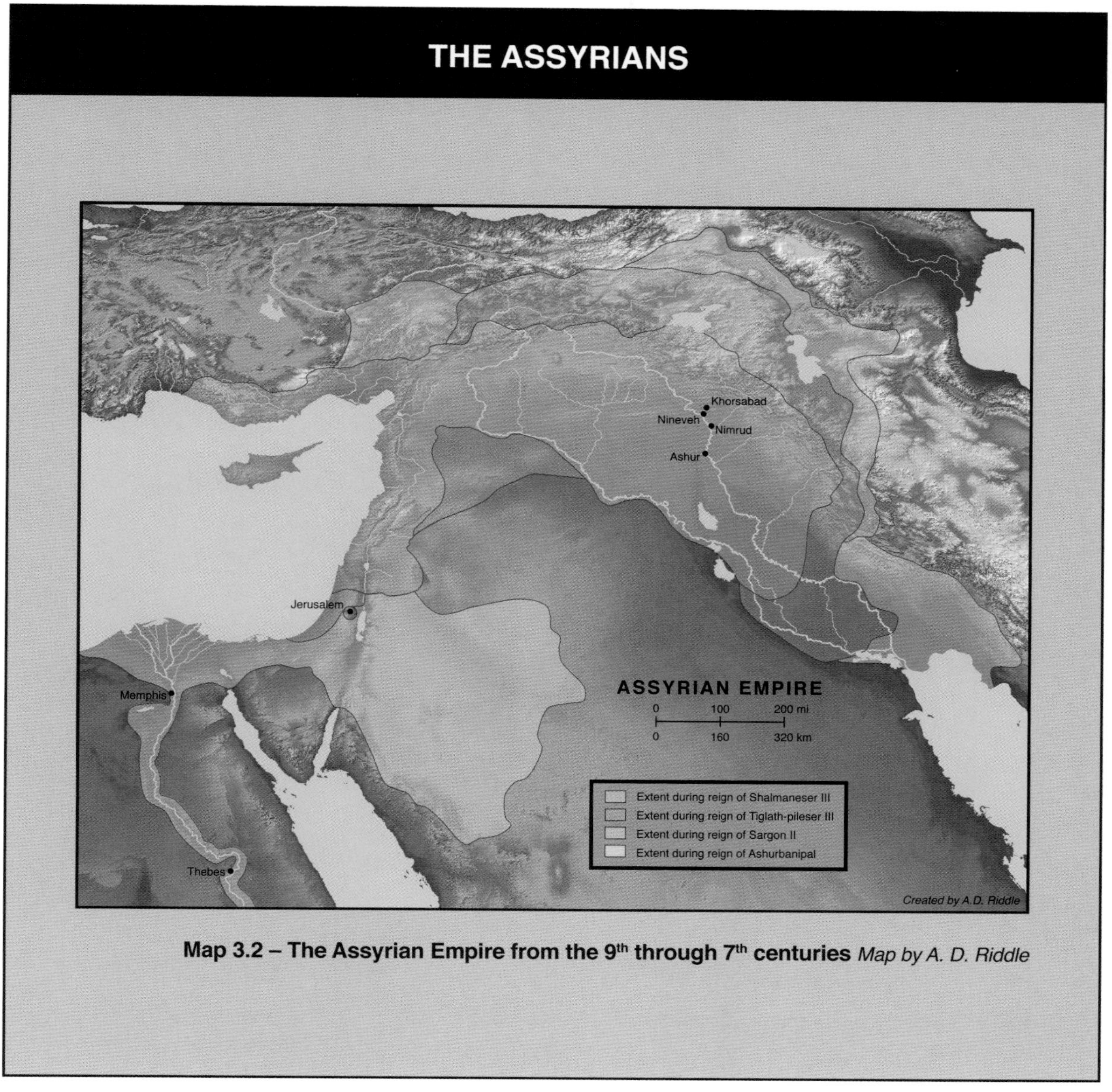

Map 3.2 – The Assyrian Empire from the 9th through 7th centuries *Map by A. D. Riddle*

The heartland of ancient Assur or Assyria was situated in northern Mesopotamia along the Tigris river, north of the Lower Zab River (which flows southwest into the Tigris about 40 k / 25 miles south of the city of Assur). Its principal cities Nimrud and Nineveh are located in the triangular area between the Upper Zab River and the Tigris River.

Assyria enjoyed several periods of power and prominence in the region, separated by down times where it exercised little or no influence in the Near East. The relevant period from biblical history involves the Neo-Assyrian Empire, which began to emerge from obscurity late in the tenth century B.C. The early Neo-Assyrian period reaches its zenith during the reigns of Ashurnasirpal II (883–859 B.C.) and his successor Shamaneser III (859–824 B.C.). The former established the city of Calah (modern Nimrud) as the royal capital. The palace of Ashurnasirpal II was the first architectural feature excavated by archaeologists in Mesopotamia, beginning in 1845 by A. H. Layard (see Fig. 2.33 & 3.1).

Fig. 3.32 – Assyrian armies engaged in siege warfare on an enemy city from Nimrud palace. Panel in British Museum
Photo by James K. Hoffmeier

Ashurnasirpal II conducted fourteen major campaigns, three of which the king personally led.[54] He pushed across the Euphrates and across Lebanon to the Mediterranean Sea. Shalmaneser III continued his father's warring ways, engaging in battles during thirty-two of his thirty-five years on the throne. Many of his campaigns were directed against the rising power of Urartu (Ararat of the Bible), his neighbor to the north. In 856 B.C. he dealt them a major setback to his hostile expansionist neighbor. On his stela from Kurkh (in present-day Turkey) he recalls of facing a coalition of twelve kings from Syria and the Levant in 853 B.C. at Qarqar on the Orontes River.[55] Included in this force was Ahab the Israelite, who is reported as contributing two thousand chariots and ten thousand infantry.

In 841 B.C., under circumstances that remain unclear, Jehu king of Israel paid tribute to Shalmaneser III. Depicted on the famous Black Obelisk is a group of Israelite tribute-bearers approaching the

Fig. 3.33 – Section from the Black Obelisk of Shalmaneser III with Israelite tribute-bearers
Photo by Todd Bolen/Bibleplaces.com

54 ABD 4:741.
55 *COS* 2:262–64.

king in one panel, while Jehu (or his emissary) prostrates himself before Shalmaneser III. The Assyrian claims, "I received the tribute . . . of Jehu of the House of Omri" (see Fig. 3.3).

After Shalmaneser III, Assyria slumped into a period not as robust known as "the Interval" (782–745 B.C.), a period of local autonomy rather than centralized rule.[56] Then a new king, Tiglath-pileser III, took the throne in 745 and ruled to 727 B.C. He quickly regained adjacent lands. He also took unprecedented steps to control the perpetually independent-minded Babylon, Assyria's southern neighbor, and thereby united Mesopotamia politically.

Tigalth-pileser introduced policies that would guarantee that Assyria would be a dynamic and expanding empire for the next century. First, he reorganized the military as a permanent

Fig. 3.34 – Tiglath-Pileser III from Nimrud palace, in British Museum *Photo by A. D. Riddle/Bibleplaces.com*

56 *ABD* 4:743–44.

fighting force rather than just a seasonal militia made up of Assyrian farmers and laborers. He also expanded the practice of mass deportation of conquered enemies so as to minimize nationalism and rebellions.

In his annals he mentions receiving tribute from Menahem (752–542 B.C.), king of Samaria. In 734 B.C. he ventured west to put down rebellions and conquered parts of Syria and northern Israel during Pekah's kingship in Samaria. The Bible states that Tiglath-Pileser captured the northmost parts of Israel. Recent excavation of Bethsaida (Geshur of the OT Period) on the northern shore of the Sea of Galilee uncovered the city gate that had been devastated and left as a massive pile of debris.[57] This campaign marked the beginning of the exile of some of the northern Israelite tribes (2 Kings 15:29).

A decade later, Israel once again was in rebellion against Assyria, prompting Shalmaneser V, Tiglath-pileser's successor, to respond (2 Kings 17:3). This led to a three-year campaign against Israel and its capital Samaria (17:5). It fell in 722 B.C., significant portions of the population were deported, and they were settled "on the Habor River and in the towns of the Medes" (17:6), that is, in the area of present-day northern Iraq and Iran. As the war was ending, Shalmanseser V died and was succeeded by Sargon II in 722, who claims that he conquered Samaria and took 27,290 prisoners.[58]

Fig. 3.35 – The ruins of the Iron Age city gate destroyed by Assyrian forces at Bethsaida/Gesher
Photo by Todd Bolen/Bibleplaces.com

Further rebellion in Philistia brought Assyrian armies back to the region, led by the "supreme commander" according to Isaiah 20:1. Beyond his military prowess, Sargon II proved to be an ambitious builder, founding a new capital named after himself, *Dur-Sharrukin* ("Fort Sargon"), just north of Nineveh. It

57 Rami Arav, *Bethsaida: A City on the North Shore of the Sea of Galilee*, vol. 4 (Kirksville, MO: Truman State University, 2009), 1–122.
58 *COS* 2:296.

Fig. 3.36 – Monumental statuary from Fort Sargon (Khorsabad), in Louvre
Photo by James K. Hoffmeier

included impressive temples, a palace with reliefs detailing Sargon's military activities, and protective winged bulls with the king's visage on them.

Sennacherib succeeded his father in 704 B.C. and elevated the Assyrian empire to new heights. He is best remembered for his efforts against Judah that had avoided Assyrian invasion up to 701 B.C. (Isa. 36–37; 2 Kings 18–19; 2 Chron. 32–33). While many cities of Judah fell, including Lachish (celebrated on the king's detailed reliefs from his palace in Nineveh), Jerusalem was spared (see below "701 B.C." in Chapter 4).

Esarhaddon (680–669 B.C.) engaged in a program of ameliorating the Babylonians after his father's brutal treatment of the historic city by rebuilding various structures including the temple of Marduk. Under his leadership Egypt was conquered in 671 B.C. Although the Cushite pharaoh Taharka (Tirhaka of the Bible) apparently fought valiantly, he was defeated and escaped to his homeland in Sudan. After receiving tribute and appointing governors, the Assyrians withdrew, taking with them members of the royal family, including the Cushite crown prince who is depicted on the stela discovered in Zincirli, Turkey.

Fig. 3.37 – Stela of Esarhaddon from Zincirli (Turkey), in Berlin Museum. The Nubian prince is the shorter kneeling figure.
Photo by James K. Hoffmeier

The ruler of Babylon, Ashurbanipal's brother, with the aid of neighboring Elam to the east, sought independence from Nineveh. This forced Ashurbanipal to take on Babylon in a siege that lasted two years, followed by a large-scale invasion of Elam. Elam's king, Teuman, was slain and decapitated. His head was transported to Nineveh, where it was hung on a tree in the royal garden, where Ashurbanipal is depicted reclining on his couch while the queen sips wine from a bowl (see Fig. 3.15).

The battles in southern Mesopotamia, especially the costly civil war with Babylon, in many ways mark the beginning of the end of the Assyrian Empire. With Ashurbanipal's passing, a number of weak rulers followed, inviting hostility from the Medes to the east and Babylon from the south. In 614 B.C. the city of Ashur fell when these two neighbors joined forces. Nineveh met its fate in 612 B.C., and with its demise, the Assyrian empire and its feared power were gone, as the prophet Nahum announced.

A HARD-HEARTED PROPHET, A CALLOUS NATION: THE BOOK OF JONAH

"When God saw what they did and how they turned from their evil ways, he relented and did not bring on them the destruction he had threatened" (Jonah 3:10).

The book of Jonah only discloses the prophet's name: "Jonah son of Amittai" (Jonah 1:1), but provides no further information about the period in which he lived and prophesied. Neither the king of Israel nor Assyria is named. A helpful note, however, is found in 2 Kings 14:25 which explains how Jeroboam II succeeded in his military expansion to the north and west of Israel: "He was the one who restored the boundaries of Israel from Lebo Hamath to the Sea of the Arabah, in accordance with the word of the LORD, the God of Israel, spoken through his servant Jonah son of Amittai, the prophet from Gath Hepher."

This information suggests that Jonah was either a contemporary of Jeroboam II (782–753 B.C.), or he that lived just before his time. We also learn that Jonah's home was Gath Hepher, a village situated in Northern Israel in

Fig. 3.38 – Gath Hepher from the air *Photo by WS/Bible places.com*

the territory of Zebulun (ca. 30 km/19 miles) west of the Sea of Galilee.[59] This location clearly situates him in the northern part of Israel.

Jonah's Story

The well-known story of Jonah occupies a significant portion of the book, namely chapters 1, 3, and 4, with chapter 2 containing the prophet's prayer. The emphasis on biography makes this book conspicuously different than the other prophetic books.

The story begins with a command from God to Jonah: "Go to the great city of Nineveh and preach against it, because its wickedness has come up before me" (Jonah 1:2). Nineveh was one of the greatest cities in the ancient world, and at times during the Neo-Assyrian empire, it was the capital. It was situated on the

Fig. 3.39 – Ashurbanipal lion hunt scene from Nineveh in British Museum
Photo by A. D. Riddle/Bibleplaces.com

59 *ABD* 2:909–10.

eastern shore of the Tigris River, the Khosr branch of which ran east-west through the walled city. A glimpse into Nineveh's glory can be seen from the later remains from the seventh century B.C. The city had a double-walled defensive system that measured approximately 5 km by 2 km (ca. 3 miles by 1 1/3 miles), or 12 km (7 miles) in circumference. The lower outer wall was made of dressed stone, while the larger, inner bastion was made of mud brick and was believed to have been 25 m (ca. 80 ft) high. The walls were punctuated by no fewer than fifteen massive gates.[60] And the palaces within the walls were approached by broad, paved avenues, and at their gates enormous winged bulls (often with the king's image serving as the head) stood guard. Within the palaces (both at Nineveh and other Assyrian cities such as Khorsabad) detailed limestone reliefs decorated the walls in which the king's heroics in battle and hunting were displayed. These often reveal how violent and brutal the Assyrians could be (see "The Assyrians" excursus).

Fig. 3.40 – Ashurnasirpal's army besieging an enemy city, using a wheeled battering ram
Photo by A. D. Riddle/Bibleplaces.com

60 *OEANE* 4, 145–146.

It is to this dreadful and violent metropolis that the little country prophet from Israel was directed to go. Furthermore, the Assyrians had been Israel's enemy for some decades since Ashurnasirpal II and Shalmaneser III had extended Assyrian domination to the Mediterranean coast. If bad news was in the offing for Nineveh, this was good news for Israel! Jonah's reluctance to go, therefore, is totally understandable.

Rather than obey God's directive, Jonah headed in the opposite direction, boarding a freighter for Tarshish. Tarshish is believed to correspond to Tartessus in southwest Spain, which was being exploited by the Phoenicians for its metals.[61] Shortly after sailing from the port city of Joppa (present-day Jaffa), located just south of present-day Tel Aviv, "the Lord sent a great wind on the sea, and such a violent storm arose" (Jonah 1:4). The boat, its crew, and cargo were threatened, prompting the sailors to pray for divine intervention. They then decided to cast lots to determine the culprit on the belief that someone on board had angered his deity who needed to be appeased. Casting lots, it will be recalled (see chap. 1), was one ancient form of divination.[62] The finger pointed to Jonah (1:8), who confessed, "I am a Hebrew and I worship the Lord, the God of heaven, who made the sea and the dry land" (1:9), and acknowledged that the storm was on his account. So, Jonah offered a remedy: "throw me into the sea . . . and it will become calm" (1:12). They called on the name of the God of Israel and asked that they not be judged for Jonah's sin. Then they tossed the prophet overboard. At this point, while flailing in the boisterous sea, "the Lord provided a great fish to swallow Jonah, and Jonah was in the belly of the fish three days and three nights" (1:17).

Fig. 3.41 – Phoenician naval vessel in service to the Assyrians sailing on the Mediterranean during the reign of Sennacherib
Photo by James K. Hoffmeier

From inside the fish, the narrative continues, Jonah prayed. The recorded prayer of chapter 2 (vv. 2–9) actually indicates that this prayer was made after deliverance as he celebrates God's salvation and promises to make good on his vows by sacrificing to the Lord at the temple (2:9). At God's command, the fish spewed the prophet "onto dry land" (2:10). The Lord again ordered Jonah to go to Nineveh, and this time he obeyed.

61 *ABD* 6:332.
62 John Walton, "Jonah," in *Zondervan Illustrated Bible Backgrounds Commentary*, ed. J. H. Walton (Grand Rapids: Zondervan, 2009), 107.

There he proclaimed, "Forty more days and Nineveh will be overthrown" (3:4). "Forty" is an important and symbolic number in the Bible, and not necessarily meant literally.[63] The number forty is often connected to divine judgment, such as forty days and nights of rain in Noah's flood (Gen. 7:12), forty years of the Israelites wandering in the wilderness (Num. 14:33–34), and the Philistines oppressing Israel for forty years (Judg. 13:1). For Nineveh, the period was to give an opportunity to respond positively to God's word delivered by Jonah.

To the prophet's surprise, the Ninevites believed God, declared a fast, and donned sackcloth—tokens of mourning and humbling oneself. Even "the king and his nobles" decreed a national repentance hoping that "God may yet relent" (Jonah 3:7, 9). The change of heart seems to have been genuine, as God had "relented and did not bring on them the destruction he had threatened" (3:10).

Jonah, a good Israelite nationalist, was distraught that the Assyrians would repent and avoid divine judgment (Jonah 4:1–3). As the "forty days" passed, Jonah enjoyed the shade of a vine, possibly the fast-growing castor oil plant, which was later attacked by a worm, causing the plant to wither and die. This development angered the prophet. In response the Lord said, "You have been concerned about this vine, though you did not tend it or make it grow. It sprang up overnight and died overnight. And should I not have concern for the great city of Nineveh, in which there are more than a hundred and twenty thousand people who cannot tell their right hand from their left—and also many animals?" (4:10–11). With this statement, the book ends, leaving the reader to ponder the message of the book.

Allegorical Interpretation

The story has some rather sensational elements, including the claim of being swallowed by "a large fish." To resolve the tension caused by the hard-to-swallow element of the story, some interpreters suggest that this story is an allegory and does not reflect reality. Furthermore, the notion that a Hebrew prophet would actually go to a Nineveh to prophesy seems farfetched to some, not to mention that Jonah's message was actually believed (Jonah 3:5). In the allegorical approach Jonah represents Israel that was reluctant to obey God and represent the Lord to the nations before the exile. The large fish, in turn, symbolizes the exile that swallowed up Israel. After a period of repentance and calling to God from distant Babylon, the Jews return to their lands and become faithful to God, and as Isaiah reports God as saying,

63 Stuart, *Hosea–Jonah*, 489.

> It is too small a thing for you to be my servant
> to restore the tribes of Jacob
> and bring back those of Israel I have kept.
> I will also make you a light for the Gentiles,
> that my salvation may reach to the ends of the earth. (Isa. 49:6)

In the allegorical approach, the story as presented in the books is not historical. While Jonah son of Amittai may have been a historical figure, the story is fictitious, made up to teach the lesson of God's compassion for the nations and to rebuke Israel for its spiritual intransigence.

Historical-Symbolic Interpretation

Because Jonah is clearly a historical figure who likely lived just before or during the reign of Jeroboam II (793–753 B.C.)[64] as reported in 2 Kings 14:25, others believe that the story is authentic. Certainly this is the view of Jesus in the New Testament. He said, "For as Jonah was three days and three nights in the belly of a huge fish, so the Son of Man will be three days and three nights in the heart of the earth. The men of Nineveh will stand up at the judgment with this generation and condemn it; for they repented at the preaching of Jonah, and now one greater than Jonah is here" (Matt. 12:40–41).

Clearly the message of the book of Jonah is not found in the prophet's preaching, as is the case with other prophetic books. In the book of Jonah, just one verse is given to his public proclamation, namely, "Forty more days and Nineveh will be overthrown" (Jonah 3:4). As we have seen elsewhere, elements of prophets' lives are interwoven with their message, such as Hosea's unfaithful wife and the names of his children, Jeremiah's purchase of a field from his cousin (Jer. 32), or the death of Ezekiel's wife (Ezek. 24). So there are cases where episodes of the lives of prophets are integral to the message—or they are, in fact, the message! This is the case, it is suggested here, with the book of Jonah. The message is to be found in narratives just as with biographical episodes found in other prophetic books.

While the story of the prophet being swallowed by a large fish sounds farfetched, similar great fish stories have been reported in modern times. There are documented cases of sperm whales swallowing men who survived. One celebrated case took place near the Falkland Islands that was reported

---

64 Thiele, *Hebrew Kings*, 75.

in 1927.[65] In this case a seaman was swallowed and lived for three days in the whale before being rescued! Perhaps a similar thing occurred with Jonah.

Israelite and foreign prophets are known to have traveled beyond the borders to prophesy elsewhere in the Old Testament. As noted previously, Balaam the prophet from distant Amaw in Syrian came to Moab (Num. 22:1–21), Elisha traveled to Damascus, the capital of Syria (Aram) to anoint Hazael to be king (2 Kings 8:7–15), and Amos left Judah to travel to hostile Israel to denounce their golden calf worship (Amos 7). Then too in the sixth century B.C., Jeremiah went to Egypt where he preached to the Judean community scattered throughout the land (Jer. 43–44).

The exact dating of Jonah's visit to Assyria is not provided by the narratives. Had the name of the king of Nineveh or Israel been included, the "when" of the story would be settled. The absence of this vital information serves to remind the reader that while the story does have a historical, social, and political setting, that is not the concern of this book. The lack of historical markers, however, does not mean the story is fictitious. The chronological datum provided by 2 Kings 14:25 that associates Jonah with the period of or just prior to the reign of Jeroboam II does provide a probable window between 800 and 750 B.C. (For a more detailed review of the history of the Assyrian Empire, see "The Assyrians" excursus above.)

The first half of the eighth century is something of a dark age between two great periods of empire building under the conquering ninth-century kings Ashurnasirpal II (883–859 B.C.), Shalmaneser III (859–824 B.C.), and Tiglath-pileser III (745–727 B.C.) and his successors. By the end of the ninth and beginning of the eighth century, Assyria was in decline. The period of 782–745 B.C. has been called the "Interval" by historians, characterized by political, military, and economic paralysis.[66] Although there were three kings during this period, the nation was divided into districts ruled by governors. It may be during this period of weakness that Jonah conducted his mission to Nineveh. This fragmented political reality may be reflected in the statement in Jonah 3:7 that a decree was issued by "the king and his nobles" and may also explain why the ruler is called "king of Nineveh" (3:6) rather than the "king of Assyria."[67] In a period of royal impotence, one might expect an Assyrian ruler would be

65 Harrison, *Introduction*, 907–8.
66 *ABD* 4:743–44.
67 This expression has been used by some critics to argue that the story of Jonah is fictitious, as one might expect the ruler to be called King of Assyria. For some sound explanations for the usage in Jonah, see Stuart, *Hosea–Jonah*, 440–42.

Fig. 3.42 – Plaque with possibly image of the goddess Ishtar from the Old Babylonian Period
Photo by Todd Bolen/Bibleplaces.com

reduced to a position that required the support of nobles or governors to make an authoritative decree to the nation.

One of these three rulers was Ashur-dan III (771–754 B.C.), whose reign was marred by failed military campaigns in central Syria, an epidemic, revolts, and a solar eclipse that was viewed as a bad omen. Under such circumstances one can certainly understand why the residents of Nineveh would respond positively to Jonah's message. Additionally, the Assyrians like other nations respected and appealed to prophets, and they were notoriously superstitious. The second largest collection of prophetic texts from the ancient Near East was discovered in Nineveh, and the prophetic works are typically the seer's responses to a question posed by the king himself! One prophetic message to king Esarhaddon (680–669 B.C.) offered words of warning and encouragement: "Fear not, Essarhaddon! I am Bel, I speak to you! I watch over the supporting beams of your heard" . . . Do not trust in humans! Lift up your eyes and focus on me! I am Ishtar of Arbela. I have reconciled (the god) Ashur to you. I protected you when you were a baby. Fear not; praise me!."[68]

So there is no real problem with Jonah the prophet traveling to Assyria (except his own understandable reluctance!) or that the foreign prophet would be favorably received. And, given the scenario of political and national turmoil in the first half of the eighth century, Jonah's mission to Nineveh seems quite plausible.

One of the main themes of the book of Jonah from this approach is that non-Israelites can come to faith in the LORD. Notice that the foreign sailors on Jonah's boat "greatly feared the LORD" (Jonah 2:10–16), and then the people of Nineveh, when they heard Jonah's warnings, "believed God" (3:5). These two reports were also intended to rebuke the people of Israel who were reluctant to respond positively to God's word via the prophets.

Second, and arguably the main lesson of the book, is the fact that God directs his prophet to warn the Assyrians of pending doom demonstrates his concern and care for non-Israelites. When Jonah was upset that his shade vine withered and died, God rebuked him for his misplaced compassion, which contrasted with God's concern for the people of Nineveh. The book concludes with the probing questions to the Jonah: "And should I not have concern about that great city . . . ?" (Jonah 4:11). Posing this question as God's final word in the book demonstrates that this is the dominant issue the book sought to address. God cares for all his creation, not just his covenant people.

---

68 Nissinen, *Prophets in the Ancient Near East*, 105.

DISCUSSION QUESTIONS

- Given the peace and prosperity of the period of Amos and Hosea and the public religious piety, how do you think their audiences reacted to hearing of God's displeasure?
- Look at the exodus/wilderness related passages in Amos (2:10; 3:1–2; 4:10; 9:7) and Hosea (11:1; 12:9; 13:4–5), and think about the role they play in shaping these prophets' messages to Israel.
- Amos and Hosea denounce Israel for failing on issues of justice. What is the relationship between issues of justice and God's law? Discuss how "justice" in the prophets has interrelated moral, religious, and social dimensions.
- In the light of the previous question, discuss the meaning and applications to Hosea 6:6.
- How are you challenged or encouraged by the fact that Amos was a shepherd and fruit farmer?
- Hosea uses the husband-wife and father-son relationships to describe God's relationship with Israel. Discuss how these vivid motifs help drive home the prophet's message.
- The books of Hosea (14) and Amos (9:11–15) both end on a positive message of restoration for the nation after a period of exile. Compare these passages. What hope do they offer the people for the near future and for the distant future?
- How do you identify with Jonah's reluctance to take God's word to people in general and those with whom you have a history of animosity?
- Discuss the ways God demonstrates his sovereign control in the book of Jonah.
- What is the main theological point of the book of Jonah?

4

"Zion Shall Be Plowed Like a Field"

THE EIGHTH-CENTURY PROPHETS OF JUDAH

"Writhe in agony, Daughter Zion, like a woman in labor,
for now you must leave the city to camp in the open field."
—Micah 4:10

The prophecies of Hosea, Amos, and Jonah were primarily, though not exclusively, directed at the northern kingdom of Israel during the eighth century while Assyrian power overwhelmed Aram (Syria) and Phoenicia, and began its aggression against the northmost reaches of Israel in the mid-eighth century B.C. By 722 B.C. Assyria had destroyed Israel's principal cities, including Samaria, the capital (see the introduction to chap. 3 and excursus "The Assyrians"), and deported large numbers of Israelites (2 Kings 17:1–13). Judah did not completely escape the Assyrian juggernaut. Judah's contemporaries of Hosea, Amos, and Jonah were Isaiah and Micah. Judah experienced the full force of the Assyrian war machine in 701 B.C. after king Sennacherib smashed the Philistine coastal region around 711 B.C. A decade later Nineveh's armies took on rebellious Hezekiah (Isa. 36–37), who enjoyed Isaiah's support and delivered communications from God during this crisis (see further below).

Micah, who lived in the Shephelah region between the Philistine zone on the west and the hill country of Judah where Jerusalem was situated, was surely aware of the developing military crisis that was brewing nearby and warned the Judeans of coming calamities. Samaria's demise was naturally a cautionary tale for Judah. Judah's failure to faithfully uphold the covenant demands in the Law would ultimately lead to its destruction, even though it had been led by godly kings like Hezekiah and, later on, Josiah. The mission of Isaiah and Micah was, like other messengers of God, to warn Israel and Judah: "Turn from your evil ways. Observe my commandments and decrees, in accordance with the entire Law that I commanded your fathers to obey and that I delivered to your through my servants the prophets" (2 Kings 17:13).

"THE HOLY ONE OF ISRAEL" SPEAKS: THE BOOK OF ISAIAH

> "They have rejected the law of the LORD Almighty and spurned the word of the Holy One of Israel."
>
> —Isaiah 5:24

Isaiah Son of Amoz, and His Personal Life

The title of the book is "the vision (*ḥazôn*) of Isaiah son of Amoz." While Isaiah was a recipient of visions (e.g., Isa. 6), the word in this title applies to the entire book, but not all chapters are vision reports. Therefore the title more broadly "refer(s) to truth disclosed by God; not necessarily in visual experience but by supernatural revelation."[1]

Isaiah is often viewed as the greatest of the Hebrew prophets. Certainly, the New Testament contains more prophecies that its writers connect to Jesus of Nazareth than any other OT book. But it does not end there. By one reckoning, there are "almost 100 citations and some 500 allusions," making Isaiah "the most frequently referenced single work in the New Testament."[2] (See further "Isaiah and the New Testament" below.)

Jerusalem appears to be the home of the prophet, although nowhere in the book is this explicitly stated. Recently, a seal impression or bulla was uncovered in excavations in Jerusalem in the Ophel site, just south of the temple mount. Though broken and thus only partially preserved, the bulla reads "belonging to Yesha'yah[u] Nvy" (i.e. Isaiah [the] prophet)."[3] Since the reading is partial, certainty that this is Isaiah the prophet of the Bible is impossible but is certainly plausible, especially since it was discovered just 10 feet (3 meters) away from a contemporary bulla of King Hezekiah. Certainly his preaching activity is centered in Jerusalem, and he is personally engaged in the major events covered in the book, namely the threat of Damascus and Samaria alliance (cf. Isa. 7) against Jerusalem, and Sennacherib's invasion in 701 B.C. (Isa. 36–37). In one narrative, his son Shear-Jashub appears with him in Jerusalem in an encounter with King Ahaz in 734/5 B.C. (Isa. 7:3; see below). Isaiah's wife,

---

1 J. Alec Motyer, *The Prophecy of Isaiah: An Introduction and Commentary* (Downers Grove, IL: InterVarsity Press, 1993), 41.

2 Rikk E. Watts, "Isaiah in the New Testament," in *Interpreting Isaiah: Issues and Approaches*, eds. D. G. Firth and H. G. M. Williamson (Downers Grove, IL: IVP Academic, 2009), 213.

3 Eilat Mazar, "Is This the Prophet Isaiah's Signature?," *BAR* 44, nos 2-3 (2018): 65–92.

Fig. 4.1a – Seal impression possibly that of Isaiah the prophet discovered in Jerusalem
Photo by Ouria Tadmor, courtesy Eilat Mazar/Ophel Excavations

Fig. 4.1b – Seal impression reading "Belonging to Hezekiah [son of] Ahaz, king of Judah"
Photo by Ouria Tadmor, courtesy Eilat Mazar/Ophel Excavations

known to us only as "the prophetess," is mentioned in another episode when describing the birth of another son (Isa. 8:3). Beyond these references, we know little about personal life of Isaiah.

There is an interesting Jewish rabbinic tradition that Isaiah's father Amoz was a younger brother of the Judean king, Amaziah (800–783 B.C.), meaning that Isaiah had connections to the royal family.[4] Supporting evidence for this theory is lacking, however, Isaiah seems to be well connected to the royal court and appears to have unfettered access to kings Ahaz (Isa. 7) and Hezekiah (Isa. 36–39). The only occurrence of the name Amoz in the Bible was Isaiah's father, thus further information about his identity is lacking. Consequently, we are unable to firmly conclude much about Isaiah's family history.

We are reminded that Isaiah's wife and names of his sons (cf. Isa. 8) are symbols to illustrate his message to Israel and Judah. In fact the prophet well understands this point, claiming, "Here am I, and the children the LORD has

4 Herbert Wolf, *Interpreting Isaiah* (Grand Rapids: Zondervan, 1985), 12.

given me. We are signs and symbols in Israel from the LORD Almighty, who dwells on Mount Zion" (Isa. 8:18).

In the biographical sections of the book (Isa. 6–8 and 36–39) we catch glimpses of Isaiah interacting with Judean rulers and with his family (the latter will be treated in more detail below). The earlier passages date to the reign of Ahaz and the invasion of his nation by the kings of Syria/Damascus and Israel occurred "in late 735 or early 734, the purpose of which was to replace Ahaz with a more pliant non-Davidic leader," according to Hayes and Irvine,[5] so that they would support their alliance against Assyria. The second crisis where

Fig. 4.2 – Traditional Jewish wedding ceremony, in which the couple signs the Ketubah or contract to make marriage legal
Photo by Todd Bolen/Bibleplaces.com

5 John Hayes and Stuart Irvine, *Isaiah the Eighth-Century Prophet* (Nashville: Abingdon, 1987), 118–19.

Isaiah takes a major role is during the invasion of Judah by the Assyrian emperor Sennacherib in 701 B.C. (see excursus "701 B.C.: The Assyrian Invasion of Judah").

Fig. 4.3 – Image of Sargon II from Khorsabad Oriental Institute
Photo by A. D. Riddle/Bibleplaces.com

In Isaiah 20, in a historical narrative dated to "the year that the commander in chief, who was sent by Sargon the king of Assyria, came to Ashdod and fought against it and captured it" (20:1 ESV). The Ashdod campaign occurred in 711 B.C. Concurrently the prophet engaged in a bizarre symbolic act at God's command—God instructed Isaiah: "'Go, and loose the sackcloth from your waist and take off your sandals from your feet,' and he did so, walking naked and barefoot" (20:2 ESV).[6] And he did this for three years "as a sign and portent" or "an object lesson and omen" (NET) "against Egypt and Cush" (20:3). Some commentators believe that the prophet paraded about naked (*'ārôm*), that is, totally stripped. "Naked" (*'ārôm*) is the same word used of the unclothed Adam and Eve in the garden (Gen. 2:25). Others consider that the sackcloth was worn over his undergarments (i.e., loincloth, see Jer. 13:1–11), and therefore was barely clothed.

Alternatively, the "sackcloth" Isaiah wore may refer to a man's underpants,[7] whereas some interpreters consider this garment to be the attire specific to the prophet at that time.[8] Elijah's characteristic "garment of hair, with a belt of leather about his waist" (2 Kings 1:8 ESV) made him identifiable,[9] and John the Baptist apparently replicated the attire of the great prophet. "Now John wore a garment of camel's hair and a leather belt around his waist" (Matt. 3:4 ESV). If this understanding is followed, when Isaiah's signature outfit was removed, he would have been virtually naked, parading in his underwear. The three years likely

6 Marvin Sweeney, *Isaiah 1–39: Forms of Old Testament Literature* (Grand Rapids: Eerdmans, 1996), 268.
7 John Watts, *Isaiah 1–33*, World Biblical Commentary (Waco, TX: Word, 1985), 264.
8 Motyer, *The Prophecy of Isaiah*, 171.
9 Some interpreters think that this expression means that Elijah was a hairy man, and not that he wore a woven animal hair garment. This understanding is reflected in the NET Bible translation. Others maintain that the "hairy" description points to his garb, not his beard of body hair (D. Wiseman, *1–2 Kings* [Downers Grove, IL: Inter-Varsity Press, 1993], 193).

refers to periodic appearances over this span of time in order to regularly communicate rather than three years of nonstop public exposure.[10] After all, winters in Jerusalem are rainy and average low temperatures are in the low 40s° F (4–5° C). Occasionally during cold snaps, the temperatures dive below freezing, and even snow falls. In acting out his dramatic message, Isaiah precedes Jeremiah and Ezekiel, who were known for their symbolic acts.

The Chronicler concludes his report on Uzziah with this citation: "Now the rest of the acts of Uzziah, from first to last, Isaiah the prophet, son of Amoz

Fig. 4.4 – Egyptian workers making bricks in the tomb of Rekhmire strip down to underwear to do menial work
Photo by Alexander Schick/bibelausstellung.de

10 Herbert Wolf, *Interpreting Isaiah* (Grand Rapids: Zondervan, 1985), 126.

wrote" (2 Chron. 26:22 ESV). As noted above (cf. chap. 1), the prophets often served as historians recording the acts of the kings of Israel and Judah. This means that Isaiah, like his other colleagues, recorded the deeds of the kings who were contemporary with them. Prophets were keenly interested in the history as it revealed the unfolding plans of God for Israel and Judah. The prophets offer evaluations of each king in the books of Kings and Chronicles relative to how they upheld the Law. Each king was to have his own copy of the Book of the Law: "he shall read in it all the days of his life, that he may learn to fear the LORD his God by keeping all the words of this law and these statutes, and doing them . . . and that he may not turn aside from the commandment, either to the right hand or to the left, so that he may continue long in his kingdom, he and his children, in Israel" (Deut. 17:19–20 ESV).

Fig. 4.5 – A recent covering of snow in Jerusalem
Photo by Todd Bolen/Bibleplaces.com

Fig. 4.6 – Modern Eilat (biblical Eloth) was home to a vital port on the Gulf of Aqaba (Red Sea).
Photo by Todd Bolen/Bibleplaces.com

The Political and Economic Context of Isaiah's Ministry

The opening verse of the book records that Isaiah received visions "during the reigns of Uzziah, Jotham, Ahaz and Hezekiah." Based on the names of these Judean rulers, he clearly overlaps with Micah. These same four monarchs were also mentioned as contemporaries of Hosea (cf. Hos. 1:1). The prophet's call is found in chapter 6, dated to "the year that king Uzziah died" (v. 1), which falls around the year 740 B.C. Hezekiah's reign spans from 715–686 B.C. It appears, then, that Isaiah had a prophetic career that lasted around a half-century (ca. 740–690 B.C.), through good times and bad.

Fig. 4.7 – Assyrian deities and protective spirits are typically shown with wings. Relief in Louvre Museum
Photo by James K. Hoffmeier

King Uzziah, known as Azariah in 2 Kings 15,[11] reigned for fifty-two years (792–740 B.C.), with coregencies with his father Amaziah and for a decade at the end of his life with Jotham his son.[12] Thanks to Uzziah's successful military operations in Edom, Judah gained control of the strategic Red Sea port of Eloth (2 Chron. 26:20), meaning that he controlled and taxed maritime trade that contributed to Uzziah's riches. This wealth enabled him to expand his military and dominate neighboring states such as Philistia (26:6–9), and his prowess grew further so that "his fame spread far" (26:15). The indictment against him, however, was that "when he was strong, he grew proud, to his destruction" (26:16 ESV). Uzziah did the unthinkable when he invaded the holy place of the temple to burn incense, which was an exclusively priestly prerogative (26:16–21). When confronted by Azariah "the priest," meaning the High Priest, the king pushed back against the cleric's rebuke. In response, "the LORD had struck him" with leprosy (26:20 ESV). Uzziah was summarily expelled by priests and had to spend the final ten years of his life isolated in his quarters; and the duties of the kingship fell to his son Jotham (26:21).

---

11 The names of kings of Israel vary between books. In the case of Uzziah and Azariah, it could be that one is his name from birth while the other is a throne name adopted at coronation. It might be recalled that David's son when born was named two names are pronounced, Solomon (2 Sam. 12:24) and Jedidiah (2 Sam. 12:25). Solomon may well have been his throne name.

12 Theile, *Hebrew Kings*, 41–42.

Fig. 4.8 – Burial shrine of Tutankhamun with winged goddesses and sun discs to protect the remains of the king *Photo by James K. Hoffmeier*

Fig. 4.9 – Defense walls and tower in Ophel, the area between the City of David and the Temple Mount
Photo by James K. Hoffmeier

Additionally, due to his leprous condition he was ceremonially defiled and was thus forever banned from the temple precinct and its activities (26:21).

Uzziah's impurity stands in stark contrast to the call vision of Isaiah. The very year the leprous king died, Isaiah received a visionary call that was characterized by a dramatic vision of God's holiness. The prophet sees the Lord "seated on a high, elevated throne" (Isa. 6:1 NET), and the winged Seraphim,[13]

---

13 Seraphim (Heb. *śerāp̱îm*) occurs only here in the Bible, but they seem to share characteristic of the cherubim, also winged beings that appear more frequently in the OT. Thus they are one type of angelic being whose task is to worship God and protect his holy presence (as is suggested by the function of their wings). Cherubim first appear

angelic beings that surround God on this throne (cf. Rev. 4:1–11), cry out, "Holy, holy, holy is the LORD of hosts; the whole earth is full of his glory" (Isa. 6:3 ESV). The holiness of Yahweh the God of Israel sharply contrasts with the unclean monarch whose death was just announced. This awesome vision must have forever impressed Isaiah concerning the holiness or otherness of God, and so the holy character of the LORD becomes one of the main themes in the book.

Fig. 4.10 – Sargon II who completed the deportations of Samaria
Photo by Todd Bolen/Bibleplaces.com

Jotham (750–732 B.C.) continued his father's policies and enjoyed continued economic success, building cities and reinforcing walls in the hill of Ophel in Jerusalem (2 Chron. 27). Jotham's name does not occur in the book of Isaiah; no message or events are connected to this king. During the period of Jotham and Uzziah's coregency, however, Tiglath-Pileser III came to power in Assyria in 745 B.C., and he quickly began to expand Assyria into an empire that soon impacted the northern kingdom of Israel (2 Kings 15:17–20).

It was Ahaz, the next ruler of Judah (732–715 B.C.), who had direct dealings with Tiglath-Pileser III as a result of the events recorded in Isaiah 7 (see further below) and in the expanded report in 2 Kings 16:5–16. He also ruled Judah during the years that the Assyrian kings Shalmaneser V (726–722 B.C.) and Sargon II (721–705 B.C.) demolished the kingdom of Israel, and thousands were taken as POWs and exiled to Assyria and northern Media (northern Iran) in 722 B.C. (2 Kings 17). Samaria, Israel's capital, is mentioned a half dozen times in Isaiah 7–10, anticipating this crucial period. One might think that God's judgment on his northern neighbor might give Ahaz pause and motivate him to repentance, but the opposite happened. Under the pressures of potential conquest, he crumbled. "In the time of his distress he became yet more faithless to the LORD" (2 Chron. 28:22 ESV).

Fig. 4.11 – Seal impression which reads "belonging to Ahaz [son of] Jehotham [i.e., Jotham] king of Judah"
in Shlomo Moussaieff-Collection

---

in the garden of Eden as protectors to the Tree of Life to prevent sinful humans from access to the sacred tree (Gen. 3:22–24).

Ahaz is the central figure in the "Immanuel" passages in Isaiah 7–8 (see further below). Even though God gave him signs and urged him to be faithful to his commandments, Ahaz failed and receives the worst possible epithet: "he did not do what was right in the eyes of the Lord his God . . . he walked in the way of the kings of Israel" by engaging in vile pagan religious practices. He "even burned his son as an offering" (2 Kings 16:2–3 ESV). Ahaz closed the temple of the LORD and took sacred vessels from it to make pagan paraphernalia (2 Chron. 28:24). The Chronicler reports on the military setback at the hands of Syria and Israel that Judah experiences as a result of Ahaz's rebellion against God. With the temple of the LORD closed and pagan practice abounding, the wicked king died, but was not honored with a royal burial in "the tombs of the kings of Israel" (2 Chron. 28:27). This exclusion is "a mark of God's judgment."[14]

Hezekiah, one of the most righteous kings in Judah's history, succeeded his evil father. After the ominous notice that Ahaz had closed the doors of the temple (2 Chron. 28:24), Hezekiah's reign began by stressing, "In the first year of his reign, in the first month, he opened the doors of the house of the LORD and repaired them" (2 Chron. 29:3 ESV), followed by reactivating the priests and Levites whose duties had been cut off during the final, dark years of Ahaz, and the temple was consecrated for proper worship (2 Chron. 29:4–36). Additionally, Hezekiah started an aggressive program to stamp out pagan religious practices by demolishing "high places and [breaking] the pillars and cut down the Asherah," and even the bronze serpent that Moses had made for healing the snake bitten Hebrews in the wilderness was destroyed as it had become an object of veneration (2 Kings 18:3–4 ESV). He reinstated celebration of Passover as a national, corporate observance (2 Chron. 30). As a consequence of these reforms and faithfulness, he earned accolades by the writer of 2 Kings, who declared that "there was none like him among all the kings of Judah after him, nor among those who were before him" (18:5 ESV). Because he trusted the LORD and the counsel of Isaiah, he did not submit to the imperial designs of Assyria and survived the attack on Jerusalem that resulted. Isaiah 36–38 and 2 Kings 36–38 contain identical, parallel accounts of the crisis of 701 B.C. In this episode we see that Isaiah and Hezekiah had an unusually cooperative working relationship. More often than not, such relationships were adversarial. Hezekiah's submission to God's word by his prophet, no doubt, was a key to his success as the leader.

---

14 Martin Selman, *2 Chronicles*, Tyndale Old Testament Commentaries (Downers Grove, IL: InterVarsity Press, 1994), 483.

During Hezekiah's near fatal illness (2 Kings 20:1–11 // Isa. 38:2–8), Isaiah advised the king that his passing approached, and accordingly, he should appoint his successor. Hezekiah prayed fervently and wept, which prompted God's extending his life an additional fifteen years. This also involved a sign, the backward movement of the sun's shadow on the sundial (2 Kings 20:8–11; Isa. 38:7–8). The cure involved Isaiah offering the following prescription: "Let them take a cake of figs and apply it to the boil, that he may recover" (Isa. 38:21 ESV). The deadly ailment of Hezekiah called *šeḥîn* is often render "boil" (e.g., KJV, ESV, NIV), but this term applies to a range of skin diseases. Pemphigus is suggested as a possible diagnosis of Hezekiah's condition.[15] "Pemphigus can occur at any age, but it's most often seen in people who are middle-aged or older. It tends to be a long-lasting (chronic) condition, and some types can be life-threatening without treatment," according to the Mayo Clinic.[16] In this case, God prescribed the treatment that would bring healing, namely a cake or poultice of figs applied to the affected area. Medical use of figs is attested among Israel's neighbors, including Mesopotamia, Ugarit, and Egypt.[17] It is noteworthy that God indicates his intent to heal Hezekiah through Isaiah, then gives a miraculous sign to convince the sickly and panicked king that he would be restored to health. God then employs a known medical remedy of the day. This illustrates that God heals through natural and supernatural means.

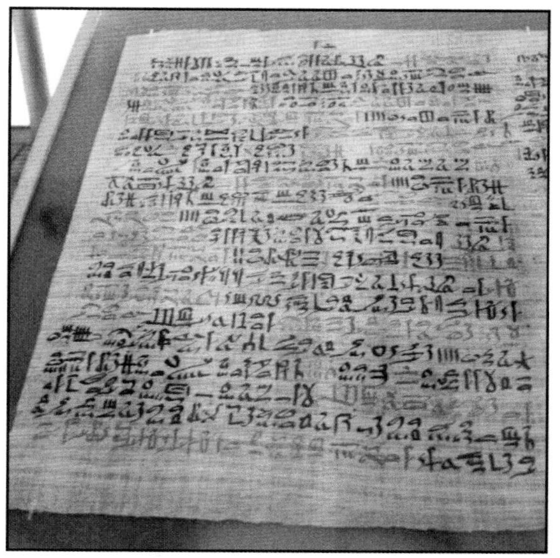

Fig. 4.12 – Ebers Medical Papyrus, a 2nd millennium B.C. document containing medical prescriptions used in Egypt
Photo by Wikimedia Commons

15 Mordechai Cogan and Hayim Tadmor, *2 Kings,* The Anchor Bible (New York: Doubleday, 1988), 255.
16 "Pemphigus," Mayo Clinic, https://www.mayoclinic.org/diseases-conditions/pemphigus/symptoms-causes/syc-20350404.
17 John Watts, *Isaiah 34–66*, World Biblical Commentary (Waco, TX: Word, 1985), 52.

The final personal interaction between Isaiah and Hezekiah was a rebuke over the king's diplomatic gestures with envoys of the Babylonian king, Merodoch-Baladan, in which Hezekiah flaunted the riches of the palace and temple treasury (Isa. 39:1–4). This seems to have been a matter of personal and national pride, for Isaiah rebukes the good king (more on this below). Despite these several occasions of prophetic confrontation, Hezekiah never rebuffed the prophet or sought to harm him as other defiant kings did.

Fig. 4.13 – Merodach-Baladan on right
Photo by James K. Hoffmeier

The Structure and Authorship of Isaiah

The sixty-six chapters of Isaiah makes it one of the longest in the Bible. The book's authorship, formation, and structure have been long debated among scholars.[18] The complexity of the book is readily recognized. As long ago as A.D. 110, Rabbi Moses ben Samuel thought that chapters 1–39 were made up of the genuine words of Isaiah, but that the content from chapter 40 onward was written during the post-exilic or second temple period. This understanding was followed a millennia later by the Spanish rabbinic scholar Ibn Ezra (A.D. 1092–1167). The late-nineteenth to early-twentieth-century German scholar Berhard Duhm promoted the view that Isaiah could be divided into three sections, 1–39, 40–55 (i.e. Deutero or Second Isaiah), and 56–66 (i.e. Trito or Third Isaiah), the product of multiple authors working as later as the mid-fifth century.[19] Duhm's analysis remains widely accepted by many biblical scholars to this day.

Jewish and Christian commentators who accept the traditional approach to Isaianic authorship typically dismiss the multiauthored theory for the book.[20] The latter point to statements by the New Testament authors, writing in the second half of the first century A.D., who quote passages from so-called Second Isaiah

18 Geoffrey Grogan, *Isaiah*, Expositor's Bible Commentary, vol. 6, ed. F. Gaebelein (Grand Rapids: Zondervan, 1986), 6–7.

19 Brevard Childs, *Isaiah: Old Testament Library* (Louisville: Westminster/John Knox, 2001), 1.

20 For a thorough survey of the history of criticism of Isaiah and a defense of its literary and authorial unity, see Harrison, *Introduction to the Old Testament*, 764–800.

Fig. 4.14 – Synagogue of Capernaum. The visible structure is from the Byzantine period that was built over the one from the 1st century A.D. where Jesus taught and healed. *Photo by James K. Hoffmeier*

Fig. 4.15 – Cyrus as a winged figure and wearing an Egyptian style crown at Pasargadae
Photo by Todd Bolen/Bibleplaces.com

and identify the author as "Isaiah the prophet" (e.g., Matthew 3:3 quotes Isaiah 40:3; Matthew 8:17 quotes Isaiah 53:4; Matthew 12:7 quotes Isaiah 42:1–3; Romans 10:16 quotes Isaiah 53:1). Then too, when invited to read Scripture in the synagogue in Nazareth, Jesus was handed "the scroll of the prophet Isaiah," which he unrolled until he reached Isaiah 61:1–2 and read out loud. This narrative and the other New Testament references noted here demonstrate that what "critical scholars" believe to be the product of later authors was considered to be a single work of Isaiah of Jerusalem by the New Testament writers.

This consideration is an important one, but sound arguments have been made for both positions. The following represent only a few arguments for and against the multiple-authorship theory.

Reasons for multiple authorship

1. It has been noted that in chapter 40–66, Isaiah is not mentioned, nor is the name of any Judean king. Cyrus (*kôreš*) alone is named in this section, and God refers to him as "my shepherd" Isa. 44:28 and "my anointed" (i.e., "my messiah") (Isa. 45:1) in order to fulfill God's intent that Jerusalem and the Lord's temple be reconstructed. In hindsight Cyrus king of the Medes and Persia is understood. He was born around 590/589 B.C and assumed the kingship in 559/8 B.C.[21] He conquered Babylon in 539 B.C and died in 530/29 B.C. Upon gaining control of Babylon, he issued an edict that freed the Jews to return to their homeland and rebuild their temple (2 Chron. 36:22–23; Ezra 1, 4:3; 6:1–5).
2. Babylon, it is argued, was not Judah's foe in Isaiah's day. Rather it was Assyria. Babylon, however, is the focus of God's judgment in Second Isaiah (cf. Isa. 43:14; 47:1; 48:14, 20).[22]

---

21 *ABD* 1:1231.

22 For a review of the internal arguments for dating and locating Deutero-Isaiah see *ABD* 3:490–501 and Third Isaiah (*ABD* 3:501–7).

3. Differences in theology, terminology, and literary style have been noticed between the two sections, and differences of theme and emphasis between the sections have been observed, such as the dominance of doom and gloom in first Isaiah, whereas restoration and hope are stressed in second Isaiah.

A response to multiple-authorship arguments

1. Concerning the naming of Cyrus the Persian emperor, traditionally minded scholars follow one of three interpretive options. First, some maintain, while acknowledging that the specificity of this prophecy is without parallel in the prophetic corpus, this is an unusual instance where a prophet, aided with divine insight, is able to name Cyrus (more on this below).[23] A second approach

Fig. 4.16 – Qumran, Cave 1 where great Isaiah Scroll was discovered
Photo by Alexander Schick/bibelausstellung.de

23 Grogan, *Isaiah*, 269.

Fig. 4.17 – Closeup of Qumran Cave 1
Photo by Alexander Schick/bibelausstellung.de

is to see that this is a genuine prophecy that originally had the prophet referred to "my shepherd" (44:28) and God's "anointed" (45:1); but after the restoration of Jerusalem, it was clear that Cyrus had fulfilled this prophecy, and later editors inserted "Cyrus" into the text.[24]

Third, it has been noted that Cyrus the king of Persia, who reigned ca. 559–530 B.C., was actually Cyrus II. His grandfather was Cyrus I, who would have reigned some decades earlier, and still earlier another "Cyrus" is attested who was a contemporary of Ashurbanipal of Assyria (668–627 B.C.). Even earlier Cyruses may have existed.[25] Thus the name, or perhaps title, "Cyrus" was used in the seventh century (or even earlier?), which overlaps with final years of Isaiah's ministry. In Isaiah's day, or shortly thereafter, the name Cyrus may have signaled that the LORD's anointed would come from the area of Medo-Persia.[26]

2. The claim that Babylon is the foe and the place of exile in Isaiah 40–55 is simply not the case. In fact Babylon is mentioned nine times in Isaiah 1–39 and only four times in 40–55. Two passages after chapter 40 (43:14 and 47:1) anticipate God's eventual judgment on Babylon, while 48:12 and 20 are closely connected to the release of the Jews from Babylon—an exile which Isaiah himself announced in 39:5–7 when Hezekiah ruled and Merodoch-Baladan (*Marduk-apla-iddina* in Babylonian) the Chaldean ruled in Babylon (Isa. 39:1). The date of the Babylonian embassy to Jerusalem remains unclear, but 721–710 B.C. and 704–703 B.C. are possibilities[27]; the latter date seems more likely. These are known periods during his nearly

24 Harrison, *Introduction*, 794.
25 The numerical designation of a king is based on the information available to modern historians (e.g., five Shalmanesers in Assyrian, two Nebuchadnezzars in Babylon, three Persian kings named Darius). Because these rulers are historically well established, should an earlier king by the same name be discovered, a renumbering typically does not occur. This is the case with the name Cyrus I and II in the sixth century, but the name occurs during the seventh century (Kitchen, *On the Reliability,* 380). Records of the Medio-Persian region of the seventh century and earlier have not survived, but mention of Median kings are known from Assyrian records.
26 Kitchen, *On the Reliability*, 379–80.
27 Hayes and Irvine, *Isaiah*, 385–86.

sixty-year reign that he ruled from Babylon, while at other times he was on the run from Sennacherib or exiled in neighboring Elam.[28]

3. Many of the issues surrounding style, theology, and the absence of "historical" data from chapter 40 onward are resolved once a different approach to the structure of the book is taken. A breakthrough in understanding the structure of the book of Isaiah occurred with the discovery of the Dead Sea Scrolls in 1947. A total of nineteen copies of Isaiah were discovered at Qumran, and most of them were just fragments.[29] Among the cache of scrolls and scraps in Cave 1 at Qumran was a complete manuscript of Isaiah, measuring 7.3 m (24 feet) long. It was found in a cylindrically shaped clay jar, specially designed to store and preserve manuscripts. Based on the style of writing, a date in the middle of the second century B.C. is assigned to this manuscript, making it the oldest witness to this prophetic book. Chapter divisions that are used today in Bibles were not introduced to the text until centuries later. The great Isaiah scroll, then, has neither chapter nor verse notations, and no breaks or spaces between chapters. It might be thought that if the book was originally consisted of two or more separate books that a joining of Isaiah 1–39 might be somehow indicated from the later prophet or prophets responsible for chapters 40–66 (or 40–55 and 56–66). No such notation or spacing, however, was found on the Qumran Isaiah Scroll between chapters 39 and 40. But to the surprise of the first scholars who examined the text, there was a three-line break at the end of page 28 of a fifty-four-page manuscript (i.e., this scroll is made up of fifty-four sheets of parchment that are sewn together to make a single scroll). This break occurs

Fig. 4.18 – Inside Cave 1 where scrolls were found
Photo by Alexander Schick/bibelausstellung.de

Fig. 4.19 – Dead Sea scroll jar in the Metropolitan Museum
Photo by Alexander Schick/bibelausstellung.de

28 *ABD* 4:704–5.
29 *ABD* 3:470–71.

between chapters 33 and 34, the exact midpoint by chapter of a sixty-six-chapter book!

One of the first scholars who examined the Isaiah Scroll was William Brownlee, a research fellow of the American Schools of Oriental Research in Jerusalem in 1947.[30] Brownlee, along with John C. Trevor, who first photographed the manuscript, were the first academics to study the scroll and to identify it as the book of Isaiah. Brownlee spelled out his structural analysis of the book of Isaiah based on the information provided by the scroll.[31] He proposed that the book was thematically arranged (seven sections each), and not chronologically ordered. Even scholars from the nineteenth century recognized that Isaiah's call to be a prophet occurs in chapter 6, not in chapter 1. By way of contrast, Jeremiah's and Ezekiel's prophetic calls and initial visions are found in the opening chapter/s of their respective books. Isaiah's call, it is plain to see, introduces a section (chaps. 6–8) that is biographical or historical

Fig. 4.20 – Isaiah Scroll (facsimile) showing the division between chapters 33 and 34 at bottom of page 28
Photo by Alexander Schick/bibelausstellung.de

---

30 William Brownlee, "My Eight Years of Scroll Research," *Duke Divinity School Bulletin* 21, no. 3 (1956): 68–81.

31 William Brownlee, *The Meaning of the Qumran Scrolls for the Bible* (Oxford: Oxford University Press, 1964).

in nature. Brownlee, followed by other scholars, believed that the Isaiah Scroll is made up of two original volumes of a single work, and that the structural pattern observed in volume 1 (chaps. 1–33) is mirrored in volume 2 (chaps. 34–66).[32] Recently some scholars have so organized their commentaries. John Watts' two-volume Isaiah commentary, for example, follows this twofold division.[33] Brownlee's thematic pattern is as follows:

Brownlee's thematic pattern		
Chapters	***Subject***	***Chapters***
1–5	1. Ruin and restoration	34–66
6–8	2. Biographical/historical material	36–39
9–12	3. Agents of divine blessing and judgment	40–45
13–23	4. Foreign-nation oracles	46–48
24–27	5. Universal redemption and deliverance for Israel	49–55
28–31	6. Ethical sermons	56–59
32–33	7. Restoration of the nation	60–66

More recent studies of Isaiah as a two-volume anthology or bifid work with parallel structure, suggest that other literary themes are also in play. Examples of a threefold plot narrative include (1) trouble at home, (2) exile abroad, and (3) happy homecoming.[35] This narrative sequence applies to Israel as (1) Israel before the exile (Isa. 1–39), (2) Israel during the exile (Isa. 40–54), and (3) Israel after the exile (Isa. 55–66). This pattern, it is suggested, demonstrates that the book is a unified work.

Because of this thematic arrangement, it is clear why hopeful and positive themes tend to be found later in the book. We also notice that if the book is divided between chapters 33 and 34, the presence of the biographical unit of chapters 36–39, which deal with the events of 701 B.C., means that the second half of the book is not devoid of historically datable narratives, as would be the case if the book is artificially divided between chapters 39 and 40.

---

32 Harrison, *Introduction*, 787–88; and Kitchen, *On the Reliability*, 379.
33 Watts, *Isaiah 1–33*; Watts, *Isaiah 34–66*.
34 Avraham Gileadi, *The Apocalyptic Book of Isaiah* (New York: Hebraeus, 1982), 173.

Fig. 4.21 – Merodach-Baladan on a boundary stone, in Berlin Museum
Photo by James K. Hoffmeier

Mention was made above that Babylon is considered the foe of Judah from Isaiah 40 onward (cf. Isa. 43:14, 47:1, 48:14, 20), which would seem to point to events after 605 B.C. when Nebuchadnezzar first campaigned against Judah and Jerusalem (2 Kings 24:1; Jer. 25:1). To understand why the focus of the second half of Isaiah shifts from Assyria to Babylon as Judah's real foe, one must recognize the significance of the events recounted in chapter 39, which reports:

> At that time Merodach-baladan the son of Baladan, king of Babylon, sent envoys with letters and a present to Hezekiah, for he heard that he had been sick and had recovered. And Hezekiah welcomed them gladly. And he showed them his treasure house, the silver, the gold, the spices, the precious oil, his whole armory, all that was found in his storehouses. There was nothing in his house or in all his realm that Hezekiah did not show them. (Isa. 39:1–2 ESV)

It is thought that the emissaries of Merodach-Baladan came in connection with this Chaldean king's declaration of independence 705 B.C.[35] Although the content of this king's communiqués to Hezekiah of Judah is not disclosed, it seems that Merodach-Baladan was encouraging Judah and its neighbors to rebel against the recently crowned Sennacherib who had just come to the throne. Concurrent distractions in the southern Levant and Babylon, it was thought, might have proved too challenging for the new king to handle, thus giving both regions freedom from Assyrian hegemony. If this interpretation of Merodach-Baladan's mission to Jerusalem is correct, it may explain the timing of Hezekiah's revolt shortly thereafter, followed by Sennacherib's retaliatory invasion of Judah in 701 B.C. It would also mean that the events of chapter 39 actually predate the Assyrian invasion as recorded in chapters 36–38.

35 Hayes and Irvine, *Isaiah*, 385–86.

In response to Hezekiah's friendly reception of the Babylonian envoys, Isaiah offers a startling denunciation and prophetic warning:

> Then Isaiah said to Hezekiah, "Hear the word of the LORD Almighty: The time will surely come when everything in your palace, and all that your predecessors have stored up until this day, will be carried off to Babylon. Nothing will be left, says the LORD. And some of your descendants, your own flesh and blood who will be born to you, will be taken away, and they will become eunuchs in the palace of the king of Babylon." (39:5–7 ESV)

Who would have thought that at time when the Assyrian Empire was reaching its zenith of power, and Babylon was only a troublesome southern province of the Assyria, that Isaiah would foresee this region as the place to which Judah would be deported beginning a century in the future? It is not surprising, then, if Isaiah considered Babylon the ultimate enemy and the prospective destroyer of Judah and that it, not Assyria, would be the focus of oracles from chapter 40 to 66. Micah the prophet, who was also active at this time, also pointed to Babylon as Judah's place of exile (Mic. 4:10).

701 B.C.: THE ASSYRIAN INVASION OF JUDAH

"In the fourteenth year of King Hezekiah's reign, Sennacherib king of Assyria attacked all the fortified cities of Judah and captured them" (Isa. 36:1). This invasion is one of the best-documented events of OT history. The Bible offers several accounts of this event (cf. Isa. 36–37; 2 Kings 18–19; 2 Chron. 32), and Sennacherib's annals and palace reliefs depict the siege and surrender of Hezekiah's defense city of Lachish. Isaiah was not only a witness to what happened in Jerusalem (Isa. 36–37), but he advised Hezekiah on how to respond to the Assyrian threat. Then there is the witness of archaeological data from ancient Judah.

While Judah's outlying cities were under attack, especially Lachish (Isa. 36:2; 37:8), some senior Assyrian military officers went to Jerusalem to pressure the city with psychological intimidation into surrendering in order to avoid the full force of the Assyrian war machine (Isa. 36:4–20). They offered a persuasive case. No other city or nation in the area had withstood the Assyrian advance, and none of their gods had protected their homelands: "Has any of the gods of the

Fig. 4.22 – Sennacherib enthroned on palace reliefs from Nineveh
Photo by Todd Bolen/Bibleplaces.com

nations delivered his land out of the hand of the king of Assyria?" (Isa. 36:18 ESV). They ask, what makes Hezekiah think his god will come to Jerusalem's aid? When this humiliating news was presented to King Hezekiah by his officials, Eliakim and Sheba, the king sent them to consult Isaiah. He told them to report the following to the king: "Do not be afraid of what you have heard. . . . Listen! When he hears a certain report, I will make him want to return to his own country, and there I will have him cut down with the sword" (37:6–7).

The Assyrian peril to Jerusalem was real. The palace reliefs from Nineveh in the British Museum depict Lachish under a relentless attack from archers, slingers, and siege machines with battering rams. The relief also shows a siege ramp in use, which Sennacherib reports that he had constructed. In his annals he declares: "As for Hezekiah, the Judean, I besieged forty-six of his fortified walled cities and surrounding smaller towns. . . . Using packed-down ramps and applying battering rams, infantry attacks by mines, breeches, and siege machines, I conquered them."[36] Recent excavations at the site of Lachish revealed the scars of the Assyrian war against it. The partially intact ramp was revealed, as were slings stones and arrowheads. The victory at Lachish proved to be the highlight of Sennacherib's campaign. Judeans are shown leaving the city for exile, some on foot with sacks over their shoulders, and better-off families are shown riding ox-drawn carts

36 *COS* 2:303.

Fig. 4.23 – Approach to gateway of Lachish *Photo by James K. Hoffmeier*

Fig. 4.24 – Siege ramp built by Assyrians at Lachish to facilitate battering ram attacks on upper walls *Photo by James K. Hoffmeier*

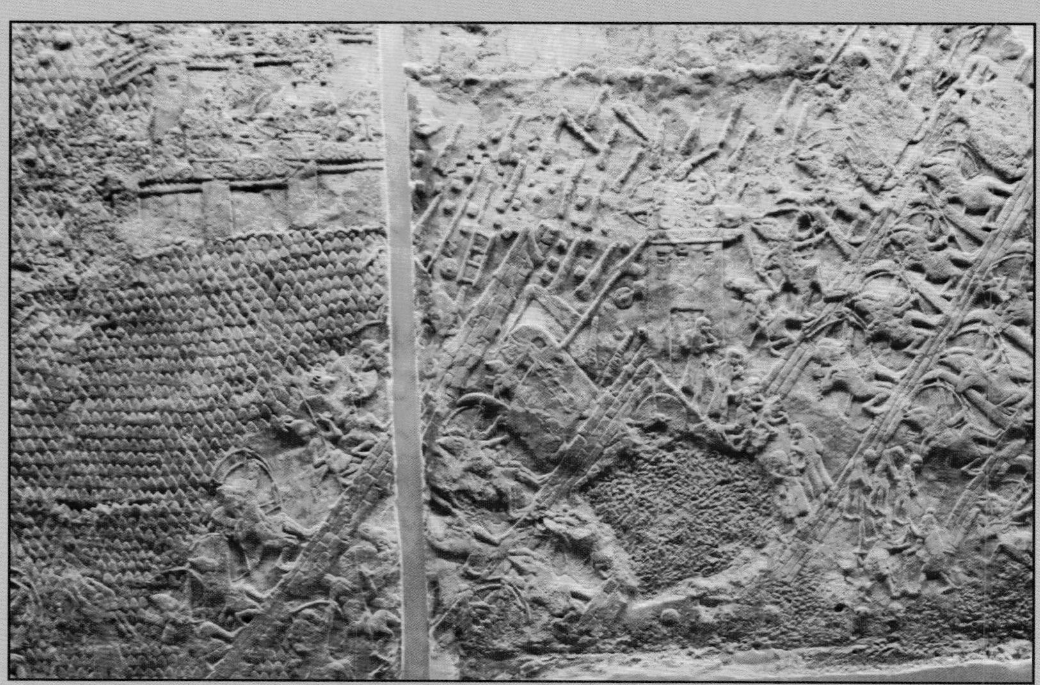

Fig. 4.25 – Lachish reliefs of Assyrian battering ram assaulting city wall, from Nineveh, now in British Museum *Photo by James K. Hoffmeier*

along with their possessions. Some beleaguered Judean men are shown bowing to Sennacherib, who is seated on a portable throne (see Fig. 4.22).

Concerning Hezekiah and Jerusalem, Sennacherib claims: "He himself, I locked up within Jerusalem, his royal city, like a bird in a cage."[37] Jerusalem was not completely caught off guard by this invasion and had, in fact, taken several measures to prepare for battle. The so-called "Hezekiah's Tunnel" was cut at this time from the Gihon Spring on the eastern slopes of Jerusalem to bring water inside the city, rather than letting its waters flow outside into the Kidron Valley, where the Assyrians might have access to the water (2 Kings 20:20; 2 Chron. 32:2–4). This project may have been undertaken while the king was indisposed

37 *COS* 2:303.

Fig. 4.26 – Closeup of battering ram at Lachish *Photo by James K. Hoffmeier*

Fig. 4.27 – Exiles leaving the city gate of Lachish *Photo by James K. Hoffmeier*

due to his illness and Shebna acted without consulting the king and seeking God's approval (Isa. 22:9–11, 15).[38] An inscription within the 533-meter (1,748-foot)–long tunnel marked the midpoint of the tunnel. Surprisingly, Hezekiah's name is not included on this inscription, which supports the theory that Shebna alone acted in this project. From this text it is evident that two teams of workers started at either end and met at the place where the inscription was found. Today a sign marks the meeting point on the surface above the tunnel.

38 Hayes and Irvine, *Isaiah*, 277–78, and Wolf, *Interpreting Isaiah*, 131.

Fig. 4.28 – Judean men groveling before Sennacherib
Photo by James K. Hoffmeier

Fig. 4.29 – Judean family riding into exile with possessions on an oxcart
Photo by James K. Hoffmeier

Fig. 4.30 – Sennacherib prism in the British Museum that contains a report on the siege of Hezekiah's Jerusalem
Photo by James K. Hoffmeier

Fig. 4.31 – Hezekiah's tunnel
Photo by James K. Hoffmeier

Fig. 4.32 – Tunnel inscription at the meeting point, at the Istanbul Archaeological Museum
Photo by Mark Fairchild

Furthermore, Hezekiah refortified walls of Jerusalem and built a new defense wall (Isa. 22:11). A 65-meter (213-foot) long and 7-meter (22.9-foot)–wide section of this stone wall was discovered in "Jewish Quarter" of the old city of Jerusalem. A final measure taken in anticipation of the Assyrian onslaught was that the king organized the distribution of grains and olive oil to key cities. These commodities were stored in clay vessels identified by having a stamp impression on the jar handle that read in Hebrew *lmlk*, that is, "to/for the king," and are identified by a two- or four-winged scarab beetle. In some cases, the name of a city is included, such as Lachish, Hebron, Socoh, and Ziph.[39] More than two thousand *lmlk*-seal impressions have now been discovered, the greatest number of which (more than four hundred) were uncovered at Lachish, which faced the brunt of the Assyrian attack. Nearly three hundred have been found in Jerusalem. So it seems that provisions were distributed to help survive a prolonged siege.

At some point during the assault, Sennacherib hears of the approach of the Cushite king, Tirhaka, who came from Egypt with his armies (Isa. 37:9). At this time, Egypt was under control of rulers

39 William Dever, *Beyond the Texts: An Archaeological Portrait of Ancient Israel and Judah* (Atlanta: SBL Press, 2017), 550–54.

Fig. 4.33 – The road built by Hezekiah to defend from Sennacherib's invasion in 701 B.C.
Photo by James K. Hoffmeier

from Napata in present-day Sudan, also known as the twenty-fifth Dynasty.[40] Tirhaka, that is, Taharka of Egyptian inscriptions, managed to momentarily distract Sennacherib from his attacks on Judah, and met the Egypto-Nubian force at Eltekeh, east of Jerusalem, near the coast. The force from the Nile Valley, likely acting in its own self-interest, was turned back. Jerusalem, however, averted a degrading defeat. The Bible reports that the angel of the LORD struck down the Assyrian camp, forcing Sennacherib to return to Nineveh (Isa. 37:36–38).

40 László Török, *The Kingdom of Kush: Handbook of the Napatan-Meroitic Civilization* (Leiden: Brill, 1997) 131–188.

Fig. 4.34 – *LMLK* jar seal, designating the contents of the jar as distributed by the king
Photo by Alexander Schick/bibelausstellung.de

The fact that the Assyrian palace reliefs only show the assault on Lachish and not Jerusalem indicates that it was not taken. In his annals, Sennacherib remains silent on the fate of Jerusalem, merely reporting that Hezekiah sent him booty back in Nineveh: "Hezekiah . . . sent me after my departure to Nineveh, my royal city . . . 30 talents of gold, 800 talents of silver."[41] This statement seems to unwittingly admit that something disastrous happened; Jerusalem had not been taken. Twenty years later, Sennacherib was assassinated by two of his own sons (Isa. 37:38). Isaiah proved to be right. Jerusalem survived, and never again did Assyria try to take Jerusalem. That was left to the Babylonians (i.e., Nebuchadnezzar), also as the prophet forewarned (Isa. 39:6–7).

41 *COS* 2:303.

Fig. 4.35 – Colossal statue of Tirhaka (Taharka), in Khartoum Museum
Photo by James K. Hoffmeier

Isaiah and the New Testament

In the introduction, mention was made of the "almost 100 citations and some 500 allusions," of Isaiah in the New Testament.[42] After his resurrection, Jesus himself made the connections between the OT prophets and the events surrounding his birth, life, ministry, suffering, death, and resurrection for his disciples. When Jesus joined two of his followers who were walking to Emmaus, he rebuked them for failing to connect the dots between the old prophecies and the recent events surrounding his own death and resurrection: "'How foolish you are, and how slow of heart to believe all that the prophets have spoken! Did not the Christ have to suffer these things and then enter his glory?' And beginning with Moses and all the Prophets, he explained to them what was said in all the Scriptures concerning himself" (Luke 24:25–27).

Jesus expanded on this point to a larger group of disciples in the upper room:

> He said to them, "This is what I told you while I was still with you: Everything must be fulfilled that is written about me in the Law of Moses, the Prophets and the Psalms." Then he opened their minds so

Fig. 4.36 – Present-day Moza, thought to be Emmaus of NT times
Photo by Todd Bolen/Bibleplaces.com

42 Watts, "Isaiah in the New Testament," 213.

> they could understand the Scriptures. He told them, "This is what is written: The Christ will suffer and rise from the dead on the third day, and repentance and forgiveness of sins will be preached in his name to all nations, beginning at Jerusalem." (Luke 24:44–47)

The point is that each part of the OT canon, Moses (i.e., the Torah or Law books), the Prophets, and the Psalms pointed to the coming of Christ, especially the events of holy week that had just occurred.[43] It is fair to conclude that the correlation between the OT prophecies and the life, death, and resurrection of Jesus made in the NT were made by the Lord himself and was a product of later guesswork.

What follows is a list of quotations, many of which "as is written in Isaiah the prophet" or "was spoken by the prophet Isaiah." It seems reasonable to think that these labels were used, and these Isaiah passages cited because Jesus Christ had linked these particular references to him.

NEW TESTAMENT CITATIONS FROM ISAIAH[44]

Matthew 1:23: Virgin with child: Isaiah 7:14
Matthew 3:3: A voice in wilderness: Isaiah 40:3
Matthew 4:15: A light in darkness: Isaiah 9:1
Matthew 8:17: He carried our diseases: Isaiah 53:4
Matthew 12:18: My Chosen Servant: Isaiah 42:1
Matthew 12:21: Justice on the earth: Isaiah 42:4
Matthew 13:14: Closed eyes and ears: Isaiah 6:9
Matthew 15:7: They worship in vain: Isaiah 29:13
Matthew 21:13: A house of prayer: Isaiah 56:7
Mark 1:2: Voice in wilderness: Isaiah 40:3
Mark 4:12: Closed eyes and ears: Isaiah 6:9
Mark 7:6: They worship in vain: Isaiah 29:13

---

43 The book of Psalms heads up the third division of the Hebrew Canon of the OT, Law, Prophets and Writings. See Canon charts in Chapter 1 and discussion there.
44 Compilation from Ron Graham, "Background to Isaiah," https://www.simplybible.com/f591-isaiah-in-new-testament.htm.

Mark 9:48: Fire is not quenched: Isaiah 66:24
Mark 11:17: A house of prayer: Isaiah 56:7
Mark 15:28: Numbered with transgressors: Isaiah 53:12
Luke 2:32: Light to the Gentiles: Isaiah 42:6; 49:6
Luke 3:4: Voice in wilderness: Isaiah 40:3
Luke 4:17: He anointed me to preach: Isaiah 61:1
Luke 8:10: Closed eyes and ears: Isaiah 6:9
Luke 19:46: A house of prayer: Isaiah 56:7
Luke 22:37: Numbered with transgressors: Isaiah 53:12
John 1:23: Voice in wilderness: Isaiah 40:3
John 6:45: All will be taught of God: Isaiah 54:13
John 12:38: Who has believed our report?: Isaiah 53:1
John 12:39: Closed eyes and ears: Isaiah 6:10
Acts 7:48: Heaven is my throne: Isaiah 66:1
Acts 8:32: A lamb to the slaughter: Isaiah 53:7
Acts 13:34: The blessings of David: Isaiah 55:3
Acts 13:47: A light for the Gentiles: Isaiah 49:6
Acts 28:25: Closed eyes and ears: Isaiah 6:9
Romans 2:24: Blasphemy among Gentiles: Isaiah 52:5
Romans 3:15–17: Feet swift to shed blood: Isaiah 59:7–8
Romans 9:19–21: Potter and the clay: Isaiah 29:16
Romans 9:27: Remnant shall be saved: Isaiah 10:22
Romans 9:29: As Sodom and Gomorrah: Isaiah 1:9
Romans 9:33: Stone of stumbling: Isaiah 8:14
Romans 9:33 & 10:11: Believers not disappointed: Isaiah 28:16
Romans 10:15: How beautiful the feet: Isaiah 52:7
Romans 10:16: Who has believed our report?: Isaiah 53:1
Romans 10:20: Found by those who sought me not: Isaiah 65:1
Romans 10:21: Disobedient and obstinate people: Isaiah 65:2
Romans 11:8: A spirit of stupor: Isaiah 29:10
Romans 11:26: Deliverer from Zion: Isaiah 59:20
Romans 11:26: When I forgive their sins: Isaiah 27:9
Romans 11:34: The mind of the LORD: Isaiah 40:13

Romans 14:11: Every knee shall bow: Isaiah 45:23
Romans 15:12: Hope for Gentiles: Isaiah 42:4
Romans 15:12: The Root of Jesse: Isaiah 11:10
Romans 15:21: They shall understand: Isaiah 52:15
1 Corinthians 1:19: The wisdom of the wise: Isaiah 29:14
1 Corinthians 2:9: Eye has not seen: Isaiah 64:4
1 Corinthians 14:21: Speak in strange tongues: Isaiah 28:11
1 Corinthians 15:32: Tomorrow we may die: Isaiah 22:13
1 Corinthians 15:54: Death swallowed up: Isaiah 25:8
2 Corinthians 6:2: Acceptable time, day of salvation: Isaiah 49:8
2 Corinthians 6:17: Come out from among them: Isaiah 52:11
Galatians 4:27: Rejoice barren woman: Isaiah 54:1
Ephesians 6:14–17: Belt, breastplate, helmet: Isaiah 11:5; 59:17
Hebrews 2:13: The children God has given me: Isaiah 8:17–18
1 Peter 1:25: God's word abides forever: Isaiah 40:6
1 Peter 2:6: Precious cornerstone: Isaiah 28:16
1 Peter 2:8: Stone of stumbling: Isaiah 8:14
1 Peter 2:22: He committed no sin: Isaiah 53:9
1 Peter 2:24: By his stripes you were healed: Isaiah 53:5
1 Peter 3:14: Do not be in fear: Isaiah 8:12
Revelation 3:7: The key of David: Isaiah 22:22

Themes in Isaiah

An anthology the size of the book of Isaiah, with all its complexities, has many theological messages, and various themes are introduced. A number of important themes are discussed here. The focus is on those that are mentioned in more detail and are treated in more than one passage, thus stressing their importance to the prophet's overarching message.

Holiness is a fundamental, defining quality of God. Holy (*qādôš*) refers to a quality of being set apart from that which is normal or mundane, and thus is something "other" than the profane or common, that is, the human realm.[45] A

45 *NIDOTT* 3:877–87.

Fig. 4.37 – Statue of Isaiah at St. Mary's on the Lake Seminary, Mundelein, IL
Photo by James K. Hoffmeier

manifestation of God is a theophany, which overwhelms a person, as it does Isaiah. In Hebrew to express a superlative idea, a twofold repetition of a word is used, like king of kings, lord of lords, and holy of holies, that is, "holiest." Here, however, there is a threefold occurrence of "holy" acting as a "super superlative" used here for the first time in Scripture to denote Yahweh's glorious unique, holy quality;[46] God is, as it were, the "most holiest!" The threefold use of holy only occurs again in Scripture the heavenly, apocalyptic vision of God in Revelation 4:8.

Awestruck by this vision of the holiness of the God, Isaiah utters, "'Woe to me! . . . I am ruined! For I am a man of unclean lips, and I live among a people of unclean lips, and my eyes have seen the King, the LORD Almighty'" (Isa. 6:5). This awesome encounter left a powerful and indelible impression on the prophet, so much so that he apparently coined the epithet "the Holy One of Israel" for Yahweh, the God of Israel. This expression occurs twenty-five times in the book, twelve times in Isaiah 1–39 and thirteen times in Isaiah 40–66. If we include the lone variant "the Holy One of Jacob" in Isaiah 29:23, there are thirteen occurrences each in first and second Isaiah. This equal distribution throughout the book illustrates that there are thematic and theological similarities between the two halves of the book.

There are a limited number of occurrences of "the Holy One of Israel elsewhere in the OT: two times each in Jeremiah and Ezekiel, three times in the Psalms, and just once in a historical book, 2 Kings 19:20, where Isaiah himself is the speaker! Then too, the word "holy" (including those in the title "Holy One of Israel") occurs more than sixty times in Isaiah, whereas in Jeremiah (a slightly longer book) there are only ten occurrences. Could it be that Isaiah's dramatic encounter with God in the vision described in chapter 6 shaped the prophet's understanding of God, which caused him to repeat this word spread evenly throughout the book?

46 Motyer, *The Prophecy of Isaiah*, 77.

God's holy character is often paired with some of his other eminent attributes: "the lord your Redeemer is the Holy One of Israel" (Isa. 41:14, 43:14, 47:4, 48:17, 49:7, 54:5); "I am the LORD your God, the Holy One of Israel, your Savior" (Isa. 43:3); "I am the LORD, your Holy One, Israel's Creator, your King" (Isa. 43:15); "the LORD . . . the Holy One of Israel, and its Maker"[47] (i.e., creator: Isa. 45:11); "their Maker . . . the Holy One of Israel" (Isa. 17:7). There is thus a close connection between God's holiness, his saving and redemptive works, and his role as creator.

> ***"The Holy One of Israel"***
>
> First, let us consider those literary and thematic similarities that occur in both halves of Isaiah, regardless of how one divides the book (i.e., 1–39; 40–66 or 1–33; 34–66), the holiness of the Lord is a major emphasis. Mentioned already is the vision of Isaiah in chapter 6 in which the prophet's call occurs. The description of the vision includes:
>
> I saw the Lord, high and exalted, seated on a throne; and the train of his robe filled the temple. Above him were seraphim, each with six wings: With two wings they covered their faces, with two they covered their feet, and with two they were flying. And they were calling to one another:
>
> "Holy, holy, holy is the LORD
> Almighty;
> the whole earth is full of his
> glory." (Isa. 6:1–3)

God Judges

The fact that God judges wrongdoing in order to establish justice vis-à-vis the covenant stipulations is consistent with his holy character. Centuries before, Abraham raised the question when he wrestled with the prospect that the righteous might feel God's wrath when judging the guilty: "Will not the Judge of all the earth do right?" (Gen. 18:25). Abraham was confident that because God is a righteous judge, he will adjudicate things in a fair way. That God Yahweh is recognized as "Judge of all the earth" is acknowledged in the biblical name Jehoshaphat, meaning "Yahweh is Judge."

Like his contemporaries Micah and Hosea, Isaiah uses juridical language to issue warnings of judgment on Judah. "Hear me, you heavens! Listen, earth!" (Isa. 1:2) is an appeal to the covenant witnesses of the Deuteronomy covenant renewal (Deut. 4:26, 31:28), and stands as the opening statement of the book. The court setting is unmistakable.[48] God is bringing legal complaints against his covenant people, here called "children" (literally "sons"). "Son" is a term used in ancient treaty texts of a vassal (see note 50 in Chapter 3; cf. 2 Sam. 7:14). God describes his rebellious vassal as follows:

> I reared children [literally "sons"] and brought them up,
> but they have rebelled against me.

---

47 "Him" in this context is the aforementioned "Cyrus."
48 Sweeney, *Isaiah 1–39*, 63–67.

> The ox knows his master,
>   the donkey his owner's manger,
> but Israel does not know,
>   my people do not understand. (Isa. 1:2–3)

The images of farm animals are especially belittling. Oxen and donkeys know who their master is, but "Israel does not know." As was observed in the book of Hosea, "knowing" God is emphasized in the prophets to characterize the intimate relationship God expects that is expressed by fidelity to him and obedience to the covenant stipulations.[49] A slightly different nuance is also intended here. The expression "does not know" and "do not understand" are synonymously paired, as if to say that Israel does not recognize who is her master (*ba'al*) and owner who provides for her.[50] By contrast even common farm animals realize who feeds and cares for them.

Isaiah denounces the leaders of Jerusalem: "Hear the word of the LORD, you rulers of Sodom; listen to the instruction of our God, you people of Gomorrah!" (Isa. 1:10). To equate Jerusalem with Sodom and Gomorrah, cities demolished by God in Abraham's day, would have been shocking and offensive to the prophet's audience. God was not impressed with the religious observances and pious prayers that were not coupled with living according to God's laws (1:11–15). Once again "seek justice. . . . Take up the cause of the fatherless, plead the case of the widow" is the prophet's cry (1:17).

The theme of doing what God desires is found in the song of the vineyard in Isaiah 5:1–7. Israel is likened to a choice vineyard (*sôrēq*), named after the Sorek Valley, west of Jerusalem in the Shepheleh region. It might be likened the Napa Valley of ancient Israel, where the best vintages grew (cf. Jer. 2:21). God's design for Israel was that through obedience and faithfulness to God they were to produce rich, delicious fruit, namely justice (*mîšpāṭ*) and righteousness (*ṣᵉdāqâ*) (Isa. 5:7). But alas, only bad and useless grapes were produced. In this case, the prophet employs a striking wordplay in which similar-sounding words are used, but they have the opposite meaning. Thus God looked for *mîšpāṭ*, justice, but instead found *mîśppāḥ*, bloodshed or "legal

49 *NIDOTT* 2:409–10.

50 "Baal" means "lord," "master," and "husband." "Baal," when associated with the Canaanite deity, is a title for the god whose name is Hadad.

infringement,"[51] and he sought *ṣᵉdāqâ*, righteousness or "fairness" (NET), but instead discovered *ṣe'āqâ*, a cry "for help from the oppressed."[52]

As a consequence of the failure of the people to obey the Torah and do what is just and right, God would remove his protection from the vineyard,

Fig. 4.38 – The Sorek Valley and Nahal (stream) Sorek
Photo by David Biven/Bibleplaces.com

51 *HALOT* 641.
52 *HALOT* 1043.

Israel, and "it will be destroyed . . . it will be trampled. . . . I will command the clouds not to rain on it" (5:5–6). The lack of rain signals an unleashing of covenant curses on the people and the land (Lev. 26:20; Deut. 28:23–24).

This illustrative song surely stands behind Jesus's parable of the tenants found in the Synoptic Gospels (Matt. 21:33–41; Mark 12:1–12; Luke 20:9–19). Here Jesus applies Isaiah's vineyard parable to the people of Jerusalem in his day. It is noteworthy that while most interpretations of the parables of Jesus escaped the hearers, this one did not because Isaiah included its interpretation (5:5–7). Hence there was no uncertainty as to its meaning when Jesus retold Isaiah 5. Matthew reports, "When the chief priests and the Pharisees heard his parables, they perceived that he was speaking about them" (Matt. 21:45 ESV), and so they wanted to do away with him. Thus, as Brevard Childs observed of Jesus's retelling the parable, it "evoked such a violent rejection from the tenants that they murder the son,"[53] precisely as the leaders of the first century did to Christ.

God's judgment falls hard on Israel over the final years of the Northern Kingdom, culminating in fall of Samaria in 722 B.C. (2 Kings 17). Isaiah lived through these dark days and would have been well aware of the demise of his northern neighbor. In fact, as the noose of Assyria tightened around Samaria's neck, King Hoshea sought help from Egypt (2 Kings 17:4). Isaiah warned that Pharaoh and Egypt were unreliable and weak allies (Isa. 30:1–5, 7; 31:1–3).[54] Divine judgment would not be averted by any human agent.

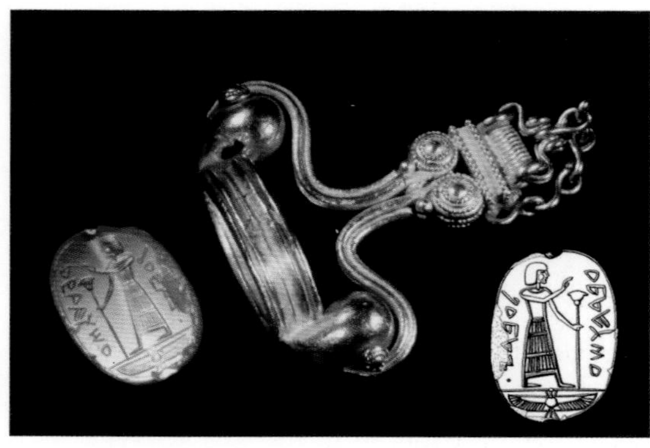

Fig. 4.39 – Seal of 'Abdi the high official of King Hoshea is Samaria, in Shlomo Moussaieff-Collection
Photo by Richard Wiskin / drawing Robert Deutsch, provided by Alexander Schick

In 701 B.C. Judah and Jerusalem experienced the heavy hand of Assyria (see excursus "701 B.C." above). In chapter 10, Assyria is called "the rod of my anger, in whose hand is the club of my wrath! I send him against a godless nation, I will dispatch him against a people who anger me" (vv. 5–6). The point is that Assyria's aggression against Israel and Judah was no accident of history, but a vehicle of God's chastisement on his people.

53 Childs, *Isaiah*, 46.

54 Scholars differ over whether Egypt's assistance was being sought by Samaria in 726/5 B.C. or by Hezekiah in connection with Sennacherib's invitation of Judah in 701. I have argued in favor to the earlier crisis; see James K. Hoffmeier, "Egypt's Role in the Events of 701 B.C.: A Rejoinder to J. J. M. Roberts," in *Jerusalem in Bible and Archaeology*, eds. A. Vaughn and A. Killebrew (Atlanta: Society of Biblical Literature, 2003), 285–90.

Divine warnings and judgments in Isaiah are directed primarily at Israel and Judah. As Isaiah 1 (the beginning of volume 1) summons the covenant witnesses to announce judgment, Isaiah 34 (the beginning of volume 2) starts with a strikingly similar appeal, this time all nations and peoples, not just Israel, are called to account: "Let the earth hear, and all that is in it, the world, and all that comes out of it! The LORD is angry with all nations" (vv. 1–2). God's condemnation of foreign lands is the focus of oracles in chapters 13–23, and 46–48 in the fourth section of each volume, demonstrating the universal nature of God's judgment and his sovereignty over the entire world.

It is unclear whether the prophecies against foreign nations were just for the benefit of the covenant people—that is, so that they would realize that God's judgment was not limited to Israel—or whether prophetic messages were taken to neighboring nations to communicate divine warnings. There is, indeed, some evidence to suggest that efforts were made to send prophetic messages to other nations. Jonah (see chap. 3), it will be recalled, traveled to distant Nineveh. Elisha went to Damascus to communicate God's word to king Ben Hadad (2 Kings 8:7–8). Not only did Jeremiah travel to Egypt to delivery his message (Jer. 43–44), but he also sent a scroll with a prophetic word to Babylon with a Judean official to read the oracle publicly (Jer. 51:59–63). Furthermore, God also instructed Jeremiah to communicate a divine message to kings of the neighboring states of Edom, Moab, Ammon, Tyre, and Sidon through their respective ambassadors who had convened a summit in Jerusalem on how to deal with the advancing Nebuchadnezzar (Jer. 27:1–7). The fact that God extends warnings of coming judgment to foreign nations illustrates his grace on them.

Isaiah 22:1, an oracle "concerning the valley of vision," is apparently a symbolic name for Jerusalem.[55] God removes Judah's (supernatural?) protection (22:8a). Verses 22:8b–11 constitute a prose unit that is introduced with the formula "in that day," usually signaling a future event, even an eschatological one in some contexts (Isa. 22:12). The breached walls and vulnerable defenses are mentioned (22:9). The location of these two messages is curious as it occurs in the foreign nation section (Isa. 13–23). The recipient of God's warning or judgment in the first section is obscure. The pronoun in the phrase "*You* looked to the weapons" (22:8b ESV) is masculine singular. Does this refer to Judah collectively as a man or Hezekiah the king? In the following verses of this passage, "you" occurs five times in the plural form. So who is evaluating Jerusalem's weakened

55 Motyer, *Prophecy of Isaiah*, 182.

state, restoring and building defense walls and making a new reservoir for the city's water supply (22:9–11a)? If Hezekiah and the people of Jerusalem, they are condemned for not completely trusting God through the Assyrian crisis.

In the following section Shebna, the manager of the palace and perhaps the equivalent of the prime minister, receives strong condemnation (22:13–19).[56] Interestingly, this is the only time a specific individual is singled out for judgment in the book of Isaiah, and a nonroyal figure at that. Could it be that Shebna and his associates are the ones judged in the previous passage?

Shebna is charged with arrogantly cutting an impressive tomb out of rock for himself (Isa. 22:15–16). Verse 11 adds, "You built a reservoir between the two walls for water of the Old Pool." This seems to refer to "Hezekiah's Tunnel," even though King Hezekiah is not mentioned in this chapter. The tunnel inscription also does not mention Hezekiah, which one might expect of a major public works project. It has been suggested that Shebna's offense was that when the king was seriously ill (Isa. 38), that he arrogated to himself kingly responsibilities by making the tunnel and then carving out his extravagant tomb.[57] Just outside the walled city of Jerusalem in the present-day village of Silwan, an elegant rock-cut tomb was discovered that some have suggested was Shebna's. Its inscription has a critical break where the name is written. It reads, "This is [the tomb of Sheban] iah who is over the [royal] household."[58] This is likely Shebna's tomb.

Shebna's judgment as announced by Isaiah 22:17–18 is, "Beware, the Lord is about to take firm hold of you and hurl you away, you mighty man. He will

Fig. 4.40 – Shebna inscription from Silwan tomb, now in the British Museum
Photo by James K. Hoffmeier

56 *ISBE* 4:547–58.
57 Hayes and Irvine, *Isaiah*, 283–86.
58 *COS* 2:180.

roll you up tightly like a ball and throw you into a large country. There you will die and there the chariots you were so proud of will become a disgrace to your master's house." His ultimate fate is not recorded in the OT.

Exile Anticipated—a Remnant Will Return

The theme of exile is met quite early in Isaiah. "My people will go into exile for lack of understanding" (literally "knowledge": Isa. 5:13). It occurs again in the name of Isaiah's son, Shear-jashub, which means "a remnant will return." The introduction of the Shear-jashub occurs in the narrative regarding the threat to Jerusalem by the Syro-Israelite coalition in 734 B.C. His name symbolically anticipates and exile and the return of a remnant (see chap. 7; for further treatment on this, see the next section).

Fig. 4.41 – Scene of Israelites from Trans-Jordan being led into exile in Tiglath-Pileser's day, from the British Museum. *Photo by A. D. Riddle/Bibleplaces.com*

Return from exile is found Isaiah 35:10 in "those the LORD has rescued will return. They will enter Zion with singing; everlasting joy will crown their heads. Gladness and joy will overtake them, and sorrow and sighing will flee away," a verse which incidentally occurs word-for-word in so-called "Second" Isaiah (Isa. 51:11). Thus even in the early days of Isaiah, as the northern tribes were being deported (and a similar fate was anticipated for Judah), the idea of a surviving and returning remnant was held out as a note of hope.

Isaiah 3 contains warnings of judgment—"woe to them" (3:9)—for Judah and Jerusalem; their sins are likened to that of Sodom (3:8), whom God destroyed in Abraham's day (Gen. 19:23–29). With this prospect of obliteration forthcoming, Isaiah 4 likens God's people to "the Branch of the LORD" that will be among "the survivors in Israel" (4:2). The branch metaphor is "family tree" related,[59] the idea being that just as a tree might be cut down, a branch will grow out of the roots once again. So too with Israel, like a tree that has been felled,[60] God will start over again with new shoots and will cover and protect them with "a cloud of smoke by day and a glow of flaming fire by night" (4:5), just as the Lord watched over Israel in the wilderness after the exodus (Exod. 13:22; 14:24).

Previously, mention was made of Cyrus, king of Persia in Isaiah 44:21–45:4. Under his authority as God's "anointed," Jerusalem and the house of the LORD will be rebuilt (44:28). What is remarkable here is that a pagan king is God's chosen instrument, "messiah," who was brought to power to fulfill God's purposes to restore Judah for God's remnant even though "you [Cyrus] do not know me" (45:4 ESV). This detail shows us that God sovereignly controls the rise and fall or kings and nations, and uses different types of individuals, even nonbelievers, to fulfill his purposes.

God with Us

During times of crisis—and the book of Isaiah deals with two them historically (the Syro-Ephraimite war against King Ahaz and the Assyrian invasion in Hezekiah's day), as well the future exile in Babylon—God comforts his people and is with them. Even with Judah's exile a century away, once announced (Isa. 39:5–7), God offers words of comfort and consolation to his people (Isa. 40:1–2; 51:12).

Perhaps the best-known illustration of God's presence with his people occurs in the Immanuel passage in Isaiah 7. "The virgin will conceive and give

---

59 Motyer, *Prophecy of Isaiah*, 65.

60 The "branch" (*ṣemaḥ*) image is used elsewhere in the prophets for the messianic king (cf. Jer. 23:5; Zech. 6:12).

birth to a son, and will call him Immanuel," which means, "God with us" (v. 14). These familiar words from the Gospel of Matthew (1:23) are customarily recited at Christmas time and associated with the annunciation of the birth of Jesus of Nazareth. These familiar words, however, were originally delivered to wicked King Ahaz (735–715 B.C.) of Judah in Jerusalem around 734/5 B.C. by Isaiah, when the combined forces of King Pekah of Samaria (752–732 B.C.) and Rezin king of Damascus threatened Jerusalem (Isa. 7:1–2). One obvious way that God is with his people is through his communicating through Isaiah the prophet to guide them through this calamity. God, however, offers even more than that.

Isaiah meets Ahaz in Jerusalem to offer words of assurance that Judah will survive this onslaught: "If you do not stand firm in your faith, you will not stand at all" (7:9); put positively, if you trust God in this crisis, you will survive. Additionally, God offers him a sign to assure the fearful king that the LORD will be with Jerusalem in its hour of need, by pointing to the birth of "Immanuel." Clearly in this context of 734/5 B.C., it would be of little consolation that Jesus would be born in Bethlehem seven hundred years later! This suggests that something of a more immediate nature was in view, as well as a future application.[61]

"Therefore the Lord himself will give you a sign: The virgin will conceive and give birth to a son, and will call him Immanuel" (Isa. 7:14). In the Old Testament context, the "virgin" was not expected to miraculously give birth to a child without the agency of a man. In fact, a Ugaritic (Canaanite) text from five centuries earlier reads "a virgin will give birth," which "means that a particular virgin would soon be engaged and that after her marriage she would become the mother of a son."[62] With this understanding in mind, it suggests that within a year, this birth will take place and the child will be named Immanuel, signaling God's presence to save Jerusalem out of this invasion.

Who then is the mother and child that illustrate God's presence in Isaiah 7? In the very next chapter we are informed, "I went to the prophetess and she conceived and bore a son" (8:3 ESV). "I" must be the prophet himself, and "the prophetess" is his wife, and suggests that she too prophesied,[63] or that as "the bearer of the Lord's word" even if she did not speak publicly.[64] One might expect that the son who was born would be named "Immanuel" to symbolize God's presence, but this is not the case. Rather, he receives the unusual but

---

61 Grogan, *Isaiah*, 59–65.
62 Wolf, *Interpreting Isaiah*, 91.
63 Watts, *Isaiah 1–33*, 113.
64 Motyer, *Prophecy of Isaiah*, 90.

figurative name Maher-shalal-hashbaz (8:1, 3), meaning "swift to come is the spoil, speedy is the prey."[65] A clarifying statement is offered. Before the boy is old enough to speak, "the wealth of Damascus and the spoil of Samaria will be carried away before the king of Assyria" (8:4 ESV). While this son's name points to the how the current enemies will be defeated by the Assyrians, the down side is that it opens the door to future and greater destruction by the Assyrians.[66]

Two questions must be asked relative to the historical context of King Ahaz. First, did he stand firm and trust God in the midst of the current emergency, a condition for Judah's survival? And second, does this historical narrative section (Isa. 6–8) record the birth of a child named Immanuel?

Fig. 4.42 – Nimrud relief of an enemy who submitted to Tiglath-Pileser III, literally depicted under the king's foot *Photo by Todd Bolen/Bibleplaces.com*

65 Childs, *Isaiah*, 72.
66 Avraham Gileadi, *The Literary Message of Isaiah* (New York: Hebraeus, 1994), 82–83.

Concerning the first point, 2 Kings provides further information on the Damascus-Samaria attack on Jerusalem. Under this stress, Ahaz caved and summoned Tiglath-Pileser III, with gold and silver as gifts, he submitted to his authority: "I am your servant and vassal [lit. "your son"]," he said, thus agreeing to be the vassal of Assyria (16:7–8). Indeed Tiglath-Pileser III's inscriptions indicate that his forces attacked Damascus in 733 B.C. Many leaders were killed and POWs taken,[67] but King Rezin fled. Assyrian records for the next year have not survived.[68] The Assyrians, 2 Kings 16:9 states, caught up with the king of Damascus and slew him. This means that King Ahaz neither trusted God nor believed Isaiah's message.

What became of Immanuel (Isa. 7:14)? In the next chapter, we learn Isaiah's wife, "the prophetess," "conceived and gave birth to a son," who was named Maher-shalal-hash-baz (Isa. 8:3), not Immanuel. We recall that it is Isaiah who later in this chapter mentioned the symbolic nature of his children (8:18). Due to Ahaz failing God's test, could it be that the name that the sign-son, "Maher-shalal-hash-baz," signified that Judah would not experience the long-term peace and God's protective presence that "Immanuel" would have represented?

The Immanuel prophecy is left dangling. Alec Motyer proposes that "Isaiah released Immanuel from the then present and pointed on to his birth 'in the afterwards.'"[69] In the very next chapter, the section after the "biographical/historical material" (Isa. 6–8), we read familiar words: "The people walking in darkness have seen a great light; on those living in the land of tdeep darkness a light has dawned" (Isa. 9:2), followed by news of the birth yet another child.

> For to us a child is born, to us a son is given, and the government will be on his shoulders. And he will be called Wonderful Counselor, Mighty God, Everlasting Father, Prince of Peace. Of the greatness of his government and peace there will be no end. He will reign on David's throne and over his kingdom, establishing and upholding it with justice and righteousness from that time on and forever. (Isa. 9:6–7)

The Gospel writer Luke connects the birth of this child from the royal line of David with Jesus (Luke 2:11), just as Matthew connected the birth of

---

67 *COS* 2:284–86.
68 Younger, *The Arameans*, 651.
69 Motyer, *The Prophecy of Isaiah*, 90–91.

Immanuel in Isaiah 7:14 with that of Jesus in Bethlehem (Matt. 1:23). The ultimate fulfillment of God's promise to be with his people comes in the form of the incarnate Son of God: "The Word became flesh and made his dwelling among us" (John 1:14).

The God Who Alone Knows the Future is God!

Ever since the Enlightenment (eighteenth century), with its rationalistic and antisupernaturalistic assumptions, many critical scholars have looked askance at the miraculous in Scripture, and this skepticism has carried over to the predictive element of prophecy. Interpreters of the Bible who have adopted this worldview maintain that prophets only could speak in the vaguest of terms about the future. Isaiah may be able to speak of pending exile for Judah in the aftermath of the northern kingdom's demise and deportation in 722 B.C. One may even allow that he anticipated that the attack on Jerusalem by Samaria and Damascus in 734 B.C. would not succeed (see previous section). But for Isaiah in the late eighth or early seventh century to announce that Judah would be deported to Babylon when they were not a dominate power (Isa. 39) and that Jerusalem would be rebuilt along with its temple by a king named Cyrus a century and a half later is

Fig. 4.43 – Assyrian Soldiers carrying of the statues of deities from a conquered temple in Nimrud relief of Tiglath-Pilerser III *Photo by A. D. Riddle/Bibleplaces.com*

deemed impossible for such critical scholars. Hence chapters 44 and 45 (as well as the other chapters surrounding this unit) must have been written after the fact. Even Brevard Childs, a biblical theologian who upheld the entire canon of Scripture to be theologically important, demurred with the traditional view that Isaiah predicted the role of Cyrus in Jerusalem's re-establishment, asserting, "I strongly doubt that the problem can be resolved by portraying the eighth-century prophet as a clairvoyant of the future".[70] Nevertheless, the following discussion suggests how essential it is for Israel's God to know the future.[71]

Fig. 4.44 – Egyptian priests carry the sacred bark of the god, Amun-Ra, at Medinet Habu Temple of Ramesses III *Photo by James K. Hoffmeier*

70 Childs, *Isaiah*, 3–4.
71 Gileadi, *The Apocalyptic Book of Isaiah*, 186–89.

One of the important themes that runs like a thread through the tapestry of Isaiah 40–45 is that Yahweh, the God of Israel, is incomparable to pagan deities who are represented by idols. "With whom, then, will you compare God? To what image will you liken him?" (40:18); a similar question is asked by God: "'To whom will you compare me? Or who is my equal?' says the Holy One" (40:25). In Isaiah 45:20 the pagans gods are mocked for having to be carried about, rather than moving about on their own.

Consequently, the challenge is issued to idol worshipers: "'Present your case (*rîb*),' says the LORD. 'Set forth your arguments,' says Jacob's King. 'Tell us, you idols, what is going to happen. Tell us what the former things were, so that we may consider them and know their final outcome. Or declare to us the things to come, tell us what the future holds, so we may know that you are gods'" (Isa. 41:21–23a). As elsewhere in Isaiah and the prophets, a legal case is used to argue God's position. He is differentiated from and hence superior to any manmade deity because he knows and controls the future. In this instance Yahweh not only brought invading armies from the north (41:25), but he "foretold it" . . . "I was the first to tell Zion" through "a messenger" (vv. 26–27). His messenger, or prophet(s), had warned of what was coming.

The argument continues in chapter 42: "I am the LORD; that is my name! I will not yield my glory to another or my praise to idols. See, the former things have taken place, and new things I declare; before they spring into being I announce them to you" (vv. 8–9). God's ability to plan and announce the future continues in the next chapter, as the "case" continues and witnesses testify to God's unique ability:

> Do not be afraid, for I am with you; I will bring your children from the east and gather you from the west. I will say to the north, "Give them up!" and to the south, "Do not hold them back." Bring my sons from afar and my daughters from the ends of the earth. . . . All the nations gather together and the peoples assemble. Which of them foretold this and proclaimed to us the former things? Let them bring in their witnesses to prove they were right, so that others may hear and say, "It is true." (43:5–6, 9)

Isaiah 44 picks up the theme of God's unique foreknowledge.

> "This is what the LORD says—Israel's King and Redeemer, the LORD Almighty: I am the first and I am the last; apart from me there is no God. Who then is like me? Let him proclaim it.
>
> Let him declare and lay out before me what has happened since I established my ancient people, and what is yet to come — yes, let him foretell what will come.
>
> Do not tremble, do not be afraid. Did I not proclaim this and foretell it long ago? You are my witnesses. Is there any God besides me? No, there is no other Rock; I know not one."
>
> All who make idols are nothing, and the things they treasure are worthless. Those who would speak up for them are blind; they are ignorant, to their own shame.
>
> Who shapes a god and casts an idol, which can profit nothing? (Isa. 44:6–9)

In what follows, Isaiah brings his argument to its climax. Not only does the prophet divinely predict that Judah will be exiled in Babylon (cf. Isa. 39:5–7), as does Micah (4:10), but that God the Creator will bring the exiles back to the Promised Land, Jerusalem and the temple will be rebuilt—and to clinch the case for Yahweh's sovereignty and foreknowledge, the name of the leader is disclosed under whose command this will occur!

> I am the LORD,
> the Maker of all things,
> who stretches out the heavens,
> who spreads out the earth by myself . . .
> who carries out the words of his servants
> and fulfills the predictions of his messengers,
> who says of Jerusalem, "It shall be inhabited,"
> of the towns of Judah, "They shall be rebuilt,"
> and of their ruins, "I will restore them,"
> who says to the watery deep, "Be dry,
> and I will dry up your streams,"
> who says of Cyrus, "He is my shepherd
> and will accomplish all that I please";
> he will say of Jerusalem, "Let it be rebuilt,"
> and of the temple, "Let its foundations be laid." (Isa. 44:24, 26–28)

Fig. 4.45 – "He is my shepherd" – A Pharaoh from 19th century B.C. portrayed with a shepherd's crook, in Metropolitan Museum, New York *Photo by A. D. Riddle/Bibleplaces.com*

The entire case being made is that Yahweh alone is God, along with proof that he is God and that the idols are nothing is his ability to plan, announce, and orchestrate the future, including naming his anointed one Cyrus, who is God's agent to end the exile of the Jews and to bring them back their ancestral land, and rebuild Jerusalem and its temple. The case hinges on being able to announce well in advance the role of Cyrus and to name him: "I summon you by name" (Isa. 45:4). Remove "Cyrus" from the narrative, the climax of Isaiah's argument, and the case crumbles. From this point of view, it is hard to explain the occurrence of Cyrus in 44:28 and 45:1 as later additions to the text, and worse still to view the entire section of 40–45 as happening after the exile and rebuilding of Jerusalem for that would make the argument of Yahweh and his messenger's ability to announce the future a sham.

The key piece of evidence having been presented in this hearing, the verdict is obvious: "I am the LORD, and there is no other; apart from me there is no God," a claim that is made repeatedly throughout the balance of chapter 45 (vv. 5, 6, 11, 14, 18, 21, 22).

The argument comes to a conclusion by saying: "Declare what is to be, present it—let them take counsel together. Who foretold this long ago, who declared it from the distant past? Was it not I, the LORD? And there is no God apart from me, a righteous God and a Savior; there is none but me" (Isa. 45:21).

THE BOOK OF MICAH: ZION A PLOWED FIELD

"What does the LORD require of you?"
—Micah 6:8

This prophet lived in the small village Moresheth, a satellite or suburb of Gath, hence the name Moresheth-Gath (Mic. 1:1). The mention of Gath (1:10) and nearby Lachish (1:13) shows that this village was in the Shephaleh, the transitional zone between the Mediterranean coastal plain and the Judean hill country.[72] The book bearing his name reveals very little about Micah the man and his social status, although based on the nature of the area where he lived, it has been suggested that he was small farmer or craftsman.[73] A century after he proclaimed his messages, his words are recalled when the prophet Jeremiah was in trouble with the religious leaders in 609 B.C. for prophesying the doom of Jerusalem. The elders of Jerusalem rejected angry calls for Jeremiah's death because his prophecy was consistent with that of "Micah of Moresheth" who "prophesied in the days of Hezekiah king of Judah." He told all the people of Judah, "This is what the LORD Almighty says: 'Zion will be plowed like a field, Jerusalem will become a heap of rubble, the temple hill a mound overgrown with thickets'" (Jer. 26:18 > Mic. 3:12).

Fig. 4.46 – The Shephelah region, the transitional zone between the hill country of Judah and the coastal plain occupied by the Philistines *Photo by Todd Bolen/Bibleplaces.com*

72 Rainey, *Sacred Bridge*, 223.
73 Bullock, *An Introduction*, 126.

Fig. 4.47 – View of Moresheth-Gath
Photo by Todd Bolen/Bibleplaces.com

They pointed out that Hezekiah and the leaders of his day did not kill Micah, and since Jeremiah and Micah's messages agreed, Jeremiah should not be harmed. What this citation illustrates is that Micah's prophecies were known in Jerusalem and considered authoritative at the end of the seventh century.

His name, a shortened form of "Micaiah" (like that of the prophet from the previous century; see chap. 2) means "Who is like Yahweh?" This in turn is a variation on the name Michael, "Who is like God?" The obvious point of the prophet's name is that there is no deity comparable to the God of Israel. Hence in the close section of the prophecy, he asks, "Who is a God like you, who pardons sin and forgives the transgression?" (Mic. 7:18)

The Times of Micah

Micah prophesied during the reigns of the Judean kings Jotham (750–732 B.C.), Ahaz (735–715 B.C.), and Hezekiah (715–686 B.C.), according to the introductory verse. This makes him a contemporary of Hosea (see chap. 3) and Isaiah (see above). The audience is clearly named: "the vision he saw concerning Samaria and Jerusalem" (Mic. 1:1). When Jotham assumed the throne in 740 B.C. after a decade of coregency with his father Azariah/Uzziah (2 Chron. 26:21), Tiglath-pileser III was already in power, with eyes focused on the east Mediterranean world. In 742 B.C. Menahem of Israel paid tribute to the Assyrian, and again in 737 B.C. Israel was forced to pay tribute to him (2 Kings 15:19–20).[74] So it is no surprise that Israel should feel vulnerable to Assyria, and in 732 B.C. Israelite territory was encroached and the earliest deportation of Israelite citizens occurred (2 Kings 15:29). Micah's warnings to the northern kingdom came at a desperate time.

Fig. 4.48 – Ancient Ashdod from the air
Photo by Todd Bolen/Bibleplaces.com

74 *COS* 2:285–87.

Fig. 4.49 – Cuneiform fragment from a basalt stela of Sargon II discovered at Ashdod *Photo by A. D. Riddle/Bibleplaces.com*

The outlook for Judah was equally foreboding. In 734 B.C. Tiglath-pileser III marched south through Philistia to capture nearby Gaza, but not before its king Ḫanunu fled to Egypt.[75] Then, with the accession of Sargon II (721 B.C.) and the destruction completed, he marched south to control rebellious Philistia. Having deposed the Assyrian puppet king around 713 B.C. and organized an opposition alliance against Sargon, the city of Ashdod became the new target. In 711 B.C., he struck back against its ruler and rebel leader, Yamani, besieging and conquering the city. Yamani himself had fled to Egypt, and continued south to Nubia,[76] the seat of the twenty-fifth Dynasty Cushite kings. Philistia, which bordered Judah on the east, became an Assyrian province under the rule of Assyrian officials.

With these events, it was clear to Micah that pressure was mounting on Judah. Perched on the hills around his village, the prophet could possibly have seen plumes of smoke arising from Philistine cities to the east by the coast as they were attacked. Having witnessed or directly heard of the horrors of Assyrian terror in just 20 miles (32 km) away, there was a real sense of urgency about his messages for his homeland Judah. Assyria was an existential threat! When the prophet announced God's intentions: "I will bring a conqueror against you" (Mic. 1:15), Assyria would have been understood as the unquestioned foe.

Warnings and Judgment

This book is composed in the form of a warning to Israel (before 722 B.C.) and Judah of anticipated judgments on the two nations. Due to their persistent violations of the Sinaitic Covenant, there was no recourse for God but to bring judgment on them. Only if there was a genuine and heartfelt repentance could their doom be averted. The seriousness of the situation is reflected immediately after the introductory verse:

> Hear, you peoples, all of you,
> listen, earth and all who are in it,

75 COS 2:288.
76 COS 2:296–97.

> that the Sovereign LORD may bear witness against you,
> the Lord from his holy temple.
> Look! The LORD is coming from his dwelling place;
> he comes down and treads on the heights of the earth. (Mic. 1:2–3)

The appeal to the earth to listen is a direct reference to one of the witnesses of the covenant in the book of Deuteronomy, which were "heaven and earth" (30:19; 31:28; 32:1); furthermore, God too will be a witness. As is the case in Hosea (see chap. 3) and Isaiah (see above), the portrayal as court action is plain. God is bringing charges, making a lawsuit against his covenant partner as if the scene were in a courtroom.[77] This passage also stresses that Yahweh is present in his earthly abode, his temple in Jerusalem, and he will come down from his heavenly realms to judge the earth. When he "treads the

Fig. 4.50 – High place on a mountaintop at Petra, Jordan *Photo by Alexander Schick/*

77 Walter Kaiser, *Micah–Malachi*, The Communicator's Commentary (Dallas: Word, 1992), 70.

Fig. 4.51 – 'Ain Dara Temple in Syria; Dr. John Monson standing in footsteps of deity
Photo courtesy of John Monson

high places," this is not merely a reference to an enormous deity stomping on mountains, but specifically those heights that contain pagan or illicit Judean sanctuaries that are known as "high places" (*bāmôṯ*), the standard term for such worship centers.[78] The people of the Near East viewed their deities as gigantic, as reflected in the Syrian Temple at Ain Dara where massive footprints measuring 94 cm (ca. 30 in.) long and 38 cm (ca. 14.5 in.) are carved in the steps and entryway to the temple that represent the impressions left by the deity when he entered the sanctuary.

The strong warnings for Israel and Judah are further wrapped in legal language in a "prophetic lawsuit" in chapter 6. A five-part pattern has been recognized, variations of which are found elsewhere in prophetic literature

78 Thomas McComiskey, *Micah*, Expositor's Bible Commentary, vol. 7 (Grand Rapids: Zondervan, 1985), 403–4.

(see Jeremiah 2). Sometimes called the *rîḇ* (lawsuit) pattern,[79] it is made of the following components:

An appeal to the covenant partner to pay attention and a summons to the covenant witness

Micah 6:1–2 (emphasis added): "Stand up, plead my *case* before the mountains; let the hills hear what you have to say. Hear, you mountains, the LORD's *accusation;* listen, you everlasting foundations of the earth. For the LORD has a case against his people; he is lodging a *charge* against Israel." Three times in these two verses is the word *rîḇ* is used, and can be translated "legal case," "accusation," and "lawsuit."[80] In the first instance, Israel is being asked to "defend yourself" (NET) against the accusation and case God is making. Mountains and hills are summoned, a variation of the witness "earth" in 1:2.

A series of questions which carried an implied accusation

In Micah 6:3 God asks, "What have I done to you? How have I burdened you?" In other words, what did God do to deserve infidelity when he had been faithful to his covenant obligations to Israel?

A reminder of past benefits granted to the covenant partner with some statement of the offenses by which the covenant had been violated

In Micah 6:4–5, the prophet recalls how God brought Israel out of Egypt at the exodus, and then provided needed leadership for early Israel in the form of Moses, Aaron, and Miriam, and protected the travels through the wilderness to the Promised Land, declaring, "Remember [your journey] from Shittim to Gilgal, that you may know the righteous acts of the LORD" (Mic. 6:5). Shittim marks the final campsite of the Israelites before entering Canaan in the book of Joshua (Num. 25:1, 33:49; Josh. 2:1, 3:1), while Gilgal was the initial campsite of the Israelites in Canaan (Josh. 4:19, 5:9–10; 10:6). Gilgal became a site of sacral significance in later times (see "Gilgal" in chap. 2 & Map 2.3).

---

79 J. Harvey, "Le 'Rîb-Pattern', réquisitoire prophétique sur la rupture de l'alliance," *Biblica* 43 (1962): 172–196.

80 *HALOT* 1224–26.

Reference made to the futility of ritual acts and sacrifices

In Micah 6–7 a series of rhetorical questions are asked to determine if God will be mollified and withhold judgment and exile if the people make offerings and sacrifices "with thousands of rams and ten thousand rivers of oil" (Mic. 6:7). The implied answer to all of these is "no," as the next verse makes clear. Not even if the people were to offer their firstborn children as an ultimate sacrifice would the LORD be satisfied.

God's Response

Micah 6:8 answers the question, What does God want? It is not ritual acts, not that they are unimportant within the covenant relationship with God, "but in and of itself without proper relationship to God and neighbor, sacrifice was useless."[81] Verse 8 is perhaps the best known in the book: "He has shown you, O mortal, what is good (*ṭôḇ*). And what does the LORD require of you? To act justly (*mîšppāṭ*) and to love mercy (*ḥeseḏ*) and to walk humbly with your God." The prophet answers the question of God's expectations for Israel is nothing new. No vision or revelation is needed. Rather Micah refers them the law that God has already revealed by alluding to Deuteronomy 10:12. The point is that the people need no new revelation from God about his expectations. They need only obey the stipulations of the covenant as recorded in the Torah. The heart of the Sinaitic Covenant is fulfilled by carrying out justice, to love mercy (or be loyal or faithful to the covenant), and to live a life of humbleness and submission to God as the Law requires.

Micah 6:8 stressed that God's priority was not on temple worship and cultic acts, but on the quality of one's life and obedience to the Mosaic Law. "To act justly and to love mercy" signals to some commentators that justice and mercy, especially applied in the social arena (i.e., social justice) means that Micah and other Hebrew prophets were social reformers. To be sure, at the heart of the Sinaitic law stands the command to "love your neighbor as yourself. I am the LORD" (Lev. 19:18), and from it flows other social laws, for instance, "Do no mistreat or oppress a foreigner. . . . Do not take advantage of of the widow or the fatherless" (Exod. 22:21–22); "Do not deny justice to your poor people in their lawsuits" (Exod. 23:6). So it is not surprising that in calling the nation back into a right covenant relationship with God, social issues are addressed. Clearly social issues are a concern of the prophets, but they must be

81 Ralph L. Smith, *Micah–Malachi*, World Biblical Commentary (Waco, TX: Word, 1984), 51.

regarded as symptoms of a deeper religious or spiritual malady: faithlessness to God. For this reason, Hassell Bullock argues that "the prophets were not social reformers. They were theological reformers, for their basic motivation was generated within their commitment to the fundamental laws of God."[82] The point is that the prophets, Micah included, point to moral, religious, and social issues, all of which are based on the Sinaitic Covenant. This is what Micah and other prophets were concerned about when he spoke of "justice."

Micah seems to hold out no hope that there would be meaningful repentance. Therefore, judgment is a major theme throughout the book. Indeed, Samaria's day of doom came at the hands of the Assyrians in 722 B.C., relatively early in Micah's career. Judah too experienced invasion in 701 B.C. at the hands of Sennacherib king of Assyria, but narrowly escaped thanks to divine intervention!

Fig. 4.52 – Farmer plowing a field near Mt. Gerazim *Photo by Todd Bolen/Bibleplaces.com*

82 Bullock, *An Introduction*, 29.

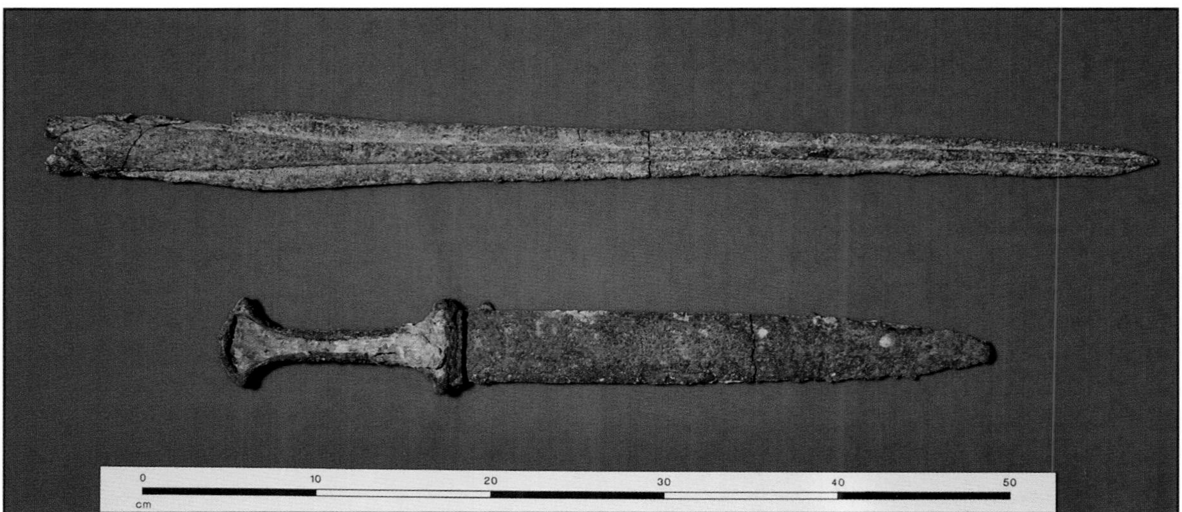

Fig. 4.53 – "Swords into plowshares and their spears into pruning hooks." Sword and lance blade from 14th century B.C. from Tell el-Borg, Egypt. *Photo by James K. Hoffmeier*

The announcement that the temple would be destroyed and Zion plowed up like a field was quoted above. This was surely a provocative thing for a prophet to say. In the minds of most Judeans, Jerusalem was sacrosanct and protected by the Yahweh himself. As long as the LORD was in his temple (Mic. 1:2), it was thought Jerusalem was safe. Consequently, Micah's warning was not only shocking,[83] but it was the first time that a prophet went on the record with such a prophecy concerning Jerusalem. He also speaks of Zion convulsing in labor pains and giving birth to exile in Babylon (Mic. 4:10). Mention of Babylon makes this one of the earliest indications that Assyria would not be Judah's destroyer, but a little-known, rising power at the end of the eighth century B.C. (see Isaiah section above).

Restoration and Future Hope

The book of Micah moves back and forth between doom and gloom, and restoration and hope. The prophet could anticipate Jerusalem being a heap of ruins, but also speaks of a surviving remnant (Mic. 5:7). He too looks forward to Jerusalem's restoration and a golden age at the end of time: "in the last days the mountain of the LORD's temple will be established as the highest of the

83 J. Gordon McConville, *A Guide to the Prophets: Exploring the Old Testament*, vol 4. (Downers Grove, IL: InterVarsity Press, 2002), 198.

mountains; it will be exalted above the hills, and peoples will stream to it" (Mic. 4:1). The prophet looks beyond the mere restoration of temple worship in Jerusalem to a time of universal access to hear God's laws and an era of peace, when peoples "will beat their swords into plowshares and their spears into pruning hooks. Nation will not take up sword against nation, nor will they train for war anymore" (Mic. 4:3), and the LORD himself will reign over Jerusalem and the nations (Mic. 4:7). This vision of a future Jerusalem is shared in almost identical words with Isaiah 2:2–4.

Fig. 4.54 – 1839 water color of Bethlehem by David Roberts *Photo by Todd Bolen/Bibleplaces.com*

In the Gospel of Matthew, when the Magi or wise men came from the east in search of the newly born "king of the Jews," they called on King Herod the Great in Jerusalem for assistance. The following unfolds:

> When he [Herod] had called together all the people's chief priests and teachers of the law, he asked them where the Messiah was to be born. "In Bethlehem in Judea," they replied, for this is what the prophet has written: "But you, Bethlehem, in the land of Judah, are by no means least among the rulers of Judah; for out of you will come a ruler who will shepherd my people Israel" (Matt. 2:4–6).

The prophet cited is Micah (Mic. 5:2). According to the interpretation of the sages during the reign of Herod (40–4 B.C.), the Messiah was a descendant of David who would, like the great king, be born in Bethlehem in a future day after the return from exile. Like David the shepherd king, this future king "will stand and shepherd his flock" (Mic. 5:4), anticipating the good shepherd who "lays down his life for the sheep" (John 10:11).

The book also concludes on a hopeful note, speaking of God's forgiveness and compassion, and the anticipation of a return to the land.

> Who is a God like you,
> who pardons sin and forgives the transgression
> of the remnant of his inheritance?
> You do not stay angry forever
> but delight to show mercy.
> You will again have compassion on us;

you will tread our sins underfoot
and hurl all our iniquities into the depths of the sea.
You will be faithful to Jacob,
and show love to Abraham,
as you pledged on oath to our ancestors
in days long ago. (Mic. 7:18–20)

The prophet bases his future hope for the remnant that will survive the destruction of Samaria and Jerusalem due to God's mercy and compassion. With exile in view and the population scattered, a profound theological question emerges: What of God's covenant promise of the land made long ago to Abraham and his descendants? God indeed will "show mercy" (*ḥese<u>d</u>*), or covenant loyalty, to Israel. God will remain faithful to his covenant promises even where Israel had failed. Therein lies the nation's hope beyond the dark days ahead.

THE EIGHTH-CENTURY PROPHETS: CONCLUDING THOUGHTS

With the passing of Isaiah in the first or second decade of the seventh century, as best we can tell, the golden era of Israelite prophecy came to an end. During this period, the prophets of the eighth century warned of God's judgment against Israel and witnessed the demise of Samaria and the deportation of tens of thousands of Israelites at the hand of the brutal Assyrian armies. Judah, however, miraculously survived that onslaught in 701 B.C. In the century that followed, the Assyrian Empire would likewise crumble, and a new foe from the north would threaten the little nation of Judah, and this period is the focus of the next chapter.

DISCUSSION QUESTIONS

- Discuss the role of holiness in Isaiah.
- Explain the Immanuel prophecy (Isa. 7:14) in its eighth-century context and how it is related to Matthew 1:22–23.
- What role do the wife and children of Isaiah play in chapters 7 and 8?
- What are some of the literary, thematic, and theological features of the book of Isaiah that support the unity of the book?
- What are the issues surrounding the appearance of King Cyrus in Isaiah 44 and 45? What are some possible explanations?
- Discuss the relationship between King Hezekiah and Isaiah during the crisis of 701 B.C. (Isa. 36–38).
- What was so shocking about Micah's prophecy in chapter 3:12: "Therefore because of you, Zion will be plowed like a field, Jerusalem will become a heap of rubble, the temple hill a mound overgrown with thickets"?
- Discuss Micah 6:1–8 from a legal and juridical context.
- What is God looking for from his people, according to Micah 6:8? What is the significance of his demands?

5 "Amend Your Ways and Your Deeds" The Seventh- and Sixth-Century Prophets of Judah

"I am bringing disaster on this people, the fruit of their schemes, because they have not listened to my words and have rejected my law."

—Jeremiah 6:19

THE POLITICAL SETTING OF THE SEVENTH AND SIXTH CENTURIES

King Hezekiah is held up as one of the best kings of Judah because of his radical reforms against pagan elements in Israelite religion. Second Kings offers him kudos: "Hezekiah trusted in the LORD, the God of Israel. There was no one like him among all the kings of Judah, either before him or after him" (18:5). His faithfulness to God and his obedience to the Law and acting on the instructions of Isaiah were exemplary. But his son Manasseh, who was coregent with his father Hezekiah 697–686 B.C. and reigned on his own 686–642 B.C.,[1] completely undid all the good that his father had done by reintroducing foreign deities, even placing an Asherah pole in the temple. In the words of the biblical author, "Manasseh led them [the people] astray, so that they did more evil than the nations the LORD had destroyed before the Israelites" (2 Kings 21:9). Not surprisingly, prophets stepped forward to condemn this apostasy (2 Kings 21:10), but these apparently were not among the literary prophets whose messages are preserved in the Bible. The Chronicler records, "The LORD spoke to Manasseh and his people, but they paid no attention. So the LORD brought against them the army commanders of the king of Assyria, who took Manasseh prisoner" (2 Chron. 33:10–11). Although this king turned back to God later in life while imprisoned by the Assyrians and his kingship was subsequently restored (2 Chron. 33:10–19), he had set the nation on a downward spiral from which it never fully recovered.

1 Thiele, *Hebrew Kings*, 75.

Fig. 5.1 – Stela of Esarhaddon, in Berlin, showing the captured king of Sidon (on right) and a Nubian prince (kneeling on the left) in shackles and manacles before the Assyrian monarch, just as Manasseh was treated
Photo by James K. Hoffmeier

Josiah, grandson of Manasseh, ruled 640–609 B.C.,[2] a period which saw the collapse of the Assyrian empire between 614 and 612 B.C.[3] Assyria's demise was brought about by the Chaldean/Babylonians under the leadership of Nabopolassar who were joined by the forces of Cyaxares king of the Medes (northern part of modern Iran), and is reported on in the Babylonian Chronicle.[4]

Ranked among the best kings of Judah, Josiah promoted religious reforms in Jerusalem and was hailed for his pursuit of justice (cf. Jer. 22:16). These efforts notwithstanding, the nation did not turn back to God wholeheartedly. Jeremiah put it this way: "'Judah did not return to me with all her heart, but only in pretense,' declares the LORD" (Jer. 3:10). Consequently God ordered the termination of Judah and the deportation of thousands "because of what Manasseh son of Hezekiah king of Judah did in Jerusalem" (Jer. 15:4). It is in this context of decline and exile that the Hebrew prophets of the seventh and sixth were called to address the nation and its leaders.

THE BOOK OF ZEPHANIAH: REDEFINING THE "DAY OF THE LORD"

"Be silent before the Sovereign LORD,
for the day of the LORD is near."
—Zephaniah 1:7

Zephaniah's Royal Pedigree

The book opens with the only known personal information about Zephaniah, namely that his genealogy is traced back four generations. Most prophets are known as X, son of Y. Zephaniah names Cushi, Gedaliah, Amariah, and Hezekiah (Zeph. 1:1). So naming male ancestors to the fourth

2 Theile, *Hebrew Kings*, 75.
3 *ABD* 4:746–47.
4 *ANET* 304–5.

generation is unparalleled among the prophets, likely signaling that that last individual named was an obviously reputable individual, namely Hezekiah. Since prior to Zephaniah no man bore that name save the good king of Judah, it stands to reason that this was Zephaniah's renowned ancestor.[5] This being the case, Zephaniah was a person of royal ancestry who likely resided in Jerusalem among the elites and probably had access to the king. His name means "Yahweh has protected/hidden,"[6] suggesting possibly that he survived the atrocities of king Manasseh who is said to have "shed so much innocent blood" (2 Kings 21:16).[7]

Fig. 5.2 – Tablet of the Babylonian Chronicle mentioning the fall of Nineveh in 612 B.C.
Photo by Todd Bolen/Bibleplaces.com

The Troubled Times of Zephaniah

His prophetic activity is also placed in the reign of Josiah (640–609 B.C.) (Zeph. 1:1). Zephaniah describes the religious corruption in Judah and Jerusalem, his primary audience, condemning "every remnant of Baal" and those "who bow down on the roofs to worship the starry host, those who bow down and swear by the LORD and who also swear by Molek" (Zeph. 1:4–5). The identity of Molech (or Molek) is disputed. He is sometimes connected to a Canaanite underground deity to whom sacrifices were offered.[8] Some translations (e.g., RSV and ESV) render "Molech" as "Milcom," which better reflects what is actually written in Hebrew (*malkām*). "Milcom" is associated with the Ammonites, Israel's neighbors in the Trans-Jordan (1 Kings 11:7; 2 Kings 23:13). Literally *malkām* means "their king," which is a reference to Baal.[9] Thus the people were swearing (making oaths) by their king, that is, Baal, who is mentioned in the previous verse (v. 4), even as they evoke the name of Yahweh.

---

5 David Baker, *Nahum, Habakkuk, Zephaniah: An Introduction and Commentary* (Downers Grove, IL: InterVarsity Press, 1988), 91.
6 *HALOT* 1049.
7 Kaiser, *Micah–Malachi*, 207.
8 *ABD* 4:895–97.
9 Smith, *Micah–Malachi*, 127.

Fig. 5.3 – Ashurnasirpal II stela in British Museum with astral deities in sky behind his head
Photo by A. D. Riddle/Bibleplaces.com

Mention of the "starry host" (1:5) or astral deities clearly connects the popularity of these foreign deities with Manasseh's apostasy. Among the grievances that the biblical historian had with this king was that "in the two courts of the temple of the LORD, he built altars to all the starry host" (2 Kings 21:5). Depictions of astral deities grew significantly in Assyrian art and may have influenced Manasseh's actions. Astral deities naturally include the sun, moon, and stars, including Venus, which is associated with Babylonian goddess Ishtar.[10] She is equated with goddess Astarte in west Mediterranean and Israel. These heavenly divinities are regularly depicted at the top of royal stelae, just over the head of the figure of the king.

Zephaniah's references to pagan practices in Jerusalem suggests that he is describing the religious picture in Judah during Manasseh's period of apostasy, which continued into the early years of Josiah's reign. In 628 B.C., when only in his mid-teens, Josiah began to purge the pagan images and practices (2 Chron. 34:3), but not likely until six years later, 622 B.C., did his reforms fully take hold when the Book of the Law was discovered in the temple (2 Chron. 34:8–33).

The Message of Zephaniah

God's response to the apostacy described in Zephaniah 1:2–6 is "the day of the Lord," a day of judgment and a military assault. The expression "the day of the Lord," however, first occurs in the book of Amos (5:18–20) and is also found in Isaiah (13:6, 9), Joel (see next chapter), and other prophets. "The day of the Lord" derives from an ancient Near Eastern idea of the day that a deity or king goes to war against its enemies.[11] After the battles, the victors and their forces naturally enjoyed a sumptuous banquet from the spoils to celebrate. The OT usages of this expression sets the stage for an eschatological "day of the Lord," which the New Testament informs us, "will come like a thief in the night," a theme used both by Peter (2 Pet. 3:10) and Paul (2 Thess. 5:2) when referring to the final return of Jesus Christ to do judgment on the earth. Thus "the day" is not a twenty-four-hour period, but the time period when the Lord

10 Hruša, *Ancient Mesopotamian Religion*, 51–54.
11 Stuart, *Hosea–Jonah*, 230–31.

returns to earth to carry out judgment and establish his kingdom based in Jerusalem (Zech. 14:16).[12]

Among the Hebrew prophets, the day of the Lord was the occasion when God would defeat Israel's enemies and the Israelites would eat from the spoils of war. Zephaniah offers a vivid description of this day, but instead of it being when God takes on the enemies of Judah, Judah becomes the victim of the day of the Lord, not the beneficiary of it.[13] Instead of being invited to participate in the glorious banquet, they become like the animals slaughtered for others to consume! The members of the royal family were to be the primary targets:

> Be silent before the Sovereign Lord, for the day of the Lord is near. The Lord has prepared a sacrifice; he has consecrated those he has invited. On the day of the Lord's sacrifice I will punish the princes and the king's sons (Zeph. 1:7–8).

He goes on the further describe the tumultuous warfare surrounding that day:

> The great day of the Lord is near—near and coming quickly.
> The cry on the day of the Lord is bitter,
>   the Mighty Warrior shouts his battle cry.
> That day will be a day of wrath—
>   a day of distress and anguish,
>   a day of trouble and ruin,
>   a day of darkness and gloom,
>   a day of clouds and blackness—
>   a day of trumpet and battle cry
> against the fortified cities
>   and against the corner towers. (Zeph. 1:14–16)

The military nature of the day of the Lord is made clear in this passage. And while Judah is the primary focus of this military action, the day of the Lord is then extended to neighboring nations. Gaza, Ashkelon, and Ashdod—Philistine cities—and Moab and Ammon are named, as is distant Cush, located south of Egypt (Zeph. 2:4, 7–9, 12). Even mighty Assyria and its capital

---

12 Kaiser, *Micah–Malachi*, 220.

13 Larry Walker, *Zephaniah*, Expositor's Bible Commentary, vol. 7 (Grand Rapids: Zondervan, 1985), 546.

Nineveh are targeted for destruction (Zeph. 2:13). No doubt this latter reference would be welcomed in Jerusalem.

The possibility of righteous individuals in Judah being spared is extended to those who "Seek the LORD, all you humble of the land, you who do what he commands. Seek righteousness, seek humility; perhaps you will be sheltered on the day of the LORD's anger" (Zeph. 2:3).

Despite the pending day of the Lord, probably anticipating the Babylonian devastation and deportation of Jerusalem and Judah (although not explicitly stated), restoration was prophesied. God would be with them through this horrific experience.

> The LORD has taken away your punishment,
> he has turned back your enemy.

Fig. 5.4 – Painted box of Tutankhamun in Cairo Museum depicts the day of battle as the king charges on his chariot at a group of Cushites *Photo by James K. Hoffmeier*

The LORD, the King of Israel, is with you;
never again will you fear any harm. (Zeph. 3:15)

The LORD your God is with you,
the Mighty Warrior who saves.
He will take great delight in you,
in his love he will no longer rebuke you,
but will rejoice over you with singing. (Zeph. 3:17)

Yahweh will not only be with them, loving and saving them, but he will deal with Judah's enemies—the Babylonians no doubt—that have exiled and scattered the covenant people. Prophets Habakkuk (2:6–20) and Jeremiah (50–51) address Babylon's doom.

At that time I will deal
with all who oppressed you;
I will rescue the lame
anI will gather the exiles.
I will give them praise and honor
in every land where they have suffered shame.
At that time I will gather you;
at that time I will bring you home.
I will give you honor and praise
among all the peoples of the earth
when I restore your fortunes
before your very eyes,"
says the LORD. (Zeph. 3:19–20)

Zephaniah addressed the people of Judah when the nation was still entangled with the apostasies of Manasseh and those of the short-lived Amon (2 Kings 21:19–26) that lingered into Josiah's reign. Because of his royal familial pedigree, which would give him uncommon access to the king, he may be regarded as the prophet who encouraged young king Josiah with his religious reforms which included demolishing pagan shrines and images while returning temple worship to its orthodox form (2 Kings 22–23; 2 Chron. 34–35). Nevertheless, as we learn from Jeremiah, the greatest prophet of the seventh and sixth centuries, those reforms did not have an enduring effect (Jer. 3:6–10).

THE CHALDEANS

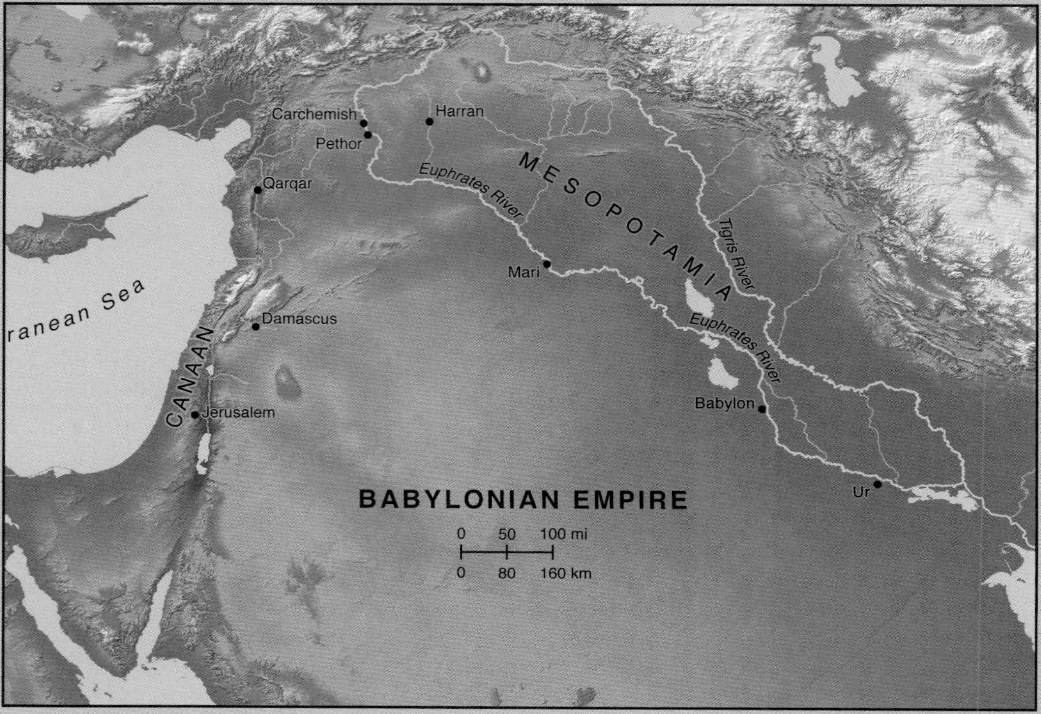

Map 5.1 – Babylonian Empire *Map by A. D. Riddle*

The city of Babylon was an ancient marvel that had a long and glorious history. The name Babel in "tower of Babel" seems related to Babylon, which means "gate of god."[14] The earliest textual references to this site that comes from the end of the third millennium B.C. during the reign of Sharkalisharri (2217–2193 B.C.), the king of Akkad.[15] It was the ancestors of Hammurabi early in the twentieth century B.C., however, who built up the city and made it their capital.[16] Babylon flourished throughout the second millennium, but it experienced its apex in the first millennium B.C., when under the Assyrians it functioned as a second capital and then under the Chaldeans achieved its legendary grandeur.

14 *ISBE* 1:382.
15 Joan Oates, *Babylon* (London: Thames & Hudson, 2003), 37.
16 Bill Arnold, *Who Were the Babylonians?* (Atlanta: Society of Biblical Literature, 2004), 35–47.

The earliest reference to the Chaldeans in Mesopotamia dates to about 1100 B.C. Then during the reign of Ashurnasirpal II (883–859 B.C.), when the Assyrian wrestled control of Babylon from the *Kal-du,* that is, Chaldeans.[17] Clearly the Chaldeans controlled much of southern Mesopotamia in the ninth century, but how much earlier these Aramean/Chaldean tribes arrived in this region remains uncertain. Based on their language, Aramean, and other factors, it appears that Aramean tribes migrated from the northeastern region of present-day Syria. Close affinity between these tribes, and a common foe in the Assyrians prompted alliances and an eventual coalescence, resulting in the terms Chaldean and Aramean becoming virtually synonymous. The Aramaic language is closely connected with Hebrew and originally spoken in northern Syria. During the Neo-Assyrian period, it started to be used in international diplomacy (cf. Isa. 36:11; 2 Kings 18:26). Its widespread use grew during the Persian Empire (539–332 B.C.), and became the language of the Jewish diaspora in Mesopotamia and Egypt, and remained the dominant language for centuries. In Jesus's day, Aramaic was the standard language spoken in Palestine.

Fig. 5.5 – Code of Hammurabi shows the king (left) standing before the god Shamash to receive laws *Photo by James K. Hoffmeier*

Merodach-baladan, who sought an alliance with Hezekiah of Jerusalem just before 700 B.C. (Isa. 39:1–4; 2 Kings 20:12–15), was a Chaldean ruler of Babylon who proved to be thorn in the flesh of the Assyrians. Sennacherib described him as "an evil rebel, of treacherous mind, doer of evil, for whom truth is sinful"[18] (see Fig. 4.21). Babylon was crushed by the Assyrians, resulting in

17 Younger, *Arameans*, 674.
18 *COS* 2:300.

Chaldeans escaping to the marshlands in the Tigris-Euphrates delta. Carved depictions from Sennacherib's palace in Nineveh provide details of these swamp battles. Merodach-baladan, meanwhile, fled to the land of Elam in for refuge.[19]

In the year 626 B.C., as the Assyrian Empire was in serious decline, a chieftain named Nabopolassar (probably a Chaldean, but proof is lacking) seized the throne in Babylon,[20] calling himself "son of a nobody," indicating his non-royal origins.[21] Beginning with his reign, the "Babylonian Chronicle"—preserved on clay tablets—contains rather objective reports of the major events of the Chaldean Dynasty down to 539 B.C., though some years are missing. Nabopolassar joined forces with the king of the Medes, Cyaxares, to bring the Assyrian Empire to its knees when

Fig. 5.6 – British Museum relief showing a boat in the southern marshes with elite Chaldean women captured by Assyrians during reign of Ashurbanipal (668–631 B.C.)
Photo by A. D. Riddle/Bibleplaces.com

19 *COS* 2:300.
20 *ABD* 4:764.
21 *ABD* 4:977.

Fig. 5.7 – Ishtar Gate from Nebuchadnezzar's Babylon, reconstructed in the Berlin Museum *Photo by A. D. Riddle/Bibleplaces.com*

Nineveh fell in 612 B.C.[22] Nabopolassar, thereby, was the undisputed ruler of Babylon and the surrounding regions. His crown prince, Nebuchadnezzar (605–560 B.C.), actively led the armies of Babylon against the Egyptians (Assyria's allies) who had occupied Carchemish on the Euphrates River in 605 B.C., an event reported in Jeremiah (46:2).

Nabopolassar died later that year and was succeeded by his son Nebuchadnezzar, who proved to be the most powerful ruler of the Near East during his lengthy reign (605–562 B.C.). Syria, Phoenicia, and Judah experienced the full force of his power. Between 605 and 582 B.C., Nebuchadnezzar's forces attacked Judah four times, deporting thousands (2 Kings 24–25; Jer. 52:28–30; Dan 1). He also attacked Egypt in 582 B.C. and 568 B.C., although he did not try to occupy it. During his protracted reign, Babylon was built into a magnificent city with colorful glazed tile outer walls and lofty gates. Associated with his palace complex was the fabulous "hanging garden," one of the seven wonders of the ancient world. Archaeology has not been able to shed any light on this famous garden. It was during the reign of his short-lived successor Evil-Merodach that the Judean king Jehoiachin was released from prison in 562 B.C. (Jer. 52:31–34; 2 Kings 25:27–30). In less than a quarter century, the Chaldean Dynasty was removed by Cyrus the Persian king in 539 B.C., who defeated Nabonidus, the last Chaldean king.

THE BOOK OF JEREMIAH: BROKEN COVENANT, NEW COVENANT

> "The days are coming," declares the LORD, "when I will make a new covenant with the people of Israel and with the people of Judah."
>
> —Jeremiah 31:31

Jeremiah's Roots

Of all the prophets, more is known about Jeremiah than any other. He was the son of Hilkiah the Priest, and his home was Anathoth (Jer. 1:1), a small priestly village located about 5 km (3 miles) north of Jerusalem in Benjaminite territory.[23] The name Anathoth first occurs when the tribal allotments were

22 *ANET* 304–5.
23 *ABD* 1:227–28.

made in Joshua 21:18, where it is described as a pastureland for the high priest Aaron's descendants. Ironically at the root of this toponym is the Canaanite goddess Anat,[24] who is a bloodthirsty, warlike deity but is also associated with fertility in Ugaritic (Canaanite) literature of the thirteenth-twelfth centuries, and her epithets further connect her to the sky.[25] Indeed, during recent excavation in north Sinai, Egypt, the writer discovered a block dating to the thirteenth century with the title "Anat, Lady of Heaven"[26] (see Fig. 2.52)

Likely with the establishment Jerusalem as the religious and political capital under King David, Anathoth became residential space for priests. This is clear when King Solomon dismissed Abiathar, who had sided with Adonijah and against Solomon's accession to the throne. He banished the priest with the following condemnation: "To Abiathar the priest the king said, 'Go back to your fields in Anathoth. You deserve to die'" (1 Kings 2:26). Jeremiah's family could well be related to this renegade priest.[27]

Fig. 5.8 – Present-day Anata/Anathoth *Bibleplaces.com*

---

24 Richard Hess, *Israelite Religions: An Archaeological and Biblical Survey* (Grand Rapids: Baker Academic, 2007), 100.

25 *ABD* 1:225–27.

26 James K. Hoffmeier, *Tell el-Borg I* (Winona Lake, IN: Eisenbrauns, 2014), 101.

27 Jack Lundbom, *Jeremiah 1–20*, Anchor Bible Commentary (New York: Doubleday, 1999), 223.

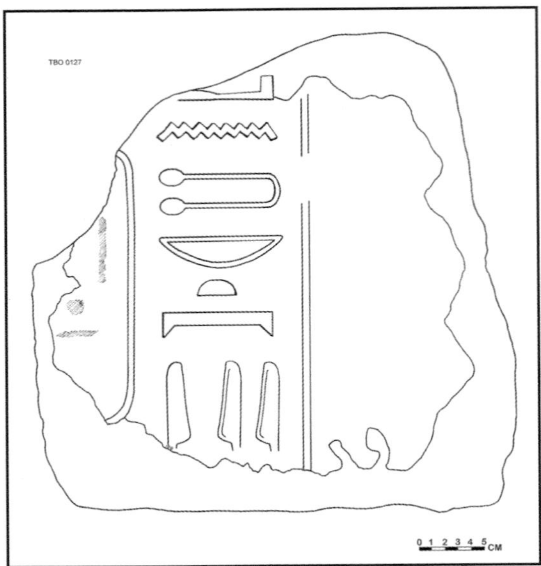

Fig. 5.9 – Inscription with the name, "Anat Lady of the Sky (or Heaven)" discovered at Tell el-Borg Sinai
Drawing by Lyla Pinch-Brock

Fig. 5.10 – Goddess Anat (on the right) with Ramesses II; inscription identifies "the Lady Sky (or Heaven)"
Photo by A. D. Riddle/Bibleplaces.com

The high priest named Hilkiah discovered "the book of the Law" in 2 Kings 22:9–10 in Josiah's reign (640–609 B.C.). Scholars tend to dismiss the connection between this priest and Jeremiah's father,[28] but offer no reason for this conclusion. Walter Brueggemann for one considers the connection to be "at least plausible."[29] The name Hilkiah, meaning "Yahweh is my part/portion,"[30] mostly occurs in the OT among Levites and priests.[31] The timing of the discovery in 622 B.C. falls a few years after Jeremiah's prophetic call, a period when Jeremiah's father would have been active in the temple. Consequently there is no really good reason for rejecting out of hand the possibility that Jeremiah's father may have been the high priest named in the discovery of the missing law scroll.

28 Roland Harrison, *Jeremiah and Lamentations* (Downers Grove, IL: InterVarsity Press, 1973), 48, and Lundbom, *Jeremiah 1–20*, 223. I can only deduce that their rejection is based on Hilkiah in 2 Kings 22 is identified as the high priest (lit. "the great priest"), whereas Jeremiah's father is not so identified in Jeremiah 1:1.

29 Walter Brueggemann, *The Theology of the Book of Jeremiah* (Cambridge: Cambridge University Press, 2007), 28.

30 *HALOT* 324.

31 *ABD* 3:200–201.

The Prophet's Call

Chapter 1 contains the prophet's call, which is dated to the thirteenth year of Josiah, or 626 B.C. In response to the divine call to be a prophet, Jeremiah tries to disqualify himself by saying that he was "a child" (NIV) or a "youth" (ESV; Jer. 1:6). This statement, coupled with God's directive later on for him not to marry (Jer. 16:1), which normally occurred for men by age twenty,[32] suggests that he may only have been in his early to mid-teens when his prophetic career began. These considerations mean that Jeremiah was likely born around or just before 640 B.C. Though just teenager, God called him to be "a prophet to the nations" (Jer. 1:6).

Since the prophetic calls are not regularly recorded in the OT, its inclusion here is noteworthy. Like Samuel and Isaiah before him and Ezekiel who follows, God speaks to the candidate, and visions of some sort accompany the experience. To young Jeremiah, the LORD uttered a tri-colon in which each line follows the same grammatical pattern:[33]

> Before I formed you in the womb I knew you,
> and before you were born I consecrated you;
> I appointed you a prophet to the nations. (Jer. 1:5 ESV)[34]

God was not only trying to assure the lad that his life was to be dedicated to ministry and appointed him to the prophetic office, but that even before he was conceived, God's plan for Jeremiah was in place. "I knew you" could be rendered "I knew you intimately,"[35] a further testimony of the Lord's purpose and care for his prophet.

The reluctant prophet appeals to his youth and inexperience as a reason not to be God's spokesman. God assures Jeremiah of his presence with him and then, similar to the touching of Isaiah's lips during his call (Isa. 6:6–7), "the LORD reached out his hand and touched my mouth and said to me, 'I have put my words in your mouth'" (Jer. 1:9). This statement echoes the

---

32 This figure is based on ancient Near Eastern data, and inferences drawn from Numbers 1:3. Twenty is the age a man can be conscripted into the military, and it was expected that he would be married and have a child before enlistment (cf. Deut. 20:7).

33 Holladay, *Jeremiah, Chapters 1–25*, 25–26.

34 Translation by the author to reflect the poetic nature of this three-line declaration by the LORD.

35 John Thompson, *The Book of Jeremiah* (Grand Rapids: Eerdmans, 1980), 143.

LORD's words to Moses and Israel on how he would raise up prophets like Moses: "I will put my words in his mouth" (Deut. 18:18).

Jeremiah's fears were not unfounded, given the abusive treatment he regularly received. He even met strong opposition from his own family, as well as the political and religious establishment, including fellow prophets who challenged his messages (see below). His discomforting messages brought shame to his own community of Anathoth. As a result, some from his village even tried to kill him (Jer. 11:21–23), including family members (Jer. 12:6; 18:18, 23). These attacks, general opposition, and anxiety about the fate of his people prompted Jeremiah to offer prayers, laments, and bitter complaints (e.g. Jer. 8:18–9:3; 10:23–25; 12:1–4; 17:14–18; 18:19–23; 20:14–18). These factors contribute to Jeremiah being traditionally called the weeping prophet.

Foes and Friends of Jeremiah

Jeremiah was a strong supporter of Josiah and his reforms. He praised him as a model of a righteous and just king (Jer. 22:15–16). There is, however, no report of a working relationship between the king and Jeremiah in the

Fig. 5.11 – Necho II (right) makes offering to goddess Hathor
Photo by A. D. Riddle /Bibleplaces.com

book bearing his name. When the king met his untimely death at the hands of Pharaoh Neco in 609 B.C., it was Jeremiah who composed a song of lament (2 Chron. 35:25) that may have been used in the period of mourning for the godly monarch. Jehoiakim and Zedekiah, Josiah's sons and successors, did not follow in his ways. To them, Jeremiah proved to be an irritation.

The prophet defied the status quo with regard to temple worship that ignored the moral aspects of the law (Jer. 7; see below), and as a result he was banned from entering the temple precinct (Jer. 36:5) and was despised by the religious and political establishment (Jer. 26:10–11). When he dramatically announced that Jerusalem would be shattered like a vessel (see below), he was beaten and imprisoned by Pashhur (Jer. 19). Jeremiah recognized that Babylon had been raised up by God to punish Judah for its sins, even identifying King Nebuchadnezzar as God's "servant" (Jer. 25:9; 27:6). Consequently the prophet thought the better path to take was to surrender to Babylon rather than resist God's purposes. For this he was charged with treason, beaten, and incarcerated (Jer. 37:11–15). King Zedekiah then had him released, but when Jeremiah continued with what his opponents considered to be his seditious announcements, the king permitted certain officials to apprehend him. They cast him into a deep, water cistern with muddy sludge in it (Jer. 38: 1–6). The conditions were putrid, horrid. The timing of this episode, shortly before the fall of Jerusalem in 586 B.C., falls around the month of July (cf. Jer. 39:1–2),[36] which was at the height of the dry season.

Despite all the antagonism, Jeremiah did have some friends who supported his work and assisted during his various incarcerations. His closest ally was Baruch son of Neriah, the scribe who not only physically wrote the book of Jeremiah (chap. 36) but took the prophet's recorded messages to the temple and read them publicly because Jeremiah had been barred from the temple precinct (Jer. 36:4–10).

Baruch also drafted the contract for Jeremiah's purchase of property (Jer. 32:9–14). The fact that he is called "the scribe" and engaged in these activities suggest that Baruch was a professional scribe, probably a civil servant.[37] A tiny seal impression came to light some years ago which reads:

---

36 Jack Lundbom, *Jeremiah 37–52*, Anchor Bible Commentary (New York: Doubleday, 2004), 68.

37 Gerald Keown, Pamela Scalise, and Thomas Smothers, *Jeremiah 26–52*, Word Biblical Commentary (Dallas: Word, 1995), 154–55; King, *Jeremiah*, 6–8.

Fig. 5.12 – A cistern plastered walls at Tell Hesban *Photo by Todd Bolen/Bibleplaces.com*

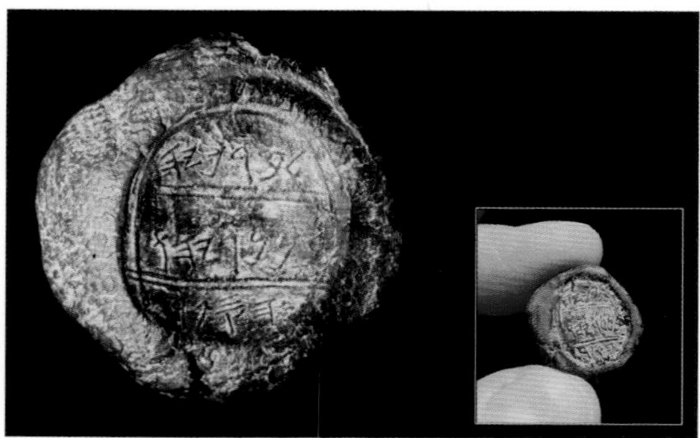

Fig. 5.13 – The seal impression of "Beruchiah son of Neriah the scribe" in Shlomo Moussaieff-Collection *Photo by Richard Wiskin*;
Fingers with replica of the seal *Photo by Alexander Schick/bibelausstellung.de*

Fig. 5.14 – A first millennium B.C. relief in Berlin Museum of a scribe from Zincerli (Turkey)

"Belonging to Berechyahu son of Neriyahu, the scribe."[38] Recently the authenticity of this sensational find has been questioned, leading to uncertainty about it.[39]

---

38 The element "yahu" is a fuller spelling of the divine name Yahweh that frequently appears in personal names written on archaeological materials like seals, seal impressions, stone, and pottery. King, *Jeremiah*, 95–96.

39 The so-called *Baruch bulla* (seal impression) was not discovered by archaeologists on a controlled excavation, but came to the antiquities market, which adds to the suspicion of the object's antiquity.

Baruch's brother Seraiah also proved to be supportive of Jeremiah.[40] He carried the scroll with Jeremiah's prophecies about Babylonia when he journeyed to Babylon with king Zedekiah in 593 B.C. (Jer. 51:59–60). The king himself personally delivered tribute or taxes as a show of loyalty to Nebuchadnezzar. There, like his brother Baruch did in Jerusalem, Seraiah publicly read the message from God (Jer. 51:61–64).

Jeremiah, interestingly, received aid from foreigners in his most trying times. When imprisoned in the cistern (Jer. 38:1–6), where he might have died from lack of water and food, a court official named Ebed-melech went to King Zedekiah to plead for the prophet, informing him, "My lord the king, these men have acted wickedly in all they have done to Jeremiah the prophet. They have thrown him into a cistern, where he will starve to death when there is no longer any bread in the city" (Jer. 38:9). The king permitted Ebed-melech to rescue the prophet. Out of compassion for Jeremiah, who was an older man in 586 B.C. (mid- to late fifties), Ebed-melech got pieces of cloths for Jeremiah to place in his armpits so that the ropes did not cut him while pulling him out of the cistern (See Fig. 5.12). Ebed-melech's access to the royal wardrobe where he got the old cloths (Jer. 38:11) suggests that his duties were more domestic, perhaps associated with the royal harem. His title *sārîs* refers to eunuchs who sometimes served the royal woman.[41] Four different times Ebed-Melech is identified as "the Cushite" (NIV, NET) or an Ethiopian (ESV) (Jer. 28:7, 10, 12; 39:16) to stress his foreign identity. Cush in the Bible, and also in Egyptian texts, refers to the area south of Egypt in modern-day northern Sudan.[42] How Ebed-Melech came to Judah and landed a position in the royal household is not known. But it is clear from his appearance in the narrative that Ebed-Melech feared the word of God, and respected Jeremiah the prophet.

Surprisingly, Jeremiah had supporters in the Babylonian regime. At Nebuchadnezzar's instruction, the "commander of the imperial guard," Nebuzaradan, was to "take him [Jeremiah] and look after him; don't harm him but do for him whatever he asks" (Jer. 39:11–12). Jeremiah had been captured by Babylonian troops and put in "chains" (Jer. 40:1), actually handcuff-like fetters rather than chains were the binding instrument used. Depictions of POWs or deportees of Egyptian armies used such manacles as did the Assyrians on prisoners.

40 *ISBE* 4:409.
41 Edwin Yamauchi, *Africa and the Bible* (Grand Rapids: Baker Academic, 2004), 147–48; Lundbom, *Jeremiah 37–52*, 70.
42 Yamauchi, *Africa and the Bible*, 40–46.

Fig. 5.15 – Manacled Philistine prisoner
Photo by Peter Brand

At Ramah (Jer. 40:1), 5 miles (9 km) north of Jerusalem, likely a staging area where deportees were assembled for the march to Babylon,[43] Nebuzaradan encountered Jeremiah. There he carried out the king's directive to free Jeremiah, and he went a step further, offering the prophet to come live with him in Babylon: "I am freeing you from the chains on your wrists. Come with me to Babylon, if you like, and I will look after you; but if you do not want to, then don't come. Look, the whole country lies before you; go wherever you please" (Jer. 40:4). Jeremiah opted to say in his homeland and was left in the care of Gedeliah the grandson of Shaphan, the high official under king Josiah. Gedeliah had been appointed governor over the surviving remnant in Judah, setting up his base of operations at Mizpah (Jer. 40:5–6). A seal impression with Gedeliah's name on it was discovered as Mizpah (see Fig. 2.10–11).

It is remarkable to realize that the powerful, imperial ruler Nebuchanezzar was familiar with Jeremiah and his prophecies, and had such respect for him. This fact was a rebuke to the Judean rulers and officials who spurned and persecuted the prophet. When Nebuzaradan released Jeremiah he acknowledged, "The Lord your God decreed this disaster for this place. And now the Lord has brought it about" (Jer. 40:2–3). Jeremiah thus proved to be an authentic prophet whose word came true—the ultimate test of a prophet (Deut. 18:21–22). No doubt the Babylonians were pleased with that outcome. The fact that Nebuchadnezzar, Nebuzaradan, and Ebed-Melech, all foreigners, respected Jeremiah and his message is obviously a reprimand to the religious and political leaders in Jerusalem who rejected both message and messenger.

Jeremiah after the Fall of Jerusalem

Sometime later after the destruction of Jerusalem, an act of tyranny against the Babylonian-appointed governor took place, inspired by Baalis king of Ammon, east of the Jordan River (Jer. 40:13–14). He and some Judean allies were still opposed to submitting to the Chaldeans. "In the seventh month" (Jer. 41:1), presumably after Jerusalem's demise,[44] Gedeliah was assassinated, along

43 William Holladay, *A Commentary on the Book of the Prophet Jeremiah, Chapters 26–52* (Philadelphia: Fortress, 1989), 293–94.

44 Holladay, *Jeremiah*, 296.

with some of the Babylonian garrison (Jer. 41:3). Anticipating a return of Babylonian forces to deal with this rebellion, a band of Judean's survivors fled to Egypt, forcing Jeremiah to accompany them even though he had warned against looking to Egypt for sanctuary (Jer. 42–43).

The Judean escapees made the long trek across the sands of northern Sinai from their starting point in Mizpah in about two weeks' time. Jeremiah entered Egypt at the frontier site of Migdol (Jer. 44:1), identified with the recently discovered fort at Tell Qedua, located about 9 m (15 km) east of the Suez Canal.[45] It was a substantial fort, measuring 200 x 200 m (40,000 m^2), and probably the official entry point for travelers coming from some southern Israel.

From there the Judean escapees continued farther east to the city of Tahpanes, which is commonly identified with the site of Tell Defenneh, situated slightly west of the present-day Suez Canal.[46] At Tahpanes Jeremiah delivered a message to the Judeans, who were scattered around Egypt at "Migdol, Tahpanes and Memphis—and in Upper Egypt" (Jer. 44:1). Judeans had settled from the northern to the southern frontiers of Egypt. Some may have fled during the Babylonian attack on Jerusalem in 597 B.C., while others may have escaped ahead of the campaign of 586 B.C.[47] How Jeremiah's message reached such a dispersed audience is not stated. We cannot rule out the possibility that he actually traveled to the major centers where his compatriots lived with his colleague Baruch the scribe who had accompanied him to Egypt.

Jeremiah warned his audience that Nebuchadnezzar would also invade Egypt because they were still engaged in pagan worship and religious syncretism as they had been in Judah. "But, heedless of their past," Charles Feinberg observed, "they went and served the gods of Egypt."[48] Jeremiah 44 informs us that the people persisted in worshiping the Queen of Heaven (vv. 18–19). Whether Jeremiah lived to witness Nebuchadnezzar's invasion, we are not told. By then he would have been an old man in his seventies. It is assumed that he lived the balance of his life in Egypt after a career of more than fifty years of prophetic activity.

---

45 Eliezer Oren, "Migdol: A New Fortress on the Edge of the Eastern Nile Delta," *BASOR* 256 (1984): 7–44.

46 François Leclère, "Tell Dafana: Identity, Explorations and Monuments," in *Tell Dafana Reconsidered: The Archaeology of an Egyptian Frontier Town*, eds. F. Leclère and A. J. Spencer (London: The British Museum, 2014), 1–40.

47 Lundbom, *Jeremiah 37–52*, 126.

48 Charles Feinberg, *Jeremiah: A Commentary* (Grand Rapids: Zondervan, 1982), 285.

Fig. 5.16 – Defense walls of the 6th century fort at Tell Qedua (Migdol)
Photo by Hesham Hussein

Fig. 5.17 – Isometric plan of the fort Migdol
Created by Hesham Hussein

JEREMIAH TRAVELS TO EGYPT

Map 5.2 – Paleo-environmental map of Egypt's northeastern frontier with Sinai *Map prepared by Stephen Moshier*

The route Jeremiah and his compatriots took to Egypt can be basically plotted on a map based on the placenames mentioned in Jeremiah 44:1. Recent archaeological and geological investigations, however, have enabled us to clarify the picture in greater detail by offering new details. In Jeremiah 2:18 (RSV) Judah's shifting political alliances between Assyria and Egypt are referred to in geographical terms. God asks, "now why go to Egypt to drink water from the Shihor? And why go to Assyria to drink water from the River?" "The River" clearly points to the Euphrates, east of which lies Assyria's heartland. Shihor is the comparable body of water for Egypt, marking its frontier.[49] Shihor is an Egyptian term meaning the waters or lake of Horus (the most prominent deity in the region).[50] New investigations in northwestern Sinai, based on the study of satellite images and geological work on the ground, have demonstrated that this body of water was a lagoon in the second millennium B.C., and it was fed by two Nile distributaries that in turn emptied into the

49 ESV and NIV render this as "the Nile."

50 James K. Hoffmeier, *Tell el-Borg I* (Winona Lake, IN: Eisenbrauns), 38–39.

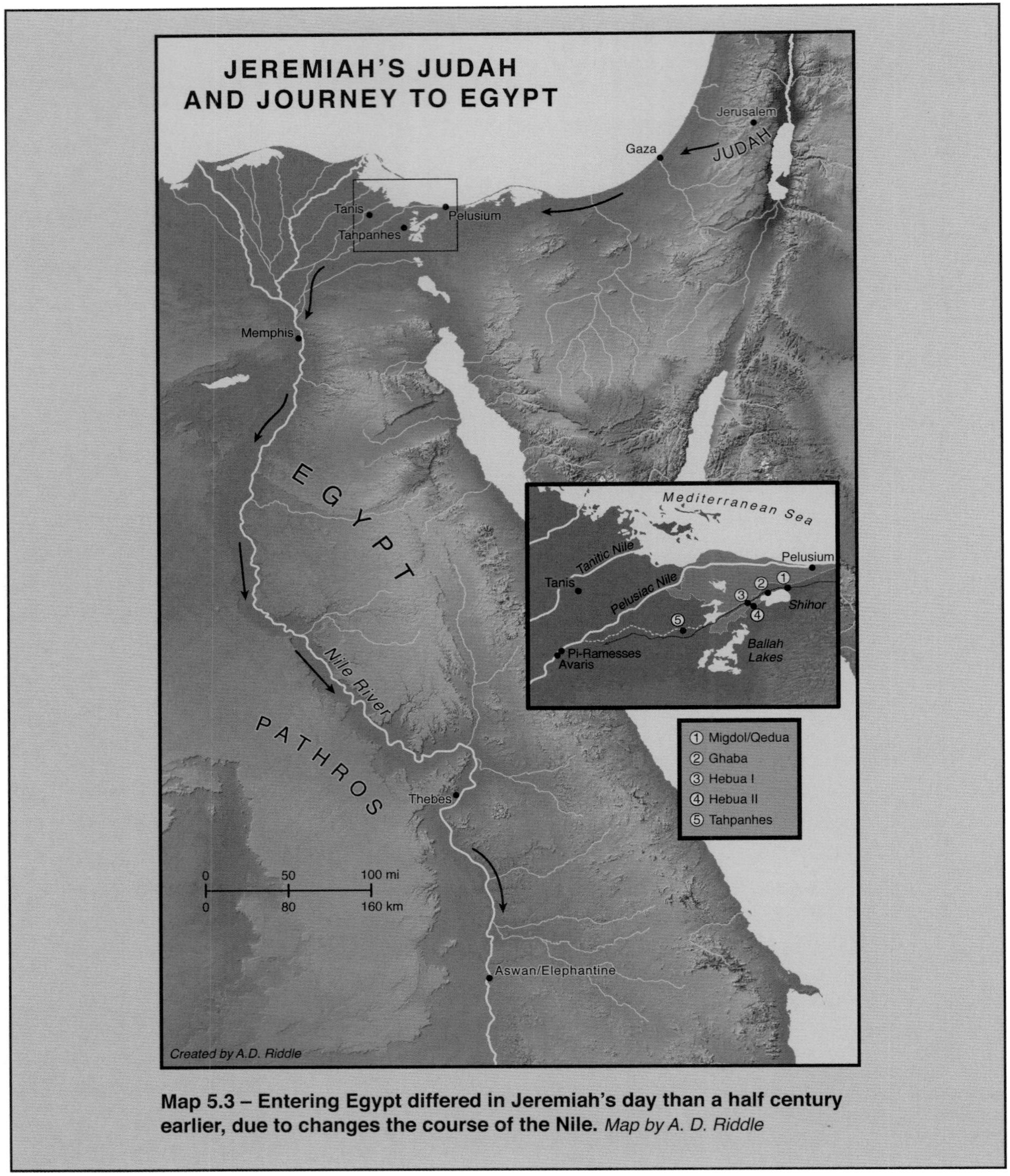

Map 5.3 – Entering Egypt differed in Jeremiah's day than a half century earlier, due to changes the course of the Nile. *Map by A. D. Riddle*

Mediterranean. The southern branch was discovered in 2000 by a team of researchers directed by this author and geologist Stephen Moshier.[51]

The new data mean that the ancient road between Egypt and Canaan traversed around this lagoon, with a number of fifteenth-twelfth century B.C. forts guarding the way, before turning east toward the Levant. Seven hundred years later by Jeremiah's day, this circuitous route had been abandoned because the two Nile branches desiccated, and the Pelusiac branch formed north of this area as the Nile's Delta built to the north and east. The Lake of Horus (Shihor) had turned into a marshland, and the former opening to the Mediterranean had silted up and a new route for travel was established across the former opening. At the northeast section of the lake is where the aforementioned fort called Migdol (Jer. 44:1; 46:14; Ezek. 29:10; 30:6) was discovered. It was Egypt's east frontier entry point where Jeremiah would likely have had to report to authorities to be cleared for entry.

From Migdol, the Judean party would have passed the recently established town at Tell Ghaba (the ancient name is not known) in the midst of the former opening between the lake and the sea, about 3 miles (4.5 km) west of Migdol. Next they would have come to another fort at Tell Hebua, about 4.5 miles (7.5 km) to the west. Centuries earlier Tell Hebua was the eastern border town with two massive forts of earlier period, but it was now reduced in size and importance, and yet with a fort and temples. Continuing on the road another 7.5 miles (12 km), Jeremiah would have reached Tahpanes (Tell Defenneh) where he delivered a message to his fellow countrymen who had preceded him to Egypt. He warned that Nebuchadnezzar's armies would soon come to Egypt, meaning that Egypt offered no real deliverance for them (Jer. 43:8–15).

Shortly after the band of Judeans fled Judah due to the assassination of the governor Gedeliah, Babylonian forces returned to the region to round up rebels in 582 B.C. (Jer. 52:30). This action close to Egypt's sphere of interest may have prompted Pharaoh Hophra (Apries) to send troops to the other side of Sinai to discourage Babylonian forces from entering Egypt. In 2011, an inscription of Hophra's was discovered at Tell Defenneh, which may allude to such a military action.[52] It was not until 568 that Nebuchadnezzar's armies followed the route taken by Jeremiah into Egypt to fulfill the prophet's warnings of an invasion of Egypt.

---

51 James K. Hoffmeier and Stephen O. Moshier, "New Paleo-Environmental Evidence from North Sinai to Complement Manfred Bietak's Map of the Eastern Delta and Some Historical Implications," in *Timelines: Studies in Honour of Manfred Bietak II* (Leuven: Peeters, 2006), 167–76.

52 Mohamed Abd el-Maksoud and Dominique Valbelle, "Une Stèle de la'an 7 d'Apries découverte sur le site de Tell Défenneh," *Revue d'Egyptologie* 64 (2013): 1–13.

Jeremiah's Book

The book offers some information about how the prophet received his messages. God tells Jeremiah that "I have put my words in your mouth" (Jer. 1:9), but how that happened is not explained during his call. Jeremiah reports (see below) of his audience in the divine council where he hears God's utterances. In Jeremiah 31 the prophet records God's word about the restoration of the land: "People will live together in Judah and all its towns—farmers and those who move about with their flocks. I will refresh the weary and satisfy the faint" (Jer. 31:24–25). This prophecy is followed by a rare glimpse into the reception of God's word: "At this I awoke and looked around. My sleep had been pleasant to me" (Jer. 31:26). Clearly, the LORD had spoken to the prophet during his sleep in a dream or an audible vision.

This book is the longest in the entire Hebrew canon. Grasping how the book was organized has presented a challenge to readers of Jeremiah. Chronological order was evidently not the organizing principle as can been seen from the fact that, for example, chapter 24 is dated to 597 B.C., while chapter 25 dates to 605 B.C., but then chapters 27–28 return to 597 B.C. Some sections, like the so-called "Book of Consolations" (chaps. 30–33), is a compilation of a variety of messages from different times that are united of the theme of Israel's future restoration and blessings. This thematically based section may have circulated as an independent unit. Furthermore, it is conceivable that the "Book of Consolations" was sent to the exiles already in Babylon with those were taken in 586 B.C., or even sent before that date.

Fig. 5.18 – Recently discovered inscription of Pharaoh Hophra/Apries from Tell Deffeneh/ Tahpanhes *Photo by James K. Hoffmeier*

Letters were sent between Jerusalem and the exiles in Babylon (Jer. 29), and the scroll of Jeremiah's oracle of doom was carried to Babylon to be read (Jer. 51:59–64). Thus it is certainly possible that the Book of Consolations and other portions of Jeremiah's work had been sent to the Babylonian exiles along with these letters. When the Persians seized Babylon in 539 B.C., Daniel the prophet concluded that the exile was over in accordance with the seventy-year period specified in "the Scriptures, according to the word of the LORD given to Jeremiah the prophet, that the desolation of Jerusalem would last seventy years" (Dan. 9:2). The word "Scriptures" (NIV) or "books" (ESV), Hebrew *sēp̱er*, is better rendered "scroll,"[53] and in the Daniel reference, the word is plural, "scrolls." This suggests that by the end of the exile, Daniel had in his possession at least two scrolls. The reference to the seventy-year exile occurs in Jeremiah's letter to the exiles (Jer. 29:1–10).

Fig. 5.19 – Group of bullae from Jerusalem; some show the impression of papyrus and the string that was tied around the scroll. *Photo courtesy of BibleLandPictures*

We can learn much about the history of the book and how the book originated in chapter 36. In 605 B.C., twenty-one years after Jeremiah's career began, God instructs the prophet to record the messages he had received since 626 B.C. (Jer. 36:1–2). "So Jeremiah called Baruch son of Neriah, and while Jeremiah dictated all the words the LORD had spoken to him, Baruch wrote them on the scroll" (36:4). Later in the same chapter, Baruch is called "the scribe" (vv. 26, 32), which identifies his profession (see Fig. 5.14). When the first edition of the book was complete, Baruch read it publicly at the temple. Then the scroll was read to King Jehoiakim, who cut it up and burnt it (v. 23). This brazen act of defiance against God's word by the king, who represented the nation, in a sense sealed the fate of Jerusalem.

Fig. 5.20 – Aramaic Papyrus from Jewish community on Elephantine Island (Aswan), ca. 449 B.C. *Photo courtesy of the Brooklyn Museum*

Scrolls in this period were largely made of Egyptian papyrus.[54] Though no papyrus from the pre-exilic period has survived in Israel, the clay seal impressions or bullae prove that papyrus was used due to the impression of papyrus texture on the underside of most bullae, and often the imprinted of the string that was wrapped around the scroll can also be detected.

God ordered that a second scroll recorded: "So Jeremiah took another scroll and gave it to the scribe Baruch son of Neriah, and as Jeremiah dictated, Baruch wrote on it all the words of the scroll that Jehoiakim king of Judah had burned in the fire. And many similar words were added to them" (vs. 32). The initial copy of the second edition, then, included the contents of the destroyed version, and other messages that were added in 605 B.C. Since the prophet's work continued for

53 *HALOT* 766.
54 King, *Jeremiah*, 87–88a.

Fig. 5.21 – Papyrus plants grow in marshy waters *Photo by Gloria Suess/ Bibleplaces.com*

Fig. 5.22 – Molds made it easy to make clay plaques of deities. Astarte (Ashtaroth) standing on back of horse
Photo by Christian Walker/bibelausstellung.de, courtesy Israel Museum, Jerusalem by Amalyah Keshet)

another twenty-five to thirty years, obviously still more was added, and the book grew over time.

When Jeremiah went to Egypt, Baruch accompanied the prophet (43:6–7). Clearly the chapters that covered his travel to Egypt and preaching there must come from the final stage of his ministry (Jer. 43–44). It may well be that in the ultimate years of his life in Egypt where papyrus was plentiful that Jeremiah was able to complete the book with Baruch's help. As noted above, by 539 B.C. "books (lit. scrolls)" of Jeremiah the prophet were cited authoritatively by Daniel (Dan. 9:2), suggesting that parts or all of the book were available in Babylon before the end of the exile. Nothing is known about Jeremiah's death and burial, but he likely died in Egypt.

Warning and Judgment

Like his eighth-century colleagues Hosea, Isaiah, and Micah, Jeremiah frames his early messages as a lawsuit because of the violation of the Sinaitic Covenant.[55] After describing how Israel like a bride had faithfully followed God in the wilderness after the exodus from Egypt (Jer. 2:2–3), the people had lapsed into infidelity, and the religious and political leaders had turned away from the LORD (Jer. 2:8), leading Jeremiah to declare, "I will bring charges (*rîḇ*) against your children's children" (Jer. 2:9). He further likens Israel to a woman divorced for adultery (Jer. 3:1). Jeremiah uses the word "Israel" for the remnant of the northern tribes still in northern Israel, as well as those in captivity since the eighth century.[56] According to a law in Deuteronomy (24:1–4), spouses should not take back their adulterous partners. Despite this, the LORD would do the unthinkable; namely, invite wayward Israel back to him, just as Hosea had done. "'Return faithless people," declares the LORD, "for I am your husband'" (Jer. 3:14). The offer of restoration required the people

55 Harrison, *Jeremiah and Lamentations,* 54.
56 Feinberg, *Jeremiah: A Commentary*, 44.

to "acknowledge your guilt" (Jer. 3:13), and then he demands: "'If you, Israel, will return, then return to me,' declares the LORD. 'If you put your detestable idols out of my sight and no longer go astray. . . . Circumcise yourselves to the LORD, circumcise your hearts, you people of Judah and inhabitants of Jerusalem, or my wrath will flare up and burn like fire because of the evil you have done—burn with no one to quench it" (Jer. 4:1, 4).

By referring to the circumcising of the heart, a spiritual severing of sin from one's life rather than a physical act of cutting the male foreskin, Jeremiah was quoting from the recently discovered book of Deuteronomy (10:16; 30:6). The prophet was advocating a painful process that would require getting rid of pagan practices that had been so intertwined with the worship of the LORD that the people were unable to distinguish orthodox from illicit religious practices. In addition to placing pagan images in the temple (Jer. 7:30), in the Valley of the Son of Hinnom that surrounds south and west sides of Jerusalem, some Judeans were engaged in the heinous practice of infant sacrifice. God's anger is palpable:

> They have built the high places of Topheth in the Valley of Ben Hinnom to burn their sons and daughters in the fire—something I did not command, nor did it enter my mind. So beware, the days are coming, declares the LORD, when people will no longer call it Topheth or the Valley of Ben Hinnom, but the Valley of Slaughter, for they will bury the dead in Topheth until there is no more room. (Jer. 7:31–32)

Fig. 5.23 – Hinnom Valley south of the walls of Jerusalem *Photo by Alexander Schick/bibelausstellung.de*

New insights into the meaning of "Tophet" came to light during excavations in present-day Tunisia. There archaeologists have uncovered the remains of Carthaginian culture.[57] This culture was made up of Phoenician colonists from Tyre who settled in North Africa in the ninth

57 Lawrence Stager and Samuel Wolff, "Child Sacrifice at Carthage: Religious Rite or Population Control?" *BAR* 10 (1984): 35–51.

Fig. 5.24 – Tombs cut into the stone ridges of the Hinnom Valley
Photo by James K. Hoffmeier

century B.C.[58] They brought with them their religious traditions and practices, including infant sacrifice. The Tophet of Carthage was uncovered where infants of various ages were burnt as sacrifices, and then their charred bones were placed in urns for burial, along with inscribed tombstones indicating that they were in some cases sacrificed to fulfill a vow (*nzr*). An estimated twenty thousand urns were buried there, and only infant bones, never those of adults, were uncovered. This vile practice had a history of around six hundred years at Carthage and was

58 The term Phoenicia/n applies to the area or people of present-day Lebanon, but they are essentially Canaanites who lived in the region north of the area known as Canaan, which in turn was mostly the Promised Land.

Fig. 5.25 – A votive stela from the Tophet at Carthage with Punic inscription dedicated to Baal Hammon, including a vow. Dated to the Iron II period in Hecht Museum (Haifa). *Photo by A. D. Riddle/ Bibleplaces.com*

taking place in the valley outside of Jerusalem, within sight of the temple of the Lord. No wonder God was going to punish Jerusalem and turn the same valley where innocents were sacrificed into a "Valley of Slaughter" (Jer. 7:32) where the guilty would pay the ultimate price.

Jeremiah's most famous sermon was preached at the entrance to the temple in chapter 7, and is paralleled in chapter 26, which is a prose accounting of the Temple Sermon, focusing more on the reaction to the message than the content of the message itself.[59] Based on the chronological data

59 Thompson, *Jeremiah*, 523–24.

offered in 26:1, the event fell on the year 609, the beginning of Jehoiakim's reign.[60] More precisely, the time of the year was later summer or early fall.[61] Three annual agricultural pilgrimage festivals were observed in Israel, where every family was to be represented (Exod. 23:14–17). The Feast of Ingathering was observed in September–October, and this may be the occasion of Jeremiah's Temple Sermon, when a large audience would be entering the temple precinct for ceremonies (Jer. 7:2).

First the prophet announces that only if the people truly amend their ways will they be able to remain in their homeland (Jer. 7:3). Then he accused them of placing faith in the temple rather than the God of the temple: "Do not trust in deceptive words and say, 'This is the temple of the LORD, the temple of the LORD, the temple of the LORD!'" (Jer. 7:4). It appears that the religious establishment believed that the mere presence of the temple was a guarantee that Jerusalem was invincible.[62] God challenged the people to consider what happened to Israel's first sanctuary: "Go now to my place at Shiloh where I first made a dwelling for my Name, and see what I did to it because of the wickedness of my people Israel" (Jer. 7:12). Here reference is made to the destruction of Shiloh, where the tabernacle stood from the days of Joshua until the time of Eli and Samuel (Josh. 18:1; 2 Sam. 4—see Fig. 2.7 & 2.9). The people seemed to think that they could live as they wished, engage in pagan religious observances, and then come to the temple of the LORD in Jerusalem and believe they would still enjoy God's blessings. This false "temple" theology is challenged when Jeremiah queried: "Will you steal and murder, commit adultery and perjury, burn incense to Baal and follow other gods you have not known, and then come and stand before me in this house, which bears my Name, and say, 'We are safe'—safe to do all these detestable things?" (Jer. 7:9–11). In this statement, five of the Ten Commandments are referenced. The only hope for Judah, then, was to return to a right relationship with God by obeying the commandments laid out in the Sinai Covenant.

In his sermon, the prophet urges people to practice justice (Jer. 7:5), it is noteworthy that in his sermon the biblical idea of justice (*mîšpāṭ*) is clarified. It includes the moral (i.e., adultery, murder), religious or spiritual (i.e., idolatry) and social areas (care for the alien, fatherless, and widow [7:6]). This is

---

60 Thiele, *Hebrew Kings*, 75.
61 Holladay, *Jeremiah*, 240.
62 Peter Craigie, Page Kelley, and Joel Drinkard, *Jeremiah 1–25*, Word Biblical Commentary (Dallas: Word, 1991), 120–21.

because biblical justice is based on God's covenantal stipulations or laws from Exodus 20 onward through the book of Deuteronomy.

The prophet's many messages can be summed up by what he said in Jeremiah 11:6–8:

> The LORD said to me, "Proclaim all these words in the towns of Judah and in the streets of Jerusalem: 'Listen to the terms of this covenant and follow them. From the time I brought your forefathers up from Egypt until today, I warned them again and again, saying, "Obey me." But they did not listen or pay attention; instead, they followed the stubbornness of their evil hearts. So I brought on them all the curses of the covenant I had commanded them to follow but that they did not keep.'"

Fig. 5.26 – Plan of Solomon's Temple

Illustration taken from the ESV® Study Bible [The Holy Bible, English Standard Version®], copyright ©2008 by Crossway, a publishing ministry of Good News Publishers. Used by permission. All rights reserved.

Jeremiah sees the covenant relationship with God to be irreparably broken; Israel was a faithless wife who could not be rehabilitated from her insatiable desire to violate the marital covenant. At the end of this message, God instructs Jeremiah not to pray or intercede for his people (Jer. 11:14). The only hope is a new covenant, which will be treated below.

Jeremiah's Dramatic Acts

More than any other prophet, Jeremiah used dramatic acts to communicate his messages to his audience. While some of these actions were played out in public, some were private and for his benefit in order for him to understand God's plans and actions. In ancient Near Eastern cultures, that were devoid of all the modern visual mediums, acting out a message would have had a powerful and graphic effect on the audience. Jeremiah was a master of communicating via dramatic acts, often by employing actual objects. Sometimes the medium was the message, or it reinforced or illustrated the point.

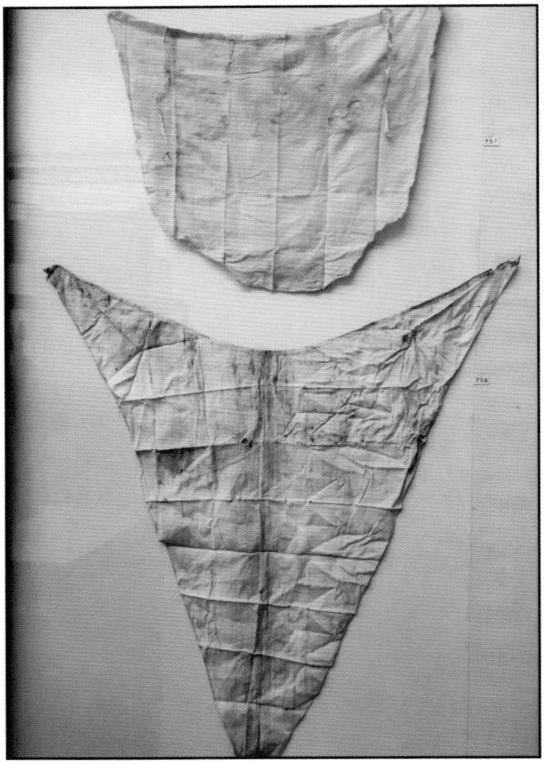

Fig. 5.27 – Linen underpants from the tomb of Tutankhamun in Cairo Museum
Photo by James K. Hoffmeier

The linen belt

Jeremiah was ordered by God to "buy a linen belt and put it around your waist" (Jer. 13:1). The NIV's "linen belt" does not fit the description of 13:11, which indicates that this item was worn directly beside the body, not over other clothes like a belt.[63] This item of clothing would be like tight-fitting underpants. Hence the translation "linen loincloth" (ESV) or "linen shorts" (NET) better fits the description. Linen undergarments were found in Tutankamun's tomb and in that of an architect names Kha from the same general period in Egypt.

Then he was told to bury it along the banks of "Perath" (so NIV, NET), which in some English translations reads "the Euphrates" (ESV). Indeed the Hebrew word *p*^{e}*rāt* is the term for the Euphrates River that flowed through Mesopotamia (e.g. Gen. 2:14;

63 Lundbom, *Jeremiah 1–20*, 667–68.

15:18; Num. 22:5; Jer. 46:2). If the great Euphrates were the location in view in Jeremiah 13:1, the prophet would have had to journey around three hundred miles (480 km) to carry out this command. Alternatively, "Perath" is also the name of a spring-fed stream known today as Wadi Farah, situated just 3 miles (5 km) from Jeremiah's home in Anathoth.[64] The Arabic name "Farah" actually preserves the Hebrew "Perath." It would have taken just over an hour for the prophet to hike from his home to this stream. The local stream seems more likely than the distant Euphrates River.

An undisclosed time later he was directed to return and dig up the cloth, only to discover that "it was ruined and completely useless" (Jer. 13:7). The word of the LORD followed, explaining that just "'as a belt is bound around the waist, so I bound all the people of Israel and all the people of Judah to me,' declares the LORD, 'to be my people for my renown and praise and honor. But they have not listened'" (13:11).

"Bound" (NIV), "cling" (ESV), or "cling tightly" (NET) are good translations of the word *dāḇaq*.[65] The same term is used in Deuteronomy to describe the ideal relationship between the people of Israel and their God: "Fear the LORD your God and serve him. Hold fast to him" (Deut. 10:20). A more expanded statement occurs again in Deuteronomy where it is closely connected with the renewing of the Sinai covenant and the witnesses are summoned:

> This day I call heaven and earth as witnesses against you that I have set before you life and death, blessings and curses. Now choose life, so that you and your children may live and that you may love the LORD your God, listen to his voice, and hold fast to him. For the LORD is your life, and he will give you many years in the land he swore to give to your fathers, Abraham, Isaac and Jacob (Deut. 30:19–20).

Dāḇaq also is used to describe God's design the closeness within the marriage relationship between a man and a woman: "FThat is why a man leaves his father and mother and is united (*dāḇaq*) to his wife, and they become one flesh" (Gen. 2:24). The linen belt or waist cloth was to illustrate how God desired his people to be close to him, intimately bound together. By virtue of disobeying God, however, the people not only lost closeness to the LORD, but

---

64 John Bright, *Jeremiah*, Anchor Bible Commentary (New York: Doubleday, 1965), lxxxvii.
65 *HALOT* 209.

failed in their mission "to be my people for my renown and praise and honor. But they have not listened" (Jer. 13:11). Just like the linen cloth that was spoiled and useless, so too Israel had lost its divine purpose.

We can only speculate whether or not this dramatic act was witnessed only by the prophet to teach him the lesson, or whether Jeremiah actually took the spoiled and soiled clothing public and used it as a stage prop for his message. Certainly displaying the linen before an audience is in keeping with other acts of the prophet.

The potter's house

In chapter 18, Jeremiah was directed to go to a potter's house or workshop and watch him molding a vessel. As he was shaping a jar, "the clay was marred in his hands; so the potter formed it into another pot, shaping it as seemed best to him" (18:4). The point of this observation is that as the potter could shape the vessel as he saw fit, so too the sovereign God could shape Israel's destiny as he wished: "Like clay in the hand of the potter, so are you in my hand, Israel" (18:6). God's "shaping" (*yaṣār*) a clay vessel is reminiscent of the LORD's creative actions in Genesis 2:7 where he "formed" (*yaṣār*) Adam out of the dust or soil. During Jeremiah's call, God told the young man "before I formed (*yaṣār*) you in the womb, I knew you" (Jer. 1:5). Simply put, Israel's fate was in hands of God the Creator, and their future would be shaped according to his will. Their only hope to not be ruined was to respond positively to his warnings through his prophets.

Fig. 5.28 – Potter forming a vessel in the tomb of Amenemhet at Beni Hasan
Photo by James K. Hoffmeier

Fig. 5.29 – In Jeremiah 18:3, the prophet sees the potter forming a vessel "on his wheel," which literally reads "on the two stones." Here is a pair of stones used by ancient potters, a lower fixed stone and the top one that rotates.
Photo by James K. Hoffmeier

The broken vessel

Once again the prophet exposes the abominable practices at the Tophet in the Valley of the Son of Hinnom or Hinnom Valley (see discussion above regarding Jer. 7). Jeremiah is told by God to buy a clay vessel, perhaps bottle-shaped, and go out of the Potsherd Gate that led to the Hinnom Valley (Jer. 19:1–2). The Potsherd Gate is otherwise unattested in the Bible, but may be the same as the Dung Gate (Neh.

2:13; 3:13–14; 12:31), and signifies the gate through which people went to dump refuse.[66] Jeremiah took with him some of the elders and priests of Jerusalem, and there announced God's judgment on the nation because "They have built the high places of Baal to burn their children in the fire as offerings to Baal—something I did not command or mention, nor did it enter my mind. So beware, the days are coming, declares the LORD, when people will no longer call this place Topheth or the Valley of Ben Hinnom, but the Valley of Slaughter" (Jer. 19:5–6).

Fig. 5.30 – Broken vessels are typical irreparable and useless.
Photo by James K. Hoffmeier

Then he threw down the jar, shattering it, while announcing: "This is what the LORD Almighty says: I will smash this nation and this city just as this potter's jar is smashed and cannot be repaired" (Jer. 19:11). This dramatic act, coupled with the announcement of doom, not only got the attention of his audience, but they clearly understood its meaning. Perhaps they saw in Jeremiah's act more than something just symbolic. Rather the breaking jar could be regarded as some sort of magical act that they feared.

From the Valley of Hinnom, Jeremiah returned to the city, entering the temple courts (Jer. 19:14), where to a wider audience he proclaimed: "This is what the LORD Almighty, the God of Israel, says: 'Listen! I am going to bring on this city and the villages around it every disaster I pronounced against them, because they were stiff-necked and would not listen to my words'" (Jer. 19:15).

At this point, Pashhur, the chief officer in the temple, arrested Jeremiah (Jer. 20:1). The text does not indicate whether Pashur was among the priests who joined the prophet in the Hinnom Valley. If not, he was surely informed by his colleagues who had witnessed Jeremiah's breaking vessel act. The use of stocks was particularly harsh as it appears, based on the literal meaning of the Hebrew term derives from *hap̄āḵ*, which means "to turn = change, distort. An instrument of punishment therefore is imagined that held the body in a bent or crooked position."[67] On the priest's orders, Jeremiah was beaten and put in stocks, where he was kept at the Benjamin Gate by the temple. This is a clear case of "shooting the messenger." Harming Jeremiah

66 Holladay, *Jeremiah*, 539–40.
67 Lundbom, *Jeremiah 1–20*, 846.

would not change God's intentions, but it demonstrated that the religious authorities had no intention of reforming the land as Josiah had done. By rejecting Jeremiah's message, they were dismissing God's word and his correction. They were stiff-necked (Jer. 19:15).

Jeremiah wears a yoke

"Early in the reign of Zedekiah son of Josiah king of Judah, this word came to Jeremiah from the LORD: This is what the LORD said to me: 'Make a yoke out of straps and crossbars and put it on your neck'" (Jer. 27:1–2). So decked with a wooden yoke and straps to secure it to his body, Jeremiah went about announcing God's word. This event took place shortly after the Babylonian deportation of King Jehoiachin in 597 B.C. Judah had already to a degree capitulated to Nebuchadnezzar. Yokes were worn by animals to pull carts or plows. When an animal pushes back against its master's design to wear a yoke, it stiffens its neck and thus the animal resists submission.[68] It is this image that stands behind the expression "stiff-necked," a symbol of defiance and resisting God.

Jeremiah's act was coupled with the announcement that God had ordained Nebuchadnezzar and therefore the nation should simply yield to him as an animal submits to its master by wearing the yoke. Since Jeremiah actually wore a yoke to communicate his message, it is not surprising that he alone of the prophets uses the expression "stiff-necked" (Jer. 7:26, 17:23; 19:15). Israel is first called a stiff-necked people after the golden calf incident in the wilderness when the Hebrews rebelled against the LORD by making and worshiping the molten image (Exod. 32:9; 33:3, 5). No doubt, when Jeremiah's audience heard this indictment, it must have evoked memories of the wilderness episode. In the New Testament, when Stephen called those who stubbornly rejected the gospel of Jesus Christ "you stiff-necked people" (Acts 7:51), his execution summarily followed.

Jeremiah also directed this message at King Zedekiah, saying, "I gave the same message to Zedekiah king of Judah. I said, 'Bow your neck under the yoke of the king of Babylon; serve him and his people, and you will live. Why will you and your people die by the sword, famine and plague with which the LORD has threatened any nation that will not serve the king of Babylon?'" (Jer. 27:12–13).

Then he discloses that his message was being opposed by fellow prophets: "Do not listen to the words of the prophets who say to you, 'You will not serve the king of Babylon,' for they are prophesying lies to you. 'I have not sent them,'

---

68 *ISBE* 3:619.

declares the LORD. They are prophesying lies in my name. Therefore, I will banish you and you will perish, both you and the prophets who prophesy to you" (Jer. 27:14–15). This reference to the prophets who opposed Jeremiah's message leads to a most dramatic result.

The showdown with false prophets

In the next chapter, one of these prophets, Hananiah of Gibeon, approached Jeremiah, removed the wooden yoke, and broke it, proclaiming that God was going to break the yoke of Nebuchadnezzar within two years, and Jehoiachin and the exiles taken in 597 B.C. would return to Jerusalem (Jer. 28:2–4). A complete reversal of Jeremiah's message is intended by Hananiah's dramatic act. Who was right? Jeremiah expresses his wish that Hananiah was correct; after all, he does not want to see his beloved land devastated and the population deported and thousands killed. He warned, however, "From early times the prophets who preceded you and me have prophesied war, disaster and plague against many countries and great kingdoms. But the prophet who prophesies peace will be recognized as one truly sent by the LORD only if his prediction comes true" (28:8–9). In essence Jeremiah is alluding to the test of a prophet introduced by Moses in Deuteronomy 18:15–22. The way to distinguish a genuine word from God versus that of false prophetic utterance is quite simple: "If what a prophet proclaims in the name of the Lord does not take place or come true, that is a word that the LORD has not spoken. That prophet has spoken presumptuously" (v. 22). Jeremiah's point was that his own message was consistent with earlier prophets (like Amos, Micah, and Isaiah), whereas Hananiah's word, as appealing as it was, stood outside of the mainstream of recent prophetic thought over the past century or more and should therefore be suspect. "It is far easier," writes Brueggemann, "to break a symbolic yoke than it is to override Yahweh's tough verdict or to break the reality of Babylonian power."[69]

Fig. 5.31 – Yoked oxen in rural Egypt in the 1950s *Photo by Charles S. Hoffmeier*

Jeremiah offers two correctives to Hanniah's assertions. First, to illustrate Nebuchadnezzar's mastery over Judah was inevitable, Jeremiah was now divinely

69 Walter Brueggemann, *A Commentary on Jeremiah* (Grand Rapids: Eerdmans, 1998), 253.

instructed to make and wear a new yoke, but this time made out of iron (28:14), that is, out of a nearly indestructible material when compared to wood. Second, chapter 28 ends with the announcement that Hananiah died two months later, signaling that the false hope he promoted died with him. Jeremiah was vindicated.

THE DIVINE COUNCIL: THE ULTIMATE TEST OF A PROPHET

In Jeremiah 28 we met Hananiah, a leader of the band of false prophets in Jerusalem who attempt to quash Jeremiah's preaching about the coming destruction of the city. In Chapter 29 we learn, through a series of letters between the Jeremiah and the exiles, and others between the exiles and temple leaders in Jerusalem, that there were false prophets in Babylon too. Two are named, Ahab and Zedekiah, who were fomenting unrest among the exiles by promising quick return to their homeland (Jer. 29:21–24). It is unclear whether the misguided belief of a very brief exile was started in Babylon and then repeated in Jerusalem by Hananiah, but this seems plausible as there is indication of a possible revolt against Nebuchadnezzar which prompted Ahab and Zedekiah to advance this false hope.[70] Because these prophets had stirred up the exiles, Nebuchadnezzar had Ahab and Zedekiah executed by being burned to death (Jer. 29:22–23), the same manner of death that was attempted by the same king on Daniel's associates Shadrach, Meshach, and Abednego (Dan. 3:19–25).

This unfortunate episode leads us back to the question of knowing whether a prophet speaks authoritatively for God or not. Prophets like Micah and Isaiah, who proclaimed the coming exile followed by a return to the land, did not live to see the outcome as prescribed in Deuteronomy 18. As Jeremiah repeatedly is confronted about his message, he had another recourse. He could claim that he was in the divine council (*sôḏ*), a privilege unique to a genuine prophet as has been noted: "no humans being apart from the prophet is ever described in the bible as being allowed to attend God's council meeting."[71] The story of Micaiah the prophet in 2 Kings 22 provides some insight into the prophet's participation in the *sôḏ* (see discussion in chap. 2). It may be that Isaiah's call and vision of God who speaks to the prophet could also be an example of the divine council.[73] In Jeremiah's case we have God pushing back against the false prophets in chapter 23 and showing that "the true prophet is one who first stands in Yahweh's council."[74]

---

70 Thompson, *Jeremiah*, 544–50.
71 Meier, *Themes and Transformations*, 21.

Bogus prophetic utterances are identifiable: "Thus says the LORD of hosts: 'Do not listen to the words of the prophets who prophesy to you, filling you with vain hopes. They speak visions of their own minds, not from the mouth of the LORD'" (Jer. 23:16 ESV). The rhetorical question is posed, "For who among them has stood in the council of the LORD to see and to hear his word, or who has paid attention to his word and listened?" (Jer. 23:18 ESV). This seems to be Jeremiah's claim that he had attended the divine conclave and has spoken accordingly.[75] God continues by dismissing the prophets who had not been in the divine council but speak as if their messages came from the LORD. "I did not send these prophets, yet they have run with their message; I did not speak to them, yet they have prophesied. But if they had stood in my council, they would have proclaimed my words to my people and would have turned them from their evil ways and from their evil deeds" (Jer. 23:21–22). Verse 22 draws a contrast between Jeremiah who had stood in the divine council and the other prophets who offer their own erroneous prognostications.

Messages of Hope and Restoration

In the days after the deportation of 597 B.C., a series of letters were sent between Jeremiah in Jerusalem and the exiles in Babylon that are preserved in chapter 29. These communiqués were sent along with Judean envoys to Babylon for King Zedekiah (perhaps to bring tribute; Jer. 29:3). One letter is clearly designed to refute the false prophecy of Hananiah and his counterparts in Babylon among the captives who were claiming that there would be a two-year exile and a return to Judah (Jer. 28:1–4; 29:21). Here is Jeremiah's response:

> Build houses and settle down; plant gardens and eat what they produce. Marry and have sons and daughters; find wives for your sons and give your daughters in marriage, so that they too may have sons and daughters. Increase in number there; do not decrease. Also, seek the peace and prosperity of the city to which I have carried you into exile. Pray to the LORD for it, because if it prospers, you too will prosper." Yes, this is what the LORD Almighty, the God of Israel, says: "Do not let the prophets and diviners among you deceive you. Do not listen to the dreams you encourage them to have. They are prophesying lies to

72 Meier, *Themes and Transformations*, 21–22.
73 Craigie, Kelley, and Drinkard, *Jeremiah 1–25*, 345.
74 Brueggemann, *Commentary on Jeremiah*, 211–12.

> you in my name. I have not sent them," declares the LORD. This is what the LORD says: "When seventy years are completed for Babylon, I will come to you and fulfill my gracious promise to bring you back to this place. For I know the plans I have for you," declares the LORD, "plans to prosper you and not to harm you, plans to give you hope and a future. Then you will call upon me and come and pray to me, and I will listen to you. You will seek me and find me when you seek me with all your heart. I will be found by you," declares the LORD, "and will bring you back from captivity. I will gather you from all the nations and places where I have banished you," declares the LORD, "and will bring you back to the place from which I carried you into exile." (Jer. 29:5–14)

Rather than two years in exile, Jeremiah announces seventy years. So he urges the people to settle down and make the best of life in Babylon. Return would only come after a genuine turning back to God, and then they would be restored to their homeland.

NEW COVENANT

Undoubtedly, Jeremiah's new covenant is the most significant theological development in the book of Jeremiah, and it is located in the Book of Consolations (Jer. 31:31–34). Jeremiah announces that in the future, a new covenant would be instituted that would be different than the one made at Mt. Sinai:

> "The days are coming," declares the Lord, "when I will make a new covenant with the people of Israel and with the people of Judah. It will not be like the covenant I made with their ancestors when I took them by the hand to lead them out of Egypt, because they broke my covenant, though I was a husband to them,'" declares the LORD. "This is the covenant I will make with the people of Israel after that time," declares the LORD. "I will put my law in their minds and write it on their hearts. I will be their God, and they will be my people." (Jer. 31:31–33)

When Jesus celebrated the Passover meal or Seder with his disciples (often called "the last supper" by Christians), he passed the cup of wine which he identified as "the new covenant in my blood, which is poured out for you" (Luke 22:20). Jeremiah 31:31–33 is actually quoted verbatim in the New Testament book of Hebrews (8:8–12) and is regarded as fulfilled in Jesus Christ: "But in fact the ministry Jesus has received is as superior to theirs as the covenant of which he is mediator is superior to the old one, since the new covenant is established on better promises" (Heb. 8:6). As a consequence, Jeremiah's new covenant is viewed within Christian theology as a turning point that anticipates the coming to Jesus and the establishment of the church.

Fig. 5.32 – DaVinci's Last Supper in the Church of Santa Maria delle Gracie in Milan
Photo by joyofmuseums.com / Wikimedia Commons, CC BY-SA 4.0

Restored Kingship

After David became king of Israel (ca. 1000 B.C.) and established Jerusalem as his capital, he was informed through Nathan the prophet that God would establish an enduring kingship through his son: "I will establish the throne of his kingdom forever" (2 Sam. 7:13). To Solomon God appeared in a dream and confirmed the promise made to his father: "I will establish your royal throne over Israel forever, as I promised David your father when I said, 'you shall never fail to have a successor on the throne of Israel'" (1 Kings 9:5). Obviously the removal of King Jehoiachin and then

Zedekiah the last king of Judah by Nebuchadnezzar, along with the destruction Jerusalem, cast doubt on God's commitment to the Davidic Covenant.

Through Jeremiah, God assures the Judean exiles that his promise was intact, declaring:

> "The days are coming," declares the LORD, "when I will fulfill the good promise I made to the house of Israel and to the house of Judah. In those days and at that time I will make a righteous Branch sprout from David's line; he will do what is just and right in the land. In those days Judah will be saved and Jerusalem will live in safety. This is the name by which it will be called: The LORD Our Righteous Savior." (Jer. 33:14–16)

Initially the word "branch" (*ṣemaḥ*) was applied to the remnant of Israel in Isaiah 4:2. The Branch of David becomes a motif for the future messianic king (cf. Zech. 3:8, 6:12; see chap. 7). When the Persians permitted the Jews to return to Judah in 539 B.C., it was Jehoiachin's grandson Zerubbabel who was appointed governor and helped restore Jerusalem (Ezra 3). Zerubbabel, however, is never called "king" in the Bible (see further chapter 7). So while members of David's line survived and returned to Jerusalem, the kingship was not restored during the Old Testament or intertestamental period.

The final chapters of Jeremiah (40–52) are devoted to events in Judah after the destruction of Jerusalem and the prophet's experiences preaching to the exiles in Egypt (43–44), followed by prophecies that announce the judgment on foreign nations, including Egypt (46) and Babylon (50–51). The last chapter reviews the events surrounding the fall of Jerusalem and the four campaigns against Judah by Nebuchadnezzar's armies between 605 and 582 B.C. This all sounds like a depressing way to conclude a book, until we read the final paragraph. It announces the release of Jehoiachin in 568 B.C. He had been incarcerated thirty years earlier (Jer. 52:31–34). Further it is reported that he lived the remainder of his life in luxury, dining at the king's table and receiving an allowance for his daily needs. A tablet dating from before his prison release was discovered in Babylon early in the twentieth century that actually contains the

Fig. 5.33 – Babylonian tablet mentioning Jehoiachin in Berlin Museum
Photo by James K. Hoffmeier

ration list for "Jehoiachin king of Judah" and the "sons of the king of Judah."[75] By concluding this lengthy book with this notice, Jeremiah signals that just as Jehoiachin was released from prison, so too Israel's captivity would soon end, and the Davidic line was still intact.

THE BOOK OF NAHUM

"The LORD takes vengeance on his foes."

—Nahum 1:2

Nahum: The Man and His Home

This short book offers no details about the prophet. Nahum's home is identified as Elkosh, the location of which remains uncertain (Nah. 1:1), a village that is otherwise not mentioned in the OT. St. Jerome in the fourth century proposed a location in Galilee and suggested it might be associated with the name of the present-day site of el-Kauzeh.[76] Another tradition is that the New Testament fishing village on the Sea of Galilee, Capernaum, is the prophet's hometown as the name means "village of Nahum,"[77] but there is no historical or archaeological evidence to show that Capernaum was occupied between 1000 and 500 B.C.[78] Given the fact that the northern kingdom of Israel had been destroyed in 722 B.C. and only a remnant survived, it seems more likely that Nahum would be from Judah.[79]

Fig. 5.34 – Amon-Ra Temple in Thebes
Photo by James K. Hoffmeier

The title of the book is "A prophecy concerning Nineveh," the target of God's judgment. The downfall of Nineveh and the Assyrian Empire occurred in 612 B.C. When Nineveh's doom is announced, it is likened to that of Thebes (the Hebrew reads No-Amon, which in Egyptian means "City of Amon") in southern Egypt (Nah. 3:8). Thebes, like Nineveh on the Tigris River, was situated on Nile. Egypt was invaded in 671 B.C. by

75 *ANET* 308.
76 *ABD* 2:476.
77 Beitzel, *Moody Bible Atlas*, 241.
78 *NEAEHL* 1:292.
79 Baker, *Nahum, Habakkuk, Zephaniah*, 19.

Fig. 5.35 – Ashurbanipal firing arrows from his chariot in British Museum
Photo by A. D. Riddle/ Bibleplaces.com

the Assyrian king Esarhaddon,[80] but it was his successor Ashurbanipal who penetrated Egypt south to Thebes in 663 B.C. and devastated the sacred city dedicated to the God Amon.[81] Though a mighty city, it fell, and so would the great city of Nineveh. Based on these chronological benchmarks, Nahum must have prophesied within a fifty-year period between 663 and 612 B.C.

The Message of Nahum

With Nineveh's doom announced, we complete the story begun in the book of Jonah. When Jonah warned Nineveh of God's judgment, the city responded at some level. But the violent expansion of the Assyrian Empire for more than a century after 745 B.C. shows that the revival had no lasting effect. To justify

80 *ABD* 4:745.
81 *ABD* 4:746.

coming judgment on Nineveh, Nahum reminds his Judean audience that it was "the city of blood, full of lies, full of plunder, never without victims! . . . Many casualties, piles of dead, bodies without number, people stumbling over corpses" (Nah. 3:1, 3). This description well illustrates the inhumane and barbarous treatment of Assyria's enemies (see Fig. 3.32, 3.40, 4.24–29).

Fig. 5.36 – Judeans from Lachish being impaled by Assyrian soldiers; relief in the British Museum *Photo by A. D. Riddle/ Bibleplaces.com*

God is described as an "avenging God . . . the LORD takes vengeance on his foes and vents his wrath against his enemies" (Nah. 1:2). Some readers of this text might find the description of God as vengeful to be disconcerting. It has been shown, however, that such vengeance is carried out as part of the covenant relationship.[82] In this case, God is coming to the aid of his covenant partner, Judah, and avenging injustice done to her. At the same time, in words that echo Jonah's description of God (Jon. 4:2), Nahum insists that "the LORD is slow to anger but great in power" (Nah. 1:3). Indeed God had shown patience toward Nineveh and withheld destruction in the eighth century, but now after a century and a half of Assyrian brutality against various peoples, including Israel, this "city of blood" would experience God's legitimate wrath.

Obviously this development was welcome news for Judah. After such a long period of oppression, taxation, warfare, deportation, and death, God intervenes to do justice for his people. News of Nineveh's obliteration was carried by messengers to Judah: "Look, there on the mountains, the feet of one who brings good news, who proclaims peace! Celebrate your festivals, O Judah, and fulfill your vows. No more will the wicked invade you; they will be completely destroyed" (Nah. 1:15). This announcement of "good news" (*basēr*) echoes the words of Isaiah (40:9), and when translated into Greek in the Septuagint uses the word *euaggelion* (evangel) which is the term used in the New Testament for "the gospel." From the perspective of the residents of Jerusalem, the announcement of "good news" had to do with the end of Israel's enemy Assyria, but St. Paul in the New Testament saw beyond the immediate history to the future when Jesus would triumph over humanity's ultimate enemy, death (Rom. 10:9–15).

---

82 Smith, *Micah-Malachi*, 73.

Fig. 5.37 – An Assyrian soldier threatens to behead a prisoner and other soldiers are waving decapitated heads; relief in the British Museum
Photo by James K. Hoffmeier

Nahum's name derives from the word meaning "compassion" or "comfort."[83] Ironically, God had shown compassion on Nineveh in Jonah's day, but now the time for appropriate judgment has come after over a century of divine grace, which demonstrates that indeed Yahweh is "slow to anger."

THE BOOK OF HABAKKUK

"I am doing a work in your days."
—Habakkuk 1:5 (ESV)

The "good news" of the termination of the Assyrian empire offered by Nahum was short-lived relief from foreign foes, for the Babylonians who were instrumental in the fall of Nineveh in 612 B.C. would soon be Judah's new nemesis (see excursus "The Chaldeans" above). Habakkuk's short "oracle," the term used of the book itself (Hab. 1:1 ESV), seems to have been given in the waning years of the Assyrian empire, but before the emergence of the Babylonian-based Chaldeans (Hab. 1:6). The period of Habakkuk's activity can be established to around 626 B.C., when the Chaldeans established Babylon as its capital and down to 605 B.C., when Nebuchadnezzar's forces first marched on Jerusalem. This window of time makes Habakkuk a contemporary of Jeremiah. Nothing is offered in this book about the prophet himself, neither his hometown nor even his father's name is given. Given the chronological framework of the book, it appears that Habakkuk was based somewhere in Judah, and possibly the temple in Jerusalem. The reasoning behind this suggestion is that chapter 3 contains "A prayer of Habakkuk the prophet. On *shigionoth*" (3:1) and concludes with the musical notation: "For the director of music. On my stringed instruments" (3:19) (see Fig. 2.49). These are the hallmarks of a formal psalm like those in the book of Psalms that were connected with temple liturgy.[84] Habakkuk, then, may have been a Jerusalem-based temple prophet.

---

83 *HALOT* 689.
84 Bullock, *Introduction*, 211.

Message of Habakkuk

Fig. 5.38 – Egyptian musicians playing stringed instruments in the tomb of Rekhmire in western Thebes
Photo by A. D. Riddle/ Bibleplaces.com

The first chapter of the "oracle" is given as a dialogue between the prophet and God, in which the prophet offers a complaint in the form of a question (1:2–4), followed by God's response (1:5–11), a second complaint (1:12–2:1), and then God's retort (2:2–5). The prophet is angered by ongoing injustice and violence around him, presumably in Judah:

> Therefore the law (*tôrâ*) to is paralyzed,
> and justice (*mîšpāṭ*) never prevails.
> The wicked hem in the righteous
> so that justice (*mîšpāṭ*) is perverted.
> (Hab. 1:4)

Habakkuk is rightly concerned that God's laws are ignored, and so "justice is perverted." Put another way, "since the Law was no longer consulted for moral or spiritual guidance, 'true justice' could no longer come to light."[85] Given these circumstances, the frustrated prophet asks God, "How long" (Hab. 1:2) must this perversion of God's law continue? And "why do you tolerate wrong?" (Hab. 1:3).

The response he received was unexpected, if not shocking. "I am raising up the Babylonians (lit. Chaldeans), that ruthless and impetuous people who sweep across the whole earth to seize dwelling places not their own" (Hab. 1:6). God was already directing the geopolitical events of the day to address the remedy the problem Habakkuk rightly recognized. By saying "I am going to do something in your days" (1:5), God signals that the prophet would see the unfolding of God's judgment on Judah in the immediate rather than the distant future. A theological point emerges from God's response to Habakkuk, namely, that his divine purposes were at work to resolve injustice even when it appears nothing is happening.

Troubled by this response, the prophet first acknowledges God's holiness and the fact that he is an immovable "Rock" (1:12), "indicating his changeless stability."[86] He struggles, however with why God would allow a "treacherous" people like the Babylonians to punish unjust Judah. He does, however, accept God's purposes in ordaining Babylon to punish Judah, not obliterate

---

85 Kaiser, *Micah–Malachai*, 154.
86 Baker, *Nahum, Hababkkuk, Zephaniah*, 55.

it, to promote "justice and redemptive correction."[87] God then orders the prophet to "write down the revelation and make it plain on tablets so that a herald may run with it" (2:2). Here the opposite of messengers bringing "good news" is presented. A tablet (*lûaḥ*) would be a writing surface, made of wood, stone, or metal,[88] that was intended for public viewing. God's Law at Sinai, similarly, were engraved on tablets of stone (Exod. 24:12, 31:18, 32:15, 32:19). Habakkuk's recorded message could be circulated and posted as a warning of the invading Babylonians. (see Fig. 2.20)

Assured by God's sovereign control over the nation and the fate of his own people, Habakkuk can taunt the Babylonians in the form of five "woes" (Hab. 2:6, 9, 12, 15, 19), cries, and warnings of judgment.[89] Ultimately, the Chaldeans are a defeated enemy, even before they fully come to power, because their gods are idols (2:18), whereas "the LORD is his holy temple" (2:20). He is present and real, so that Judah's future was assured. Babylon is the recipient. Convinced now of God's sovereign purposes, the prophet can conclude his book by praising God (chap. 3).

Habakkuk's Prayer

The closing chapter is described as a "prayer," a particular genre of psalm known in the Psalter (e.g. Ps. 17, 90, 102). "LORD, I have heard of your fame; I stand in awe of your deeds, LORD" (Hab. 3:2) marks the opening this song. The musical note at the end of the psalm shows that it was accompanied by stringed instruments (3:19). Reference to God's deeds and the prophet's awe at the LORD's actions takes the prophet back to the Sinai theophany (3:3–6). At God's advance, "Sun and moon stood still" (3:11), reflecting on Yahweh's controlling the forces of nature when Joshua and the Israelites were conquering Canaan.[90] From there, God proceeds as a warrior to deliver Israel (3:13).

Inevitably, the coming of the Babylonians would mean prolonged siege, hardship, hunger, and thirst. Habakkuk recognized this. Despite these realities, "yet I will rejoice in the LORD, I will be joyful in God my Savior. The Sovereign LORD is my strength; he makes my feet like the feet of deer, he enables me to go on the heights" (Heb. 3:18–19). Habakkuk clearly was

---

87 Baker, *Nahum, Hababkkuk, Zephaniah*, 55.
88 *HALOT* 522–23.
89 *ISBE* 4:1088.
90 Smith, *Micah–Malachi*, 116.

putting into action the LORD's answer to the prophet's second complaint, "the righteous person will live by his faithfulness" (Hab. 2:4). Because Habakkuk believe in a God who had acted powerfully in the past for his peoples, he could by faith be saved through the coming crisis. St. Paul quotes this most important verse, applying to the gospel, that righteousness before God comes by faith.

Fig. 5.39 – Edomite shrine with deities and cultic vessels, in Israel Museum
Photo by Todd Bolen/ Bibleplaces.com

THE VISION OF OBADIAH

> "The day of the LORD is near for all nations."
>
> —Obadiah 15

The Book and Its Setting

This is shortest book in the entire Old Testament, a single chapter consisting of only twenty-one verses. Obadiah means "servant of Yahweh," but nothing is known about him. He apparently was active in the period just after the fall of Jerusalem in 586 B.C., but the historical setting is somewhat obscure. Its placement after Amos is not indication that Obadiah dates to the eighth-century books that precede or follow it. Rather, it is proposed that "the first five verses of Obadiah connect the book to the end of Amos" (9:11–15) where the focus is on the restoration of the Davidic kingdom in future days,[91] whereas Obadiah opens by announcing the doom of the Edomite kingdom. The contrast between Edom being cut off (1:10) and Israel's future glory (1:17–21) is a major theme in this short book.

The target of Obadiah's vision is Edom, the territory from the southern end of the Dead Sea in the Trans-Jordan and south to the Gulf of Aqaba. Edom is equated with the descendants of Esau, Jacob's (Israel) brother (Gen. 25:23–34). There had been a long history of hostility between the two brother nations ever since the Edomites refused to allow the Israelites safe passage through their lands after the exodus and the forty-year stay in Sinai (Num. 20:14–21). In Psalm 137 when the Israelites lament their fate in Babylon, they recall Edom's role in Jerusalem in 586 B.C.: "Remember,

91 Shepherd, *Book of the Twelve*, 209.

Fig. 5.40 – The mountains of the Arabah in Edom, leading south to the Gulf of Aqaba
Photo by David Biven/ Bibleplaces.com

Fig. 5.41 – "The Treasury" at Petra
Photo by James K. Hoffmeier

Lord, what the Edomites did on the day Jerusalem fell. 'Tear it down,' they cried, 'tear it down to its foundations!'" (v. 7). This bitter memory suggests that in some way Edom encouraged the Babylonians when they sacked Jerusalem rather than aiding his brother. A historical allusion to this complicity is likewise found in Obadiah, when God's doom is announced against Edom:

Because of the violence against your brother Jacob,
you will be covered with shame;
you will be destroyed forever.
On the day you stood aloof
while strangers carried off his wealth
and foreigners entered his gates
and cast lots for Jerusalem,
you were like one of them. (vv. 10–11)

The Edomites took advantage of the collapse of Jerusalem's political and social structures to plunder the remains "like vultures for the city's leftovers."[92]

Message of Obadiah

Just as messengers are actors in circulating news of Assyria's demise in Nahum and word of the advancing Babylonian armies on Judah, a messenger appears in Obadiah. This time he is "sent to the nations" to rally them against Edom (v. 1). Just as Judah had experienced "the day of the Lord" (see discussion above regarding Zephaniah), God's judgments would be expanded to deal with other nations, including Edom: "The day of the Lord is near for all nations" (v. 15). For Edom, "there will be no survivors from the house of Esau" (v. 18), "but on Mount Zion will be deliverance; it will be holy, and Jacob will possess his inheritance" (v. 17). Here the vision indicates that while Edom will cease to exist as a nation, the Judeans will occupy their homeland (1:17), and

92 Stuart, *Hosea–Jonah*, 419.

Map 5.4 – Transjordanian Kingdoms, including Edom *Map by A. D. Riddle*

furthermore, they will occupy the former lands of Esau, as will other neighboring peoples. Most significantly, Mt. Zion will serve as center of Yahweh's kingdom, and Edom's former territory will be governed from Jerusalem (1:21). One of the tribes that eventually settled in Edom was the Nabatean Arabs, whose origins are still debated, but by 312 B.C. the Nabateans had established their base in the city of Petra, the magnificent "rose city."[93]

Fig. 5.42 – Rock-cut structures at Petra
Photo by James K. Hoffmeier

93 *ABD* 4:970.

DISCUSSION QUESTIONS

- What is the Day of the Lord, and how does Zephaniah describe it and redirect it against Judah?
- What do we know about the personal life of Jeremiah, his calling, home, family, and the challenges he faced?
- Who were some of Jeremiah's friends and allies? What roles did they play in his life and ministry? Who were some of his opponents, and how does Jeremiah deal with them?
- Discuss some of Jeremiah's dramatic acts. What were they intended to teach, and how effective might those illustrations have impacted the original audience? modern hearers?
- What are the social and spiritual issues raised by Jeremiah's temple sermon in chapter 7, and what light does chapter 26 shed on this momentous challenge to God's people?
- Jeremiah 11 treats the covenant as broken by Israel, while Jeremiah 31:31–34 introduces the new covenant. How are the Sinaitic covenant and the new covenant similar and different?
- How can we understand God as a loving and compassionate God in the book of Nahum, when he is exacting vengeance on the Assyrians?
- What is the basis for Habakkuk's confidence in God, even though he knows his nation will be destroyed and exiled?
- Why are the Edomites the focus of God's judgment in Obadiah, and why ultimately is the Day of the Lord a good thing in verses 15–21?

6

"By the Rivers of Babylon We Sat and Wept"

THE PROPHETS OF THE BABYLONIAN EXILE

THE EXILIC PERIOD: 605–539 B.C.

In 605 B.C. Nebuchadnezzar defeated the Egyptian garrison of Pharaoh Neco II at Charchemish on the Euphrates River (Jer. 46:2; 2 Kings 23:29). With this obstacle removed, the Babylonians pushed south to Judah and besieged Jerusalem its capital. King Jehoiakim quickly submitted, becoming Nebuchadnezzar's vassal (2 Kings 24:1; Dan 1:1). At that time a select group of young potential leaders were taken to Babylon to be educated in Chaldean traditions and ways (Dan. 1:3–4). This small deportation would be the first, and three more would follow (Jer. 52:28–30). (see Map 5.1)

Fig. 6.1 – Tablet of the Babylonian Chronicle in the British Museum reporting the seizure of Jerusalem in 597 B.C. and the capture of its king, Jehoiachin, according to 2 Kings 24:10–17
Photo by Todd Bolen/ Bibleplaces.com).

In his seventh year as king of Babylon (597 B.C.), Nebuchadnezzar ordered his armies to march back to Judah and lay siege to Jerusalem in response to King Jehoiakim's rebellion. Before he faced the wrath of Babylon, however, the Judean king died, leaving his young successor, Jehoiachin, to face Nebuchadnezzar's wrath. Large numbers of Judeans fled to Egypt for refuge.[1] The Babylonian Chronicle further reports that "he captured its king (i.e., Jehoiachin). He appointed there a king of his

---

1 When Jeremiah arrived in Egypt (ca. 584 B.C.) after the fall of Jerusalem, there was a significant community of Judeans living in Egypt from the northern borders to the southern frontier at Aswan on Elephantine Island (Jer. 44:1–10).

Fig. 6.2 – Judean captive playing lyres as they are taken into captivity by Sennacherib in 701 B.C. from Lachish
Photo by James K. Hoffmeier

Fig. 6.3 – Judean captives carrying bag over shoulders and a leather canteen for water in their hands as they are led to exile
Photo by James K. Hoffmeier

own choice" (i.e., Zedekiah).[2] Only eighteen when this occurred (2 Kings 24:8), Jehoiachin had barely ruled three months when his reign abruptly ended as a captive of Nebuchadnezzar. The king and other members of the royal family, military leaders and other elites were taken, along with craftsmen and artisans for a total of ten thousand were marched to distant Babylon (2 Kings 24:14–17). These Judeans were settled in communities in and around Babylon.

The words of the Psalmist reflect the anxiety and displacement the exiles felt in this distant land: "By the rivers of Babylon we sat and wept when we remembered Zion. There on the poplars we hung our harps, for there our captors asked us for songs, our tormentors demanded songs of joy; they said, 'Sing us one of the songs of Zion!' How can we sing the songs of the LORD while in a foreign land?" (Ps. 137:1–4).

The image of the captives being forced to sing their songs, possibly laments sung to remember their homeland, is depicted a century earlier in when Judeans of Lachish are shown playing their lyres as a soldier drives them off into exile. The pain of being forced to live in a foreign land away from the comforts of home was profound. But things would only get worse when a decade later Zedekiah too rebelled against his Babylonian master by withholding taxes and allying with Egypt (2 Kings 24:20). This treachery led to the utter destruction of Jerusalem and its temple in 586 B.C.

The thousands of Judean exiles would have had to make the long and arduous march of about 900 miles (1450 km). They would have traveled north into Syria and east to the Euphrates, then following its southern course to Babylon. Most would have walked, though

2 *ANET* 306.

some well-to-do individuals may have ridden on carts or on the backs of horses and donkeys (see Fig. 4.29)

Two prophets, Daniel and Ezekiel, emerge from these captives who offered encouragement and helped the people grapple with their plight and God's purposes, as well as pointing to God's future plan for Israel. Ezekiel's book stands as the third of the major prophets along with Isaiah and Jeremiah. The book of the prophet Daniel follows Ezekiel in the Greek and English book order. In the Hebrew tradition, however, Daniel is placed in the writings section, not with the prophets. The reasons for the different placement are not clear, although the New Testament certainly refers to "the prophet Daniel" (Matt. 24:15). One of the features used in both of these books is apocalyptic literature.

Map 6.1 – The route to travel from Judah to Babylon in Mesopotamia *Map by A. D. Riddle*

APOCALYPTIC LITERATURE

Readers of the New Testament are familiar with the book of Revelation, which is introduced with the "the revelation of Jesus Christ." The Greek word for "revelation" is *apokalupsis*, from which derive the English words "apocalypse" and "apocalyptic." It is evidence from a cursory reading of the book of Revelation that it contains highly symbolic language, including bizarre, colorful beasts and visionary scenes. In addition to the Revelation of John, apocalyptic material occurs in the gospels in what has been called "the little apocalypse": Matthew 24, Mark 13, Luke 21,[3] and also in some Pauline literature: 1 Corinthians 15 and 2 Thessalonians 2.[4] Apocalyptic literature is not limited to the New Testament but is found in writings of various OT prophets, especially exilic and post-exilic period books like Ezekiel, Daniel, Zechariah, and Joel, but apocalyptic material goes back to the book of Isaiah.[5]

What precisely is apocalyptic literature, and why does it especially appear in the tumultuous times of the exilic and post-exilic periods? A simple definition is that it is "symbolic prophecy."[6] A more nuanced explanation is that apocalyptic is:

> a group of writings concerned with the renewal of faith and the reordering of life on the basis of a vision of a prototypical heavenly order revealed to a religious community through a seer. The author tends to relativize the significance of existing realities by depicting how they are about to be superseded by God's universal reign in an eschatological event that can neither be hastened nor thwarted by human efforts, but which will unfold, true to an eternal plan, as the result of divine action.[7]

Thus unlike traditional prophecy that concentrates on the present and the immediate future, apocalyptic moves the readers to the distant, the eschatological future.

---

3 *ABD* 2:1081–84.

4 Leon Morris, Revelation: Tyndale New Testament Commentaries (Downers Grove, IL: InterVarsity Press, 1984), 72–74.

5 Paul Hanson, *Old Testament Apocalyptic* (Nashville: Abingdon, 1987), 75–113. Over against the prevailing view of critical scholarship that Isaiah 39–66 is from the exilic and post-exilic periods, I follow the view of Harrison and Gileadi that the book is largely pre-exilic in date (see discussion in chap. 4), with possible editorial work occurring after the death of the great prophet.

6 Gary V. Smith, *Interpreting the Prophetic Books* (Grand Rapids: Kregel Academic, 2014), 27.

7 Hanson, *Old Testament Apocalyptic*, 27–28.

Because of the complexity of the symbols used in this genre, interpretation is challenging, if not impossible, without an interpretive key. In the case of apocalyptic literature, that key is provided in the form of an angel. The dramatic visions are typically mediated by an angel who functions as a kind of tour guide through the vision (e.g. Ezek. 8:2–18), and he also serves as an interpreter of the enigmatic revelations. In Daniel 8, for example, we read: "While I, Daniel, was watching the vision and trying to understand it, there before me stood one who looked like a man. And I heard a man's voice from the Ulai calling, "Gabriel, tell this man the meaning of the vision" (vv. 15–16). Other cases are found in Ezekiel 8:2–18, Zechariah 1:8–4:7, and Revelation 22:1–16.

Because of the dislocation of the Israelites and the termination of the Davidic kingship in Jerusalem, apocalyptic writings are intended to offer comfort and hope to the afflicted by shifting focus toward the future and the establishment of God's kingdom. The shift toward the eschatological, rather than just the more immediate future, draws the reader to the spiritual realities of the future, and not the immediate crisis and suffering. Consequently, the apocalyptic is ultimately about the "triumph of God" and that "in the end God will prevail."[8]

EZEKIEL: GOD'S WATCHMAN

> "Son of man, I have made you a watchman for the house of Israel; so hear the word I speak and give them warning from me."
>
> —Ezekiel 3:17

The Exiled Prophet

Ezekiel explains, in first-person form, that he was one of the exiles taken to Babylonia along with Jehoiachin in 597 B.C. (Ezek. 1:1). The introduction also dates the call vision occurred in "the fifth year of the exile of King Jehoiachin," or 593 B.C. (Ezek. 1:2). Further he states that he lived within the community of exiles by the Chebar Canal, where he received his initial vision. This canal is known from Babylonian texts as "Kabaru Canal" that was located near the city of Nippur, about 44 miles (70 km) southeast of the city of Babylon.[9] He also identifies himself as a priest and the son of Buzi, who

8 Morris, *Revelation*, 41–43.
9 *ABD* 1:893.

Fig. 6.4 – Statue of Ezekiel at St. Mary's on the Lake Seminary, Mundelein, IL
Photo by James K. Hoffmeier

must have also been a priest. A final biographical detail offered in the introductory paragraph of the book is an obscure reference to "the thirtieth year" (Ezek. 1:1 ESV). Scholars are baffled by this atypical date, as it is not tied to anything: "the thirtieth year" of what?[10] Some interpreters follow the church father Origen's suggestion from the third century A.D. that the thirtieth year may refer to Ezekiel's age at the beginning of his prophetic work.[11] Should this be the correct understanding of the thirtieth year, it is an unusual datum as other than Jeremiah's youth, a prophet's age is simply never disclosed. If indeed Ezekiel's age is in view, it takes on special significance as priests actually began formal service in the temple at age thirty (Num. 4:3). In Ezekiel's case, temple service was impossible, nevertheless, God had another noble form of service to the exiled community in lieu of cultic duties.

Assuming Ezekiel was thirty at the beginning of the book means that he had spent his first twenty-four to twenty-five years in Judah and would have been familiar with Jerusalem, the temple, and the religious state of the nation. As a prophet, his task is likened to a "watchman for the house of Israel" (Ezek. 3:17). "Watchman" is the word *ṣōp̱eh*, meaning "to look out."[12] Just as a sentry's work was primarily in defense of a city,[13] he was to look for coming dangers and alert the city. So too, Ezekiel was to look for God's prophetic words and visions, and then warn people of what was coming.

Only a few other insights into the prophet's life are found in the balance of the book. The prophet reports in the sixth year of the exile (591 B.C.), "while I was sitting in my house and the elders of Judah were sitting before me, the hand of the Sovereign LORD came upon me" (Ezek. 8:1). From this brief statement we gain three important insights. First, Ezekiel took seriously his colleague and contemporary Jeremiah's instruction in his letter to the exiles to "build houses and settle down" (Jer. 29:5; for further discussion of Jeremiah's letter, see chap. 5). The Judean exiles did not live in concentration camps, but resided in individual homes that they were free to build.

Second we learn that there was freedom for the Judean exiles to gather for religious purposes. In this case the reason the elders of the community come to the prophet, is not specified, but in Ezekiel 20:1 they came "to inquire

---

10 For a review of opinions, see Leslie Allen, *Ezekiel 1–19*, Word Biblical Commentary (Nashville: Thomas Nelson, 1994), 20.

11 Harrison, *Introduction*, 837.

12 *HALOT* 1044.

13 Daniel I. Block, *The Book of Ezekiel, Chapters 1–24*, New International Commentary of the Old Testament (Grand Rapids: Eerdmans, 1997), 144.

Fig. 6.5a – Bearded Judean men from Lachish in 701 B.C. *Photo by Todd Bolen/ Bibleplaces.com*

Fig. 6.5b – Barber shaving the head of a man in the tomb of Userhet, Western Thebes *Photo by J. J. Shirley*

of the LORD" and to hear the prophet's response. The meaning of inquiring of the LORD is explained in 1 Samuel 9:9. Since there are three references to the elders assembling with Ezekiel in the book (Ezek. 8:1, 14:1; 20:1), it apparently was a regular practice, which may have laid the foundations for the synagogue movement. The Greek word "synagogue" means "to bring/come together." There the faithful would gather to hear the word of the LORD (read and study Torah), receive instruction, and pray.[14]

Third, "the elders of Judah" were meeting in Ezekiel's home. The fact that elders are mentioned, probably already recognized community leaders before the exile, suggests that there was a degree of self-governance during the Babylonian sojourn.[15]

Two other personal notes emerge about the prophet. Not surprisingly, Ezekiel had a beard. Assyrian carved reliefs show that Israelites and Judean men were usually bearded. God instructed Ezekiel to shave off his hair and beard in a bizarre prophetic act (Ezek. 5:1–4). God instructed him to divide his hair into three equal parts. A third was burned, another third cast to the wind and blown away, and the last third was chopped up with a sword. This graphic illustration was meant to show the fate of the nation.

Last, we know that the prophet was married. His unnamed wife died at the beginning of the siege of Jerusalem that lasted about eighteen months (cf. Ezek. 24:1–2; 2 Kings 25:1–8). Her death was intended to mirror what was happening between God and his wife, Israel/Judah, and its capital, Jerusalem. It would be snuffed out. No mention of children from this marriage are found in the book of Ezekiel.

14 *ISBE* 4:676–677.
15 Allen, *Ezekiel 1–19*, 137.

Visions of Judgment

The Opening Vision

This book begins with the unfolding of an apocalyptic vision of the glory of God to Ezekiel (Ezek. 1–3), that was intended to "impress on him the majesty, holiness, and wonder of the God who was about to execute judgment on the people of Israel."[16] The reader of this vision will be struck by the use of the same symbols and images that occur in the book of Revelation in the NT. The four-winged, living creatures in Ezekiel 1:5, for example, are the same as those in Revelation 4:6–8. When the mobile throne of Yahweh moved, the wings emitted a rumbling noise "like the roar of rushing waters" (1:24 NIV) or "like the sound of many waters" (ESV), the very same roaring that John heard in the opening vision of the apocalypse (Rev. 1:15). Awestruck, the prophet falls prostrate (Ezek. 1:28), but he is ordered: "Son of man, stand up on your feet and I will speak to you" (Ezek. 2:1). "Son of man" (*ben 'āḏām*) is a nickname used by God for addressing Ezekiel as it occurs just over ninety times through the book. This epithet is intended to draw a contrast between the overwhelming sanctity and otherness of God by "emphasizing the lowly creaturely character of the prophet."[17] After the opening display of the glory of God, the prophet receives his call and career change to be the LORD's watchman. Overwhelmed by what he had witnessed, Ezekiel went to join a group of exiles where he "sat among them for seven days—overwhelmed" (Ezek. 3:15), or in a "state of shock."[18]

Fig. 6.6 – One of four winged creatures on the great supporting pillars of the dome in Hagia Sophia Church, Istanbul
Photo by Steven Sanchez/ Bibleplaces.com

The exiles of 597 B.C. complained that God's judgment had fallen unjustly on them for the sins of their fathers. After all, Jeremiah had announced that enemies would visit Judah "because of what Manasseh son of

---

16 Ralph Alexander, *Ezekiel*, Expositor's Bible Commentary, vol. 6, ed. F. Gaebelein (Grand Rapids: Zondervan, 1986), 756.
17 John Wevers, *Ezekiel*, New Century Bible Commentary (Grand Rapids: Eerdmans, 1969), 48.
18 William Brownlee, *Ezekiel 1–19*, World Biblical Commentary (Waco, TX: Word, 1986), 40.

Hezekiah king of Judah did in Jerusalem" (Jer. 15:4). To this seeming unfairness toward their plight, the people coined the following proverb: "The parents eat sour grapes, and the children's teeth are set on edge" (Ezek. 18:2). Jeremiah spoke of a day when this same proverb, which he fully quotes, will no longer be repeated (Jer. 31:29). Evidently, this complaint was the subject of the correspondence between the exiles taken in 597 B.C. and the leaders in Jerusalem (Jer. 29).

The book of Ezekiel is structured so that the first twenty-four chapters lay bare the sins of the people and chiefly what was currently occurring in Jerusalem in order to challenge the erroneous claim that the current generation was suffering solely for the sins of previous generations, and to disabuse the people of their claim of innocence. Rather they were guilty of violating the covenant by failing to uphold God's laws. Ezekiel clarifies the situation:

> This is Jerusalem, which I have set in the center of the nations, with countries all around her. Yet in her wickedness she has rebelled against

Fig. 6.7 – A composite, mythical beast from the Ishtar Gate from Babylon, now in Metropolitan Museum, NY
Photo by A. D. Riddle/ Bibleplaces.com

> my laws and decrees more than the nations and countries around her. She has rejected my laws and has not followed my decrees. Therefore this is what the Sovereign Lord says: "You have been more unruly than the nations around you and have not followed my decrees or kept my laws. You have not even conformed to the standards of the nations around you. Therefore this is what the Sovereign Lord says: I myself am against you, Jerusalem, and I will inflict punishment on you in the sight of the nations. (Ezek. 5:5–8)

Visionary Journey to Jerusalem

In response to the assertion that somehow the people of Judah were blameless of wrongdoing against God, Ezekiel is transported to Jerusalem to witness personally the various apostasies occurring in Jerusalem at that very time (Ezek. 8–11). This scene is reminiscent of Ebenezer Scrooge's experience in Dickens's *Christmas Carol.* He was carried by spirits from place to place to visit the past, present and future. Ezekiel recounts his vision:

> I looked, and I saw a figure like that of a man. From what appeared to be his waist down he was like fire, and from there up his appearance was as bright as glowing metal. He stretched out what looked like a hand and took me by the hair of my head. The Spirit lifted me up between earth and heaven and in visions of God he took me to Jerusalem, to the entrance to the north gate of the inner court, where the idol that provokes to jealousy stood. (Ezek. 8:2–3)

God asks the prophet, "do you see what they are doing—the utterly detestable things the house of Israel is doing here, things that will drive me far from my sanctuary? But you will see things that are even more detestable" (Ezek. 8:6). Within the temple complex, Ezekiel sees a group of seventy elders of Israel in a chamber decorated with the images of various "detestable animals" and idols engaged in burning incense (Ezek. 8:10–12). The prophet recognized the ringleader, Jaazaniah the son of Shaphan, suggesting that he may have known him from his days in Jerusalem before 597 B.C.

Fig. 6.8 – Seal and impression of "Jaazaniah, servant of the king," the same name as the leader of the apostacy in Jerusalem. Another man by the same name is mentioned in Ezekiel 8:16–17. There is no way of knowing if the name is one of these men, since the father's name is not included.
Photo courtesy of BibleLandPictures

Shaphan had been an important official from the court of King Josiah who received the newly discovered "book of the Law" and read it to the king (2 Kings 22:3–10). Three of Shaphan's sons are named in the book of Jeremiah— Ahikam (Jer. 26:24), Gemeriah (Jer. 36:10–11), and Elasah (Jer. 29:3)—and they were generally supportive of Jeremiah. Though not mentioned in Jeremiah, Jaazaniah was no doubt a fourth son of Shaphan,[19] as this name is otherwise unattested in

Fig. 6.9 – Women mourning the dead in the tomb of Ramose (ca. 1350 B.C.) in Western Thebes
Photo by James K. Hoffmeier

19 Allen, *Ezekiel 1–19*, 143.

the Bible.[20] Knowing this history may explain Ezekiel's alarm. The son of the official who had read the law and witnessed the godly king's reforms (and perhaps helped to promote them) was now the instigator of pagan acts in the temple! This is why Jaazaniah has been called "the black sheep if the family."[21]

Next the prophet's vision takes him to northern entrance of the temple where he saw a woman "mourning the god Tammuz" (8:14). Tammuz was the old Sumerian fertility deity Dumuzi. In the region surrounding Israel he was

Fig. 6.10a – Sun worship was practiced in Egypt from earliest times. Pharaoh Akhenaten was especially a devotee of the sun disc, Aten. This scene is in the Luxor Museum.
Photo by James K. Hoffmeier

20 "Shaphan" is the word for a rock badger (*HALOT* 1633).
21 John B. Taylor, *Ezekiel*, Tyndale Old Testament Commentary (Downers Grove, IL: InterVarsity Press, 1969), 99.

associated Baal-Hadad, a dying-resurrecting fertility deity.[22] During the previous Assyrian period, "a statue of the god was exhibited so that lamentations could be offered by his devotees."[23] The fact that these women are engaged in these acts show the extent to which Mesopotamian religious influences had made inroads into Jerusalem. It also suggests that the land was experiencing a severe drought, which may explain the extraordinary measures taken by the people in Jerusalem to remedy the problem. Mention of a drought at this approximate time is made in the book of Jeremiah: "This is the word of the LORD that came to Jeremiah concerning the drought: 'Judah mourns, her cities languish; they wail for the land, and a cry goes up from Jerusalem'"(Jer. 14:1–2). The wailing Jeremiah mentions is likely the same as the "mourning" cited by Ezekiel. Rather than recognizing drought as a covenant curse (Lev. 26:18–20; Deut. 28:15–23), or warning to return to Yahweh as Amos announced (Amos 4:6–8), the people did not turn to God for his intervention but sought the aid of foreign deities.

A group of twenty-five men are spotted in front of the temple, bowing down to the sun in the east (Ezek. 8:16), presumably as it rose over the Mount of Olives, across the Kidron Valley from the temple. Adoring the sun has been associated with Baal-Shamen, "Lord of the Sky."[24] It has also been suggested that as part of his religious program against pagan worship, king Josiah removed "the horses of the kings of Judah had dedicated to the sun" that had stood at the entrance to the temple.[25]

Finally, Ezekiel witnesses a group of twenty-five men in the temple plotting evil (Ezek. 11:1–2), although what they were planning is not disclosed. They may well be the same men mentioned in Ezekiel 8:16–17.[26] Two municipal leaders are mentioned by name, another man named Jaazaniah son of Azzur and Pelatiah the son of Benaiah. By naming these officials and the son of Shaphan previously drives home the point that these offenses are real, not imagined, by known individuals and leaders rather than nameless people.

Early in his tour to witness the gross sins if Jerusalem, God asks the prophet, "Son of man, do you see what they are doing—the utterly detestable things the house of Israel is doing here, things that will drive me far from my sanctuary? But you will see things that are even more detestable" (Ezek. 8:6). That which is detestable, or an abomination (*tô'ēḇâ*), is one of the strongest words in the OT

---

22 Hess, *Israelite Religions*, 263.
23 Hruša, *Ancient Mesopotamian Religion*, 93.
24 Brownlee, *Ezekiel 1–19*, 136–37.
25 Taylor, *Ezekiel*, 100; cf. 2 Kings 23:11.
26 Block, *The Book of Ezekiel*, 297.

Fig. 6.10b – The Egyptian motif of the winged sun disc spread across the Near East in the 2nd and 1st millennia B.C. (see also Fig. 3.3, 4.8, 4.34). This painted relief is from the Medinet Habu Temple of Ramesses III. *Photo by James K. Hoffmeier*

to express what is repugnant to God and defiling to what is sacred.[27] Having been trained in priestly matters for around twenty years, Ezekiel would understand the severity of defiling the temple. God's holy presence, his glory, could no longer tolerate the desecration, therefore, "The glory of the LORD went up within the city and stopped above the mountain east of it" (Ezek. 11:23).

The weight of the departure of the glory of Yahweh and presence in the temple represents a cataclysmic rupture in Israel's relationship with God. That glory had appeared on Mount Sinai during the covenant ceremony (Exod. 19:16–20; 24:15–17), and then settled in the tabernacle (Exod. 40:34). The glory of the LORD remained in the tabernacle, presenting God's tangible presence, until Solomon's temple was dedicated. It then occupied the holiest place in the temple (1 Kings 8:11). For more than six hundred years, that glory hovered in the temple, but the holy God of Israel would tolerate the abomination no longer, and that tragic departure is recorded in Ezekiel 11. With God's protective presence gone from the temple, it was reduced to being a building like any other. Now its destruction was a certainty.

---

27 *NIDOTTE* 4:314–18.

With the series of visions over, Ezekiel "told the exiles everything the Lord had shown me" (Ezek. 11:25). There could be no longer any doubt that the punishment of Jerusalem was justifiable. The people were equally guilty of gross violations of the Sinaitic covenant, and the covenant curses would be experienced, especially their removal from the land (see Deut. 4:27–28; 28:64–65). To illustrate the deportation of the rest of the people of Judah, God instructs Ezekiel to pack a bag like one going into exile and carry it around over his shoulder among the community of exiles so that they would realize what was coming (Ezek. 12:1–7). The image of exiles with sacks of belongings through on the shoulder is illustrated in the reliefs of king Sennacherib when Judean exiles were taken to Mesopotamia in 701 B.C. (Fig. 6.3)

Allegories and Dramatic Acts

The term "allegory" is frequently applied to some of Ezekiel's poetic narrative, namely, chapters 15, 16, 17, 19, 23, 27 and 37.[28] Nine times the word *māšāl* occurs in the book and can be rendered "allegory" or "proverb," and it can also mean "similar" or "similarity."[29] In Arabic (*mithal*) it means "example" or "illustration." Ezekiel uses graphic and occasionally bizarre illustrations or word pictures, while others are dramatically played out.

Fig. 6.11a – Necklaces of semi-precious stones from Jerusalem during the period of Ezekiel's ministry *Photo by Todd Bolen/ Bibleplaces.com*

The allegory of Israel as God's wife is treated in two different passages. In the first, Israel's birth is described (Ezek. 16). The little girl was born to a Hittite mother and an Amorite father (Ezek. 16:3). This mix of ethnicities is odd, but perhaps challenges the notion that the people believed they were of noble and pure stock. There was nothing special about Israel's origin—a point made elsewhere by God, who speaks of her election: "The Lord did not set his affection on you and choose you because you were more numerous than other peoples, for you were the fewest of all peoples" (Deut. 7:7). Tragically, the neonate was discarded naked into field, and not even her navel cord had been cut (Ezek. 16:4–5). She would have died had God not passed by and rescued her:

28 Bullock, *Old Testament Prophetic Books*, 283.
29 *HALOT* 648.

> Then I passed by and saw you kicking about in your blood, and as you lay there in your blood I said to you, "Live!" I made you grow like a plant of the field. You grew and developed. . . . Later I passed by, and when I looked at you and saw that you were old enough for love, I spread the corner of my garment over you and covered your naked body. I gave you my solemn oath and entered into a covenant with you, declares the Sovereign LORD, and you became mine. (Ezek. 16:6–8)

By covering her with his garment, God was claiming the young woman for marriage,[30] followed by the consummation of a covenant of marriage for which he decked her as a glorious bride! Israel became God's wife, but soon she trusted in her beauty and used her fame to become a prostitute (Ezek. 16:15), an "adulterous wife" (Ezek. 16:32), and is likened to Sodom (Ezek. 16:46–49). Israel in general, and Judah in particular at that time, is shown to be ungrateful and faithless to God who had saved and nurtured her, and then entered into a marriage covenant with her. She committed adultery when she violated the first and second commandments.

The second marital illustration is that of the prophet and his wife. The death of Ezekiel's wife was already introduced. Her death is described as occurring in "one blow" (Ezek. 24: 16), which typically suggests "a plague or disease,"[31] something that struck quickly. The prophet's love and endearment with his wife is stressed when God describes her as "the delight (*maḥmāḏ*) of your eyes" (Ezek. 24:16); that is, she was precious to him.[32] As she was a relatively young woman, her death therefore was a painful shock. Her passing was meant to symbolize the death of Jerusalem, a strong and well-defended city whose demise was unthinkable to the people of Judah. When people died in Old Testament times, inconsolable mourning occurred. The Egyptians mourned the dead for seventy days (Gen. 50:3), while lamenting in ancient Israel lasted thirty days (Num. 20:29; Deut. 34:8). Ezekiel, on the other hand, was instructed by God not to mourn, but to go about his work. Summarizing this

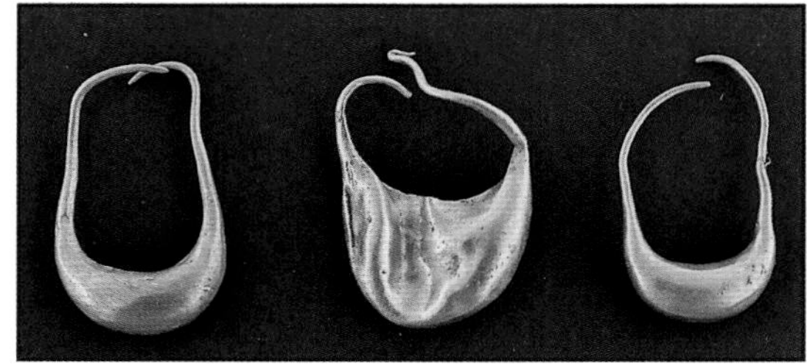

Fig. 6.11b – Gold earrings discovered at Tell el-Borg, Sinai *Photo by James K. Hoffmeier*

30 Allen, *Ezekiel 1–19*, 238; cf. Ruth 2:4–9.
31 Alexander, *Ezekiel*, 862; cf Exod. 9:14.
32 *HALOT* 325.

dramatic scene, Leslie Allen opines: "The pain of this bereavement is utilized as a reflection of his people's imminent catastrophe. The pain is intensified in that it must remain bottled up instead"[33] as he was denied the traditional period of intense mourning and grief. (See Fig 6.9)

Ezekiel seems to expand on Jeremiah's illustration of the kingdoms of Israel and Judah being sisters (Jer. 3:6–10); however, he gives them the names Oholah for Samaria and Oholibah for Jerusalem (Ezek. 23:4). The former means "her tent," and the latter translates as "my tent is in her." *'Ōhel* means tent,[34] and is used of the "Tent of Meeting," an alternative expression for the tabernacle (e.g., Exod. 27:21; 28:43; 29:4; 29:10). Jerusalem, of course, was home to the house of the LORD, and specifically, the old tent of meeting from the wilderness days was actually preserved and brought into the new temple when it was dedicated by Solomon (1 Kings 8:3). Quite literally, then, God's tent was in Jerusalem, whereas "her tent" signifies that from the start, the kings of the north built their own cult centers at Bethel and Dan (1 Kings 13:25–33) (see Fig. 2.28, 3.9). Jerusalem is more culpable because they had the real deal, God's presence and temple, and it could see how the northern kingdom was judged for their infidelities. On the political side, both nations had attempted to pacify her foes with peace treaties, Samaria with Assyria and Judah with Babylon (Ezek. 23:11–27). Rather than trust God to protect them, they relied on failed diplomacy, and thus committed adultery in the political sense with their enemies.

Major Theological Developments

The tumultuous experiences of the destruction of the temples, loss of the Davidic kingship, and exile in Babylon and elsewhere proved to be fertile grounds for important theological developments.

The soul who sins shall die

The complaint that God was unjustly punishing Israel for the sins of earlier generations was addressed above. In part, God's response was to show Ezekiel's contemporaries that they were every bit as guilty as earlier generations as those uncovered in the prophet's visionary journey to Jerusalem (Ezek. 8–11). Over against the proverb "The parents eat sour grapes, and the children's teeth are set on edge," the LORD counters, "The one who sins is the one who will die" (Ezek. 18:2, 20), and one "will not die for his father's sin" (Ezek. 18:17). Similarly, "the

33 Leslie Allen, *Ezekiel 20–48*, Word Biblical Commentary (Dallas: Word, 1990), 60.
34 *HALOT* 19.

righteousness of the righteous will be credited to them" (Ezek. 18:20). This perspective reveals a movement away from corporate responsibility, a hallmark of the old covenant. "The great contribution of the prophet Ezekiel to the doctrine of man," R. K. Harrison maintained, "lies in his emphasis upon the personal responsibility."[35] One was physically born into the covenant community and maintained one's relationship with God and the community by virtue of living according to the demands of the covenant, by loving "the LORD your God with all your heart and with all your soul and with all your strength" (Deut. 6:5). Entry into the New Covenant results not from physical birth but from spiritual birth or rebirth (John 3:1–8); Ezekiel's message paves the way for the coming reality.

I will give you a new heart

Jeremiah announced God's new covenant for his people, which would involve God writing his laws on the hearts of the people (Jer. 31:33). Ezekiel developed the same ideas while using different language. What the people of Israel needed was a radical transformation, a heart transplant, since their hard-heartedness was incurable. "I will give them an undivided heart and put a new spirit in them; I will remove from them their heart of stone and give them a heart of flesh. Then they will follow my decrees and be careful to keep my laws. They will be my people, and I will be their God" (Ezek. 11:19–20). The new spirit must accompany the new heart, Ezekiel acknowledges (see also Ezek. 18:31; 36:26–27). Through this spiritual transformation, the covenant relationship will be reestablished. At the exodus, God expressed his plan to "take you as my own people, and I will be your God" (Exod. 6:7), which occurred when the Sinai Covenant was ratified. This theological affirmation has been called the covenant formula, so that by reciting these words, or even the abbreviated "my people" is a shorthand for the whole line pointing to the covenant relationship with God.[36] Those who receive the new heart and spirit, God will take to be his people.

'They will know that I am the Lord"

When Moses issued Yahweh's order to Pharaoh, "Let my people go," the stubborn king responded, "Who is the LORD that I should obey him . . . ?" (Exod. 5:1–2). As if to demonstrate who the Lord was, plagues one by one struck Egypt as if framed as a battle. Pharaoh, the warrior of Egypt, would experience Israel's champion who would defeat Egypt with an outstretched arm and a mighty hand (Exod. 3:19; 6:6). Repeatedly through these acts of judgment on Egypt and yet salvation for Israel, God announces his intentions, that Egyptians and/or Pharaoh "will/shall know that I am the LORD" (Exod. 7:5, 17; 8:10, 22; 14:4, 18) and that the Hebrews would "know that am the LORD" (Exod. 6:7; 10:2). God was revealing himself through both judgment and salvation. This dual purpose is expressed in Ezekiel's use of the same expression.

---

35 Harrison, *Introduction to the Old Testament,* 853.

36 Rolf Rentdorff, *The Covenant Formula* (Edinburgh: T&T Clark, 1998).

In Ezekiel 1–24 the declaration, "They will know that I am the LORD" is repeated more than thirty times, and more than seventy times in the entire book. The ubiquity of this line suggests that one of the major points, even "the ultimate goal" of Ezekiel's message, is that God was revealing himself through his actions,[37] thereby drawing people into a relationship with him. In the prophets, knowing (*yāda'*) God has the nuance of intimacy, a special relationship.[38]

Fig. 6.12 – Pharaoh's were mighty warriors and absolute rulers. Ramesses III is shown smiting enemies of Egypt with his outstretched arm at Medinet Habu. *Photo by James K. Hoffmeier*

37 Block, *Ezekiel*, 228.
38 *NIDOTTE* 1:411–12.

Even in judgment (e.g. Ezek. 5:13; 6:7, 13–14; 7:4, 9, 27), God was trying to reveal himself to Israel. By bringing the survivors back to the land of Israel, they "will know that I am the LORD" (Ezek. 20:44). The same is said when the covenant is reinstated (Ezek. 16:62; 20:38). When the nations see how Got restored his people to their land and the temple is rebuilt, they "will know that I am the LORD" (Ezek. 37:28). God's judgment on the nations, too, was to result in Israel knowing "that I am the LORD" (Ezek. 25:5, 7), and as a consequence of God's judgment on Egypt, the Egyptians will know "that I am the LORD" (Ezek. 29:6, 9).

Visions of a Bright Future

Ezekiel's messages are not all filled with despair. Even in chapters 1–24, where the main theme has to do with Israel's sin and coming punishment, there

Fig. 6.13 – Pomegranate tree in Israel *Photo by Daniel Frese/Bibleplaces.com*

is nonetheless the hope of God's presence with his people. "I have been a sanctuary for them in the countries where they have gone" (Ezek. 11:16). Regarding the land of Israel, they will return to it, but they must remove all the vile images and detestable idols (Ezek. 20:7–8, 30; 37:23). The latter third of the book, chapters 33–48, addresses in more detail the restoration of the nation under the categories of the people, the land, the temple, and the kingship. Interpreting these prophecies has presented a challenge because in addressing a people in exile, one might think the immediate fate to the nation is of vital importance. However, due to the apocalyptic nature of some of the literature, a more eschatological perspective is expected.

The people

The people were scattered, and the nation is as good as dead (Ezek. 37:1–14). To illustrate the problem of reviving the nation, Ezekiel is taken by the Spirit of the LORD to a valley with bones strewn across it. After surveying the dismembered remains, God asks the prophet, "Can these bones live?" Naturally one would think it to be impossible, and that is the point. Only by divine agency can the dead be restored to life. God, however, commands the prophet to preach to the skeletal remains. As he does, God resuscitates the dead: the bones come together, sinew and flesh appear, and the people come back to life. When this happens, "Then you, my people, will know that I am the LORD" (37:13), and when God brings them back to the land of Israel, "You will know that I the Lord have spoken, and I have done it" (37:14).

Fig. 6.14 – Almond tree in blossom in Israel
Photo by James K. Hoffmeier

Restoring the land (Ezek. 36:16–37:14)

The LORD directs the prophet to "prophesy concerning the land of Israel" (Ezek. 36:6). The land will once again be prosperous, trees will sprout and bear fruit, fields will be farmed, cities will be rebuilt and inhabited, and the peoples will multiply. The outcome of the restored land will be that the people "will know that I am the LORD" (36:11). A return to the land was not just a matter of nationalistic pride but demonstrates that God's promise of the land to Abraham and his descendants was still in force.[39]

The future king

The prophet condemns the rulers of Judah whom he calls "shepherds" (Ezek. 34:1–10), a common term used for political leaders among the prophets (Mic. 5:2–4; Jer. 2:8; 10:21). Rather than caring for the sheep, they fleeced the flock for their own gain. Instead of feeding the sheep, the rulers had devoured them and ruled them "harshly and brutally" (Ezek. 34:4). In response, God will become the good shepherd who will gather the scattered flock, heal their wounds, and feed and protect them from wild beasts (Ezek. 34:11–22). Then the Lord will raise up for them "one shepherd, my servant David" (34:23). The mention of David here and in 37:24–25 anticipates the restoration of kingship from the line of David. It was under Zerubbabel, grandson of Jehoiachin, the last legitimate king of Judah, that Jerusalem was resettled and the temple rebuilt (Ezra 1–4), but he was never made king, only a governor (Hag. 2:2, 21). Later kings of Judea, such as Alexander Jannaeus (103–76 B.C.) and Herod the Great (37–5 B.C.), were not from the line of David and so were never viewed as messianic kings, as expected based on Ezekiel's (and Jeremiah's) prophecies. The Messianic ruler, the NT maintains, is connected to Jesus Christ (Matt. 1:17, 20, Luke 1:32–33). In John 10:1–21, Jesus identifies himself as the "good shepherd" who cares for his flock, but this image points beyond the brief period of Christ's earthly ministry two millennia ago. Hence "Christians can see the fulfillment of this expectation in the character of Christ's future Messianic rule of which the present Christian era is a mere foreshadowing."[40]

Fig. 6.15 – Head from a statuette discovered at Abel Beth-Maacah, Northern Israel, possibly an Israelite king
Photo by Caroline Schick/bibelausstellung.de, courtesy Israel Museum, Jerusalem by Amalyah Keshet

The temple

The year is 573/2 B.C., that is, the twenty-fifth year of the exile (Ezek. 40:1), fourteen years after

39 Alexander, *Ezekiel*, 920; cf. Gen. 12:1; 15:18–20.
40 Taylor, *Ezekiel*, 223.

the destruction of the temple in Jerusalem, when Ezekiel had a vision in which he is brought to the land of Israel (Ezek. 40:1–2). On the top of "a very high mountain" (Ezek. 40:2) that "represents theological geography and points to Yahweh's supremacy,"[41] the prophet witnesses a grand temple that he describes in detail (Ezek. 40:5–42:20). It shares many of the architectural features that Solomon's temple had, such as an altar in front of the temple (Ezek. 40:47), decorative cherubim and palm trees on the inner wall of the sanctuary (Ezek. 41:17–20), and it had the basic tripartite structure (porch entrance, holy place and holy of holies). There are, however, striking differences in the presentation of this future temple. From the entrance of the east-facing temple entrance a stream of water flows that becomes a river, on either side of which trees grow (Ezek. 47:3–7). The water continues east flowing down to the Dead Sea. Known for its brackish waters in which no sea life can live, this sea is transformed by the water from the temple: "When it empties into the sea, the salty water there becomes fresh. . . . There will be large numbers of fish, because this water flows there and makes the salt

Fig. 6.16 – Dead Sea by the shores of Ein Gedi *Photo by Bill Schlegel/Bibleplaces.com*

41 Allen, *Ezekiel 1–19*, 229.

water fresh. . . . Fishermen will stand along the shore; from En Gedi to En Eglaim there will be places for spreading nets" (Ezek. 47:8–10).

Additional information is offered about the trees growing along the banks of this river. All kinds of fruit are produced continually, and the leaves do not wither. Sustained by the holy waters of the sanctuary in Jerusalem, the "fruit will serve for food and their leaves for healing" (Ezek. 47:12). This miraculous and life-giving stream and the fruit trees with their healing powers evokes memories of the garden of Eden with its rivers and the tree of life.[42] But it also points forward to the New Testament book of Revelation (i.e., the Apocalypse of John). There John has a vision of the new heavens and earth where the faithful will reside with God (Rev. 21–22). He sees "the river of the water of life, as clear as crystal, flowing from the throne of God. . . . On each side of the river stood the tree of life, bearing twelve crops of fruit, yielding its fruit every month. And the leaves of the tree are for the healing of the nations" (22:1–2).

Fig. 6.17 – Waterfalls at Ein Gedi
Photo by DF/ Bibleplaces.com

The association of the river of life and the healing tree(s) of Ezekiel's vision with that of John's revelation more than six hundred years later suggests that Ezekiel's temple anticipates the rebuilding of the temple in Jerusalem after the exile, but then it goes beyond that to an eschatological world—the new Jerusalem with a different kind of temple: "I did not see a temple in the city, because the Lord God Almighty and the Lamb are its temple" (Rev. 21:22). The implication is that God controls the present, the immediate future, as well as the end of human history.

The previously discussed refrain, "that they (or you) may know that I am the LORD," is not present at all in Ezekiel's temple vision. The clue that may explain the absence of this line is found in the final verse of the book in which the new Jerusalem and with its temple that was filled with God's glory (Ezek. 44:4) is named "the LORD is there" (Ezek. 48:35). Rather than being known through his acts on behalf of Israel, he will be known by his presence with his people.

42 Alexander, *Ezekiel*, 990; Gen. 2:10–17.

Similarly the book of Revelation affirms that "the dwelling place of God is with man. He will dwell with them, and they will be his people, and God himself will be with them as their God" (Rev. 21:3 ESV).

The book of Ezekiel ends, then, with the prospect of a resurrected and unified people, a fruitful and bountiful land, a king in the line of David, and a reconstructed temple that points beyond the immediate future with an apocalyptic vision of the climax of human history and a restored relationship between God, humanity, and all creation as it was in the garden of Eden at the beginning of time.

Fig. 6.18 – The menorah in the temple represents the tree of life in the garden of Eden. The menorah shown here is on the Titus Arch in Rome. Roman soldiers carry the menorah from the Jerusalem temple in A.D. 70. *Photo by Todd Bolen/Bibleplaces.com*

THE MEDES AND PERSIANS

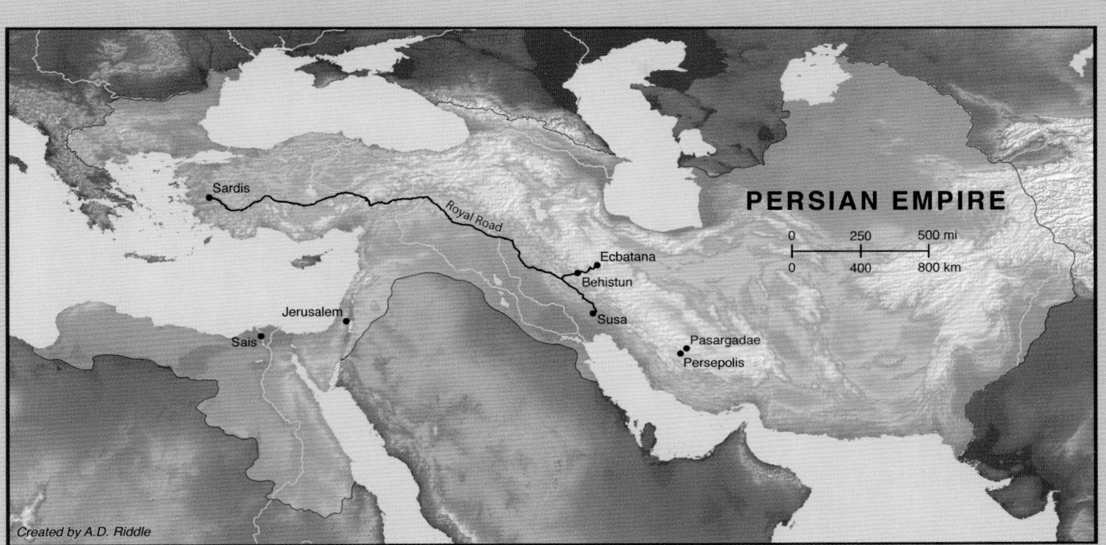

Map 6.2 – The Persian Empire *Map by A. D. Riddle*

The Medes and Persians play a decisive role in biblical history, especially in the sixth century B.C. These two people groups came to the area of modern Iran or Persia (as it was known until 1935) in a migration of Indo-Europeans or Aryans from the area of Russia at the end of the second millennium B.C.[43] The Medes were more prominent in region early in the first millennium. They were mentioned in Assyrian records of the ninth century B.C. and in the Bible in the days of Isaiah (Isa. 13:17).[44] Israelite deportees were placed in the land of the Medes after the fall of the northern kingdom in 722 B.C. (2 Kings 17:6). The Median homeland was in northern Iran, while the Persians controlled southern Iran. When the Babylonians defeated the Assyrian Empire, it was with the assistance of the King Cyaxeres of the Medes that the great cities of Assur and Nineveh were conquered.[45] During the first half of the sixth century, the Persians were subservient. A later Median

43 Edwin Yamauchi, *Persia and the Bible* (Grand Rapids: Baker Books, 1996), 33–42.
44 *ABD* 4:659.
45 *ANET* 304–5; 614–612 B.C.

Fig. 6.19 – Pasargadae, the capital of Cyrus in Iran
Photo by Todd Bolen/Bibleplaces.com

king, Astyges (585–550 B.C.) married his daughter to a Persian chieftain, Cambyses.[46] One son of this union was Cyrus, making him half-Persian and half-Median. In 550 B.C. he overthrew his Median master and father-in-law and united the two nations under Persian control. Cyrus proved to be an excellent warrior who expanded his territory and organized the armies into an effective war machine. The next decade saw Persian forces take control of most of Anatolia and regions east of Persia. In 539 B.C. Babylon fell to Cyrus (see Fig. 4.14)

46 Yamauchi, *Persia and the Bible*, 56.

Fig. 6.20 – Tomb of Cyrus at Pasargadae *Photo by Todd Bolen/Bibleplaces.com*

Cambyses succeeded his father Cyrus, and he invaded Egypt in 525 B.C., adding it to the vast empire.[47] But while in Egypt word arrived of a coup against him back home, he returned to Persia. While traveling home, he was either accidentally injured and died or committed suicide. A member of his elite force, Darius, seized the throne, even though he had no connection to the royal family. Darius the Great successfully ruled from 522 to 486 B.C.[48] Although he failed to conquer Greece, losing the decisive battles at Marathon, he established a continuous road that connected Susa in Elam (just west of Persia) to Sardis in Asia Minor. This 1,700-mile (2,735-km)–long road facilitated movement of his forces, and for communications purposes, he established a "pony express" system with stops at regular intervals, which allowed the long trek to take only a week to travel (see Map 6.2).[49] To further communication and

47 *ABD* 5:238.
48 *ABD* 5:238–39.
49 Yamauchi, *Persia and the Bible,* 174–78.

Fig. 6.21 – Darius's palace at Persepolis
Photo by Todd Bolen/Bibleplaces.com

transportation within his empire, he successfully completed the first "Suez Canal' from the Gulf of Suez to the Pelusiac Nile that ran to the Mediterranean.

When the Jews in Judah were having problems rebuilding the temple in Jerusalem because of legal obstacles caused by regional governors, it was Darius I who reissued the order to build the temple (Ezra 6:1–12) upon finding Cyrus's original edict. He also was responsible for carving

Fig. 6.22 – Glazed brick walls with Persian archers from Persepolis
Photo by James K. Hoffmeier

the "Rosetta Stone" equivalent for deciphering of cuneiform script. This trilingual inscription, written in Elamite, Babylonian, and Old Persian, is known as the Behistun (Bisitun) Monument.[50] Darius I also built the magnificent city Persepolis, that remained the capital of the Persian Empire until it was sacked by Alexander the Great in 330 B.C.

On the wall at Persepolis there is a relief showing Darius seated on his throne, and standing behind him is his son and successor, Xerxes (486–465 B.C.). He tried to fulfill his father's vision to seize Greece, but likewise failed, losing a humiliating naval battle at Salamis and a land battle at Thermopylae that included the heroics of Leonidas and his three hundred Spartans. In the Bible he is known as the great Persian emperor who married the Jewish beauty queen, Esther.

Fig. 6.23 – Darius enthroned with his son and successor Xerxes standing behind him from Persepolis *Photo by Todd Bolen/Bibleplaces.com*

50 *OEANE* 1:330–31.

DANIEL: THE STATESMAN-PROPHET

> "The God of heaven will set up a kingdom that will never be destroyed, nor will it be left to another people."
>
> —Daniel 2:44

The Book of Daniel

English Bibles follow the Greek (Septuagint) and Latin canonical ordering of books by locating Daniel after the three major prophets, Isaiah, Jeremiah, and Ezekiel, and before the Book of the Twelve, that is, Hosea to Malachi. This placement demonstrates that the Greek-speaking Jewish translators of the Old Testament considered the book to be at home with the prophetic books. In the earlier Hebrew ordering the OT Scriptures, however, the book of Daniel is not placed among the prophets, but in the Writings or Kethuvim section, between the books of Esther and Ezra. The book itself includes biographical and historical narratives, while chapters 2 and 7–12 are recognized to be apocalyptic literature.[51] Since six of the twelve chapters are prophetic/apocalyptic, the rationale for its exclusion from the prophetic corpus in the Jewish tradition is puzzling. It may be that the Jewish sages who assembled the Kethuvim saw "discontinuity" between Daniel the royal official and Daniel who was the recipient of apocalyptic visions.[52] Put another way, unlike the prophets of Israel who were professional prophets,[53] Daniel was a statesman who prophesied rather than a prophet who was a statesman. There is no record of him exercising more pastoral duties among the people like his contemporary, Ezekiel. The NT does, indeed, call Daniel a prophet (Matt. 24:15). Daniel 1:17 includes the notice regarding Daniel that he "could understand visions and dreams of all kinds." As a recipient of visions that were recorded for posterity, Daniel was clearly understood to be a prophet.

When and by whom the book was compiled is not known. Parts of the book were written in Aramaic and others in Hebrew. Fragments of the book of Daniel were discovered at Qumran among the Dead Sea Scrolls and date to the second century B.C., which suggests that the book of Daniel had to have been composed at least two centuries earlier. According to R. K. Harrison, "It is now clear from

---

51 Bullock, *Old Testament Prophetic Books*, 353.

52 Joyce Baldwin, *Daniel: An Introduction and Commentary* (Downers Grove, IL: InterVarsity Press, 1978), 53.

53 See discussion in chapter 1 about Balaam, Samuel, and other prophets and how they made a living. Amos 7:12 also implies that prophets earned their living through their ministry.

the Qumran manuscripts that no part of the OT canonical literature was composed later than the fourth century B.C."[54]

Some Historical Challenges

The authenticity and historical accuracy of the book of Daniel has long been debated. Such challenges hearken back to Porphyry the philosopher (A.D. 233–305), an anti-Christian polemicist.[55] Like critics of Daniel ever since, Porphyry recognized that the prophecies anticipating the king of Greece (i.e., Alexander the Great) whose vast empire divided into four regions upon his death and the subsequent Seleucid/Maccabean period (cf. Dan. 2:36–45; Dan. 8; 9:24–27) were so accurate that they had to originate later in the Hellenistic period (third to second century B.C.). At the heart of this rejection was Porphyry's "assumption that there could be no predictive element in prophecy."[56] In the past two centuries modern skeptics continue to embrace Porphyry's denial of divinely inspired prophecy.

Particularly, critics point to apparent historical blunders in the text that is explained by the second-century author not having an accurate grasp on the history of the Chaldean and early Persian periods. Thus historical details and the names of various rulers don't accord with the well-documented history of the sixth-century setting of the narratives of Daniel. Thanks to various archaeological discoveries, largely from ancient inscriptions, some of these issues have been resolved, or at least plausible explanations can be offered. Indeed, some of the evidence demonstrates that the biblical author was keenly aware of ancient details of the Chaldean and earlier Persian periods and was not prone to error. Here are some of the more substantive problems and explanations based on archaeological data.

The date of Nebuchadnezzar's first campaign against Judah

Daniel 1:1 dates Nebuchadnezzar's initial campaign to Jerusalem in the "third year of the reign of Jehoiakim king of Judah." This is when Daniel and other young Judean men were taken to Babylon for education in Chaldean/Babylonian language and literature (1:4). The issue is that Jeremiah 25:1 also reports on this event but dates it to "the fourth year of Jehoiakim," adding that it was Nebuchadnezzar's first regnal year. The one-year difference between the

---

54 *ISBE* 1:862.
55 Yamauchi, *Persia and the Bible*, 57–58.
56 Harrison, *Introduction to the Old Testament*, 1110.

two accounts was clarified with the discovery of the Babylonian historical records, which reveal that the period of time between the accession of the king in Babylon and the new year was called the accession year, and not regnal year one.[57] The first full year of a king's reign would be year one. In Judah where Jeremiah wrote did not follow the Babylonian means of reckoning. Hence, Jeremiah's year four and Daniel's year three of Jehoiakim are the same, and correspond to Nebuchadnezzar's first year, that is, 605 B.C.[58]

Babylonian dating used by Daniel	Judean dating used by Jeremiah	Years B.C.
Accession year	Year 1	609/8 B.C.
Year 1	Year 2	607 B.C.
Year 2	Year 3	606 B.C.
Year 3	Year 4	605 B.C.

Who is King Belshazzar?

The king of Babylonia who saw the handwriting on the wall (Dan. 5; see further below) on the eve of the Persian conquest of Babylon, and in whose reign Daniel received visions (Dan. 7:1; 8:1), is not named among the known Chaldean kings. During the reign of King Nabonidus (556–539 B.C.),[59] the final king of the Neo-Babylonian era, he recorded the sequence of his predecessors and the lengths of their reign, beginning with its founder, Nabupolassar (twenty-one years), Nebuchadnezzar (forty-three years), Evil-merodoch (Awil-Marduk; two years),[60] Neriglissar (four years),[61] and then Nabonidus himself (seventeen years), which ended abruptly when Cyrus the Great seized Babylon.

57 Alan Millard, "Daniel in Babylon: An Accurate Record?" in *Do Historical Matters Matter to Faith?* eds. J. Hoffmeier and D. Magary (Wheaton, IL: Crossway, 2012), 264–65.

58 Thiele, *Hebrew Kings*, 80–91.

59 *COS* 2:310.

60 The successor of Nebuchadnezzar who released king Jehoiachin from his prison in Babylon (2 Kings 25:27–30; Jer. 52:31–34)

61 This ruler is apparently is one and the same Nergal-sar-ezer named in Jeremiah 39:3, who was one of the officials who lead the attack on Jerusalem in 588/7 that led to its fall in 586 B.C. His young son Labashi-Marduk ruled for three months but was assassinated, allowing Nabonidus to assume the throne the same year. Arnold, *Who Were the Babylonians?*, 100–101. *ANET* 311–12.

Conspicuously absent from this sequence is Belshazzar, which led earlier generations of critics so see him as a figure invented by the writer of Daniel nearly four centuries after the purported events.

The clue to Belshazzar's identity is found in the Babylonian Chronicle, which records that Nabonidus moved to Teima in northern Arabia and thus was unable to fulfill the royal duties associated with the New Year's festival (the Akitu), while adding that "the crown prince, the officials and his army (were) in Akkad (i.e. Babylonia)."[62] A negative assessment of Nabonidus's move to Teima was recorded in a poem by priests of Babylon. In Arabia he built a temple to the moon-god Sin (patron of Ur), thus diminishing the principal deity of Babylonian, Marduk. This poem dates the king's departure to the very end of his second year, claiming "he entrusted the 'Camp' to his oldest (son), the first-born . . . [he] entrusted the kinship to him."[63] This unnamed crown prince was the *de facto* ruler or coregent in Babylon while his father was absent. We learn the name of the acting ruler in an inscription discovered in association with the Ziggurat of Ur. One clay cylinder contains a prayer to the moon god Sin, patron of Ur. Nabonidus prays that the temples of the gods be firm, and then seeks the deity's blessing: "As for me, Nabonidus, the king of Babylon, save me from sinning against your great godhead and grant me as a present a life of long days, and as for Belshazzar, the eldest son of my offspring, instill reverence for your great godhead (in) his heart."[64] This Belshazzar was certainly the one named in the book of Daniel. Furthermore, the book of Daniel contains a clue as to Belshazzar's true identity. When Belshazzar saw the handwriting on the wall, he called for its interpretation and offered a reward to whomever could decipher the mysterious text: "he will be made the third highest ruler in the kingdom" (Dan. 5:7). This notice indicates that Belshazzar could only elevate someone to the third position since he only occupied the second slot, as Nabonidus was still officially the ruler.

Fig. 6.24 – Stela of Nabonidus in the British Museum
Photo by Todd Bolen/Bibleplaces.com

62 *ANET* 306.
63 *ANET* 313.
64 *COS* 2:314.

Fig. 6.25 – Nabonidus-Belshazzar cylinder from Ur, in the British Museum
Photo by James K. Hoffmeier

Who is Darius in the book of Daniel?

In the year 539 B.C., on the very night of Belshazzar received the interpretation about the mysterious handwriting on the wall (see below), he was killed and the city taken by Darius the Mede, a sixty-two-year-old man (Dan. 5:30) identified as the son of Ahasuerus (a Mede by descent; Dan 9:1). His name also occurs in Daniel 6:1 when he organized the kingdom, and two visions are dated to his first year (Dan. 9:1; 11:1). The identity of this Darius has long been debated. Three different Persian emperors bore the name, Darius I (522–486 B.C.), Darius II (423–404 B.C.), and Darius III (335–332 B.C.). The first ruler with this name was twenty-eight years old when he usurped the throne, meaning that in 539 B.C. he would only have been around eleven years old. Some critics think that the author, writing centuries later, simply employed the name of the well-known first emperor with that name, despite the obvious chronological problem.

Fig. 6.26 – Approach to the Ishtar Gate of Babylon, in the Berlin Museum
Photo by James K. Hoffmeier

Several more positive identifications have been proposed. First, when Babylon fell to the Persians in 539 B.C., the Babylonian Chronicle reports, it occurred under the leadership of Ugbaru/Gubaru (Gk. Gobryas): "Gobryas (Ugbaru), the governor of Gutium, and the army of Cyrus entered Babylon without a battle."[65] This regional governor had defected to the Persian side and as a native of the region, he was tasked to lead the seizure of Babylon.[66] One theory is that Darius the Mede is an honorific title of Ugbaru/Gubaru, who took control of Babylon according to Daniel 5:30–31. An apparently different official also named Ugbaru/Gubaru was appointed governor of Babylon province by Cyrus.[67] Thus there were apparently two different officials with the same name associated with the fall of Chaldean Babylon and the beginnings of Persian-controlled Babylon, but why the leader who is called king in the Bible is identified as a Mede is a problem, as neither of these Ugbarus were Medo-Persian. One apparently died three weeks after the events described in Daniel 5.[68]

Darius the Mede has also been equated with King Cyrus himself. At the end of chapter 6 we are told, "So Daniel prospered during the reign of Darius and the reign of Cyrus the Persian" (v. 28). Donald Wiseman showed that the word "and" (Heb. *waw*) could be rendered "that is," which equates the two names:[69] "Darius, that is, the reign of Cyrus."[70] This view would mean that Darius the Mede is none other than Cyrus the Persian emperor, making Darius the Mede a title for the emperor of the Medes and Persians. Further in support of this theory is the stated age of Darius the Mede, namely sixty-two years (Dan. 5:31). Some scholars believe this age squares with Cyrus's age as he died nine years later, around age seventy.[71] A final salient point is that the Greek historian Herodotus wrote: "Cyrus

---

65 *ANET* 306.
66 Yamauchi, *Persia and the Bible*, 85–86.
67 For a technical review and discussion of this figures and their identities, see Yamauchi, *Persia and the Bible*, 58–58, 85–87; Baldwin, *Daniel*, 23–28.
68 Baldwin, *Daniel*, 24–25.
69 D. J. Wiseman, "Some Historical Problems in the Book of Daniel," in *Notes on Some Problems in the Book of Daniel* (London: Tyndale, 1965), 12.
70 Wiseman's understanding of the apposition of the two names is reflected in footnote translation in the NIV.
71 Wiseman, "Some Historical Problems," 14–15.

was really a mule because he was born to two people who were not of the same race, and his mother . . . was a Mede and the daughter of Astyages, king of the Medes, while his father was a Persian."[72] Thus while the identity of Darius the Mede remains uncertain, there are some credible explanations based on ancient and biblical sources, with the latter proposal being the most likely interpretation.

Daniel in Babylon

We meet Daniel when he as a young man in his teens. He is among the select group of Judean youths taken to Babylon in 605 B.C. after the recently crowned king of Babylon, Nebuchadnezzar, marched on Jerusalem to demand its submission (Dan. 1:1–7). For three years Daniel and his colleagues, only three of which are named (Hananiah, Mishael, and Azariah), were to be trained in "language and literature of the Babylonians" (Dan. 1:4). The intent of this acculturation program was to educate promising young Judeans to act as administrators for the growing Babylonian Empire. Perhaps they were to be sent back to Judah to represent Nebuchadezzar's interests. Daniel and his friends decided that even though they were in a foreign land they would stay true to their religious and dietary practices, as prescribed in the Law. Daniel stood out from the others by his ability to interpret dreams and receive visions: "Daniel could understand visions and dreams of all kinds" (Dan. 1:17b). In fact, his dream-interpreting skills made him especially valuable to Nebuchadnezzar, and he interpreted the mysterious "handwriting on the wall" for coregent Belshazzar late in his career (Dan. 5:5–15). Then under Darius the Persian king, he was appointed to be one of three senior administrators who oversaw the 120 satraps, regional governors who oversaw the 120 districts of the empire. This was because "Daniel so distinguished himself among the administrators and the satraps by his exceptional qualities" (Dan. 6:3a). Mention of serving under Persian rulers indicates that Daniel continued to serve in the administration in Babylon until at least 536 B.C. (Dan. 10:1).

This timespan offered in the book means that Daniel worked for the government from 605 to 536 B.C., a period of around seventy years (cf. Dan 1:1; 10:1). This means that he was active throughout the entire period of the Judean exile. It does not appear, however, that like Ezekiel he mingled with and pastored the other exiles. Rather, he resided within the capital and worked in official administrative capacities, and when he received visions, he recorded them (Dan. 7:1).

---

72 Walter Blanco, *Herodotus: The Histories* (New York: W. W. Norton, 1992), 34–35.

Daniel also earned the reputation for being a righteous and God-fearing man. These characteristics are recognized by Ezekiel, who associates him with Noah and Job (Ezek. 14:14, 20), and in Ezekiel 28:3 he is hailed for his great wisdom.

The Visions and Message of Daniel

The people of the Near East, including the Israelites, believed gods communicated with mortals through dreams, and therefore people sought out sages who could interpret their dreams. In Egypt, a thirteenth-century-B.C. dream interpretation manual has survived that priests could consult (See Fig. 1.16). Nebuchadnezzar had a peculiar dream, and he demanded to know its meaning (Dan. 2:1–16). To be sure that his magicians and sorcerers offered an accurate interpretation, the king insisted that they first tell him what he dreamed, followed by its meaning. The sages of Babylon knew this was impossible without some sort of divine assistance, and they were desperate since the king threatened their lives if they failed him. This crisis presented for Daniel the opportunity to use his divine gift. In a vision at night, the mystery was revealed to him (Dan. 2:17).

Fig. 6.27 – Dream omens from Sippar, north of Babylon, in the British Museum
Photo by Todd Bolen/Bibleplaces.com

Daniel, who had been given the Babylonian name Belteshazzar (Dan. 1:7), stood before the king and proclaimed that while humanly dreams cannot be explained, nevertheless, "there is a God in heaven who reveals mysteries. He has shown King Nebuchadnezzar what will happen in days to come" (2:28). Then he correctly recounts the dream the king had; he had seen an impressive metallic image.

> Your Majesty looked, and there before you stood a large statue—an enormous, dazzling statue, awesome in appearance. The head of the statue was made of pure gold, its chest and arms of silver, its belly and thighs of bronze, its legs of iron, its feet partly of iron and partly of baked clay. While you were watching, a rock was cut out, but not by human hands. It struck the statue on its feet of iron and clay and smashed them. Then the iron, the clay, the bronze, the silver and the gold were broken to pieces at the same time and became like chaff on a threshing floor in the summer. The wind swept them away without leaving a trace. But the rock that struck the statue became a huge mountain and filled the whole earth. (Dan. 2:31–35)

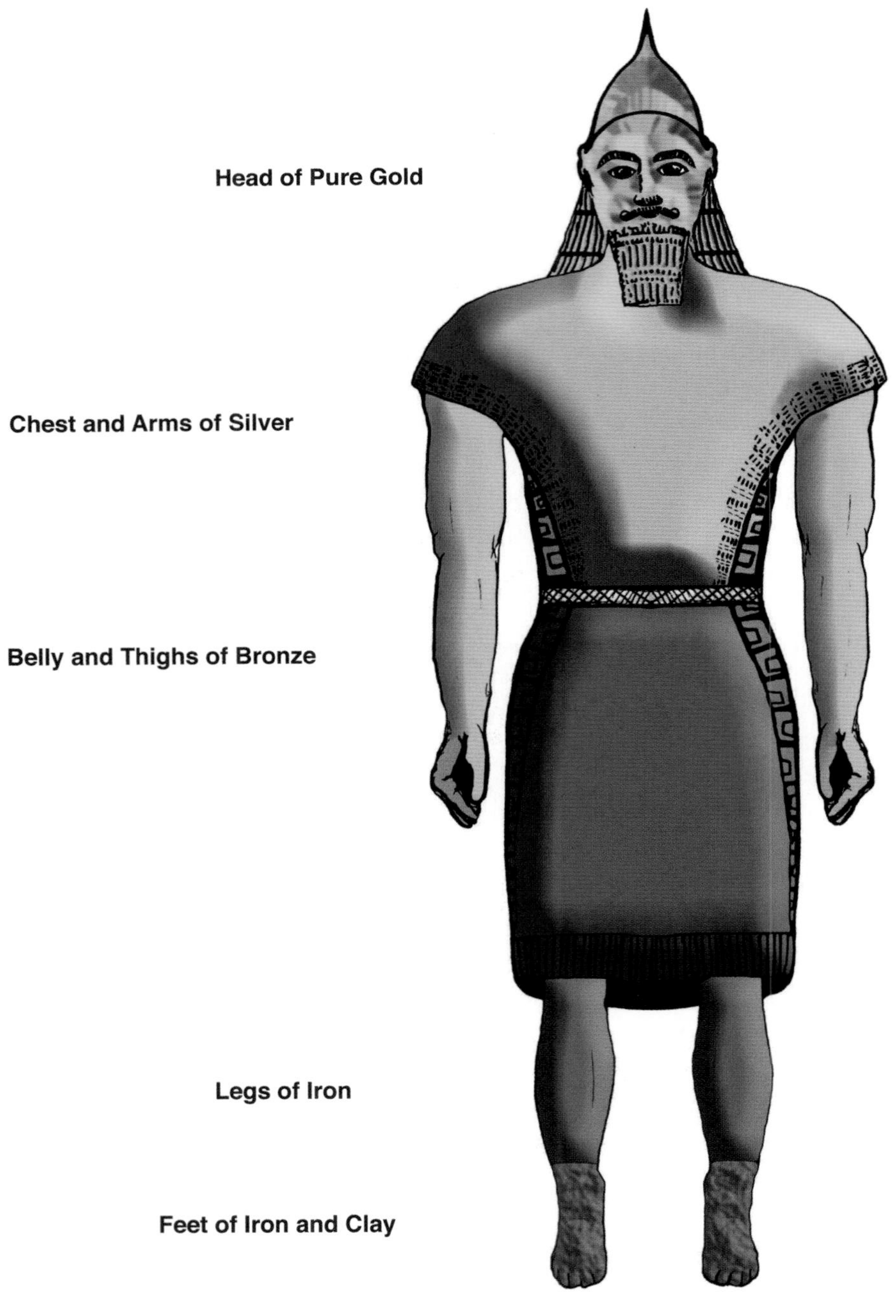

Fig. 6.28 – Statue in King Nebuchadnezzar's dream
Illustration by Hannah Vander Lugt

Daniel then explained the meaning of this bizarre dream. Moving from the head to the feet, the golden head represented Nebuchadnezzar and his empire, of which "the God of heaven has given you dominion" (Dan. 2:37). The silver chest and arms symbolize the kingdom that would replace the Babylonian, followed by a third which corresponds to the bronze belly and thighs, and then the legs of iron with feet mingled with clay was the fourth kingdom (Dan. 2:31–32). As each kingdom arose and then fell to the next, the metals change from gold, silver, bronze, to iron, indicating an increase in strength but a qualitative decline. The fourth kingdom would, however, be weakened as the feet becomes a mix of iron and mud. It would then be "smashed" by a rock not cut by human hands that then grew and expanded, covering the whole earth (Dan. 2:35).

The identity of the succeeding empires is not made in the book of Daniel. Knowing the history of the next five centuries is critical to interpreting the balance of the vision. Commentators have long debated and disagreed on how the future kingdoms correspond to history. Since Daniel lived to see the demise the Babylonian Empire and rise of the Persians, and his vision in chapter

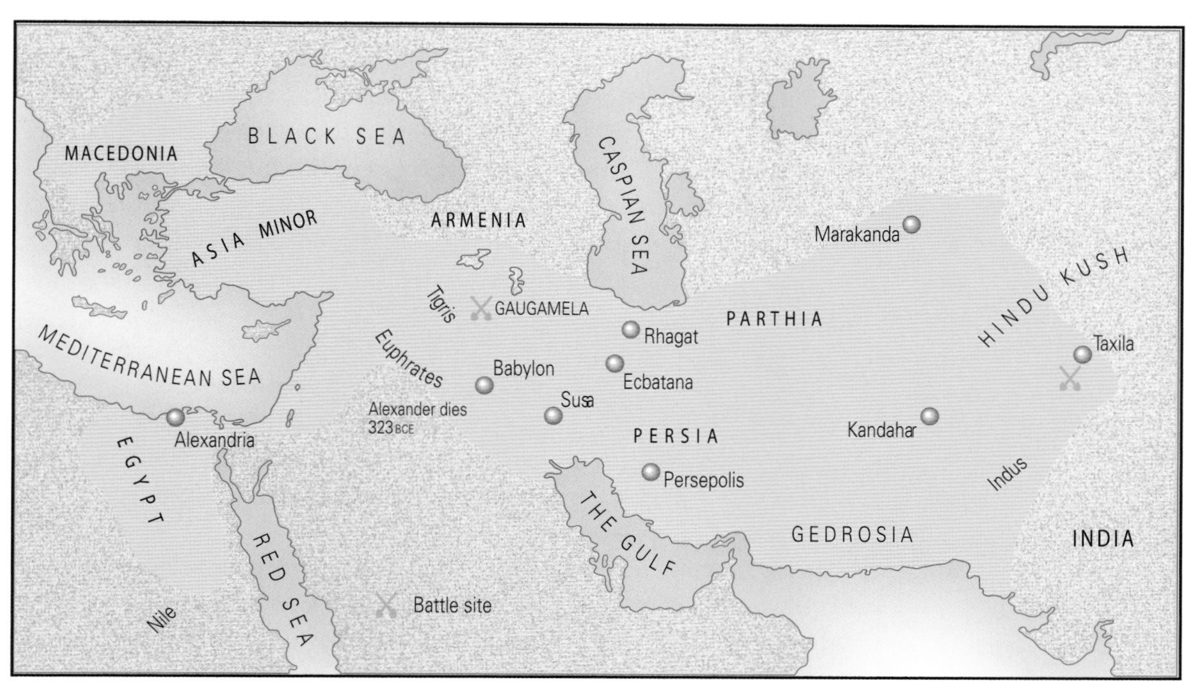

Map 6.3 – Alexander's Empire *Map from the* Kregel Bible Atlas *by Tim Dowley, copyright © 2003 Angus Hudson Ltd./Tim Dowley & Peter Wyatt trading as Three's Company. Used by permission.*

8 anticipates the defeat of Persia to an unnamed king of Greece (vv. 20–21), the first three kingdoms are apparent. Thus the likely historical sequence: Babylon, Persia, and Greece is what was envisioned in Nebuchadnezzar's dream. Certainly this represents the unfolding history as seen and anticipated in the book of Daniel and matches history as we know it.

The fourth kingdom, the one which begins with iron and ends with feet of clay (Dan. 2:40), seems to point to Rome, the heir of Greek domination of the Near East and Mediterranean world. It started out as strong as iron, expanding beyond the boundaries of the preceding empires. What then was the rock that demolished the last empire? Daniel explains that at the time of the demise of the fourth kingdom, "the God of heaven will set up a kingdom that will never be destroyed, nor will it be left to another people. It will crush all those kingdoms and bring them to an end, but it will itself endure forever" (Dan. 2:44). In place of the human kingdoms that God raises up and removes, God will establish a kingdom that will last forever. No further clarification is given in this chapter on this divine kingdom (but see 7:7–14). The theme of God's kingdom ultimately prevailing, is a central element of apocalyptic literature (see excursus "Apocalyptic Literature" above).

From this vision and others that follow in the book, it is evident that the overriding theme of the book is that while the world is in turmoil and the nation of Israel was destroyed with its survivors dispersed in different lands, God was in control of the future. Through his experiences with divine visions and Daniel's wisdom and through interaction with God-fearing Hebrews, Nebuchadnezzar makes several profound confessions of the greatness, might, and sovereignty of the God of Israel: "Surely your God is the God of gods and Lord of kings and a revealer of mysteries" (Dan. 2:47).

After Shadrach, Meshach, and Abednego survived a certain death sentence in the fiery furnace, Nebuchadnezzar makes a remarkable confession about the God who saved his faithful servants: "How great are his signs, how mighty his wonders! His kingdom is an eternal kingdom; his dominion endures from generation to generation" (Dan. 4:3). Once again, the eternal kingdom of God is praised.

Later the king undergoes some sort of bizarre mental disorder for some years, at the end of which Nebuchadnezzar makes another remarkable declaration: "At the end of that time, I, Nebuchadnezzar, raised my eyes toward heaven, and my sanity was restored. Then I praised the Most High; I honored and glorified him who lives forever. His dominion is an eternal dominion; his kingdom endures from generation to generation. All the peoples of the earth are regarded as nothing. He does as he pleases with the powers of heaven and the peoples of the earth" (Dan. 4:34–35).

In Daniel 5 the famous episode of the "handwriting on the wall" occurs. King Belshazzar, the de facto ruler of Babylon, threw a huge party on the eve of the Persian takeover of Babylon. He ordered that some of the vessels taken from the Jerusalem temple by Nebuchadnezzar be brought out to be used for further drinking (Dan. 5:2–4). In response to this sacrilege, suddenly there appeared a

Fig. 6.29 – Mural of Shadrach, Meshach and Abednego in the fiery furnace, protected under the wings of an angel; from Faras-Petros Cathedral, Sudan, 10th century A.D. *Photo by James K. Hoffmeier*

human finger writing on the plastered wall that wrote the following words: "Mene, Mene, Tekel, Parsin" (Dan. 5:25), apparently written in the Aramaic script.[73] Aramaic was the standard language of the Persian Empire and continued to dominate the Near East for centuries to come, and it was the common language spoken in the Holy Land in Jesus's day. (For Aramaic script written on a wall, see Fig. 1.6.)

Not surprisingly, the king panicked! Daniel was summoned to offer an interpretation. He reminds Belshazzar that Nebuchadnezzar before him "acknowledged that the Most High God is sovereign over all kingdoms on earth and sets over them anyone he wishes" (Dan. 5:21), and it was this God that Belshazzar had dishonored. As a result, judgment was coming to Babylon. Then Daniel explained the four words to signify that Belshazzar's reign was about to end; he had been weighed and found wanting, and his kingdom would be taken by the Persians. That very night, the narrative continues, the king was killed, and the Persians took the city (Dan. 5:30–31).

Fig. 6.30 – Lion devouring a man, in Khartoum Museum *Photo by James K. Hoffmeier*

Under Persian administration of Babylon, Daniel continued to serve in important capacities (Dan. 6; 9–12). When baseless charges by jealous officials were brought against Daniel for praying to God, he was sentenced to the den of lions. God, however, spared his life, and the next day he was released (Dan. 6:6–27). When King Darius heard from Daniel that his life was spared, once again a pagan king acknowledges the power and uniqueness of the God of Daniel: "For he is the living God and he endures forever; his kingdom will not be destroyed, his dominion will never end. He rescues and he saves; he performs signs and wonders in the heavens and on the earth. He has rescued Daniel from the power of the lions" (Dan. 6:26–27).

The topic of God's eternal kingdom introduced in chapter 2 comes into view again and is expanded in Daniel 7. As noted in the discussion of apocalyptic literature, the coming and ultimate rule of God is a central theme in this genre of prophecy. Here the prophet has a vision in which God is described as "the Ancient of Days," that is, "one

73 Archer, *Daniel*, 71.

advanced in days, very old,"[74] and he is described as having clothes "as white as snow; the hair of his head was white like wool" (Dan. 7:9). Representing God as an old man with white garments and hair is to represent "a judge (and) indicates both dignity and purity."[75] In this rare portrayal of God, he is enthroned on a flaming throne on wheels. Then Daniel reports:

> In my vision at night I looked, and there before me was one like a son of man, coming with the clouds of heaven. He approached the Ancient of Days and was led into his presence. He was given authority, glory and sovereign power; all nations and peoples of every language worshiped him. His dominion is an everlasting dominion that will not pass away, and his kingdom is one that will never be destroyed. (Dan. 7:13–14)

The vision anticipates God's kingdom being ruled by "one like a son of man," that is, one who is human-like and yet comes with the clouds like a deity. This image combines human and divine elements. In the New Testament, Jesus of Nazareth refers to himself as "the son of man" (e.g., Mark 2:28, 8:31, 38; Luke 6:22; 7:34). References like John 3:13 seems to have Daniel's idea in mind when it records, "No one has ever gone into heaven except the one who came from heaven—the Son of Man." Similarly, in Mark 13:26 Jesus discloses, "At that time people will see the Son of Man coming in clouds with great power and glory," referring to the end of the age and the return of Christ. Such statements make it clear that the New Testament considers Jesus to be the one who would receive the kingdom in fulfillment of Daniel's prophecy. It is his kingdom that will surpass all and will endure forever.

In Daniel 8, dated to Belshazzar's third year, 550–549 B.C.,[76] while Daniel was in the Elamite capital, Susa, he had another vision. In it he saw a ram with two horns on its head, although one stood higher than the other (Dan. 8:1–4). This ram charged all over the land, taking possession of great territory, and he "became great." But then from the west came a male goat with a single "prominent horn" on its head. The two animals clashed, with the goat breaking the two horns of the ram and defeating it. The horn of the goat grew until it too was broken, and four smaller horns grew in its place (Dan. 8:5–8). With the interpretive assistance

74 C. F. Keil and F. Delitzsch, *Ezekiel, Daniel*, Commentary on the Old Testament, vol. 9 (Edinburgh: T&T Clark, 1890), 230.

75 Edward J. Young, *The Prophecy of Daniel* (Grand Rapids: Eerdmans, 1949), 151.

76 Baldwin, *Daniel*, 155.

Fig. 6.31 – Goat charging
Photo by Todd Bolen/Bibleplaces.com

Fig. 6.32 – Silver coin of Alexander the Great with ram's horn protruding from his head
Photo by Todd Bolen/Bibleplaces.com

of the angel Gabriel, Daniel receives the explanation of this vision (Dan. 8:16–26). The ram and its two horns represented the Medes and the Persians, and the goat was Greece, and its long, single horn is the first king of Greece.

Alexander the Great's meteoric rise to power followed the death of his father Phillip in 336 B.C. appears to be whom the single horn of the goat represents.[77] After dislodging the Persians from Asia Minor, Alexander moved south to Phoenicia and Palestine in 332 B.C., followed by a rather easy takeover of Egypt in 331 B.C.. Later that year he fought the decisive battle against the Persian emperor Darius III at Gaugamela or Arbela (due north of Babylon), just east of the Tigris River near Nineveh. In 323 B.C. he died in Babylon after his campaigns to India.

The vision continues. The great horn was broken "at the height of his power" (Dan. 8:8), just as Alexander died after his impressive world conquest at the young age of thirty-two. Daniel's vision explains that four smaller horns grew up in place of the large one, which point to the four kingdoms that replaced the great, unified empire of the Greek king. Plainly this depicts what happened to Alexander's conquered lands after his death in 323 B.C. Four generals carved up his realm, with the largest area going to Seleucus (Mesopotamia and Syria), Ptolemy (Palestine and Egypt), Antigonus (much of Anatolia/Turkey), and Lysimachus (Thrace, the area north and east of Macedonia).[78] Meanwhile Cassandra ruled the old homeland of Macedonia (northern Greece) until Alexander's son and namesake came of age. Wars in the following decades between these powers, however, resulted in the territories shifting their configuration as borders changed.

---

77 Gleason Archer, *Daniel*, Expositor's Bible Commentary, vol. 7, ed. Frank Gaebelein (Grand Rapids: Zondervan, 1985), 97–98.

78 R. Baker III and C. Baker III, *Ancient Greeks: Creating the Classical Tradition* (Oxford: Oxford University Press, 1997), 195–1204.

Fig. 6.33 – Mosaic of the Gaugemela battle between Alexander (on left) and Darius III (on right)
Photo by A. D. Riddle

The movement toward the future kingdoms and the appearance of God's eternal kingdom begins with the end of the Judean captivity. When Cyrus took control of Babylon in 539 B.C., Daniel reckoned that the seventy years of exile that Jeremiah announced was nearing completion (Dan. 9:1–2): sixty-six years had elapsed. Daniel offers a long prayer of confession to God on behalf of his people, acknowledging that the exile was the covenant curse poured out on Judah (9:11). It will be recalled that Isaiah the prophet had named Cyrus as God's anointed one who would order the rebuilding of Jerusalem and its temple (Isa. 44:28–45:1). Indeed Cyrus decreed the release of the captive Jews and permitted them to return to their homeland. The words of this decree are found in the books of Ezra (1:1–4) and 2 Chronicles (36:22–23).

The "Cyrus cylinder" was discovered in Babylon in 1879 and reveals some features of the Persian imperial policy regarding the treatment of the temples of non-Persian deities. Cyrus claims, "I returned the (images of) the gods to the sacred centers [on the other side of] the Tigris whose sanctuaries had been abandoned for a long time, and I let them dwell in eternal abodes. I gathered all their inhabitants and returned [to them] their dwellings."[79]

---

79 *COS* 2:315.

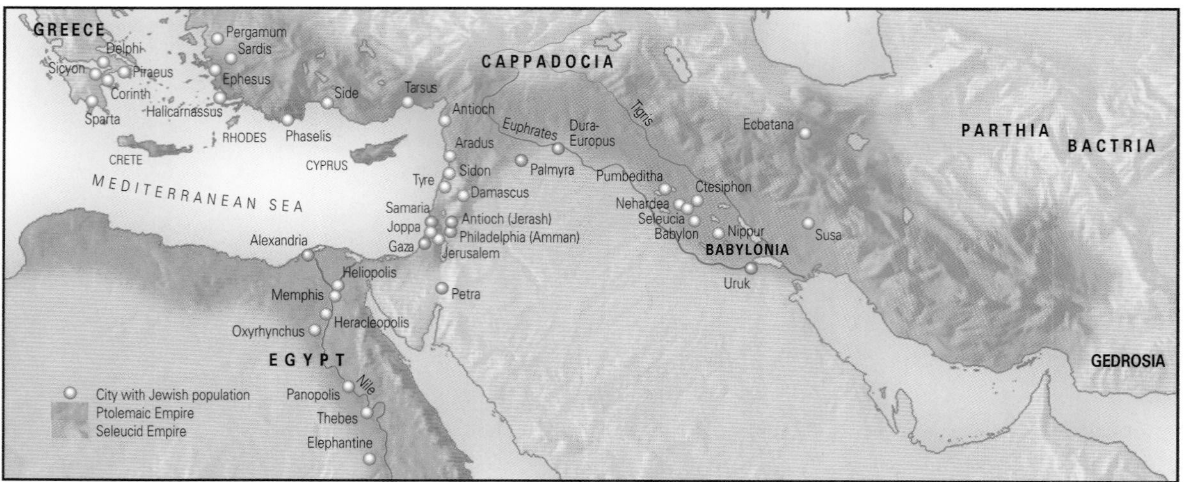

Map 6.4 – The Ptolemaic and Seleucid empires after Alexander's death
Map from the Kregel Bible Atlas *by Tim Dowley, copyright © 2003 Angus Hudson Ltd./ Tim Dowley & Peter Wyatt trading as Three's Company. Used by permission.*

Fig. 6.34 – The Cyrus Cylinder, in the British Museum
Photo by Todd Bolen/Bibleplaces.com

The Jewish exile ended and permission for people to return to their homeland and to rebuild the temple of the LORD reflects the same practice implemented by Cyrus in this important document. No doubt the Jews who returned to Judah recognized that God had reduced Babylon and elevated the Persians to fulfill God's purposes for Israel, just as Daniel's visions presaged.

CONCLUDING THOUGHTS

Daniel, as noted above, served in the administration of Babylon for nearly the entire exilic period, and periodically through this seventy-year period he received visions. As noted in the previous section, the dominant theme was that God was sovereignly controlling the kingdoms, raising up and removing rulers according to his plan. Ultimately it was God's kingdom that would be established and endure because God's appointed "son of man" (Dan. 7:13) would rule over it. For the nationless Jewish community that was scattered in Mesopotamia and Medo-Persia (as the book of Esther demonstrates), and as far away as Egypt, this message must have given great hope because "the sovereignty, power and greatness of all the kingdoms under heaven will be handed over to the holy people of the Most High. His kingdom will be an everlasting kingdom, and all rulers will worship and obey him" (Dan. 7:27).

It is noteworthy that throughout his ministry, Jesus Christ proclaimed the kingdom of God (or heaven): "the kingdom of God has come" or "is near" (Matt. 12:28; Mark 1:15; Luke 4:44; John 3:3–5), and he called himself "the son of man" thirty times in the Gospel of Matthew alone. Matthew also connects the eschatological appearance of Christ with the Daniel 7 vision: "Then will appear in heaven the sign of the Son of Man, and then all the tribes of the earth will mourn when they see the Son of Man coming on the clouds of heaven with power and great glory" (Matt. 24:30).

DISCUSSION QUESTIONS

- What are some ways in which Ezekiel's background as a priest impacts his ministry as a prophet?
- How does God impress on Ezekiel that the people back in Jerusalem were continuing their pagan ways?
- What are some of the dramatic acts and allegories that Ezekiel used, and how did they help convey his message?
- What is apocalyptic literature, and what are some examples of it in Ezekiel and Daniel?
- Describe Ezekiel's visions of the immediate future and how they related to the end times.
- Discuss Daniel's roles as statesman and prophet.
- What is the overarching message of the book of Daniel, and how does God convey this message?

7

When I Restore the Fortunes of Judah and Jerusalem

THE PROPHETS OF THE POST-EXILIC PERIOD

THE POST-EXILIC PERIOD

The last cluster of prophets in the Old Testament fall into the Persian Period (ca. 539–400 B.C.), and the restoration of Jerusalem and Judah. This focus is summed up in the prophet Zechariah's words: "Therefore this is what the LORD says: 'I will return to Jerusalem with mercy, and there my house will be rebuilt. And the measuring line will be stretched out over Jerusalem,' declares the LORD Almighty" (Zech. 1:16).

Shortly after Cyrus king of Persia took control of Babylon in 539 B.C., he issued a decree ending the captivity of the Jewish exiles, permitting those who wished to do so to return to Judah and rebuild their temple in Jerusalem (Ezra 1:1–4; 2 Chron. 36:22–23). Some months later, a sizeable group of more than 42,000 made the long journey back to Judah. Under the leadership of Zerubbabel, the grandson of king Jehoiachin, work on rebuilding the temple began almost immediately (Ezra 3). What started as a joyous endeavor quickly ground to a halt due to harassment and legal obstacles thrown up by other residents of the land (Ezra 4). The opponents included exiles from other nations who had been brought to northern Israel by Esarhaddon king of Assyria (Ezra 4:2). Some years passed, until under the emperor Darius I (522–486 B.C.) permission was reaffirmed, and the work resumed. The book of Ezra reports on these events and notes that the prophets Haggai and Zechariah helped and encouraged the people and the leaders, Zerubbabel and Joshua the high priest, in the building efforts (Ezra 5:1–2; 6:14). These two prophets left us books that bear their name. The other two prophets to the post-exilic community in Judah

Fig. 7.1 – Darius before enemy prisoners, on the Behistun Inscription
Photo by Todd Bolen/Bibleplaces.com

are Joel and Malachi, although dating their respective ministries is difficult due to lack of specific chronological details.

HAGGAI: ENCOURAGER OF LEADERS

"'I am with you,' declares the LORD."
—Haggai 1:13

The period of prophetic activity of Haggai spans merely three months and twenty-four days. The brevity of his career may be due to the fact that he was an old man in 520 B.C. when "the word of the LORD came" to him (Hag. 1:1). In all just four messages are recorded all from the second year of Darius I (i.e., 520 B.C.), from first day of the sixth month to the twenty-fourth day of the ninth month (Hag. 2:10, 20). In chapter 2, the prophet speaks to those who had seen the first temple in all its glory, and seems to identify with those who in their youth would had been in Jerusalem, and then taken to Babylon in 586 B.C. Now a half century later, these elders would be in their seventies. If this is the case, Haggai would have been an elderly man when he made the long journey back to his homeland. Rebuilding the devastated city and the temple from the heaps of stone was a daunting task. Into this situation, Haggai emerges as a figure whose prophetic task was to encourage and motivate the people and their leaders. Due to his advanced age, he may not have lived to see the second temple just five years later when it was completed, but he certainly witnessed the beginning of the reconstruction project.

His name derives from the word for "holiday," *ḥag*,[1] suggesting that he may have been born during a religious festival. Beyond his name and his possible age, little else can be said about Haggai: the expected patronym is not included.

The first of the four messages (Hag. 1:1–11) is addressed to Zerubbabel the governor and Joshua the high priest, but it was clearly intended for the whole community. The prophet chides the people because while they have rebuilt their own homes, described as "paneled" (Hag. 1:4), it seems unlikely that the homes of commoners would have wood-paneled walls like David's "house of cedar" palace (2 Sam. 7:2). "Panels" (*sāp̱anîm*) could also refer to roof beams, which seems to be the intended reading.[2] Perhaps even the governor's mansion and some administrative buildings had been restored, but the house of the Lord lay in ruins (1:4).

1 *HALOT* 289–90.
2 Baldwin, *Haggai, Zechariah, Malachi*, 20.

Fig. 7.2 – Jumble of fallen stone blocks as discovered by archaeologists from the destruction of Herod's temple in Jerusalem (A.D. 70), giving something of an impression of the piles of stone and rubble to be dealt with in rebuilding Jerusalem in 520 B.C. *Photo by James K. Hoffmeier*

The book of Ezra reports that upon return from Babylon, work began on the temple immediately but was stalled when various legal challenges were made by foreign residents of the region, possibly those known in later time as "Samaritans," who had been brought to Samaria by the Assyrians after the fall of the northern kingdom in 722 B.C. (Ezra 4:1–3; cf. 2 Kings 17:24–33). Fifteen years or so had passed since the construction work stopped, and now God was challenging the people to reassess their priorities and get back to work: "'Go up into the mountains and bring down timber and build my house, so that I may take pleasure in it and be honored,' says the LORD" (Hag. 1:8). Timber for rebuilding the temple, we are informed by Ezra 3:7, came from Lebanon and was floated by sea to the port of Joppa in Israel.

In response to Haggai's message, the text states the Zerubbabel, Joshua, and the people obeyed the word of the LORD and feared him, and they were moved to take action. Since the prophet's messages dates to the year 520 B.C., the very year that king Darius I reissued Cyrus's original edict promoting the building the temple in Jerusalem (Ezra 4:24), Haggai's prodding likely comes when news of the permission reached Jerusalem. Haggai and his fellow prophet's encouragement succeeded, and construction started.

Fig. 7.3 – Boats towing timber for building Sargon II's new capital, Khorsabad; in Louvre Museum *Photo by James K. Hoffmeier*

The second vision, dated to the twenty-first day of the seventh month, of seven weeks after the first, and the prophet is directed to speak to the governor and the high priest. There was likely some discouragement over the quality and appearance of the temple by those who saw the first temple in all its grandeur. So the prophet asks: "Who of you is left who saw this house in its former glory? How does it look to you now? Does it not seem to you like nothing?" (Hag. 2:3). So he offers words of encouragement: "'But now be strong, Zerubbabel,' declares the LORD. 'Be strong, Joshua son of Jozadak, the high priest. Be strong, all you people of the land,' declares the LORD, 'and work. For I am with you'" (Hag. 2:4). God assures the people that despite what they see, "The glory of this present house will be greater than the glory of the former house" (Hag. 2:9).

Fig. 7.4 – Temple Mount, presently covering the area expanded by King Herod for his temple
Photo by William Schlegel/Bibleplaces.com

Fig. 7.5 – Gold signet ring of Pharaoh Horemheb
Photo by Todd Bolen/Bibleplaces.com

The meaning of this statement is variously interpreted. First, it could refer to the enlarged and glorious temple built by Herod the Great, which may have begun as early as 23–22 B.C., with the bulk of the work continuing to 9 B.C. By Jesus's day work would have been underway for forty-six years (John 2:20). This massive complex covered thirty-five acres.[3] We are reminded that the disciples of Jesus pointed out to him of the splendor of that temple when they said, "What massive stones! What magnificent buildings!" (Mark 13:1). Secondly, the glorious temple could be the future, eschatological temple envisioned in Revelation 21 and 22.[4] A third view is a messianic interpretation,[5] in which the coming glory will surpass that of Solomon's sanctuary and those that follow because of Jesus, who was considered to be "the glory of the one and only Son, who came from the Father" (John 1:14). It must be remembered that when the glory of the Lord departed the temple in Ezekiel 11:22–24, its return is never described in the books that speak of the Second Temple, namely Ezra, 2 Chronicles, Haggai, Zechariah, Joel, and Malachi. It is as if the absent glory returned in the person of Jesus Christ. On one occasion when Jesus taught in the temple, he himself claimed, "I tell you that something greater than the temple is here" (Matt. 12:6). From the perspective of the New Testament, the coming glory of the temple points to Jesus Christ.

The third (2:10–19) and fourth visions (2:20–23) fell on the same day, the twenty-fourth day of the ninth month. In the fourth is a word for Zerubbabel, encouraging him that God controls the kingdoms and will bring to pass his purposes for Jerusalem. He tells Zerubbabel that he is "chosen" by God to rebuild the temple, likening him to a "signet ring" (2:23). Signet rings were worn by

3 John McRay, *Archaeology and the New Testament* (Grand Raids: Baker Book House, 1991), 101–2.
4 Shepherd, *The Book of the Twelve*, 385–86.
5 Robert Alden, *Haggai*, Expositor's Bible Commentary, vol. 7, ed. F. Gaebelein (Grand Rapids: Zondervan, 1985), 587.

kings and high-ranking officials who act for the ruler.[6] It bore the name of the king. Authority was associated with signets or seals, and so documents could be signed and edicts proclaimed. In the book of Esther, king Xerxes authorizes an order with his signet ring (Esth. 8:10). In the case of Zerubbabel the fact that he is vested with this symbol of authority is especially significant for Jeremiah wrote of king Jehoiachin, that his signet ring would be torn off, and he would be taken captive to Babylon (Jer. 22:24). The removal of his signet and the loss of his authority and kingship went together. Zerubbabel is entrusted with divine authority to carry our God's commands. In this case, it was to build the temple.

Within five years, the temple was completed (Ezra 6:15). Haggai's encouragement and urgings had a positive effect on the people and the leaders of his day despite the brevity of his ministry.

ZECHARIAH: VISIONS OF COMING DAYS

> "'Return to me,' declares the LORD Almighty, 'and I will return to you,' says the LORD Almighty."
>
> —Zechariah 1:3

Zechariah the Prophet

Haggai's prophet partner in 520 B.C. was Zechariah (Ezra 5:1–2). Together they challenged the people to get on with the task of completing the construction on the temple that had begun some fifteen years earlier. The returning Jews began their project in the second year after their return from exile (Ezra 3:8–13), although the altar had been restored almost immediately so that sacrifices and offerings could be made (Ezra 3:1–4). But owing to intimidation and legal roadblocks (Ezra 4), the temple project stalled until the new emperor, Darius, reissued Cyrus's original decree in 520 B.C., permitting the completion of the temple of the LORD (Ezra 6:1–15).

Zechariah is introduced as son of Berechiah, son of Iddo (Zech. 1:1). It may be that Iddo, his grandfather, was the priest Iddo named on the list of the priests and Levites who came with Zerubbabel to Jerusalem after 539 B.C. (Neh. 12:4).[7] If indeed he is related to Iddo the priest, then Zechariah too was a priest, which may explain his focus on the rebuilding of the temple and

---

6 *ISBE* 4:508.
7 Ralph L. Smith, *Micah–Malachi*, World Biblical Commentary (Waco, TX: Word, 1984), 183.

restoration of Jerusalem. Then too, his vision in chapter 3 deals with Joshua the high priest and his ceremonially unclean garments, which were a genuine concern for a priest serving in the sanctuary. His name means "the LORD has remembered,"[8] which may reflect his parents' recognition of God's remembering his people suffering in exile and possibly bringing them back to their land.

It is unknown whether Zechariah was born in Jerusalem after the return from Babylon around 539 B.C (or just after), or whether he was born in Babylon and returned with his parents as a child. Since introduction of the book is dated to the eighth month of the second year of Darius (520 B.C.), Zechariah could have been seventeen or eighteen when he began prophesying, or had he been born in Babylon, then would probably been in his twenties or older in 520 B.C. The last dated vision in the book (7:1) is the fourth year of Darius I, or 518 B.C. How much beyond this date his work lasted is uncertain. Beyond his possible priestly roots, and the obvious Jerusalem setting for this prophet, nothing else is recorded about Zechariah in the Bible.

The Book of Zechariah

Among critical OT scholars it is widely thought that the second part of the book (chapters 9–14) came from a different author or authors who were writing well after the life span of Zechariah.[9] It is observed that it contains very different prophetic material than in chapters 1–8 and speaks of events well after the prophet's life in the Maccabean period (second century B.C.) that require these passages be written after the fact, just as is the case with that second half of the book of Daniel (see chap. 6). Moreover, the absence of any reference to Zechariah or any of his contemporaries, and the use of dating formulae to introduce the prophetic messages, has led many commentators to conclude that these chapters do not originate with Zechariah. The same considerations have been used to distinguish Isaiah 1–39 from 40–66. In the case of Isaiah, it was argued that the book is arranged as a bifid, or two-volume work, and that thematic blocks were arranged in the same sequence in Isaiah volume 1 with volume 2, thus mirroring each other (see chap. 4).

R. K. Harrison argued that, like Isaiah, Zechariah should be considered a bifid (1–8; 9–14), and that there are words and expressions used in both

8 *HALOT* 271–72.
9 For a discussion of the history of questioning the authorship of these chapters, see Smith, *Micah–Malachi*, 242–49; *ABD* 6:1061–68.

sections suggesting a literary unity of the book as a whole.[10] Some of these are: the use of the number two (Zech. 4:3; 5:9; 11:7; 13:8), which is not typical symbolic word like three, seven, or twelve in the Bible; the vocative form of address (Zech. 2:7, 1; 3:2, 8; 4:7, 9:9, 13; 11:1–2; 13:7); the phrase "go to and fro"[11] occurs only twice in the whole OT, and they are both in Zechariah (7:14; 9:8); and lastly the use of the verb "to dwell" or "inhabit" (*yāšaḇ*) in the Qal or simple form used passively is found rarely outside Zechariah (2:8; 7:7; 12:6; 14:10). Seeing these unique, unusual, or even common features evenly distributed in both sections of the book need to be considered when evaluating the relationship between the two sections of Zechariah.

Bullock cogently expresses the problem, writing that "the authenticity of Zechariah 9–14 is one of the most formidable issues of prophetic studies," but suggests that chapters 1–8 come from early in his career when the Persian empire was at its zenith. He suggests that Zechariah "was likely still alive when the fortunes of the Persian Empire began to shift in favor of the Greeks" after the military setbacks at the Battle of Marathon (490 B.C.) and Salamis (480 B.C.) in Greece.[12] One could argue that the literary and structural observations of Harrison and the chronological differences in the two sections of Zechariah suggested by Bullock complement each other and offer a credible explanation for how the book meshes differing types of apocalyptic materials from decades apart from the same prophet to create a literarily unified book.

Visions in the Night: Zechariah 1–8

The opening paragraph contains an invitation to the people of Jerusalem: "This is what the LORD Almighty says: 'Return to me' declares the LORD Almighty, 'and I will return to you'" (Zech. 1:3). "These opening lines of Zechariah highlight a doctrinal theme that will be important throughout the book: repentance."[13] "Return" (*šûḇ*) conveys the idea of turning away from sin and evil and turning back to God. Zechariah urges the people not to be like their ancestors who had ignored the prophets in bygone days (Zech. 1:4). Following this opening are eight visions, the first of which dates to the twenty-fourth day of the eleventh month, two months after Haggai's final message.

---

10 Harrison, *Introduction to the Old Testament*, 953–56.
11 This is a more literal reading (so RSV, ESV), whereas NIV offers "marauding."
12 Bullock, *Old Testament Prophetic Books*, 381.
13 Richard Phillips, *Zechariah*, Reformed Expository Commentary (Phillipsburg, NJ: P&R, 2007), 10.

Fig. 7.6 – Myrtle bushes growing in Israel
Photo by Todd Bolen/Bibleplaces.com

Fig. 7.7 – Assyrian horsemen riding through a forested terrain
Photo by A. D. Riddle/Bibleplaces.com

These visions are classified as apocalyptic (see discussion in Chapter 6). This style of prophetic literature is known for its highly symbolic images involving exotic animals, the use of different colors, and the tendency to point to the distant future and the culmination of human history. The New Testament book of Revelation is regarded as the culmination of this type of literature. In fact, many of the images found in Old Testament books of Ezekiel, Zechariah, and Joel occur in the book of Revelation.

In the first vision, which Zechariah saw at night (in his sleep?), showed "a man mounted on a red horse. He was standing among the myrtle trees in a ravine. Behind him were red, brown and white horses" (Zech. 1:8). The "ravine" is understood as a "wadi" in Arabic, a streambed through which water flows in the rainy season, although a streambed could feed a wadi by a perennial spring. In either case, vegetation grows around such streams, including myrtle trees, an aromatic bush in the evergreen family that could stand as high as 6 to 8 feet (2–2.5 m). Myrtle can symbolize peace and divine blessing.[14]

These four horses are the inspiration for so-called "four horsemen of the apocalypse" of the book of Revelation (6:4). What exactly the colors signify is not explained, but the purpose of the horsemen is stated. An angel says, "They are the ones the Lord has sent to go throughout the earth" (Zech. 1:10), and bring back an intelligence report that "the whole world [is] at rest and in peace" (Zech. 1:11). The angel who served as the prophet's interpreter cries out to God: "Lord Almighty, how long will you withhold mercy from Jerusalem and from the towns of Judah, which you have been angry with these seventy years?" (Zech. 1:12). Sixty-six years had elapsed since the temple was destroyed; the pressing issue was, when will the temple be built? God's response is that he was "very jealous for Jerusalem and Zion" (Zech. 1:14). "I will return to Jerusalem with mercy, and there my house will be rebuilt" (Zech. 1:16). The theme of God's passion for Jerusalem and

14 *ABD* 2:807.

his plan to see it rebuilt, including the temple, sets the stage for some of the other visions to follow.

The eighth vision is closely connected to the first, in which Zechariah witnesses four men on horseback among the myrtle trees. In this case there are four chariots with different colored horses—red, black, white, and dappled—pulling the vehicles emerging from between two bronze mountains (Zech. 6:1–8). These also patrol the earth, with the focus on the north, symbolically representing the area from which enemies traditionally advanced on Israel (cf. Jer. 1:13–14; 4:6, 6:1). Just as the four horsemen patrolled "the earth and found the whole world at rest and peace" (Zech. 1:11), the chariots explore the earth, but the focus is on those that traveled north. They brought rest to this troubled region. Here too, the point seems to be that God has removed all obstacles for the people to rebuild their land and temple according to God's purposes.

Fig. 7.8 – Hittite chariots depicted at Ramesseum, Luxor *Photo by James K. Hoffmeier*

In the third vision, the prophet sees a man, possibly the rider of the red horse with "a measuring line in his hand" (Zech. 2:1).[15] The measuring line, of course, is to survey and lay out the architectural plans for the construction projects.[16] In Egypt stretching a cord was part of a foundation ceremony for building

Fig. 7.9 – Men stretching out a cord to measure a field in Egypt in the tomb of Menna *Photo by Katy Doyle for the Tomb of Menna Project [TT69]*

15 Shepherd, *Book of the Twelve*, 403.

16 Kenneth Barker, *Zechariah*, Expositor's Bible Commentary, vol. 7, ed. F. Gaebelein (Grand Rapids: Zondervan, 1985), 616.

Fig. 7.10 – Pharaoh Ramesses III wearing an ornate kingly crown and priestly garb while burning incense to the god Osiris, from tomb of that Pharaoh *Photo by James K. Hoffmeier*

or rebuilding a temple.[17] In the fifth vision, Zerubbabel is depicted laying the foundation of the temple (Zech. 4:9), and has a plumbline in his hand (Zech. 4:10; see Fig. 3.18–19). Such images are all associated with temple building rite over which a king typically presides.

After the visions, the prophet reports, "The word of the LORD came to me" (Zech. 6:9). Zechariah is to meet a group of recent returnees from Babylon who had brought silver and gold with them, possibly as offerings to assist in the building of the temple. What follows is a dramatic act in which Zechariah was to make a crown from the silver and gold and place it on the head of Joshua the high priest (Zech. 6:11), with the following proclamation from God: "Here is the man whose name is the Branch, and he will branch out from his place and build the temple of the LORD" (Zech. 6:12). This comes as a bit of an astonishment, since crowns are associated with kingship, and not the priesthood. Walter Kaiser explains, "The most surprising news here is that the high priest is given the dual role of priest and king!"[18] This portrayal is further complicated by the fact that the governor Zerubbabel has already been named as the political leader who will build the temple (Zech. 4:8–10). Furthermore, Jeremiah had previously used the same word for "branch" (*ṣemaḥ*) as pointing to the future messianic king from the line of David who would rule after the exile (Jer. 33:14–16).[19] In fact there was likely the expectation that Zerubbabel, the grandson of king Jehoiachin, and the governor responsible for the rebuilding of the temple, would be crowned king. It is evident, however, from the Bible and Persian records that he was never made king. It may be that the symbolic coronation of Joshua the priest was to signal that Zerubbabel, despite his accomplishments and pedigree, was not "the Branch" messianic king. Indeed this symbolic coronation my indicate that the Branch, the future Messianic ruler, would bring together kingly and priestly roles.

---

17 Ash Melika, "The Founding of the Temple in Ancient Egypt: Ritual and Symbolism," in *"An Excellent Fortress for His Armies, a Refuge for the People": Egyptological, Archaeological, and Biblical Studies in Honor of James K. Hoffmeier*, eds. R. E. Averbeck and K. L. Younger (University Park: Eisenbrauns/Pennsylvania State University Press, 2020), 209–10.

18 Kaiser, *Micah–Malachi*, 345.

19 Baldwin, *Haggai, Zechariah, Malachi*, 135

This fusing of priestly and kingly lines seems to be illustrated in the genealogies of Jesus as reflected in his human parentage. Joseph's line as presented in Matthew (1:1–17) is designed to emphasize the Davidic connection. Indeed David's name occurs four times in the genealogical section, and the number fourteen, which occurs three times in Matthew 1:17, which is a cryptic number for David. The Hebrew numeric value of the letters in David's name totals 14: D > 4, W > 6, D > 4 = 14. Mary clearly is related to the priestly family of Elizabeth, wife of Zechariah the priest, and mother of John the Baptist. She is identified as "a descendent of Aaron" (i.e., of the daughters of Aaron; Luke 1:5), and Mary is her relative (Luke 1:36), suggesting that she too was of priestly heritage.[20]

The Word and Visions of the Lord: Zechariah 9–14

These debated critical questions aside, it is certain that these chapters focus on Jerusalem's future and God's protection of it. Some major themes in the latter half of Zechariah are consistent with those found in chapters 1–8. Some of the prophecies in chapters 9–15 point to events from the life of Jesus Christ as recognized by the NT writers and the eschatological reign of God on earth.

Some examples of the latter refer to Jerusalem's coming king:

> Rejoice greatly, Daughter Zion! Shout, Daughter Jerusalem!
> See, your king comes to you, righteous and victorious,
> lowly and riding on a donkey, on a colt, the foal of a donkey.
> (Zech. 9:9)

Donkeys were often ridden in OT times to signify leadership, authority, and status (Judg. 10:4; 12:13–15; 2 Sam. 16:1–2, 19:24–26), whereas horses mostly pulled chariots and were used in warfare.[21] Despite the rather humble appearance of this king, and seemingly being not armed for war, because "the Lord will appear" with his weapons (Zech. 9:14) and will disarm his foes of their chariots, war horses and battle bows to protect Jerusalem so that "his rule will extend from sea to sea, and from the River to the ends of the earth" (Zech. 9:10). The militaristic language here is reminiscent of holy war and God as the Divine Warrior.[22]

---

20 *ISBE* 2:73.
21 Kaiser, *Micah–Malachi*, 372.
22 Smith, *Micah–Malachi*, 259; cf. Exod. 15:1–6.

Fig. 7.11 – Arab shepherd with his staff in hand leads his flock
Photo by Craig Dunning/ Bibleplaces.com

The Gospel of John (12:15) quotes Zechariah 9:9, as does Matthew 21:5, when Jesus rides into Jerusalem on Palm Sunday, and the people called out, "Hosanna [save us!] to the Son of David!" (Matt. 21:9), in keeping with the call for the people of Jerusalem to "rejoice greatly" and "shout" (Zech. 9:9).

A future king is also likened to a shepherd who cares for his flock (Israel), who proclaims, "In one month I got rid of the three shepherds" (Zech. 11:8). This statement has been called "probably the most enigmatic in the whole Old Testament."[23] The term shepherd applies to kings, most significantly David himself (Mic. 5:2–4), but to other Judean monarchs as well (Jer. 2:8; 10:21). Ezekiel expands on the shepherd king of Israel.

The identity of the three shepherds in Zechariah 11 is not disclosed.[24] One view is that this represents the three final Judean kings Jehoiakim, Jehoiachin, and Zedekiah whose reigns were all relatively short (i.e., "one month"), and God cut them off.[25] Alternatively the shepherds could be three preceding kingdoms that had crushed Israel (Persia, Babylon, and Assyria), or foreign enemy kings in the period after Zechariah, like Antiochus IV (Epiphanes) who reigned from Antioch in Syria between 175–163 B.C. and oppressed the Jews.[26] Despite his successes, the good shepherd was subsequently rejected by his people (Zech. 11:4–13). He was paid thirty pieces of silver as payment, but then the text reports, "So I took the thirty pieces of silver and threw them into the house of the Lord" (11:13 ESV).

Who is this good shepherd king? Once again no interpretation is offered. The incident of throwing the thirty pieces of silver the temple, whatever it meant in in Zechariah's day, the New Testament writers saw a connection with Jesus's betrayal for the thirty pieces of silver, and then how Judas the betrayer threw the silver into the temple (Matt. 26:14–15; 27:3–10).

Another puzzling passage refers to Jerusalem mourning over the death of the unidentified speaker, who reports: "They will look on me, the one they have pierced, and they will mourn for him as one mourns for an only child" (Zech.

---

23 Joyce Baldwin, *Haggai, Zechariah, Malachi* (Downers Grove, IL: InterVarsity Press, 1972), 181.
24 For a helpful review of the range of interpretations of this passage, see Smith, *Micah–Malachi*, 270–72.
25 Kaiser, *Micah–Malachi*, 393.
26 Smith, *Micah–Malachi*, 270.

12:10). Once again the interpretation of this murder and the identity of the victim are not offered. Some more immediate application like the assassination of the Jerusalem priest Onias III (170 B.C.) or Simon the Maccabee (134 B.C.) is often suggested. The New Testament saw this passage as ultimately referring to the crucified Jesus (John 19:37).

The protection of Jerusalem and the defeat of her enemies are important themes in the second half of Zechariah. The rise of Greek domination of the Mediterranean world with Alexander the Great's conquests and the subsequent Hellenistic periods meant Judah was frequently caught in middle of battles between the Ptolemaic kings of Egypt and the Seleucid kings of Syria. The period from the fourth century onward was perilous indeed. Promises of protection were no doubt welcomed.

Zechariah 12:8–9 reads: "On that day the LORD will shield those who live in Jerusalem. . . . On that day I will set out to destroy all the nations that attack Jerusalem." These dual themes reach a climax in chapter 14, in which "the day of the LORD" is in view, when God goes to war against Israel's enemies.[27] With nations gathered against Jerusalem experiencing a certain loss and exile (Zech. 14:2) and hope all but gone, the LORD comes as a warrior and rescues Jerusalem:

> Then the LORD will go out and fight against those nations, as he fights in the day of battle. On that day his feet will stand on the Mount of Olives, east of Jerusalem, and the Mount of Olives will be split in two from east to west, forming a great valley, with half of the mountain moving north and half moving south. You will flee by my mountain valley. . . . You will flee as you fled from the earthquake in the days of Uzziah king of Judah. Then the LORD my God will come, and all the holy ones with him. (Zech. 14:3–5)

This dramatic battle scene is thought by many to move beyond the immediate crises to the culminating battle of history, what the New Testament calls Armageddon (Rev. 16:16). The divine warrior motif is pervasive in the Bible. After God intervened in the exodus and defeated Pharaoh and his armies at the Sea, Moses sang, "The LORD is a warrior, the LORD is his name. Pharaoh's chariots and his army he has hurled into the sea. . . . Your right hand, LORD, was majestic in power. Your right hand, LORD, shattered the enemy" (Exod. 15:3–4, 6).

---

27 See discussion of "the day of the LORD" in chap. 2 (Amos) and chap. 5 (Zephaniah).

Fig. 7.12 – Ashurbanipal king of Assyria shown as a mighty warrior, in British Museum relief
Photo by James K. Hoffmeier

The LORD's descent onto the Mount of Olives will be a dramatic and earth-shaking phenomenon (Zech. 14:4). Similarly, in the Mt. Sinai theophany when YHWH descended, "the whole mountain trembled violently" (Exod. 19:18). In this eschatological vision, the quaking in Jerusalem is likened to the earthquake that shook Jerusalem in king Uzziah's day 250 years earlier and mentioned in Amos 1:1.[28]

God intervenes spectacularly; Jerusalem is saved. The survivors of the enemy nations who attacked Jerusalem are converted and come to "worship the King, the LORD Almighty" in Jerusalem (Zech. 14:16). The idea of the world at peace and worshiping God in Jerusalem is a repeated end-time motif (Mic. 4:1–5; Isa. 2:2–4).

EXCURSUS: "THE LORD OF HOSTS"

The title of God, "the LORD of Hosts," rendered in some more modern translations as "The LORD Almighty" (NIV) is a recurring expression found around three hundred times in the Old Testament, 247 of which occur in the prophetic books, Isaiah to Malachi. Ninety-one of these occurrences (37 percent) appear in the books Haggai (fourteen times), Zechariah (fifty-three times), and Malachi (twenty-four times). This concentration of uses in a limited period of time after the exile in a relatively small segment of the prophets is obviously significant.

The LORD of Hosts, combines the divine name Yahweh with the Hebrew term *ṣᵉḇā'ôt*, may be recognized from Martin Luther's famous hymn, "A Mighty Fortress Is Our God," which includes the verse, "Lord Sabaoth his name, from age to age the same, and He must win the battle." This divine title first occurs in connection with the birth narrative of the prophet Samuel (1 Sam. 1:3, 11; 4:4). Military associations with this word are obvious. In the exodus narratives, the armies of pharaoh are called "hosts" (*ṣᵉḇā'ôt*) (Exod. 14:4, 17, 19, 20, 24, 28). It is also applied to the Israelites

28 For a discussion of this earthquake, see chap. 3, "The Times of Amos" section.

themselves as they marched out as a force from Egypt and through Sinai (Exod. 6:26; 7:4; 12:17, 41, 51; Num. 10:28; 33:1).

When David duels with the giant, he calls out to Goliath, "You come to me with a sword and with a spear and with a javelin, but I come to you in the name of the LORD of hosts, the God of the armies of Israel, whom you have defied" (1 Sam. 17:45 ESV). In addition to "hosts" having military connotations, it also extends to the angelic armies (Ps. 148:2; Luke 2:13) and to the stars of heaven (Gen. 2:1; Deut. 4:19; Dan. 8:10).

Fig. 7.13 – A host or division of the Hittite army on the walls of the Ramesseum
Photo by James K. Hoffmeier

When King David brings the ark of the covenant to Jerusalem, this expression is connected to the ark: "the ark of God, which is called by the name of the LORD of hosts who sits enthroned on the cherubim" (2 Sam. 6:2 ESV). These two citations suggest that "the LORD of hosts" might be the full name of the God of Israel that has both military and liturgical associations.

In his temple vision, Isaiah the prophet is overwhelmed by what he saw. The angelic cherubim cry out, "Holy, holy, holy is the LORD of hosts; the whole earth is full of his glory!" and then Isaiah responds: 'Woe is me! For I am lost; for I am a man of unclean lips, and I dwell in the midst of a people of unclean lips; for my eyes have seen the King, the LORD of hosts!' (Isa. 6:3, 5 ESV).

With the temple in disrepair and the Judean exiles without a professional army, they felt alone and were especially vulnerable. It may be, then, that the expression "the LORD of Hosts" took on special significance at this time that brought together military and temple themes at this time. The returned exiles needed divine protection, while anticipating God's presence in the temple once again.

Fig. 7.14 – Greek soldier on tombstone from Athens, ca. 400 B.C.
Photo by Todd Bolen/Bibleplaces.com

JOEL: THE POURING OUT OF GOD'S SPIRIT

"I will pour out my Spirit on all people."
—Joel 2:28

The Prophet Joel and His Book

Joel son of Pethuel is generally thought to be among the post-exilic prophets of Jerusalem, but there is no clear historical datum in the book. "Joel" is an abbreviated form of the name meaning "the LORD is God."[29] The placement of Joel as the second book in the sequence of the twelve between Hosea and Amos might incline one to think the book dates to the eighth century B.C. There is nothing, however, within the book to suggest this early date. Rather, the prophet speaks of the restoring the fortunes of Judah and Jerusalem after being scattered among the nations (Joel 3:1–3). "Zion" or "Mount Zion" is used repeatedly by this prophet, a metaphorical way of referring to Jerusalem (Joel 2:1, 15, 23; 2:32), and particularly as the LORD's residence (Joel 3:17, 21). Not surprisingly, the temple, the altar and priestly activities are emphasized (Joel 1:9–16). No hints are found of the dual kingdoms or of Samaria the northern capital that would have been the case during the eighth century B.C. These factors suggest that Joel was active in the post-exilic period, after the completion of the temple in 515 B.C.[30] How much later than this date is not known. Mention of the people of Judah and Jerusalem being sold to the Greeks (i.e., Ionians: Joel 3:6) need not mean that Alexander the Great had already taken control of the region as some think. Greeks mercenaries were known to be active in Egypt and surrounding areas in the seventh century B.C. onward, and Greek merchant marines were engaged in trade through the Mediterranean world. Pharaoh Psamtik I/Psammeticus I (664–610 B.C.) employed Ionian (Greek) and Carian (southwest Anatolian) mercenaries to his formidable army.[31]

---

29 *ISBE* 2:1076.
30 Wolff, *Joel and Amos*, 5–6.

Joel's focus on temple activities, declaring fasts and religious assemblies (Joel 2:12–17), may indicate that this prophet was in fact a priest. His father's name, Pethuel—meaning "youth belonging to God"[31]—may point to his service to God from his youth like Samuel. This personal name does not occur again in the Bible. Since priestly status was based on an ancestry linked to Aaron, brother of Moses (e.g., Ezra 7:1–5), it was passed on father to son. If Pethuel was a priest, his sons, too, would be priests. Beyond the possibility that Joel was a priest, nothing more can be said personally about him. It is likely he lived in Jerusalem or a nearby village.

The location of the book of Joel, surrounded by Hosea and Amos, both eighth-century prophets, might lead readers to think that Joel falls into the same general time period. But as noted already, the internal evidence suggests a post-exilic date for the book. A factor in the organization of the Book of the Twelve, however, was thematic considerations, as Shepherd has observed with regard to Joel's location: "with the composition of the Twelve, the function of the book of Joel is to introduce the Day of the LORD theme,"[33] which is treated also by Amos (5:18–20), and both books deal with locust plagues as a mode of destructive judgment (cf. Joel 1:4; 2:25; Amos 7:1–2).

THE DAY OF THE LORD: THE LOCUST PLAGUE

The opening scene of the book portrays a devastating locust plague in vivid detail that devours the land (Joel 1:2–12).

What the locust swarm has left
    the great locusts have eaten;
what the great locusts have left
    the young locusts have eaten;
what the young locusts have left
    other locusts have eaten. (Joel 1:4)

---

31 Olivier Perdu, "Saites and Persians (664–332)," in *A Companion to Ancient Egypt*, ed. Alan Lloyd (Oxford: Wiley-Blackwell, 2010), 143.
32 *ABD* 5:288.
33 Shepherd, *Book of the Twelve*, 115–16.

Fig. 7.15 – A locust horde *Public domain*

Fig. 7.16 – Harvesting wheat in Israel
Photo by Todd Bolen/Bibleplaces.com

This locust swarm is likened to an invading army with myriads of forces (Joel 1:6). Locusts are known to devour vegetation of every sort. In Joel's words, "It has laid waste my vines and ruined my fig trees. It has stripped off their bark and thrown it away, leaving their branches white" (Joel 1:7); "The fields are ruined, the ground is dried up, the grain is destroyed, the new wine is dried up, the olive oil fails" (Joel 1:10); "the harvest of the field is destroyed" (Joel 1:11); "The vine is dried up and the fig tree is withered; the pomegranate, the palm and the apple tree—all the trees of the field—are dried up. Surely the people's joy is withered away" (Joel 1:12). Grain, olive oil, and wine were essential products, the staples of life in ancient Israel.

Locust plagues were a real source of alarm for people from the agriculturally based economies of the Middle East and Africa in ancient as well as present times. A headline from February 2020 reads: "Africa Locust Invasion Spreading, May Become 'Most Devastating Plague' in Living Memory, UN Warns."[34] This particular swarm is working its way through parts of Kenya, Somalia, and Ethiopia. The report continues: "A single swarm can contain up to 150 million locusts per square kilometer of farmland, an area the size of almost 250 football fields." Such an injurious force had attacked Judea in Joel's day.

One of the results of the vegetation being consumed was that the "grain offerings and drink offerings are cut off from the house of the Lord" (Joel 1:9), a point repeated later in the chapter (Joel

34 Stephen Sorace, "Africa Locust Invasion Spreading, May Become 'Most Devastating Plague' in Living Memory, UN Warns," FOX News, February 11, 2020, https://www.foxnews.com/world/africa-locust-invasion-spreading-united-nations.

1:13). The priests mourn over this crisis (Joel 1:9, 13) for "joy and gladness" have been cut off the temple. Joel's concern regarding the impact of the locust plague on temple activities further suggests that he was a priest. Not only were people deprived of food to eat, but they were also prevented from bringing temple offerings; consequently, the priests and Levites did not get their share, thus denying them sustenance.[35] These dramatic events turn the prophet's thinking from the present trauma or the day of the Lord, to the eschatological, universal "day of the LORD." It "is near; it will come like destruction from the Almighty" (1:15).

The Day of the Lord

The present catastrophe leads to a vision about the day of the LORD at the culmination of history. Joel does so by employing highly symbolic apocalyptic imagery. The devastating grasshoppers or locusts are transformed from insects to warhorses and a terrifying army appears.

> They have the appearance of horses;
> they gallop along like cavalry.
> With a noise like that of chariots
> they leap over the mountaintops,
> like a crackling fire consuming stubble,
> like a mighty army drawn up for battle. (Joel 2:4–5)

These invaders were led by God himself and they wreak havoc on the earth:

> Before them the earth shakes, the heavens tremble,
> the sun and moon are darkened, and the stars no longer shine.
> The LORD thunders at the head of his army;
> his forces are beyond number, and mighty is the army that
> obeys his command.
> The day of the LORD is great; it is dreadful.
> Who can endure it? (Joel 2:10–11)

35 Stuart, *Hosea–Jonah*, 243.

That these passages are eschatological portrayals, as demonstrated by their inclusion in Revelation 9:2–3 and 7–9:

> When he opened the Abyss, smoke rose from it like the smoke from a gigantic furnace. The sun and sky were darkened by the smoke from the Abyss. And out of the smoke locusts came down upon the earth and were given power like that of scorpions of the earth. . . . The locusts looked like horses prepared for battle. On their heads they wore something like crowns of gold, and their faces resembled human faces. Their hair was like women's hair, and their teeth were like lions' teeth. They had breastplates like breastplates of iron, and the sound of their wings was like the thundering of many horses and chariots rushing into battle.

Joel does not linger on the distant and universal day of the LORD, but returns to the present and issues God's invitation to "return to me with all your heart, with fasting and weeping and mourning" (Joel 2:12). God demands more than a token acknowledgment, and rather than traditional gestures of penance like tearing one's clothes, Joel promotes a heartfelt repentance, returning to God, "for he is gracious and compassionate, slow to anger and abounding in love, and he relents from sending calamity" (Joel 2:13). This confession, while following the word order of Jonah 4:2,[36] echoes those used in the wilderness episode after the golden calf apostacy when God explains his character, namely that he forgives wickedness, "Yet he does not leave the guilty unpunished" (Exod. 34:7). So too in Joel's day, God has punished the people and their land by the locust plague, but due to his gracious and compassionate nature, the LORD would restore both people and land if there was genuine contrition. In this public penitence, the priests lead the way by gathering the people who weep by the altar in the temple and call on the LORD (Joel 2:15–17).

God responded and took pity on the people and the land (Joel 2:18) and replies, "I am sending you grain, new wine and oil, enough to satisfy you fully" (Joel 2:19). "The threshing floors will be filled with grain; the vats will overflow with wine and oil" (Joel 2:24).

---

36 Wolff, *Joel and Amos*, 49.

I Will Pour Out My Spirit

With this crisis abated and the healing of the land anticipated, Joel turns to what will happen "afterward" (2:28). Although this time marker is somewhat ambiguous, it likely points to a period after "true restoration of covenant relationship has been achieved and the people have fully turned back to Yahweh."[37]

> And afterward, I will pour out my Spirit on all people.
> Your sons and daughters will prophesy,
> your old men will dream dreams,
> your young men will see visions.
> Even on my servants, both men and women,
> I will pour out my Spirit in those days. (Joel 2:28–29)

Twice in this short passage, reference is made to pouring out of God's Spirit on all humans, regardless of age, social status, or gender—that is, "all believers"[38]—and they will prophesy in the Spirit. The twofold reference to "I will pour out my Spirit" in this passage is to express certainty regarding its fulfillment. Prophecy will no longer be the domain of a professional class of seers. No further hint is offer as to how far into the future this phenomenon would occur, but it seems to be centered in Jerusalem (Joel 2:32).

Joel's prophecy regarding the outpouring of God's Spirit is identified with the events of Pentecost in the New Testament. After the resurrection of Jesus Christ and just before his ascension to heaven as reported in the book of Acts, he told his followers that "you will receive power when the Holy Spirit comes on you" (Acts. 1:8). About ten days later at the feast of harvest or Pentecost (based the Greek name for "fifty"), that is fifty days after the Sabbath of Passover, the early Christians were meeting together, when "suddenly a sound like the blowing of a violent wind came from heaven and filled the whole house where they were sitting" (Acts 2:2). These people began speaking "in other tongues as the Spirit enabled them" (2:4). They moved outdoors, where the public was startled by this inexplicable event. The apostle Peter offered an explanation to the gathering crowd concerning what was happening: "this is what was spoken by the prophet Joel" (Acts 2:16), followed by fully quoting Joel's prophecy about the outpouring of the Spirit (Acts 2:17–21 = Joel 2:28–32).

---

37 Stuart, *Hosea–Jonah*, 260.

38 Richard Patterson, *Joel*, Expositor's Bible Commentary, vol. 7, ed. F. Gaebelein (Grand Rapids: Zondervan, 1985), 255.

Fig. 7.17 – The Persian Empire extended south past the province of Judah to include Egypt. Stela with the name King Darius in the cartouche on this Egyptian stela, in the Berlin Museum.
Photo by James K. Hoffmeier

From the New Testament's perspective, then, Joel's prophecy about the outpouring of the Spirit was fulfilled at the outset of the Christian era. It would be one of the acts in God's redemptive plan that would begin moving history toward that ultimate day of the LORD.

MALACHI: "I WILL SEND MY MESSENGER"

"See, I will send my messenger, who will prepare the way before me. Then suddenly the Lord you are seeking will come to his temple."

—Malachi 3:1

Malachi and His Book

The last prophet in the Book of the Twelve and the last prophetic voice in the Old Testament is Malachi, whose name means "my messenger" (Mal. 3:1). The book is identified as "an oracle," *maśśā'* (just like Nah. 1:1 and Hab. 1:1: "of the word of the LORD"; Mal. 1:1). It is made up of six disputations where a charge or complaint is leveled, followed by the response of the accused. Thus a dialogical style is followed. The disputations of Malachi are identified as follows:

1. A dispute about God's love (1:2–5)
2. A dispute about God's honor and fear (1:6–2:9)
3. A dispute about faithlessness (2:10–16)
4. A dispute about God's justice (2:17–3:5)
5. A dispute about repentance (3:6–12)
6. A dispute about speaking against God (3:13–4:3)[39]

By virtue of the important location of this book, its message is significant, for a long period of prophetic silence settles in for the Jewish community. The book offers little information about the setting of the prophet's messages and

39 Smith, *Micah–Malachi*, 299.

nothing about Malachi himself. Neither his home nor his parentage is provided. From references to priests, the altar and the LORD's table where offerings were presented, and the doors of the temple area (Mal. 1:6–10), it is evident that the Jerusalem temple was fully functioning. A date for the prophecy must be after 515 B.C., when the temple was completed (Ezra 6:15). The fact that the Jewish community seems discouraged and disillusioned by their plight suggests that some decades had passed since the initial burst of enthusiasm when the temple was completed. Some of the social problems addressed by Malachi in chapter 2, such as marital infidelity, intermarriage with pagans, and priests failing in their duties are also decried by Ezra the priest (Ezra 8–9) when he came to Jerusalem in 457 B.C. Linguistic similarities with Haggai and Zechariah 1–8 suggest a date around 500 B.C. for the book of Malachi.[40] These issues and timing point to a period from 500 to 445 B.C. for the origin of Malachi's messages.[41]

It is thought that enough time had elapsed since the temple was rebuilt that two to three generations had passed, and that religious malaise had set in. God's people felt unloved as some of the promises associated with their restoration remained unfulfilled, and, as a consequence, the LORD was not receiving his due respect. This development is evident in the first and second disputations between God and a representative of the people. The people dispute God's claim "'I have loved you.' . . . But you ask, 'How have you loved us?'" (Mal. 1:2). God's response is startling, and at first read appears theologically inconsistent with God's loving character (John 3:16). To encourage the Jews, descendants of Jacob (Israel), he affirmed, "I have loved Jacob, but Esau I have hated" (Mal. 1:2–3). The thought that God "hates" an ethnic group, even fellow offspring of the patriarch Isaac (Gen. 25:19–34) and grandsons of Abraham, is troubling. The word "hate" (*śānē'*), like the Hebrew word "love" (*'āhab̲*), is not limited to emotional and relational affections, rather "its standard use in legal texts indicates formal renunciation or severance of a relationship, as divorce."[42] In 1 Kings 5:1 we are told that King Hiram of Tyre "loved David" (ESV), that is, "had always been on friendly terms with David" (NIV).

Śānē', which has the opposite meaning, also applies in diplomatic or treaty contexts.[43] An example of this occurs between Isaac and the king of Gerar, who

---

40 Andrew Hill, *Malachi: A New Translation with Introduction and Commentary* (New York: Anchor Bible/Doubleday, 1998), 83.
41 Baldwin, *Haggai, Zechariah, Malachi*, 213.
42 Andersen and Freedman, *Amos*, 525.
43 Hill, *Malachi*, 152.

Fig. 7.18 – Stamp seal impression with the name "Yehud" (Judah) written in Hebrew, from the 5th century *Photo by Todd Bolen/Bibleplaces.com*

at first expelled Isaac from his territory, but later sought to make a treaty (*bᵉrîṯ*) with him (Gen. 26:16–28). Isaac was incredulous, asking, "Why have you come to me, since you were hostile (*śānēʾ*) to me and sent me away?" (26:27).[44] Clearly *śānēʾ* in Malachi's context means that God rejected Esau/Edom for a covenant relationship, but in establishing a covenant with Israel, he "set his affection on you and [chose] you . . . because the LORD loved (*ʾāhaḇ*) you and kept the oath he swore to your ancestors . . . keeping his covenant of love" (Deut. 7:7–9).

The point of God's word to his people is that because of his covenant faithfulness to Israel, he not only loved them, but reestablished them in the Promised Land, whereas Esau's descendants, the Edomites, during the period of Judah's rebuilding "in some small measure rebuilt their country, though never regaining its former territory or power."[45] A couple centuries later Nabatean Arabs dominated Edom's ancient territory (see discussion of Obadiah in chap. 6).

The second disputation reads: "'A son honors his father, and a slave his master. If I am a father, where is the honor due me? If I am a master, where is the respect due me?' says the LORD Almighty" (Mal. 1:6). Such honor was expected to human parents according to the fifth commandment (Exod. 20:12); surely God as heavenly father deserved no less. The accused seems quite shocked by this charge: "How have we shown contempt for your name?" (Mal. 1:7). God goes on to explain that by presenting inferior and blemished animals for offerings that they were showing contempt for God. In what has been described as "biting irony,"[46] God challenges his people: "Try offering them to your governor!" (Mal. 1:8). The word "governor" (*peḥâ*) was applied to Zerubbabel (Hag. 1:1, 14; 2:2, 21), who was appointed by Cyrus to administer the small province of Yehud or Judah.[47]

Obviously it would be an embarrassment for one to present an inferior or damaged gift even to the local governor. God, however, is no local

---

44 ESV reads "hate."
45 Alden, *Haggai*, 710.
46 Kaiser, *Micah–Malachi*, 449.
47 Hill, *Malachi*, 71–72.

administrator. God rather describes himself as a "great king" who should be respectfully treated (Mal. 1:14), making an inferior gift insulting!

The title "great king" had special significance in the ancient Near East. While the adjective "great" is often applied to rulers like Ramesses the Great or Alexander the Great, known for their outstanding achievements and conquests, this is a modern appraisal. In ancient times, a great king is a monarch who had numerous vassal kings bound to him by treaties. A great king was a king over kings, or a king of kings. Most of the ancient treaties begin by the king introducing himself as, "Thus says My Majesty, Suppiluliuma, Great King, King of Hatti,"[48] as does "Ramesses, Great King, King of Egypt."[49] As a great king, God would prefer to have the temple closed down rather than accept such disrespectful treatment (1:7–10) (see Fig. 1.19 & 1.20).

The loss of reverence and respect between the covenant community and the Lord results in the degeneration the social fabric of society. The prophet details areas where the people are not being faithful to God's covenant demands in the third disputation. There was a general unfaithfulness in dealings with members of the community (Mal. 2:10). Then too some members of the Jewish community were marrying pagans (Mal. 2:11), a practice not permitted in the Sinaitic Law (Exod. 34:15–16), yet nevertheless was widespread at this time, judging from Ezra 9:1–5 and Nehemiah 13:23–27. Such intermarriage was watering down faith in Yahweh. Thirdly the prophet attacks men for being faithless to their spouses (Mal. 2:13–16), for God hates divorce because it destroys families and harms the development of godly offspring (v. 15). Only in Malachi 2:14 and Proverbs 2:17 is marriage specifically identified as a covenant (*bᵉrîṯ*), and that God was the witness to every marriage covenant.

Malachi harshly denounces the priests of Jerusalem. First, they accepted the inferior offerings from worshipers, showing that they too did not appropriately revere God. Second, the priests had failed the people in their duty as teachers of the law: "For the lips of the priest ought to preserve knowledge, because he is the messenger of the Lord Almighty and people seek instruction from his mouth" (Mal. 2:7).

---

48 *COS* 2:93, 96, 98, 100.

49 Gary Beckman, *Hittite Diplomatic Texts*, 2nd ed. (Atlanta: Scholars Press, 1999), 96.

GOD'S FUTURE PLANS

Nowhere are we explicitly told why the people had become indifferent toward God, but the book begins with an assurance that he loves Jacob (i.e., Israel). Consequently, the covenant relationship was intact.

The heart of the problem seems to be that the people of Judah thought that God had not come through for them in fulfilling the prophecies made by prophets like Jeremiah and Ezekiel. Where is the prosperous land? Why is the nation still under the heel of foreigners? Why was there no Davidic king or Messiah? Where is God's kingdom that the LORD himself would rule from Jerusalem?

That the latter point is on their mind is hinted at in chapter 3:1 of Malachi when God announces, "'I will send my messenger, who will prepare the way before me. Then suddenly the Lord you

Fig. 7.19 – The Persian high god Ahuramazda shown within a winged sun-disc in the center. Below this figure is a winged sun disc from Persepolis.
Photo by Todd Bolen/Bibleplaces.com

are seeking will come to his temple; the messenger of the covenant, whom you desire, will come,' says the LORD Almighty."

"The Lord you are seeking" seems to point to the source of their disappointment. They had anticipated God's coming, but that had not happened. God then discloses the sign that would precede God's sudden appearance in the temple, saying, I will send "my messenger" (*mal'āḵi*, which is what Malachi means!). The LORD's coming, called "the day" (Mal. 4:1, 3), is a variation on the "day of the LORD" (used in 4:4). This "day" would be like the blast of a furnace on evildoers who would be consumed like stubble. But those who fear or "revere my name, the sun of righteousness will rise with healing in its rays" (4:2). For the faithful, God's coming will yield a therapeutic warmth, not a scorching furnace. The image of the sun with wings was a well-known icon in the ancient world, spanning form Egypt to Persia, and symbolized divine presence and protection. Rather than equating God with ancient solar deities, this is simply figurative language.[50]

CONCLUSION OF THE OLD TESTAMENT PROPHETIC LITERATURE

The final verses of the book (Mal. 4:4–6) appear to stand apart from the sixth disputation (Mal. 3:13–4:3). Indeed, it is suggested "these verses appear to be the work of the composer of the Twelve who has consistently provided seams that connect the ends of individual books to the beginnings of the books that follow them."[51] This final charge, then, is intended to conclude both the book of Malachi, the book of the Twelve, and perhaps even the entire prophetic corpus. The prophets unanimously point the people back to the Law and the Sinaitic covenant, and, consistent with this emphasis, God declares, "Remember the law of my servant Moses, the decrees and laws I gave him at Horeb for all Israel" (Mal. 4:4). This theme echoes Jeremiah's insistence that God's people chose to walk on well-trodden, ancient paths that come from God's past revelations as the key to moving forward into the future (Jer. 6:16).

50 Hill, *Malachi*, 350.
51 Shepherd, *Book of the Twelve*, 506–7.

But these concluding remarks look forward: "I will send you the prophet Elijah before that great and dreadful day of the LORD comes" (v. 5). This passage is connected to the unnamed messenger in Malachi 3:1, thereby identifying the messenger.[52] He is identified with Elijah.[53] This prophet will restore the broken relationships that chapter 2 described. So the prophet lays out the sequence of coming events, but places no time strictures on when these events will occur. In the meantime, God urges the people to remain faithful by remembering the law of Moses (Mal. 4:4). The anticipation of Elijah's appearance serves as an important segue to the New Testament and the prophetic work of John the Baptist (see chap. 8).

---

52 Kaiser, *Micah–Malachi*, 487.
53 On the life and work of Elijah, see further chap. 1, "Elijah."

DISCUSSION QUESTIONS

- What were some of the issues facing the returned exiles to Jerusalem, and how did Haggai and Zechariah (chaps. 1–6) encourage and prod them along?
- What is the significance of "the Branch" in Zechariah 6:12 in the light of Jeremiah 23:5–6? And why does the priest wear a crown (see Zech. 6:11–13)?
- What is the significance of the divine epithet "The LORD of Hosts"? Why does it occur so frequently among the post-exilic prophets?
- In Malachi God complains that his people had lost fear or reverence for God and did not honor him. What is behind this backsliding, and how did it affect their worship? How is this problem rectified?
- Another consequence of the loss of fear/reverence for God is the lack of justice within the community of faith. Discuss the range of issues it impacts, according to Malachi 3:5.
- What is the relationship between God's messenger in Malachi 3:1 and Elijah in Malachi 4:5? How is this interpreted in the NT?
- What are some lessons we can learn about God's attitude toward marriage in Malachi 2:13–16?
- Malachi 4:5–6 is thought to be a postscript to the book of Malachi that serves as a conclusion to the Book of the Twelve. In that light, what points are emphasized as the heart of this compendium?

8

"In the Fullness of Time"

Prophets and Prophecy in the New Testament

> "The prophets, who spoke of the grace that was to come to you, searched intently and with the greatest care, trying to find out the time and circumstances to which the Spirit of Christ in them was pointing when he predicted the sufferings of Christ and the glories that would follow."
>
> —1 Peter 1:10–11

One might think the prophets flourished only in the Old Testament, and once we turn the page between the book of Malachi and Matthew in the New Testament, prophetism ceased. Jesus taught that the prophets in the traditional sense ended with John (Matt. 11:13–14). As Joel foretold, God would pour out his spirit "on all people" (Joel 2:28), ushering in a new era of prophecy in which God's spirit was not limited to select servants of God, but to all believers. Consequently, we encounter prophets in the New Testament, and the epistles promote prophecy as an ongoing spiritual gift for the church (1 Cor. 12:1–11, 14:3; Eph. 4:11).

JOHN THE BAPTIST

The birth of John the Baptist was revealed to his father, Zechariah the priest, while burning incense in the temple (Luke 1:8–23). The angel, who brought the announcement identified himself as "Gabriel. I stand in the presence of God, and I was sent to speak to you and to bring you this good news" (v. 19). Moreover, he discloses to Zechariah that his son who will be named John would "go before the Lord, in the spirit and power of Elijah, to turn the hearts of the parents to their children, and the disobedient to the wisdom of the righteous—to make ready a people prepared for the Lord" (v. 17). After John's birth, Luke reports that Zechariah "was filled with the Holy Spirit and prophesied" (v. 67), indicating the a prophetic word was a divinely inspired message. In his message, Zechariah announced that his son would be "the prophet of the Most High" (v. 76). Thus

Fig. 8.1 – Mosaic of John the Baptist (right) adoring Jesus in Hagia Sophia, Istanbul
Photo by Mark Fairchild

Fig. 8.2 – Model of priest burning incense in the tabernacle
Photo by Todd Bolen/Bibleplaces.com

Zechariah is presented as a prophet who introduces his newborn son as destined to fulfill a divinely ordained prophetic task (Fig. 8.2).

Mark, thought by many scholars to be the earliest Gospel, begins by reciting Malachi and the final prophetic word in the OT: "See, I will send the prophet Elijah to you before that great and dreadful day of the Lord comes" (Mal. 4:5). Mark 1:2 follows by a citation from Isaiah, "a voice of one calling in the wilderness, 'Prepare the way for the Lord, make straight paths for him'" (1:3). Malachi's prophecy also included that God would send Elijah the prophet before the appearance of God. The Gospel continues by reporting on the preaching of John the Baptist that motivated people to turn from their iniquity and to be baptized "for the forgiveness of sins" (1:4). Luke's Gospel contains the story of John's birth to Zechariah the priest and his wife Elizabeth, a relative of Mary mother of Jesus. The angel Gabriel appeared to Zechariah in a vision in the temple to inform him that he and his aging wife would finally have a son (Luke 1:11–19) "who will go on before the Lord, in the spirit and power of Elijah . . . to make ready a people prepared for the Lord" (v. 17).

John lived in relative obscurity for most of his life in the Judean wilderness before he went public, preaching and baptizing (Luke 1:80). Luke pinpoints the beginning of this activity in the fifteenth year of the reign of Tiberius Caesar (Luke 3:1). Tiberius's reign spanned A.D. 14–37,[1] meaning that John's prophetic work began around A.D. 29 and may have lasted only a matter of months. Some scholars have suggested that John was influenced by the Dead Sea Scrolls community, which included a sect of Judaism known as the Essenes, because of their emphasis on purity and ritual cleansings.[2] This idea lacks any tangible evidence, and some scholars are now rejecting the notion that the Essenes were even associated with the site of Qumran by the Dead Sea

1 *ABD* 6:549.
2 John McRay, *Archaeology and the New Testament* (Grand Rapids: Baker Book House, 1991), 160–61.

where the famous scrolls were discovered in the 1940s and 1950s.

Recently a cave was excavated in Israel about 2.5 miles (4 km) from Ein Kerem, the traditional birth site of John the Baptist. In 2004 and 2005, this discovery received considerable attention in the press. Shimon Gibson, the excavator, identified the cave as originally an Iron Age (eighth through sixth century B.C.) tomb that was reused in Roman and Byzantine times.[3] In this latter period, due to the presence of pottery from this era, along with a cistern and crude etchings on the cave walls, the excavator believes that this cave was associated with John the Baptist. Thus it became a pilgrimage site in the Christian era. One image shows a standing figure with a kilt-like gown with spots on it. Gibson theorizes that the spotted kilt represents an animal skin. John the Baptist, the Gospel writers report, wore a camel hair gown with a leather belt (Matt. 3:4; Mark 1:6), apparently like the unique outfit worn by Elijah himself (2 Kings 1:8). Whether or not John ever lived in this cave, we may never know, but it appears that in the Byzantine period, from the fourth century onward, Christians thought the place was linked to the forerunner of Jesus. Hundreds of fragments of juglets were found, leading to the suggestion that they were used in some sort of ritual baptizing in the early Christian period. The location of this cave is quite distant from other places mentioned in connection with John's life and ministry as reported in the Gospels (see below).

Fig. 8.3 – Judean wilderness between Jerusalem and Jericho *Photo by James K. Hoffmeier*

Fig. 8.4 – The recently excavated "Cave of John the Baptist" *Photo by Todd Bolen/Bibleplaces.com*

John shared other characteristics beyond the garb of Elijah. For example, as Elijah had confronted Ahab about his wife Jezebel, while John rebuked Herod Antipas for marrying his brother's wife Herodias (Matt. 14:1–5; Luke 3:19–20). For this criticism, Herod arrested John and subsequently had him beheaded when Herodias demanded John's head on a platter (Matt. 14:6–12).

Jesus was himself baptized by John in Jordan River (Matt. 3:13–17). One location where John's revivalist preaching was occurring, he was "at Bethany

3 Shimon Gibson, *The Cave of John the Baptist* (New York: Doubleday, 2004).

Fig. 8.5 – Traditional site where John baptized, opposite Jericho in Jordan *Photo by Alexander Schick/bibelausstellung.de*

on the other side of the Jordan" (John 1:28), although he also baptized at "Aenon near Salim" (John 3:23), the precise location of which remains uncertain, with locations on both sides of the Jordan River being candidates. One proposed site for Aenon is in area identified with Tirzah of the Old Testament (i.e., Tell Farah North) located east of the modern town of Nablus.[4] The water source would have been from the Wadi Farah.[5] The other proposed location is south of Scythopolis (Beth Shean) in Samaria. If this geographical understanding is correct, then John had taken his message of repentance and preparing the way of the Lord to the homeland of the despised Samaritans. This may explain why in the following chapter, the Samaritans warmly received Jesus and accepted his message (John 4:39–40). It seems that John's ministry of baptism took him to several locations.

When questioned by a priestly delegation sent to interview John to learn if he was Elijah, he replied, "I am not" (John 1:19–21). In Jewish thought, it was believed that Malachi's prophecy regarding Elijah, who had been miraculously taken to heaven in a fiery chariot (see above chap. 2), would physically return. John rejects the notion that he was the reincarnated Elijah, either out of humility or uncertainty. The popular consensus view was that John was a prophet (Matt. 21:11; Mark 11:32).

Jesus offered his understanding of the identity of John the Baptist. Speaking to a crowd after John's imprisonment, Jesus asked the people who had gone to see John,

> What did you go out into the wilderness to see? A reed swayed by the wind? If not, what did you go out to see? A man dressed in fine clothes? No, those who wear fine clothes are in kings' palaces. Then what did you go out to see? A prophet? Yes, I tell you, and more than a prophet. This is the one about whom it is written:
>
> "I will send my messenger ahead of you,
> who will prepare your way before you."

4 *ABD* 1:87.
5 For a review of the various options, see *Sacred Bridge*, 350–51.

> Truly I tell you, among those born of women there has not risen anyone greater than John the Baptist. . . . For all the Prophets and the Law prophesied until John. And if you are willing to accept it, he is the Elijah who was to come. (Matt. 11:7–11, 13–14)

This testimony affirms that John was a prophet, but not just another prophet, rather God's special messenger that Malachi had announced. He also affirms the conviction that he was "the Elijah who was to come," and finally he signals that John's work marked the end of the prophetic era that began with Moses in the Law, continued through the prophetic books, and ended with John who heralded the beginning of a new epoch.

SIMEON

According to the Law of Moses, Mary and Joseph took baby Jesus to the temple for the consecration of the firstborn (Luke 2:22–24). On entry to the temple precinct, they met a godly man named Simeon who is described by Luke as "righteous and devout. He was waiting for the consolation of Israel" (2:25), and we are informed that "the Holy Spirit was upon him. It had been revealed to him by the Holy Spirit that he would not die before he had seen the Lord's Messiah" (2:25b-26). Prompted by God's spirit he went to the temple at the very time that Jesus and his family arrived (2:27) where he offered words of blessing and what appears to be a prophetic utterance about Jesus as the source of God's salvation (2:30), and he offers words about the nature of Jesus's ministry that will painfully impact Mary. The role of God's Spirit in this narrative and that Simeon speaks at the Spirit's prompting suggests that he was a prophet,[6] even though the text does not explicitly make this point.

ANNA THE PROPHETESS

Apparently during the same temple visit when Simeon met Joseph, Mary and Jesus, an elderly prophetess named Anna appeared who also offered words of praise to God and "spoke about the child to all who were looking forward to the redemption of Jerusalem" (Luke 2:38). She had spent decades closely connected to the temple where she "worshipped night and day, fasting and praying" (Luke 2:37). Given her devotion to the Lord and the recognition that she was a prophetess, it is thought that she may have lived in one of the ancillary

---

6 *ISBE* 3:514.

Fig. 8.6 – Icon of Jesus Christ from St. Catherine's monastery, Sinai, dating to the 6th century A.D.
Photo by Alexander Schick/bibelausstellung.de, courtesy of Father John and Father Justin, St. Catherine's Monastery, Sinai

Fig. 8.7 – Sculpture of the Holy Family entering Egypt with pyramids in background, by Mariusz Dybich at the Cave Church, Cairo
Photo by James K. Hoffmeier

chambers in the temple precinct.[7] It is significant to note that both Simeon and Anna in the temple were pointing to the special status and role Jesus would play. In essence, they were recognizing in Jesus what the Old Testament prophets had foretold.

JESUS OF NAZARETH

The life of Jesus, from birth to death, is surrounded with references to the Old Testament prophets in the Gospel narratives. When the Magi came from the east seeking the newly born king of the Jews, king Herod's scholars in Jerusalem understood Micah 5:2 as pointing to Bethlehem as the birthplace of the messianic king (Matt. 2:1–6). When Joseph took Mary and Jesus to Egypt out of the reach of Herod's plot to kill the Christ child, Matthew sees this sojourn in Egypt as fulfilling Hosea's prophecy, "Out of Egypt I called my son" (Matt. 2:15 = Hos. 11:1). When Jesus began preaching in the area of Galilee, in the ancient tribal areas of Zebulun and Naphtali, Matthew says this action was "to fulfill what was said through the prophet Isaiah: Land of Zebulun and land of Naphtali . . . the people living in darkness have seen a great light; on those living in the land of the shadow of death a light has dawned" (Matt. 4:14–16). In his suffering, death, and the beginnings of the early church, the New Testament writers saw a correlation with various prophecies (see chap. 8, sections on Zechariah and Joel).

The New Testament, furthermore, considered Jesus to be the fulfillment of the prophecies concerning the coming messianic king, especially after his crucifixion, resurrection, and ascension. But how did the general public view Jesus during the days of his ministry? Most frequently his is called a prophet. When his teaching was well received by an audience in Jerusalem, some exclaimed, "Surely this man is the Prophet" (John 7:40).

7 Walter Liefeld, *Matthew*, The Expositor's Bible Commentary (Grand Rapids: Zondervan, 1984), 850.

Fig. 8.8 – Roman road at el-Qubeibeh by the "Emmaus" Church
Photo by Todd Bolen/Bibleplaces.com

He is also called "the Prophet who is to come into the world" after performing the miracle of feeding the five thousand (John 6:14). Calling him "the Prophet" seems to indicate that the people considered him more than just another prophet—rather, as a prophet like Moses, with messianic implications.[8] It may be that the people were recalling the words of Moses in Deuteronomy 18, when God declares that he will raise up a prophet like Moses. On another occasion when Jesus performed a miracle, people declared, "A great prophet has appeared among us" (Luke 7:16). The Samaritan woman's reaction to Jesus when he appeared clairvoyant for knowing she had had five husbands was to say "Sir," the woman said, "I can see that you are a prophet" (John 4:19). When a blind man in Jerusalem received his sight, the religious leaders pressed him to explain who Jesus was. "He is a prophet" was the answer (John 9:17). On Palm Sunday as Jesus rode into Jerusalem, the excited crowd identified him as "Jesus, the prophet from Nazareth in Galilee" (Matt. 21:11).

Some, however, questioned his status, saying that if he really were a prophet, he would not have dealings with disreputable people. Indeed the Pharisees who were present on the occasion when the woman anointed Jesus's feet said to themselves, "If this man were a prophet, he would have known who and what sort of woman this is who is touching him, for she is a sinner" (Luke 7:39 ESV). This reaction suggests the Pharisees believed that prophets were clairvoyant. Then too, when Jesus was being abused and beaten by the high priest's thugs during his trial, they mocked him when he was being punched, saying, "Prophesy to us, you Christ! Who is it that struck you?" (Matt. 26:68 ESV). Mark adds that they had blindfolded his face, as if to test his predictive abilities (Mark 1:65). These references all imply that Jews of the first century in Israel believed a prophet was somehow clairvoyant.

Luke reports on an interesting incident after stories began circulating that Jesus had risen from the dead (Luke 24:13–32). Two of Jesus's followers journeyed from Jerusalem to Emmaus not knowing what to believe. Jesus joins them on the road and asks why they were so downcast. Cleopas asks if he

8 Barnabas Lindars, *The Gospel of John*, The New Century Bible Commentary (Grand Rapids: Eerdmans, 1982), 244.

was unaware of what had transpired in Jerusalem in the preceding days (Luke 24:13–16). Not knowing that he was speaking to the resurrected Jesus, Cleopas recounts the death of Jesus of Nazareth: "He was a prophet, powerful in word and deed before God and all the people." And then he adds, "we had hoped that he was the one who was going to redeem Israel" (24:19, 21). This statement illustrates that "while in Luke's narrative Jesus is perceived as a prophet, the Resurrection affirmed him to be much more."[9]

Cleopas continues by telling of reports that Jesus had appeared to some of the disciples, to which Jesus replied: "How foolish you are, and how slow of heart to believe all that the prophets have spoken! Did not the Messiah have to suffer these things and then enter his glory?" And beginning with Moses and all the Prophets, he explained to them what was said in all the Scriptures concerning himself" (24:25–27).

From this exchange it is evident that even the closest disciples initially thought that Jesus was a prophet, although they had hoped that he would liberate Israel (from Rome), a uniquely messianic idea. For Jesus, Moses and the prophets of the Old Testament were pointing to him, his suffering and glorious resurrection. This understanding concurs with the testimony of John the Baptist who described Jesus as "the Lamb of God, who takes away the sin of the world!" (John 1:29).

For the New Testament writers, it was the correlation between scores of prophecies in the Old Testament with the life of Jesus that convinced them that he was the long-promised Messiah, who came to be the suffering servant (Isa. 53) but who would come again on the day of the Lord as a conquering warrior king to rule the earth (Zech. 14). The apostle Peter summed up the role of the Hebrew prophets and the movement toward Jesus in his first letter to Christians scattered across present-day Turkey:

> The prophets, who spoke of the grace that was to come to you, searched intently and with the greatest care, trying to find out the time and circumstances to which the Spirit of Christ in them was pointing when he predicted the sufferings of Messiah and the glories that would follow. It was revealed to them that they were not serving themselves but you, when they spoke of the things that have now been told you by those who have preached the gospel to you by the Holy Spirit sent from heaven. (1 Peter 1:10–12)

---

9 Liefeld, *Matthew*, 1052.

As was noted regarding the murder of the prophet Zechariah son of Jehoida, he was a martyr prophet to whom Jesus referred (Matt. 23:29:36; Luke 11:45–52). Jesus likened his own pending death in Jerusalem to the killing of other prophets by the religious authorities who rejected God's word. In this case, denying Jesus was not just ignoring God's word he spoke, but a denial of the incarnate word of God himself. Hence Jesus laments the fate of Jerusalem for its history of dismissing and even murdering God's messengers. Immediately after reminding his audience of the reprehensible murder of Zechariah on trumped up charges (just as Jesus would be treated), Jesus forewarns:

> Jerusalem, Jerusalem, you who kill the prophets and stone those sent to you, how often I have longed to gather your children together, as a hen gathers her chicks under her wings, but you were not willing. Look, your house is left to you desolate. For I tell you, you will not see me again until you say, "Blessed is he who comes in the name of the Lord." (Matt. 23:37–39)

Fig. 8.9 – View of Jerusalem from the Mt. of Olives *Photo by James K. Hoffmeier*

Stephen, the first Christian martyr, echoed these words of Jesus in his speech that led to his summary execution when he accused the temple leaders of rejecting and killing earlier prophets and Jesus: "You stiff-necked people, uncircumcised in heart and ears, you always resist the Holy Spirit. As your fathers did, so do you. Which of the prophets did your fathers not persecute? And they killed those who announced beforehand the coming of the Righteous One, whom you have now betrayed and murdered, you who received the law as delivered by angels and did not keep it" (Acts 7:51–53 ESV). Clearly Stephen likens Jesus to the prophets of old whose messages were dismissed and in some cases were abused (e.g., Jeremiah) or killed (e.g., Zechariah and Uriah), resulting in God's judgment—namely, the destruction of Jerusalem, the temple and exile. This is the point Jesus is making in Matthew 23 in his lament over Jerusalem.

PROPHETS AND PROPHESY IN THE EARLY CHURCH

Prophets and prophetic activity continue to play a role in the life of the early church as evidenced by the books of Acts and various epistles. Angels (Gk: *angelos*) are heavenly, spiritual, or supernatural divine messengers sent by God to communicate, warn, protect, and encourage God's people. In a sense, prophets are men and women who spoke under the prompting of the Holy Spirit, and are the human, earthly counterparts to angels. When John was experiencing apocalyptic visions that are recorded in the book or Revelation, an angel acted as his guide. At the end he saw the new heavens and earth in all their splendor (Rev. 22:1–7) (see excursus "Apocalyptic Literature"). Overwhelmed, John fell prostrate before the angel, who rebuked him: "Don't do that! I am a fellow servant with you and with your brothers the prophets and of all who keep the words of this book. Worship God'!" (Rev. 22:9). This statement is clarifying. Prophets and angels are equally servants or slaves of God; both are in the business of communicating God's word. As Leon Morris observes, "It is an intriguing thought that angels tell forth the Word of God like the prophets do."[10] The words of Old Testament prophets were often recorded, sometimes in the form of new revelations or oracles, and mostly pointed to God's existing revelation in the Torah. A prophet may, however, cite fellow prophets to validate their own messages (cf. Jer. 26:18, 20; 28:8–9).

The angel's statement to John extends the prophetic office to include apostles like John who were witnesses to the life and teachings of Jesus, and in this instance John was the recipient of apocalyptic visions. Through these human agents, the

10 Morris, *Revelation*, 258.

Spirit would work to record divine communication to be Scripture (John 14:26; 16:13; 1 Peter 1:10–12; 2 Peter 1:16–21; 3:15–16). Angels and prophets who utter God's word do so with equal authority, which is why Morris suggests, "We should not miss the importance of these words for an understanding of the proper dignity of the prophets. They rank with angels as servants of God."[11]

Angels and human prophets participate in the divine council (*sôḏ*). A well-known example of an angel being in God's presence and was thereby authorized to speak on behalf of God occurs in the Gospel of Luke. There the angel Gabriel appeared to Zechariah the priest in the temple, conveying that he and his wife would have a child, the future John the Baptist (Luke 1:11–17). Skeptical of this announcement, the aged Zechariah was told, "I am Gabriel. I stand in the presence of God, and I have been sent to speak to you and to tell you this good news" (Luke 1:19). As noted, previously prophets like Micaiah, Isaiah, and Jeremiah also witnessed the enthroned God in the divine council and heard the deliberations among the "sons of God" or angels (cf. Job 1:1–6). Uniquely, Moses had face to face encounters with God, that is, direct communication with the Almighty (Deut. 34:10–11).

Paul relates his dramatic visionary experience in 2 Corinthians 12:2–4 (ESV) where he reports cryptically about what happened to him: "I know a man in Christ who fourteen years ago was caught up to the third heaven—whether in the body or out of the body I do not know, God knows. And I know that this man was caught up into paradise—whether in the body or out of the body I do not know, God knows—and he heard things that cannot be told, which man may not utter."

Fig. 8.10 – Byzantine period painting of Paul at the Grotto of Paul, Ephesus
Photo by Todd Bolen/Bibleplaces.com

Visions, of course, were a primary means that Old Testament prophets received revelations (e.g., Isaiah, Ezekiel, Daniel, Zechariah). Paul was somehow transported to paradise, that is, heaven into what might be viewed as "the immediate presence of God."[12] There he heard "things that cannot be told," perhaps impossible for humans to comprehend or it was of such a sensitive nature that it was to be kept private.[13] Indeed it took fourteen

11 Morris, *Revelation*, 259.

12 Murray Harris, *The Second Epistle to the Corinthians* (Grand Rapids: Eerdmans, 2005), 840.

13 Harris, *Corinthians*, 844–45; Ralph Martin, *2 Corinthians*, Word Biblical Commentary (Waco, TX: Word, 1986), 405–6.

years for Paul to mention it in his writings, and he does not disclose what he heard. Reading of Paul's mystical experience and hearing things in the presence of God sounds as if Paul, like special prophets of the OT, was transported into the divine council. It is noteworthy that when Paul refers to this revelation (2 Cor. 12:1), it is part of his defense of his apostleship. Similarly, Jeremiah (23:18–22) appeals to his participation in the divine council to demonstrate his credentials as a prophet over against the false prophets who challenged him. If indeed Paul's divine encounter described in 1 Corinthians 12 represents a participation in the divine council, it elevates him to a very special circle like some of the prophets of the Old Testament.

It has been suggested that this otherwise unmentioned spiritual encounter might have occurred in Antioch when Paul and Barnabas were being commissioned for their first missionary trip.[14] Among the leadership of the church in Antioch were "prophets and teachers," including Paul and Barnabas (Acts 13:1). As they were worshiping and fasting, "the Holy Spirit said, 'Set apart for me Barnabas and Saul for the work to which I have called them'" (13:2). Whether or not the great apostle was considered a prophet, teacher, or both is not stated. Both teachers and prophets would have been "involved in the exposition . . . of Scriptures; the prophets, however, had also the gift of charismatic utterance," I. Howard Marshall maintains.[15] How the Holy Spirit spoke his will is not disclosed, but it may have been through one of the prophets who was present; and since Paul and Barnabas are the goal of the divine assignment, it seems doubtful that Barnabas or Paul was the prophetic voice used in this case.

Furthermore, Acts 11 speaks of a group of prophets visiting the Christians in Antioch: "Now in these days prophets came down from Jerusalem to Antioch. And one of them named Agabus stood up and foretold by the Spirit that there would be a great famine over all the world (this took place in the days of Claudius)" (vv. 27–28 ESV). Agabus appears again when Paul is returning to Jerusalem in Acts 21, for what turned out to be the last time. Paul and his travel companions had stopped at Caesarea Maritima and were visiting with Philip the Evangelist, whom we are told "had four unmarried daughters, who prophesied" (v. 9 ESV). It is curious that none of them foretold the trials that awaited Paul in Jerusalem. Rather, it was Agabus who had come from Judea to see Paul with the ominous warning: "he took Paul's belt and bound his own feet and hands

---

14 Martin, *2 Corinthians*, 399.

15 I. Howard Marshall, *Acts: Tyndale New Testament Commentaries* (Downers Grove, IL: InterVarsity Press, 1980), 215.

and said, 'Thus says the Holy Spirit, This is how the Jews at Jerusalem will bind the man who owns this belt and deliver him into the hands of the Gentiles'" (v. 11 ESV).

Fig. 8.11 – St. Peter's Grotto Church in Antioch
Photo by David Padfield/Bibleplaces.com

Agabus's dramatic act of tying up Paul's hands and feet with his own belt is reminiscent of the dramatic acts of prophets like Jeremiah. It is as if Agabus stepped off the stage of the seventh century B.C. Undeterred, Paul apparently decided that the divine word was not to hinder him from completing his task of taking gifts and tithes to Jerusalem, but prepare him for the trials that awaited him. His statement, "For I am ready not only to be imprisoned but even to die in Jerusalem for the name of the Lord Jesus" (Acts 21:13) might suggest that like his Lord, he was prepared to go to Jerusalem to die if that was God's purpose.

Most of the prophetic activity in the early church seems to be more pastoral in nature rather than focused on revelations and predictive matters like that of Agabus on two recorded occasions. For example, when a doctrinal dispute erupted in Antioch about what Jewish practices Gentile believers had to embrace, the council of Jerusalem was held. The apostles and elders of the mother church deliberated and issued a letter explaining the expectations for Gentile Christians. Including Paul and Barnabas, two other leaders were authorized to communicate and explain the council's position, namely Silas and Judas. These representatives of the church in Jerusalem went to Antioch to disseminate the teaching. "Judas and Silas," Acts 15:32 relates, "who themselves were prophets, said much to encourage and strengthen the believers." Clearly these men were teaching and expounding on the doctrinal letter, and their ultimate purpose was to encourage and strengthen the church. This pattern seems to follow the original model of Moses, whose task it was to "expound" upon the law revealed at Sinai (Deut. 1:5).

The pastoral dimension of prophetism in the New Testament is further evidenced by Paul's use of the expression "man of God" when addressing Timothy, his disciple who was an evangelist and pastor (1 Tim. 6:11; 2 Tim. 3:17). "Man of God" was a title for prophets in the Old Testament (see chap. 1), and Paul's usage seems to connect with the idea that the prophet speaks for God.[16] The 2 Timothy reference follows that oft-quoted and foundational statement on the nature of the Bible: "All Scripture is God-breathed and is

---

16 Ralph Earle, *1, 2 Timothy*, The Expositor's Bible Commentary (Grand Rapids: Zondervan, 1978), 386.

useful for teaching, rebuking, correcting and training in righteousness, so that the servant of God may be thoroughly equipped for every good work" (3:16–17). God's Word is the basis for any teaching ministry.

JOHN AND THE BOOK OF REVELATION

It seems fitting that the final book of the Christian Bible is prophetic in nature. The title of the book is "The revelation of Jesus Christ" (Rev. 1:1; Greek *apokalupsis* = apocalypse). The book refers to itself as "prophecy" (*prophēteias*) in Revelation 1:3, 22:7, 10, 18, 19, and is further described as "the word of God and the testimony of Jesus Christ" (Rev. 1:2). The book ends by declaring the purpose of the book: "I, Jesus, have sent my angel to give you this testimony for the churches. I am the Root and the Offspring of David, and the bright Morning Star" (Rev. 22:16).

Apocalyptic is a particular genre of prophetic literature that is attested in books like Ezekiel, Daniel, Joel, and Zechariah (see excursus "Apocalyptic Literature"). The book of Revelation is characterized by symbols and visions, characteristics of apocalyptic; in fact, many of the symbols are found in books like Ezekiel and Joel, and thus the motifs used would not be unfamiliar to a Jewish-Christian audience, even though they seem so challenging for the modern interpreter.[17] One key to interpreting this book is by studying the apocalyptic materials in the aforementioned Old Testament prophetic books that use the same or similar motifs.

The author, John—likely the beloved apostle—reports that he was on the Island of Patmos, off the coast of Asia Minor, where the seven churches were situated.[18] They were the original recipients of the book (or parts thereof) that was written in the form of a letter.[19] There John received visions, toward the end of the first century A.D., about "the things that must soon take place" (Rev. 22:6). Moreover, as is the nature of apocalyptic writings, it is eschatological, pointing toward the end of the epoch and the return of Jesus Christ, and the futuristic new heavens and new earth (Rev. 21–22). It also deals with the trials and tribulations that will face the church (Rev. 8–18), and its ultimate salvation (Rev. 19–22). Throughout the book, in keeping with apocalyptic

17 Alan Johnson, *Revelation*, The Expositor's Bible Commentary (Grand Rapids: Zondervan, 1981), 399.
18 Mark Fairchild, *Christian Origins in Ephesus and Asia Minor* (Arkeoloji ve Sanat Yayinlari Tur: Izmir, 2015), 15–16.
19 G. B. Caird, *The Revelation of St. John the Divine* (New York: Harper & Row, 1966), 27–28.

literature, an angel acts as a guide and interpreter for the prophet (Rev. 1:1; 2:1; 10:8–9; 19:9; 21:15; 22:1, 6, 8, 16).

To the Christians struggling under the boot of tyrannical Roman emperors like Nero and Domitian, who fashioned themselves divine and determined to secure everyone's devotion, Christ the Lord holds out hope for those who cling to the faith and endure. He assures them, "Yes, I am coming soon." To this promise, the author cries the aspirations of the church, "Amen, come Lord Jesus" (Rev. 22:20).

Fig. 8.12 – The Isle of Patmos, where John received his revelations
Photo by James K. Hoffmeier

DISCUSSION QUESTIONS

- How are John the Baptist and Elijah connected?
- Why was Jesus considered a prophet by many of his contemporaries?
- What is the evidence that suggests that Paul was a prophet?
- Discuss how prophecy was implemented in the early church. How is it similar and different than the practices of the OT prophets?
- What are some of the characteristics of apocalyptic literature in the book of Revelation, and how was it intended to help Christians?

Abd el-Maksoud, Mohamed, and Dominique Valbelle. “Une Stèle de la’an 7 d’Apries découverte sur le site de Tell Défenneh.” *Revue d’Égyptologie* 64 (2013): 1–13.

Alden, Robert. *Haggai*. In *Expositor’s Bible Commentary*, edited by F. Gaebelein, 7:569–94. Grand Rapids: Zondervan, 1985.

Alexander, Ralph. *Ezekiel*. In *Expositor’s Bible Commentary*, edited by F. Gaebelein, 6:737–996. Grand Rapids: Zondervan, 1986.

Allen, Leslie. *Ezekiel 1–19*. Word Biblical Commentary. Nashville: Thomas Nelson, 1994.

______. *Ezekiel 20–48*. Word Biblical Commentary. Dallas: Word, 1990.

Andersen, F. I., and D. N. Freedman. *Amos*. Anchor Bible Commentary. New York: Doubleday, 1989.

Arav, Rami. *Bethsaida: A City on the North Shore of the Sea of Galilee, vol. 4*. Kirksville, MO: Truman State University, 2009.

Archer, Gleason. *Daniel*. In *The Expositor’s Bible Commentary*, edited by Frank Gaebelein, 7:3–157. Grand Rapids: Zondervan, 1985.

Arnold, Bill. *Who Were the Babylonians?* Atlanta: Society of Biblical Literature, 2004.

Averbeck, Richard. “The Test of a Prophet.” In *“An Excellent Fortress for His Armies, a Refuge for the People”: Egyptological, Archaeological, and Biblical Studies in Honor of James K. Hoffmeier*, edited by R. E. Averbeck and K. L. Younger, 1–17. University Park: Eisenbrauns/Pennsylvania State University Press, 2020.

Baker, David. *Nahum, Habakkuk, Zephaniah: An Introduction and Commentary*. Downers Grove, IL: InterVarsity Press, 1988.

Baker, Rosalie, and Charles Baker III. *Ancient Greeks: Creating the Classical Tradition*. New York: Oxford University Press, 1997.

Baldwin, Joyce. *Haggai, Zechariah, Malachi*. Downers Grove, IL: InterVarsity Press, 1972.

______. *Daniel: An Introduction and Commentary*. Downers Grove, IL: InterVarsity Press, 1978.

______. *1–2 Samuel: An Introduction and Commentary*. Downers Grove, IL: InterVarsity Press, 1988.

Barker, Kenneth. *Zechariah*. In *Expositor’s Bible Commentary*, edited by F. Gaebelein, 7:595–700. Grand Rapids: Zondervan, 1985.

Beale, G. K. *The Book of Revelation: A Commentary on the Greek Text*. Grand Rapids: Eerdmans, 1999.

Beckman, Gary. *Hittite Diplomatic Texts*. 2nd ed. Atlanta: Scholars Press, 1999.

Beitzel, Barry. *The New Moody Bible Atlas*. Chicago: Moody, 2009.

Bietak, Manfred. *Avaris the Capital of the Hyksos*. London: British Museum, 1996.

Blanco, Walter. *Herodotus: The Histories*. New York: W. W. Norton, 1992.

Blankensopp, Joseph. *Sage, Priest, Prophet: Religious and Intellectual Leadership in Ancient Israel*. Louisville: Westminster John Knox, 1995.

Block, Daniel I. *The Book of Ezekiel, Chapters 1–24*. New International Commentary of the Old Testament. Grand Rapids: Eerdmans, 1997.
Bright, John. *Jeremiah*. Anchor Bible Commentary. New York: Doubleday, 1965.
Brownlee, William. "My Eight Years of Scroll Research." *Duke Divinity School Bulletin* 21, no. 3 (1956): 68–81.
______. *The Meaning of the Qumran Scrolls for the Bible*. Oxford: Oxford University Press, 1964.
______. *Ezekiel 1–19*. World Biblical Commentary. Waco, TX: Word, 1986.
Brueggemann, Walter. *A Commentary on Jeremiah*. Grand Rapids: Eerdmans, 1998.
______. *First and Second Samuel*. Louisville: John Knox, 2002.
______. *The Theology of the Book of Jeremiah*. Cambridge: Cambridge University Press, 2007.
Budd, Philip. *Numbers*. World Biblical Commentary. Waco, TX: Word, 1984.
Bullock, C. Hassell. *An Introduction to the Old Testament Prophetic Books*. Chicago: Moody, 2007.
Caird, G. B. *The Revelation of St. John the Divine*. New York: Harper & Row, 1966.
Carson, Donald. *Matthew: The Expositor's Bible Commentary*. Grand Rapids: Zondervan, 1984.
Chapman, Rupert. "Samaria: Capital of Israel." *Biblical Archaeology Review* 43, no. 5 (2017): 24–30, 63.
Childs, Brevard. *Isaiah: Old Testament Library*. Louisville: Westminster John Knox, 2001.
Cogan, Mordechai, and Hayim Tadmor. *2 Kings*. Anchor Bible. New York: Doubleday, 1988.
______. *1 Kings*. Anchor Bible. New York: Doubleday, 2001.
Craigie, Peter, Page Kelley, and Joel Drinkard. *Jeremiah 1–25*. Word Biblical Commentary. Dallas: Word, 1991.
Cundall, A. E. *Judges and Ruth: An Introduction and Commentary*. Downers Grove, IL: InterVarsity Press, 1980.
Davis, Theodore. *The Tomb of Thoutmôsis IV*. London: Archibold Constable, 1904.
Dearman, J. Andrew. *The Book of Hosea*. Grand Rapids: Eerdmans, 2010.
Dever, William. *Beyond the Texts: An Archaeological Portrait of Ancient Israel and Judah*. Atlanta: SBL Press, 2017.
DeVries, Simon. *1 Kings*. Word Biblical Commentary. Waco, TX: Word, 1985.
Earle, Ralph. *1, 2 Timothy: The Expositor's Bible Commentary*. Grand Rapids: Zondervan, 1978.
Fairchild, Mark. *Christian Origins in Ephesus and Asia Minor*. Izmir: Arkeoloji ve Sanat Yayinlari Tur, 2015.
Fee, Gordon, and Douglas Stuart. *How to Read the Bible for All Its Worth*. Grand Rapids: Zondervan, 1982.
Feinberg, Charles. *Jeremiah: A Commentary*. Grand Rapids: Zondervan, 1982.
Franklin, Norma, et al. "Have We Found Naboth's Vineyard at Jezreel?" *Biblical Archaeology Review* 43, no. 6 (2017): 49–54.
Gibson, Shimon. *The Cave of John the Baptist*. New York: Doubleday, 2004.
Gileadi, Avraham. *The Apocalyptic Book of Isaiah*. New York: Hebraeus, 1982.
______. *The Literary Message of Isaiah*. New York: Hebraeus, 1994.
Gordon, Robert P., ed. *The Place Is Too Small for Us: The Israelite Prophets in Recent Scholarship*. Winona Lake, IN: Eisenbrauns, 1995.
Grogan, Geoffrey. *Isaiah*. In *Expositor's Bible Commentary*, edited by F. Gaebelein, 6:1–354. Grand Rapids: Zondervan, 1986.
Guenther, Allen. *Hosea, Amos*. Believers Church Bible Commentary. Scottdale, PA: Herald, 1998.
Hanson, Paul. *Old Testament Apocalyptic*. Nashville: Abingdon, 1987.
Harris, Murray. *The Second Epistle to the Corinthians*. Grand Rapids: Eerdmans, 2005.
Harrison, Roland. *Introduction to the Old Testament*. Grand Rapids: Eerdmans, 1969.

______. *Jeremiah and Lamentations*. Downers Grove, IL: InterVarsity Press, 1973.

Harvey, J. "Le 'Rîb-Pattern', réquisitoire prophétique sur la rupture de l'alliance." *Biblica* 43 (1962): 172–196.

Hayes, John, and Stuart Irvine. *Isaiah the Eighth-Century Prophet*. Nashville: Abingdon, 1987.

Hess, Richard. *Israelite Religions: An Archaeological and Biblical Survey*. Grand Rapids: Baker Academic, 2007.

Hill, Andrew. *Malachi: A New Translation with Introduction and Commentary*. New York: Anchor Bible/ Doubleday, 1998.

Hobbs, T. B. *2 Kings*. Word Biblical Commentary. Waco, TX: Word, 1985.

Hoffmeier, James K. "The Wives' Tales of Genesis 12, 20, and 26 and the Covenants at Beer-Sheba." *Tyndale Bulletin* 43, no. 1 (1992): 81–100.

______. "Once Again the 'Plumb Line' Vision of Amos: An Interpretive Clue from Egypt?" In *Boundaries of the Ancient Near Eastern World: A Tribute to Cyrus H. Gordon*, edited by Meir Lubetski, et al., 304–19. Sheffield: Sheffield Academic Press, 1998.

______. *Ancient Israel in Egypt: The Evidence for the Authenticity of the Wilderness Tradition*. New York: Oxford University Press, 2011.

______. *Tell el-Borg I*. Winona Lake, IN: Eisenbrauns, 2014.

Hoffmeier, James K., and Stephen O. Moshier. "New Paleo-Environmental Evidence from North Sinai to Complement Manfred Bietak's Map of the Eastern Delta and Some Historical Implications." In *Timelines: Studies in Honour of Manfred Bietak* II, edited by E. Czerny, et al., 167–76. Leuven: Peeters, 2006.

Holladay, William. *A Commentary on the Book of the Prophet Jeremiah, Chapters 1–25*. Philadelphia: Fortress, 1986.

______. *A Commentary on the Book of the Prophet Jeremiah, Chapters 26–52*. Philadelphia: Fortress, 1989.

Hruša, Ivan. *Ancient Mesopotamian Religion: A Descriptive Introduction*. Münster: Ugarit-Verlag, 2015.

Hwang, Jerry. "'I Am Yahweh Your God from the Land of Egypt?': Hosea's Use of the Exodus Tradition." In *"Did I Not Bring Israel Out of Egypt: Biblical, Archaeological, and Egyptological Perspectives on the Exodus Narratives*, edited by J. Hoffmeier, A. Millard, and G. Rendsburg, 243–54. Bulletin for Biblical Research Supplement 13. Winona Lake, IN: Eisenbrauns, 2016.

Janzen, Mark, ed. *Five Views on the Exodus: Historicity, Chronology, and Theological Implications*. Grand Rapids: Zondervan, 2021.

Johnson, Alan. *Revelation: The Expositor's Bible Commentary*. Grand Rapids: Zondervan, 1981.

Kaiser, Walter. *Micah–Malachi*. The Communicator's Commentary. Dallas: Word, 1992.

Keil, C. F., and F. Delitzsch. *1–II Kings, I–II Chronicles, Ezra, Nehemiah, Esther*. Vol. 3, *Commentary on the Old Testament*. Edinburgh: T&T Clark, 1890.

______. *Ezekiel, Daniel*. Vol. 9, *Commentary on the Old Testament*. Edinburgh: T&T Clark, 1890.

Keown, Gerald, Pamela Scalise, and Thomas Smothers. *Jeremiah 26–52*. Word Biblical Commentary. Dallas: Word, 1995.

King, Philip J. *Amos, Hosea, Micah: An Archaeological Commentary*. Philadelphia: Westminster, 1988.

______. *Jeremiah: An Archaeological Companion*. Philadelphia: Westminster, 1993.

Kistenmaker, Simon. *Exposition of the Book of Revelation*. Grand Rapids, Baker Academic, 2001.

Kitchen, Kenneth. *On the Reliability of the Old Testament*. Grand Rapids: Eerdmans, 2003.

Kitchen, Kenneth, and Paul Lawrence. *Treaty, Law and Covenant in the Ancient Near East, vol. 1*. Mainz: Harrasowitz, 2012.

Klein, Ralph. *1 Samuel*. Word Biblical Commentary. Waco, TX: Word, 1983.

Leclère, François. "Tell Dafana: Identity, Explorations and Monuments." in *Tell Dafana Reconsidered: The Archaeology of an Egyptian Frontier Town*, edited by F. Leclere and A. J. Spencer, 1–40. London: British Museum, 2014.
Liefeld, Walter. *Matthew: The Expositor's Bible Commentary*. Grand Rapids: Zondervan, 1984.
Linblom, Johannes. *Prophecy in Ancient Israel.* Philadelphia: Fortress, 1962.
Lindars, Barnabas. *The Gospel of John.* The New Century Bible Commentary. Grand Rapids: Eerdmans, 1982.
Lundbom, Jack. *Jeremiah 1–20.* Anchor Bible Commentary. New York: Doubleday, 1999.
______. *Jeremiah 12–36.* Anchor Bible Commentary. New York: Doubleday, 2004.
______. *Jeremiah 37–52.* Anchor Bible Commentary. New York: Doubleday, 2004.
Marshal, I. Howard. *Acts: Tyndale New Testament Commentaries*. Downers Grove, IL: InterVarsity Press, 1980.
Martin, Ralph. *2 Corinthians.* Word Biblical Commentary. Waco, TX: Word, 1986.
Mazar, Amihai. *It Is the Land of Speech: Discoveries from Tel Reḥov, the Early Days of the Israelite Monarchy.* Jerusalem: Hebrew University, 2016.
Mazar, Eilat. "Is This the Prophet Isaiah's Signature?" *BAR* 44, nos 2-3 (2018): 65–92.
McCarter, P. Kyle. *1 Samuel: A New Translation with Introduction and Commentary*. The Anchor Bible. New York: Doubleday, 1980.
McComiskey, Thomas. *Micah: Expositor's Bible Commentary*. Grand Rapids: Zondervan, 1985.
McConville, J. Gordon. *A Guide to the Prophets: Exploring the Old Testament, vol. 4*. Downers Grove, IL: InterVarsity Press, 2002.
McLeod, W. *Composite Bows from the Tomb of Tut'ankhamūn*. Oxford: Oxford University Press, 1970.
______. *Self Bows and Other Archery Tackle from the Tomb of Tut'ankhamūn*. Oxford: Oxford University Press, 1982.
McRay, John. *Archaeology and the New Testament*. Grand Rapids: Baker, 1991.
Meier, Samuel A. *Themes and Transformations in Old Testament Prophecy*. Downers Grove, IL: IVP Academic, 2009.
Melika, Ash. "The Founding of the Temple in Ancient Egypt: Ritual and Symbolism." In *"An Excellent Fortress for His Armies, a Refuge for the People": Egyptological, Archaeological, and Biblical Studies in Honor of James K. Hoffmeier*, edited by R. E. Averbeck and K. L. Younger, 199–220. University Park: Eisenbrauns/Pennsylvania State University Press, 2020.
Millard, Alan. "Daniel in Babylon: An Accurate Record?" In *Do Historical Matters Matter to Faith?*, edited by J. Hoffmeier and D. Magary, 263–80. Wheaton, IL: Crossway, 2012.
Morris, Leon. *Revelation.* Tyndale New Testament Commentaries. Downers Grove, IL: InterVarsity Press, 1984.
Motyer, J. Alec. *The Prophecy of Isaiah: An Introduction and Commentary*. Downers Grove, IL: InterVarsity Press, 1993.
Nissinen, Martti, ed. *Prophecy in Its Ancient Near Eastern Context: Mesopotamia, Biblical and Arabian Perspectives*. Atlanta: Society of Biblical Literature, 2000.
______. *Prophets in the Ancient Near East*. Atlanta: Society of Biblical Literature, 2003.
Oates, Joan. *Babylon*. London: Thames and Hudson, 2003.
Oren, Eliezer. "Migdol: A New Fortress on the Edge of the Eastern Nile Delta." *BASOR* 256 (1984): 7–44.
Patterson, Richard. *Joel.* In *Expositor's Bible Commentary*, edited by F. Gaebelein, 7:229–66. Grand Rapids: Zondervan, 1985.

Paul, Shalom. *A Commentary on the Book of Amos*. Minneapolis: Fortress, 1991.

Perdu, Olivier. "Saites and Persians (664–332)," in *A Companion to Ancient Egypt*, edited by Alan Lloyd, 140–58. Oxford: Wiley-Blackwell, 2010.

Phillips, Richard. *Zechariah.* Reformed Expository Commentary. Phillipsburg, NJ: P&R, 2007.

Rainey, Anson, et al. *The Sacred Bridge: Carta's Atlas of the Biblical World.* Jerusalem: Carta, 2006.

Rentdorff, Rolf. *The Covenant Formula*. Edinburgh: T&T Clark, 1998.

Sasson, Jack. *Jonah*. New York: Anchor Bible, 1990.

Seitz, Christopher. *Prophecy and Hermeneutics*. Grand Rapids: Baker, 2007.

Selman, Martin. *2 Chronicles.* Tyndale Old Testament Commentaries. Downers Grove, IL: InterVarsity Press, 1994.

Shepherd, Michael. *A Commentary on the Book of the Twelve*. Grand Rapids: Kregel Academic, 2018.

Smith, Gary V. *Interpreting the Prophetic Books*. Grand Rapids: Kregel Academic, 2014.

Smith, Ralph L. *Micah–Malachi*. World Biblical Commentary. Waco, TX: Word, 1984.

Sweeney, Marvin. *Isaiah 1–39: Forms of Old Testament Literature*. Grand Rapids, Eerdmans, 1996.

Stuart, Douglas. *Hosea–Jonah*. Word Biblical Commentary. Waco, TX: Word, 1987.

Taylor, J. Glen. "Hosea." In *Zondervan Illustrated Bible Backgrounds Commentary*, edited by J. H. Walton, 2–41. Grand Rapids: Zondervan, 2009.

Taylor, John B. *Ezekiel.* Tyndale Old Testament Commentary. Downers Grove, IL: InterVarsity Press, 1969.

Thiele, Edwin. *A Chronology of the Hebrew Kings*. Grand Rapids: Zondervan, 1977.

Thompson, John. *The Book of Jeremiah*. Grand Rapids: Eerdmans, 1980.

Tigay, Jeffrey. *You Shall Have No Other Gods: Israelite Religion in the Light of Hebrew Inscriptions*. Atlanta: Scholars Press, 1986.

Török, Lászl6. *The Kingdom of Kush: Handbook of the Napatan-Meroitic Civilization*. Leiden: Brill, 1997.

Tsumura, David. *The First Book of Samuel*. Grand Rapids: Eerdmans, 2007.

Tully, Eric. "Hosea 1–3 as the Key to Literary Structure and Message of the Book." in *"An Excellent Fortress for His Armies, a Refuge for the People": Egyptological, Archaeological, and Biblical Studies in Honor of James K. Hoffmeier*, edited by R. E. Averbeck and K. L. Younger, 369–83. University Park, PA: Eisenbrauns/Pennsylvania State University Press, 2020.

Ussishkin, David. "Jezreel: Where Jezebel Was Thrown to the Dogs." *Biblical Archaeology Review* 36, no. 4 (2010): 32–42, 75.

von Rad, G. *Old Testament Theology, Vol. 1.* New York: Harper & Row, 1962.

_______. *Old Testament Theology, Vol. 2.* New York: Harper & Row, 1965.

Walker, Larry. *Zephaniah.* In *Expositor's Bible Commentary*, edited by F. Gaebelein, 7:537–65. Grand Rapids: Zondervan, 1985.

Walton, John. "Jonah." In *Zondervan Illustrated Bible Backgrounds Commentary*, edited by J. H. Walton, 100–119. Grand Rapids: Zondervan, 2009.

Watts, John. *Isaiah 1–33.* World Biblical Commentary. Waco, TX: Word, 1985.

____. *Isaiah 34–66.* World Biblical Commentary. Waco, TX: Word, 1985.

Watts, Rikk E. "Isaiah in the New Testament." In *Interpreting Isaiah: Issues and Approaches*, edited by D. G. Firth and H. G. M. Williamson, 213–34. Downers Grove, IL: IVP Academic, 2009.

Wevers, John. *Ezekiel.* New Century Bible Commentary. Grand Rapids: Eerdmans, 1969.

Williamson, H. G. M. *Variations on a Theme: King, Messiah, and Servant in the Book of Isaiah*. Carlisle, UK: Paternoster, 1998.

Wiseman, D. J. "Some Historical Problems in the Book of Daniel." In *Notes on Some Problems in the Book of Daniel*, 9–18. London: Tyndale, 1965.
______. *1–2 Kings*. Tyndale Old Testament Commentaries. Downers Grove, IL: InterVarsity Press, 1993.
Wolf, Herbert. *Judges*. In *The Expositor's Bible Commentary*, edited by Frank Gaebelein, 3:375–506. Grand Rapids: Zondervan, 1985.
______.*Interpreting Isaiah*. Grand Rapids: Zondervan, 1985.
Wolff, Hans Walter. *Joel and Amos*. Philadelphia: Fortress, 1977.
Yamauchi, Edwin. *Persia and the Bible*. Grand Rapids: Baker Books, 1996.
______. *Africa and the Bible*. Grand Rapids: Baker Academic, 2004.
Young, Edward, J. *The Prophecy of Daniel*. Grand Rapids: Eerdmans, 1949.
Youngblood, Ronald. *1, 2 Samuel*. In *The Expositor's Bible Commentary*, edited by Frank Gaebelein, 3:553–1104. Grand Rapids: Zondervan, 1985.
Younger, K. Lawson. *Judges/Ruth*. NIV Application Commentary. Grand Rapids: Zondervan, 2002.
______. *A Political History of the Arameans*. Atlanta: Society of Biblical Literature, 2016.
Zertal, Adam, and Dror Ben-Yosef. "Bedhat esh-Sha'ab: An Iron Age I Enclosure in the Jordan Valley." In *Exploring the Longue Durrée: Essays in Honor of Lawrence E. Stager*, edited by J. S. Schloen, 517–29. Winona Lake, IN: Eisenbrauns, 2009.